REPUBLICAN
ASCENDANCY

1921 ★ 1933

The New American Nation Series

Edited by Henry Steele Commager and Richard B. Morris

North America from Earliest Discovery to First Settlements:
    The Norse Voyages to 1612 *by David B. Quinn*
The Cultural Life of the American Colonies, 1607-1763 *by Louis B. Wright*
The English People on the Eve of Colonization, 1603-1630 *by Wallace Notestein*
The Colonies in Transition, 1660-1713 *by Wesley Frank Craven*
France in America *by W. J. Eccles*
The Indian in America *by Wilcomb E. Washburn*
Spain in America *by Charles Gibson*
The Rise of the West, 1754-1830 *by Francis S. Philbrick*
The Coming of the Revolution, 1763-1775 *by Lawrence Henry Gipson*
The American Revolution, 1775-1783 *by John Richard Alden*
The Federalist Era, 1789-1801 *by John C. Miller*
The Democratic Republic, 1801-1815 *by Marshall Smelser*
The Cultural Life of the New Nation 1776-1830 *by Russel B. Nye*
Society and Culture in America, 1830-1860 *by Russel B. Nye*
The Growth of Southern Civilization, 1790-1860 *by Clement Eaton*
The Awakening of American Nationalism, 1815-1828 *by George Dangerfield*
The Jacksonian Era, 1828-1848 *by Glyndon G. Van Deusen*
The Far Western Frontier, 1830-1869 *by Ray A. Billington*
The Crusade Against Slavery, 1830-1860 *by Louis Filler*
The Impending Crisis, 1848-1861
    by David M. Potter, Completed and Edited by Don E. Fehrenbacher
The New Commonwealth, 1877-1890 *by John A. Garraty*
The Transformation of American Foreign Relations, 1865-1900
    by Charles S. Campbell
The Development of the American Constitution, 1877-1917 *by Loren P. Beth*
Politics, Reform and Expansion, 1890-1900 *by Harold U. Faulkner*
America's Rise to World Power, 1898-1954 *by Foster Rhea Dulles*
The Era of Theodore Roosevelt, 1900-1912 *by George E. Mowry*
Woodrow Wilson and the Progressive Era, 1910-1917 *by Arthur S. Link*
The Constitution in Crisis Times, 1918-1969 *by Paul L. Murphy*
Republican Ascendancy, 1921-1933 *by John D. Hicks*
Franklin D. Roosevelt and the New Deal, 1932-1940
    by William E. Leuchtenburg
The United States and World War II, 2 vols. *by A. Russell Buchanan*

REPUBLICAN ASCENDANCY

1921 ★ 1933

by JOHN D. HICKS

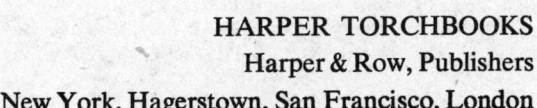

HARPER TORCHBOOKS
Harper & Row, Publishers
New York, Hagerstown, San Francisco, London

To My Grandchildren

REPUBLICAN ASCENDANCY, 1921-1933

Copyright © 1960 by John D. Hicks
Printed in the United States of America

This book was originally published in 1960 by Harper &
Brothers in The New American Nation Series edited by
Henry Steele Commager and Richard B. Morris.

First HARPER TORCHBOOK edition published 1963

Library of Congress catalog card number: 60-7528

ISBN: 0 −06 −133041 −8

80   20 19 18 17 16 15 14

Contents

	EDITORS' INTRODUCTION	viii
	PREFACE	xi
1.	THE STATE OF THE UNION	1
2.	THE RETREAT TO ISOLATION	23
3.	WHAT PRICE NORMALCY?	50
4.	THE PROGRESSIVE PROTEST	79
5.	PROSPERITY PLUS	106
6.	THE DIPLOMACY OF ISOLATION	130
7.	THE OTHER AMERICAS	153
8.	SOCIAL INSECURITY	167
9.	AGRICULTURE VS. INDUSTRY	193
10.	HOOVER TAKES OVER	215
11.	DEPRESSION DIPLOMACY	241
12.	THE YEARS OF THE LOCUST	260
	BIBLIOGRAPHICAL ESSAY	281
	INDEX	302

Illustrations

These photographs, grouped in a separate section,
will be found following page 110

1. President Harding throwing out the ball in 1921
2. Calvin Coolidge dips a hook in a Vermont trout stream
3. The American delegation to the Washington Armament Conference in 1921
4. Senator Borah, leading American advocate of the Conference
5. Calvin Coolidge and Charles G. Dawes in 1924
6. Robert M. La Follette of Wisconsin and Robert M. La Follette, Jr.
7. Albert B. Fall being assisted into the courtroom to stand trial in 1927
8. A Ku Klux Klan parade in the national capital
9. Clarence Darrow and William Jennings Bryan at the Scopes trial in 1925
10. Charles A. Lindbergh and the *Spirit of St. Louis*
11. General "Billy" Mitchell
12. Wreck of the *Shenandoah* near Ava, Ohio, September 3, 1925
13. Douglas Fairbanks, Mary Pickford, and Charlie Chaplin
14. Al Capone in Florida during his heyday
15. The Nebraska State Capitol, completed in the 1920's
16. Imperial Hotel, Tokyo, Japan, designed by Frank Lloyd Wright
17. An early radio and radio equipment store
18. Henry and Edsel Ford, with every model produced by the Ford plant from its founding to 1932
19. The New York skyline when the Woolworth Building was the tallest building in the world

20. Forty-second Street in New York, 1929

21. Alfred E. Smith

22. President-elect Herbert Hoover with Henry Ford, Thomas A. Edison, and Harvey Firestone in February, 1929

23. Combination harvester-thresher

24. Caterpillar-drawn cultivator-seeder

25. Prohibition agents make a find

26. The St. Valentine's Day massacre of 1929

27. Apple vending by the unemployed, November, 1930

28. Wall Street scene during the panic of 1929

29. General Douglas MacArthur, then Chief of Staff, during the Army's battle to oust the bonus marchers

30. Police and veterans fight a fierce battle on a Washington, D.C., lot in 1932

31. Two pages from *Oh Yeah?*, edited by Edward Angly

Editors' Introduction

HISTORICALLY a decade is a wholly artificial unit, yet the decade of the 1920's commends itself to us as having a more than artificial character. In the perspective of a generation, now, we can see that it had a tone, an atmosphere, a style, a quality of its own, and one that set it apart unmistakably from the years that came before and after. On the one side—to shift our metaphor—were the swift currents of Wilsonian liberalism and the first great plunge into world affairs; on the other the turbulent waters of the New Deal and the upheavals of the vasty depths we associate with the Second World War; the twenties stretch in between like some Sargasso Sea on the ocean of history.

It is suggestive, and not willful, that we think of the second and fourth decades of our century in positive terms, but of the third largely in negative. We remember it as the age of isolation, or as the age of disillusionment, or as the age of normalcy. And it is probably true that we have known no more negative era in our history since the days of Arthur and Cleveland and Harrison; even that decade witnessed the not unheroic enterprise of the final conquest of the West and saw the beginnings of social protest and reform. But the era of Republican ascendancy was above all one of withdrawal: withdrawal from the responsibilities of world order; withdrawal from our commitments in the Pacific; withdrawal from the political experimentation of government regulation into an individualism that was not so much rugged as sullen; withdrawal from the idealism of the recent past into irrationalism and irresponsibility.

Indeed, if we may use a moralistic term that Professor Hicks does not himself indulge in, the mark of failure is heavy on these years:

failure in the sense of responsibilities evaded, and of opportunities missed. The United States emerged from the war the leading world power, and proceeded to dissipate that power. It withdrew from participation in the postwar settlement, refusing to join not only the League of Nations but the innocuous World Court. Deeply committed to the support of the status quo in the Far East, it watched with malign but wholly passive dissatisfaction the systematic flouting of treaties guaranteeing that status. Immensely rich—and growing richer every year—those who stood at the levers of control failed even to attempt a more equitable distribution of wealth. Employing ever more efficient techniques for the exploitation of natural resources, they failed to conserve those resources for future generations, but frittered them away, heedlessly or corruptly. It was doubtless understandable that a generation still chewing the cud of Spencerian philosophy should refuse to accept responsibility for conserving and improving human resources—health, education, race relations—but it is difficult to understand how they could have failed so egregiously to perform well the elementary task to which they dedicated their thought and efforts, to preserve the economic health of the nation. Perhaps the most astonishing aspect of this "business civilization" is that it managed its business so badly.

Politically, too, the decade was one of negation: it lacked not only the glittering virtues but the lurid vices. Its sins were, on the whole, vulgar, and its failures were prosy. Rarely in our history have so many mediocrities been counterbalanced by so few men of talent. It was perhaps characteristic that the chief political achievements of that decade should have been the frustration of its greatest statesman, Woodrow Wilson, and the defeat of its most progressive and imaginative politician, Robert La Follette. "Make no little plans," the great architect Daniel Burnham used to say, but the men who sat in the seats of the mighty in these years made only little plans. Mr. Coolidge's famous aphorism about the business of America is too familiar to rehearse; it was paralleled by Mr. Hoover's astonishing verdict that "when the war closed the most vital of all issues was whether governments should continue their wartime ownership and operation of many instrumentalities of production and distribution." Not peace, world order, the end of colonialism, social justice—but laissez-faire! It was because the twenties failed to carry forward the promising beginnings of economic and social reform inherited from the Roosevelt and Wilson administrations that the thirties in turn inherited not only an acute economic depression, but a ramshackle and anachronistic political and administrative mechanism that was incapable of coping with that depression. Not since the fateful decade of the 1850's had there been so egregious a failure of leadership in American politics.

Physicians study sickness rather than health, and if it is neither gratifying nor flattering to submit the history of these years of failure to the historical microscope, it is profitable to do so. Professor Hicks has done just this, and, notwithstanding his modest disclaimer, with an almost scientific objectivity. It would be misleading to suggest that he has given us only a study in failure. He has spread before us the whole social and economic scene, and his luminous pages reflect to us the importance of such institutions as the automobile, the movies, and the radio, and the color of those practices and malpractices most conveniently suggested by the term "the jazz age." He has ranged widely over the political scene, and has not failed to fit American politics into its international setting. It is appropriate to note, however, that the full story of foreign policy, of cultural and of constitutional history of these years is reserved for other volumes in this series.

This volume is one of the New American Nation Series, a comprehensive and co-operative survey of the history of the area now embraced in the United States from the days of discovery to our own time. Each volume of this series is part of a carefully planned whole, and fitted as well as is possible to other volumes in the series; each is designed to be complete in itself. Some overlapping is doubtless inevitable, but it has seemed to the editors that repetition is less regrettable than omission, and that something is to be gained from looking at the same period from different and independent points of view.

HENRY STEELE COMMAGER
RICHARD BRANDON MORRIS

Preface

ANYONE who attempts nowadays to write on the years covered by this book suffers from one of two handicaps—either he has lived through the period or he has not. If he has lived through it as an observing adult, he has in the process formed many opinions of which he can never completely divest himself. If he has not lived through it he must conjure up, out of his experience with a later age, images of the earlier period, images that must at best depart considerably from the reality. But these, of course, are the standard dilemmas of all who undertake the writing of history. How can the writer keep his account pure from his own prejudices and preconceptions? And how can he escape the overweening influence of the world that surrounds him as he writes?

As a teacher of American history I not only lived through these years; I attempted both to make history shed what light it could on the unfolding events of the time and to digest current happenings into my lectures. My survey course in American history always got through to the present; I have never had much patience with teachers who are defeated by the difficulties involved in covering the last thirty to fifty years. I suffered most of the disillusionments of which I write in this book, and my classes suffered them with me. I have profited somewhat, I hope, from the accumulation of perspective; certainly I have changed my mind about many things many times, and I have repeatedly torn up my old notes and started over. But no doubt the pattern of thought I worked out three decades ago has left its imprint. For this I have no apologies. Objectivity is something for which one strives earnestly, knowing full well that it is unattainable.

I owe many more acknowledgments than I can make, among others

to the thousands of undergraduates who listened patiently to my classroom efforts, and to the scores of graduate students who worked with
me in seminar on problems of the 1920's and 1930's. I have had the intelligent assistance of many librarians, but particularly those of the
Manuscripts Division of the Library of Congress, and of the Doe and
Bancroft Libraries of the University of California. I owe most, undoubtedly, to the many writers and researchers whose publications I
have pillaged at will; it was Leo Gershoy, I think, who once remarked
that history may not repeat itself, but historians certainly do repeat
each other. On the bibliography I had the extraordinarily expert guidance of my former assistant, Helen E. Burke, and her husband, Dr.
Robert E. Burke, now of the University of Washington. Another assistant, Estelle Lau Gaffney, helped with the checking of footnotes, and
from her husband, Dr. M. Mason Gaffney, an economist, now of the
University of Missouri, I got many useful suggestions. My wife, Lucile
Curtis Hicks, somehow found the time to aid me in note taking and to
type most of the manuscript. From Henry Steele Commager and
Richard B. Morris, the two editors of the series, I have had the maximum of helpful co-operation. My indebtedness to Beulah Hagen and
the editorial staff of Harper & Brothers would also be hard to overstate.

JOHN D. HICKS

December 1, 1959

CHAPTER 1

The State of the Union

AMERICANS of the early 1920's who reflected on the population statistics revealed by the Fourteenth Census found in these figures ample evidence that the United States as a nation had at last achieved maturity. Within the forty-eight states that manifest destiny had located between the Atlantic and the Pacific, and between Canada and Mexico, there lived well over one hundred million people. As became an adult nation, the rate of population increase was slowing down, under 15 per cent for the second decade of the century as compared with 21 per cent for the first. Abraham Lincoln had had it wrong when he had once predicted a population of 187 million for 1920. He had assumed that a rate of increase proper for the nation's adolescent years would continue on indefinitely, whereas a full-grown nation could not be expected to maintain the spectacular growth of its youth. There was nothing abnormal about the fact that immigration had fallen off and the birth rate had begun to decline; these conditions, indeed, were only the marks of full national development. It would not be long now, census experts predicted, before the modest 10 per cent increase per decade, common to the somewhat older nations of western Europe, would become the rule in America.[1]

The evolution of a fairly homogeneous national stock seemed also well on the way. Students of the subject held that approximately half

[1] William S. Rossiter, *Increase of Population in the United States, 1910–1920*, Census Monographs (Washington, 1922), I, 9–26, 81. Cf. Warren S. Thompson, *Population Problems* (New York, 1930), p. 236.

the blood heritage of all white Americans, taken together, derived from the "native white stock" enumerated in the census of 1790, while the other half came from "immigrant" sources, that is, from those whites who had come to the United States since 1790. Through the years the mingling of the native and the immigrant blood streams had proceeded so rapidly that by 1920 far more white Americans were of mixed native and immigrant ancestry than were exclusively of the one or the other. The great influx of southern and eastern Europeans before the First World War had threatened to upset this balance, but there was now every reason to suppose that the check on immigration that the war itself had provided would soon be reinforced by appropriate legislation. In the cities large blocks of unassimilated immigrants still existed, and would no doubt continue to exist for some time; but the day seemed in sight when the number of Americans of strictly foreign birth or ancestry would decline to insignificance. According to the theorists, nothing could stop the "melting pot" from eventually completing its work.[2]

Ten million Negroes, the legacy of African slavery, required separate consideration. It was possible to speak freely about the coming amalgamation of native and immigrant stocks, but few whites were willing to admit that anything comparable would happen to whites and Negroes. Nevertheless, the census takers classified 16 per cent of the Negro population as mulatto, while it was a matter of general belief that among persons classified as "black" only a few were without white ancestors. Comprising only 10 per cent of the total population, the Negroes might not have constituted a serious racial problem had they been equally distributed throughout the Union. But the fact was that more than 85 per cent of them lived in the region where slavery had existed before the Civil War—some seventeen states and the District of Columbia. In two southern states, South Carolina and Mississippi, the Negro population exceeded the white, while in seven other states and the District of Columbia it constituted over one-fourth of the whole. Hopefully, the census takers called attention to three circumstances that were certain to affect the situation. First, the Negroes were increasing in number less rapidly than the whites, 6.5 per cent for the Negroes during the preceding decade as against 16 per cent for the whites; secondly, they were leaving the South in substantial numbers

[2] Rossiter, *Increase of Population,* pp. 95–122.

for the states where they were less numerous; and thirdly, in response to the growing demand for industrial workers, they were moving from the rural areas to the cities, both northern and southern. What the future held in store for the American Negro, none could foretell, but optimists predicted that the two races would learn to live peaceably side by side.[3]

In addition to the Negroes there were only three minority groups in the American population whose numbers warranted separate census enumeration. These were the Indians, the Chinese, and the Japanese. They accounted altogether for only four-tenths of 1 per cent of the total population: Indians, 244,437; Chinese, 61,639; Japanese, 111,000. As for the Indians, they were held to be steadily declining in numbers and "slowly merging into the national population." Nearly half of the Chinese still lived in California, but they were showing a definite tendency to spread eastward from the Pacific Coast, with "a few Chinese in every state of the union." Well over half of the Japanese were located in California, and they were increasing in numbers. But with the existing immigration restrictions, not to mention others to be expected, the Japanese problem, even in California, could hardly become serious.[4]

The homogeneity of the American people in religion, education, and language was far more significant than the average individual realized. Over 41 per cent of the population were members of some Christian church; of these about 64 per cent were Protestant and about 36 per cent were Catholic. Of the rest only an insignificant minority, mainly Jews, were actually non-Christian; the overwhelming majority, whether members of Christian churches or not, accepted in general the Christian code of ethics. Tension between Protestants and Catholics did exist, also between Christians and Jews; but there was not in the United States, nor had there ever been, the kind of religious animosity between sects that in India, for example, set Hindu against Moslem or, in the Middle East, Moslem against Jew. The educational pattern showed even fewer variants. Every state provided for its junior residents a system of free public instruction, including secondary schools and institutions of higher education. Parochial schools existed among Roman Catholics and Lutherans, and there were many privately endowed colleges and universities. But the idea of generous educational

[3] *Ibid.*, p. 129. Cf. Gunnar Myrdal, *An American Dilemma* (2 vols., New York, 1944), I, 157–181.
[4] Rossiter, *Increase of Population,* pp. 133–138.

opportunities for all who wished to learn was accepted as a fundamental factor in the American way of life. Illiteracy, in spite of the backwardness of some southern Negroes and the handicaps of some recently arrived immigrants, had declined to 6 per cent. And the English language, written and spoken after the American fashion, was all but universal.[5]

Notable among the revelations of the Fourteenth Census was the rapidity with which the American people were changing their residences from country to city. The rural to urban trend in American life was not new; it had been in evidence for a long time. The striking fact was the momentum it had attained. Rural areas were gaining only slowly in population when they gained at all; urban areas were growing by leaps and bounds. For the first time in census history the number of people living in communities of 2,500 or more inhabitants exceeded (51.4 to 48.6 per cent) the number who lived in the smaller towns and the country. Naturally the growth of the cities was most marked in the industrial areas of New England, the Middle Atlantic states, and the Old Northwest; but there were lesser urban centers on the make the whole country over, in the western Middle West, in the South, in the mountain states, and along the Pacific Coast. The decade of the twenties would see many more millions of country people move to the cities, and the proportion reach 56.2 to 43.8. Furthermore, the trend was increasingly toward the creation of a few great metropolitan districts. Such a city as New York, for example, was girdled by a series of "satellite" cities whose interests and activities were closely intertwined with those of the central city itself, and with each other's. "Suburbanization" might spread a given district over an extensive area, but there was no mistaking its essential unity. In 1920 the census takers had not yet singled out such metropolitan districts for separate identification, but they listed sixty-eight cities of 100,000 or more inhabitants, each of which was the center of a much greater population. Ten years later there were ninety-six metropolitan centers, and their combined population had reached 44.6 per cent of the whole.[6]

The shift of population from country to city reflected accurately the

[5] *The Chicago Daily News Almanac and Yearbook for 1923* (Chicago, 1922), pp. 547–548; *Statistical Abstract of the United States, 1921* (Washington, 1922), p. 80.
[6] *Fourteenth Census of the United States, Population* (Washington, 1921), I, 76; *Fifteenth Census of the United States, Population* (Washington, 1931), I, 8.

growing importance in the national economy of manufacturing as compared to agriculture. For every forty-six persons engaged in agriculture, there were now fifty-four engaged in "manufacturing and mechanical industries," while the gross value of the nation's manufactured products was now nearly three times that of agriculture. The First World War had greatly expanded the industrial plants of the nation, and had called striking attention to the effectiveness of mass production and standardization after the pattern first worked out by Frederick W. Taylor and later applied by Henry Ford. American manufacturers were making rapid headway in adapting the new system to nearly every type of production, installing improved machinery, eliminating wasteful plants, reducing transportation costs, and minimizing waste. As a result their potential output had expanded amazingly; seemingly there were no limits to the amounts they could produce. Capital goods, consumer goods, everything that a complicated civilization required, American manufacturers stood ready to create. What they worried about more than how to provide the goods was how to stimulate the need for still more and more goods. For mass production quite obviously depended on a persistent mass demand.[7]

During the last few weeks of 1918 and the first of 1919 American manufacturers suffered a temporary setback. This was due in part to the overhasty and ill-advised cancellation of war contracts, together with the dislocations naturally attendant upon the change-over from production for war to production for peace. But the recovery from this slump was so rapid that it could hardly be noticed in the annual statistics. The year 1919 saw the total gross value of American manufactured products reach $62.5 billion, the largest such figure in the history of the nation, and an increase of 150 per cent over 1914. New postwar demands from the American public helped keep the wheels of business turning. Soldiers discharged from the Army received their transportation home plus $60 in cash. A large part of the latter went for civilian clothing, and so benefited the textile industries. There was some cashing in of war bonds, and some catching up on the purchase of civilian goods in short supply during the war. Automobile output, down to less

[7] *Statistical Abstract*, 1921, pp. 299–300; *Abstract of the Fourteenth Census of the United States* (Washington, 1923), 886; *Abstract of the Census of Manufactures, 1919* (Washington, 1923), p. 12; Keith Sward, *The Legend of Henry Ford* (New York, 1948), pp. 32–43; President's Conference on Unemployment, *Recent Economic Changes in the United States* (2 vols., New York, 1929), I, 80–82.

than a million passenger cars in 1918, rose to 1.65 million in 1919 and 1.9 million in 1920. A critical housing shortage greatly stimulated the building industries.[8]

The explanation of this postwar boom could hardly be attributed wholly, as some overzealous defenders of the free-enterprise system seemed to think, to the removal of wartime restraints on business. Actually, government spending continued at a high peak; a Victory Loan, fifth in the series of fund-raising drives for the winning of the war, had to be staged in April, 1919, in order to bring 4.5 billion badly needed dollars into the Treasury. Since the government was still spending far more than it took in by way of taxes, the securities it issued to bridge the gap enhanced greatly the lending power of the banks, and so stimulated the borrowing power, and indirectly the purchasing power, of the people. In other words, credit was easy. Of fundamental importance also were American loans to the Allies, which continued for two years after the armistice, and gave European nations the money they needed to continue buying American goods. When the fighting ended, Allied borrowings from the United States stood at about $7 billion, but before November, 1920, this sum was increased by another three billion. The new credits were designed mainly to help the war-shattered nations with their pressing problems of relief and rehabilitation, and interestingly they were extended not only to the associates of the United States in the war but also to such newly formed countries as Finland, Estonia, Poland, Czechoslovakia, and Yugoslavia. A considerable part of the American loans was spent by European purchasers in the United States for agricultural products, but much of the rest went for such manufactured goods as locomotives and rolling stock, badly needed to restore the hard-hit European transportation systems.[9]

Supplementary to manufacturing, and an integral part of American industrialism, was the exploitation of the nation's mineral resources. During the year 1919, enterprises engaged in this type of activity employed nearly a million workers, and contributed to the national economy products valued at about $3 billion. The pre-eminence of

[8] George Soule, *Prosperity Decade, from War to Depression: 1917–1929* (New York, 1947), pp. 81–86; *Abstract of Manufactures, 1919,* p. 12; *Statistical Abstract, 1931,* p. 403.

[9] National Resources Planning Board, *After the War—1918–20; Military and Economic Demobilizaton of the United States,* pamphlet prepared by Paul A. Samuelson and Everett E. Hagen (Washington, 1943), pp. 23–27.

coal in the mineral field was still unchallenged; coal mining accounted for 70 per cent of the workers employed in all the nation's mines. But it was apparent that there would be trouble ahead from the competition of oil, already the second greatest mineral industry in the nation, with production figures up 17 per cent over 1919 for 1920, and in 1921, despite the general economic slump, higher than in any preceding year. Third in rank among American mineral industries was the production of iron ore, with copper fourth, lead and zinc fifth. In all these industries production continued approximately at wartime levels throughout the year 1920. Pennsylvania, with both coal and oil, led the nation in mining, with West Virginia (coal and oil) second, Oklahoma (mostly oil) third, Illinois (coal and oil) fourth, California (oil) fifth, and Texas (oil) sixth. Minnesota and Michigan produced most of the nation's iron ore; Arizona and Michigan, most of its copper; Missouri, Idaho, and Oklahoma, most of its lead and zinc.[10]

Of vital importance to both mining and manufacturing was the business of transportation, the bulk of which fell to the railroads. Here, too, as in every other aspect of the life of the nation, the legacy of war was plainly apparent. For twenty-six months preceding March 1, 1920, the Railroad Administration, an agency of the federal government, had operated the nation's railroads as one unified system, paying their owners in return a rental based on prewar earnings. When by the Transportation Act of 1920 Congress reinstituted private management, it sought to guarantee the owners against whatever losses the change-over might otherwise involve. While it charged the companies for the numerous improvements made by the government during the war, it funded this indebtedness at 6 per cent interest, allowed them a ten-year period in which to pay off the debt, and authorized the Interstate Commerce Commission to set new rates that would bring in a 5.5 to 6 per cent return on investments. The Commission might also permit limited railroad combinations, and it was charged with the duty of laying out a general plan of consolidation.[11]

In line with the letter and spirit of the law, the Interstate Commerce Commission on July 29, 1920, granted the railroads a general advance

[10] *Fourteenth Census, Mines and Quarries, 1919* (Washington, 1922), **XI**, 20–21, 31; *The New International Yearbook, 1920* (New York, 1921), pp. 155, 523; *ibid., 1921* (New York, 1922), 158, 546.

[11] Rogers MacVeagh, *The Transportation Act, 1920; Its Sources, History, and Text* (New York, 1923), pp. 67, 83–88, 268–270, 384; *Recent Economic Changes*, I, 257; *New International Yearbook, 1920*, pp. 567–570.

in freight and passenger rates. Between government aid and higher rates they found it possible by the end of the year to restore the physical condition of their property, but they were none too pleased with the financial situation. The year 1920, according to one observer, provided "the greatest traffic in railway history, the greatest operating revenues; the greatest operating expenses; the greatest wage aggregate; the greatest taxes, and the smallest net operating income in more than 30 years." When President Harding addressed Congress on April 12, 1921, he made it clear that in his opinion all was not as it should be with the railroads. He registered his opposition to Congress levying "taxes upon the people to cover deficits in a service which should be self-sustaining," but objected at the same time to the high rates the railroads charged, and insisted that some means of cutting down the costs of operation must be found.[12]

In the same message the President called attention to the tremendous importance in the national economy that the nation's highways had begun to achieve. This was hardly news, for before the outbreak of the First World War the American people were acutely conscious of the fact that the automobile had precipitated a transportation revolution comparable in its effect to the one wrought earlier by the railroads. But there was one major difference. The highways over which motor traffic must flow were by long-established custom a public rather than a private responsibility. And the local road districts, townships and counties, to which in a more primitive age road building and road maintenance could be left, were totally incapable of coping with the new situation. Realizing this fact, state legislatures felt obliged to help out; every state in the union by 1917 (and in most cases much earlier than that) had its program of state aid and state administration to supplement local activities. But state aid was not enough, for as the highway system grew its nation-wide character became too obvious to overlook. So Congress, by the Federal Highways Act of 1916, inaugurated a program of "federal aid" on the familiar dollar-matching basis—for every dollar expended by state and local authorities, the United States would expend another, provided that the states were fully organized to supervise the work and would make it conform to federal standards.[13]

[12] Julius H. Parmelee, "Railway Revenues and Expenses in the Year 1920," *Railway Age,* LXX (Jan. 7, 1921), 129; *Congressional Record,* 67th Cong., 1st Sess., LXI (Apr. 12, 1921), 169.
[13] *United States Statutes at Large* (Washington, 1917), XXXIX, 355–359;

Before the contemplated program could get fully under way, however, the United States was involved in the First World War, and as a result highway improvements ground almost to a halt. But traffic grew with the wartime needs until by the end of 1918 it was estimated that half a million motor trucks and five million motor cars were in use on the nation's highways. The havoc they caused to whatever roads existed was almost indescribable; one of the greatest postwar needs was to get the highways in order again. To do this the states usually bonded themselves heavily, amending their constitutions when necessary to make legal the huge outlays required for "internal improvements"; only a frugal few planned their programs on the "pay-as-you-go" basis. And Congress continued to provide "federal aid"; by 1921 total expenditures for road building from all sources had reached nearly a half billion dollars, about 40 per cent of which came from national appropriations. Although the funds for road building came exclusively from governmental sources, it is important to note that the work itself was done in considerable part by private contractors. Thus a whole new business interest came into existence. Over all the country companies and individuals devoted themselves primarily to the construction of roads and bridges, adding their very considerable bit to the total volume of the nation's business activities. Nor did business fail to make full use of the new roads. Privately owned bus and truck companies were quick to exploit the road network that the public had so thoughtfully provided.[14]

Problems of external commerce were hardly less stupendous than those of internal commerce. During the year 1920 the foreign trade of the United States, reflecting the spectacular changes that the war had brought, was larger both in exports and in imports than during any previous calendar year. The value of exports for 1920 stood at more than eight and a quarter billion dollars, an increase of 4 per cent over the exports of 1919, and of about 333 per cent over those of 1913. The figure for imports was substantially less, about five and three quarters

---

The New International Yearbook, 1918 (New York, 1919), pp. 548–549; *ibid.,* *1920,* p. 588.

[14] U.S. Department of Agriculture, Bureau of Public Roads, *Public Roads,* I (July, 1918), 28–30. Through this publication, which began May 1, 1918, one may trace the history of federal and state road policy. *Congressional Record,* 67th Cong., 1st Sess., LXI (Apr. 12, 1921), 169; Preston William Slosson, *The Great Crusade and After, 1914–1928* (New York, 1930), pp. 231–235; *Recent Economic Changes,* I, 272–273.

billion dollars, but the percentages of increase were equally impressive, up 35 per cent over 1919, and nearly 300 per cent over 1913. About half of the ocean-borne commerce to and from American ports was now carried in ships flying the American flag, a situation relatively new to the United States, for before the war American foreign trade, what there was of it, went mainly in foreign bottoms. The great increase in the number and carrying capacity of merchant ships was due to the efforts of the United States Shipping Board to provide replacements for Allied ships lost from submarine sinkings during the war. Unfortunately, however, most of the ships for which the Board contracted were not completed until after the war was over. The United States by 1920, with a merchant fleet second only to Great Britain's in size, and in large part government-owned, had to decide what its policy should be for the future.[15]

That same year Congress attempted to answer this question with a new Merchant Marine Act based upon two principles. First, the United States must not give up the pre-eminence it had won in shipping; and secondly, public ownership and management must give way as speedily as possible to private ownership and management. What Congress had in mind was a great "merchant marine of the best equipped and most suitable types of vessels," adequate to meet the nation's needs alike in time of peace and war, and "ultimately to be owned and privately administered by citizens of the United States."[16] This was a frank reversal of prewar policy. Before the war no one had worried much over the fact that American ships could carry only about 10 per cent of the nation's foreign trade; after the war there were many who deemed such dependence on foreign shipping altogether too hazardous to contemplate. Among the most devoted friends of a strong merchant marine, events were soon to prove, would be the new President, Warren G. Harding. The United States, he promptly announced, "intends to maintain a great merchant marine," but by means of "government encouragement not government operation."[17]

When Americans spoke of "business," or the "business world," they had in mind much more than manufacturing, mining, and transportation. Communication by telephone and telegraph bulked large in the

[15] *Ibid.*, I, 309–319; Slosson, *The Great Crusade and After,* pp. 51–54.
[16] John B. Hutchins, "The American Shipping Industry Since 1914," in *Business History Review,* XXVIII (June, 1954), 109–111.
[17] *Congressional Record,* 67th Cong., 1st Sess., LXI (Apr. 12, 1921), 169.

national economy, and was dominated almost completely by the American Telephone and Telegraph Company. Banking, both state and national, was closely controlled by the Federal Reserve System, which had survived the stress and strain of war, and had won the enthusiastic support of most of the bankers themselves. In some of the states, particularly California, branch banking was on the rise. Associated with, often even identified with, the banks, was the huge investment business through which the stocks and bonds of the various corporations were bought and sold. Public utility companies, both publicly and privately owned, supplied electric power, gas, and other necessities to the various municipalities. An infinite variety of wholesale and retail establishments catered to the marketing needs of the people. Insurance companies sold policies that provided indemnification for practically every known calamity. A huge construction business, promoted and financed in considerable part by building and loan associations, made available through thousands of operators housing for the people and buildings of every sort and kind. Amusement and entertainment; advertising; the publication of books, magazines, and newspapers; household services, such as laundering, cleaning, and dyeing; hotels and other accommodations for travelers; garages and filling stations—these and a thousand other services were a part of the huge business complex.[18]

Certain general changes in the nature of American business were increasingly in evidence. For one thing, as the total volume of business increased, the number of independent operating units tended to decrease; obviously a tremendous concentration in control was in progress. There was a difference, too, in the personnel of management; except for the Ford industry and a few others, the original entrepreneurs were giving way to new managers who might or might not be members of the founding families. Finally, there was a much wider diffusion of ownership, especially with respect to big business. Capital for expansions came not only from profits but also from the investments of thousands, even hundreds of thousands, of individual stockholders, whose test of the value of an investment lay mainly in the dividends it paid. Stockholders, whether large or small, were rarely much afraid of mere bigness; the industrial and financial combinations that went on worried them little or not at all. Nor were they much concerned about

[18] Russell M. Posner, "State Politics and the Bank of America, 1920–1934," unpublished Ph.D. dissertation, University of California, Berkeley, 1956; Slosson, *The Great Crusade and After,* pp. 162–169, 176–189.

the growth of trade associations, through which, quite within the letter of the law, many of the advantages of monopoly could be achieved.[19]

The avowed purpose of these trade associations was to promote the mutual benefit of corporations and individuals engaged in a given type of business. Through a central agency they were able to collect and distribute information of general value on prices, methods of production, standardization, shipping problems, credit ratings, insurance, public and employee relations, cost accounting, and the like. Another principal function was to scrutinize the regulatory proposals of both state and national legislative bodies, and to make sure that laws unfavorable to the interest of the particular group they represented failed of passage, while laws that might be helpful to its members went on the statute books. That such activities might run counter to antitrust legislation seemed obvious, but the Supreme Court eventually (1925) held that, since the associations were not actually engaged in fixing prices or curtailing production, they were within the law. This was apparently the opinion of Herbert Hoover, Secretary of Commerce under Harding and Coolidge, who actively encouraged their formation as a positive business good. The oldest of these organizations, the United States Brewers Association, dated back to 1862, and some others of prominence had their origins in the nineteenth century. But for the most part they were founded in the twentieth century. By the time Harding took office they were numbered by the thousands, and they grew both in numbers and in influence throughout the rest of the decade. Particularly powerful was the National Association of Manufacturers, formed in 1895, which was more responsive during the twenties to the wishes of small manufacturers than it later became.[20]

In addition to the trade associations, the Chamber of Commerce of the United States, founded in 1912 at the suggestion of President Taft, attempted "to reflect the views of American business" in general. The

[19] A. A. Berle, Jr., and G. C. Means, *The Modern Corporation and Private Property* (New York, 1932), pp. 119–125; James Burnham, *The Managerial Revolution* (New York, 1941), pp. 71–95; W. L. Thorp, *The Integration of Industrial Operation, Census Monographs* (Washington, 1924), III, 10, 45; National Industrial Conference Board, *Mergers in Industry* (New York, 1929), pp. 9–27.

[20] Emmet H. Naylor, *Trade Associations; Their Organization and Management* (New York, 1921), pp. 1–24; National Industrial Conference Board, *Trade Associations; Their Economic Significance and Legal Status* (New York, 1925), pp. 7–30; Herbert Hoover, *The Memoirs of Herbert Hoover* (New York, 1952), II, 169–173; *Industrial Progress*, V (July, 1922), 15.

Chamber was based upon the federative principle, with a voting membership consisting exclusively of business organizations, such as a state or local chambers of commerce and trade associations of every sort and kind. Individuals and firms might, for a consideration, enjoy all privileges except voting, and from these memberships the Chamber derived a substantial revenue; but, in theory at least, it represented business organizations rather than individual businesses and businessmen, just as the American Federation of Labor represented labor organizations rather than individual laborers. Chamber policy might be stated through resolutions passed at its annual meetings, or through committee reports approved by the membership on referendum. While the Chamber spoke directly for only about one-sixth of the business groups of the country, its membership provided a good cross section of American business activity, and gave credence to its claim to be the one central "clearinghouse" for American business ideas. The Chamber maintained a national headquarters in Washington, D.C., the ideal location for influencing governmental decisions.[21]

Journalistically, the voice of business was strong and clear. The Chamber of Commerce of the United States proclaimed its views through the *Nation's Business;* the world of finance spoke forcefully in the *Wall Street Journal,* and the *Commercial and Financial Chronicle;* while the newspaper world in general, itself composed of formidable business enterprises, naturally saw eye to eye with other businesses.

In effective organization American labor lagged far behind American business. The American Federation of Labor, still headed by Samuel Gompers, was at the peak of its strength in 1920, with a total membership among its affiliates of 4,078,740, the largest in its history. Other nonaffiliated unions brought the total for all organized labor to 5,110,800; but since this was out of a nonagricultural, nonprofessional working force of perhaps 25 million, union members actually constituted only a small minority of all American workers.[22] Whole great

[21] Harwood L. Childs, *Labor and Capital in National Politics* (Columbus, 1930), pp. 11–16, 66–67; D. A. Skinner, *The Chamber of Commerce of the United States* (Washington, 1925), p. 6; Galen Fisher, "The Chamber of Commerce of the United States," unpublished master's thesis, University of California, Berkeley, 1950, in Library of the University of California.

[22] Also some of the unions were international and had members outside the United States, particularly in Canada. Leo Wolman, *The Growth of American Trade Unions, 1880–1923* (New York, 1924), p. 65. See also *Statistical Abstract of the United States, 1921,* pp. 299–309.

areas and whole great industries, particularly in the South, were virtually closed to union activities. Such successes as organized labor had achieved in recent years resulted in part from the friendly attitude of the Wilson administration, and in part from the opportunities that had come labor's way during the war. In order to "do its bit" labor had virtually given up the right to strike for the duration, but in return it had achieved a degree of immunity from antiunion activities that enabled it to make substantial gains, both in influence and in numbers. There were gains, too, in the shape of higher wages, shorter hours, the extension of collective bargaining, and the improved condition of union treasuries that accompanied every increase in membership.[23]

The numerous strikes of 1919, however, and the "red scare" of the postwar years, aroused the opponents of organized labor to a new frenzy of activity. Some of the more moderate corporation executives thought they saw hope in the removal of labor grievances; if workers were satisfied, they would not be interested in union membership. So they talked in terms of better "personnel management," improved employer-employee relations, company unionism, and "welfare capitalism." But others favored more direct methods. Unions, they said, should be held responsible for the acts of their officials, and they should even be forced to respect the hated "yellow-dog" contracts by which an employee, as a condition of his employment, bound himself not to join a labor union. Of even greater appeal was the so-called "American plan," which called for an outright return to the principle of the open shop. This idea received the blessing of such influential bodies as the Chamber of Commerce of the United States, the National Association of Manufacturers, the National Metal Trades Association, and a wide variety of local as well as national organizations, many of which undertook its vigorous promotion. And when it came to combating the strike as an instrument for the enforcement of labor demands, employers were in general agreement that the authority of government should somehow be ranged on their side, with the possibilities of the injunction, despite the restraining provisions of the Clayton Antitrust Act, not to be overlooked.[24]

[23] Lewis Lorwin, *The American Federation of Labor* (Washington, 1933), pp. 146, 165–166, 177, 187–189; Selig Perlman and Philip Taft, *Labor Movements,* in John R. Commons and associates, *History of Labor in the United States, 1896–1932* (New York, 1935), IV, 603–604.

[24] *Ibid.,* pp. 343, 580; Lorwin, *American Federation,* pp. 201–203; *New International Yearbook, 1922,* pp. 405–406; Whiting Williams, "That the

In the face of this concerted attack, organized labor itself did not present a united front. There were differences as to fundamental policy. The Railroad Brotherhoods, who were not affiliated with the A.F. of L. but whose co-operation was greatly desired, had profited materially from government operation of the railroads during the war, and favored its continuation. To this end they advanced the "Plumb Plan," which proposed that the government should purchase the railroads and operate them through an agency on which labor, management, and the government should have equal representation. Contrary to the wishes of Gompers and other labor leaders, the Federation at its June, 1920, meeting endorsed the Plumb Plan, with its implications for nationalization. By this time Congress had already returned the railroads to their owners, and even the Brotherhoods soon lost interest in the Plan; but the issue remained. Should American labor push forward in the direction of state socialism, as British labor was doing, or should it continue the Gompers policy of "voluntarism," which held that labor must depend for its gains primarily upon its own economic power, and not upon governmental intervention. Gompers was re-elected president of the Federation both in 1920 and 1921, but confidence in the infallibility of his judgment was clearly on the wane.[25]

There was a division, even, among those who believed that the future of labor lay with political action. Traditional Socialists still had faith in the evolutionary process, and held that their ultimate goal could best be achieved through the ballot. But they showed a new willingness to work with other liberal groups, and at their Detroit convention in 1921 called upon the party executive to make a survey of all such possibilities. On the other hand, the success of the Russian revolution encouraged the really radical left wing to seek a similar overthrow of the American government. This was the aim of the Communist party, organized in 1919, but because of wartime legislation obliged to remain underground until 1924. Masquerading publicly as the Worker's party, communism made every effort to infiltrate the labor movement; but while this process of boring from within led to much turbulence, eventually, more often than not, it culminated in the purging of Communist leadership from the unions. In relative harmony with the Communists

People May Decide," *Collier's Weekly*, LXVIII (July 23, 1921), 7–8, 20, 22; *Open Shop Association*, II (June, 1923), 1.

[25] *New Internatinal Yearbook*, 1921, p. 407; Lorwin, *American Federation*, pp. 81, 198–199; *New Republic*, XXVI (Mar. 9, 1921), 32.

were the remnants of the Industrial Workers of the World, but the effectiveness of state and federal prosecutions of I.W.W. members during the war had reduced the influence of this organization to virtual insignificance. By the time the Republicans took over the government in 1921, the "red hysteria" that had gripped the nation during the preceding two years was beginning to abate, but the hostility of the public toward anything savoring of radicalism was still a factor to be reckoned with. Majority opinion tended even to regard Socialists with great suspicion.[26]

It is perhaps not surprising, under these circumstances, that organized labor failed conspicuously to gain ground during the 1920's. A decline in union membership during the hard times that characterized the first few years of the decade was natural enough, but the decline continued over into the years of prosperity that followed. Union membership dropped steadily from its peak of over 5 million in 1920 to about 3.4 million in 1929, and in the same years from over 12 per cent of the total labor force to only 7 per cent. Undoubtedly part of the trouble lay with the A.F. of L. itself, which showed little concern for the welfare of the workers in the great mass-production industries that in the manufacturing world were carrying all before them; in particular, the rising new automobile industry remained unorganized until the time of the New Deal. But even in mining, in textiles, and in the heavy industries union influence was declining. Gompers, no longer the dynamic leader of his youth, died in 1925, and was succeeded by the far less vigorous William Green. Indeed, the best fighters for labor during this period were not union men at all, but such humanitarians and reformers as Norris of Nebraska, La Follette of Wisconsin, and La Guardia of New York.[27]

While the clash of interests between capital and labor echoed throughout urban America, agriculture continued to dominate the

[26] David A. Shannon, *The Socialist Party of America* (New York, 1955), pp. 126–149; Theodore Draper, *The Roots of American Communism* (New York, 1957), pp. 218–225, 388–395; James Oneal and G. A. Werner, *American Communism* (New York, 1947), pp. 67 n., 229, 285; *Industrial Progress*, V (Sept., 1922), 6–8. The Sacco-Vanzetti case attracted much attention until the execution of the two principals in August, 1927.

[27] A. M. Schlesinger, Jr., *The Age of Roosevelt; The Crisis of the Old Order, 1919–1933* (Boston, 1957), pp. 111–113; Leo Wolman, *Ebb and Flow in Trade Unionism* (New York, 1936), p. 16; Rowland H. Harvey, *Samuel Gompers, Champion of the Toiling Masses* (Stanford, Calif., 1935), pp. 337–340.

countryside. Agriculture in America, like industry, was exceedingly varied. In the Northeast the farmers had long since yielded all pretense of pre-eminence to the industrialists, but the potato growers of Maine, the dairy, fruit, and viticulture farmers of New York, the wheat growers of southwestern Pennsylvania, and the market gardeners who encircled every sizable city were collectively numerous, even if not always well-to-do, and they played an important role in the section's economy. The growing of tobacco in the upper states of the Southeast and of cotton in the lower tier absorbed a disproportionate share of the southeastern farmers' time, but the production of Georgia peaches, Virginia apples and peanuts, Kentucky horses, and Florida citrus fruits was not without great local significance. The Middle West (i.e., the upper Mississippi Valley) was the greatest food-producing section of the nation, with three principal specialties: dairy products, corn and livestock, and wheat. The western states of the Old South, Louisiana, Arkansas, and Texas, produced cotton, corn and livestock, rice, sugar-cane, and citrus fruits. The ranches of the Great Plains and the Rocky Mountains concentrated mainly on cattle and sheep, but there were also areas in which the output of such items as wheat, potatoes, and sugar beets was phenomenal. The far Southwest provided abundant crops of grapes, citrus fruits, and vegetables, while the soil of north-ern California and the far Northwest yielded nearly everything that would grow anywhere. Throughout most of the agricultural areas there was also much general farming; a farmer might produce a given crop or two for the money it would bring, but he grew much else besides, both for his own use and for sale.[28]

Financially speaking, the decade of the 1920's was a bad one for American farmers, in spite of the fact that the process of mechaniza-tion had clearly begun. The census of 1920 found automobiles on 30.7 per cent of American farms, a figure raised to 58 per cent in 1930. Equally significant was the increase in motor trucks from 2 per cent in 1920 to 13.4 per cent in 1930, and of tractors from 3.6 per cent to 13.5 per cent. Before 1930 the use of electric motors and stationary gas engines on farms was not common enough to attract the attention of the census takers, but by that year they reported that over 4 per cent were equipped with the former, and 15 per cent with the latter.

[28] Foster F. Elliott, *Types of Farming in the United States,* United States Bureau of the Census (Washington, 1933), appended map.

Obviously horsepower and man power still did much of the work. No doubt, if the farmers had had the money with which to buy the new labor-saving devices, they would have had more of them. For in spite of generally good crops, the times were hard. During these years the number of American farms decreased by 2.5 per cent, the first such decline the census takers had ever reported, although in contrast the total farm acreage was up 3.2 per cent. Tenancy, which was commonest in the South (counting tenants rather than acres) but existed everywhere in the nation, was on the rise in nearly every state, from 38.1 per cent of all farms in 1920 to 42.4 per cent in 1930. The proportion of farms mortgaged rose similarly from 37.2 per cent in 1920 to 42 per cent in 1930. But the decline of the total value of farm products, from $21.4 billion in 1919 to $11.8 billion in 1929, best measured the disaster that had overtaken American agriculture.[29]

It was the wartime boom and its subsequent collapse that had brought the American farmer to the brink of ruin. During the war the demand for farm products had driven farm prices higher than had ever been known before. The net value of farm produce, according to a reliable estimate, rose between 1914 and 1918 from $4 billion to $10 billion and, in terms of purchasing power, an average of 25 per cent for all persons whose livings came from the farm. Wheat growers were particularly well off, for during the war a government guarantee assured them returns of well over $2 a bushel for all the wheat they produced, but war prices for all foodstuffs were high. With the farmers convinced that their good fortune would continue indefinitely, land prices, especially in the Middle West, soared to spectacular heights. When the war ended they were up for the nation as a whole by 40 per cent; by the end of 1919 they were up 70 per cent. Sometimes purchasers paid as high as $300 or $400 an acre for land that had been worth less than half those amounts before the war.[30]

Then came the news that after May 31, 1920, the government would no longer support the price of wheat; as a result, not only wheat prices

[29] *Fourteenth Census of the United States, Agriculture* (Washington, 1922), V, 18, 512; *Fifteenth Census, Agriculture* (Washington, 1932), IV, 11–12, 15, 22, 145, 443, 530.

[30] Willford I. King and others, *Income in the United States* (Washington, 1922), II, 313; Soule, *Prosperity Decade*, pp. 77–78; A. B. Genung, "Agriculture in the World War Period," United States Department of Agriculture, Yearbook, 1940, *Farmers in a Changing World* (Washington, 1940), pp. 277–295.

but also agricultural prices in general began to nose downward. By July, 1920, the index of farm prices had dropped ten points below the June figures; August showed an additional decline of fifteen points; September, still another fifteen points. Wheat by the end of the year sold as low as 67 cents. Exports continued in good volume, but their dollar returns declined alarmingly. By this time European farmers had begun to produce again, and with shipping released from wartime necessities other countries besides the United States were flooding the European markets with their produce. The results on American agriculture were catastrophic. Production kept up well—too well—but the low prices meant that farmers who had borrowed to buy land, or to improve their farms, were all too frequently unable to pay even the interest on their loans. Bankruptcies and foreclosures multiplied to an avalanche—a total of 453,000 farmers lost their farms in the crash. The boom had turned into the worst agricultural depression the nation had ever known.[31]

To meet this crisis the farmers were by no means unorganized. They had many societies, after the analogy of the businessmen's associations, that linked together farmers of similar interests, and they had also other and far more formidable organizations that included farmers of many different types. Oldest of the latter was the Grange, or, more accurately, the Patrons of Husbandry, which had survived many vicissitudes since its great days in the 1870's, and with the hard times took on new life. State Granges in nearly every state, and an active national headquarters in Washington, kept a close watch on all legislation that might affect the farmer. On the whole the order was conservative, with "more business in government and less government in business" as its favorite slogan. But it took an increasing interest in such farmer objectives as co-operative marketing, tax relief, and better credit facilities. Far more radical in tone was the American Society of Equity, founded in 1902 and active during the early 1920's in the Middle West. The original Equity program called for a holding movement to keep overplentiful items of farm produce, particularly tobacco and grain, off the market when prices were low, and even for a curtailment of production in order to let "the demand catch up with the supply." In practice these ideas proved to be almost impossible of

[31] Theodore Saloutos and John D. Hicks, *Agricultural Discontent in the United States, 1900–1939* (Madison, Wis., 1951), pp. 100–110.

attainment, so the leaders of Equity turned more and more toward cooperative marketing as their principal goal. Finally, they joined forces with a third and equally liberal order, the Farmers' Union, also founded in 1902, which was ready to promote almost any scheme that might bring the farmer better returns for his labor and investment.

Much more specific was the program of the National Non-Partisan League, founded in 1916, which operated principally in North Dakota, but was active also in Minnesota and other neighboring states. First the League proposed to capture political control of a given state, and then to embark on a program of socialization that the grain grower found well-nigh irresistible. League platforms demanded such items as (1) the state ownership of terminal elevators, flour mills, packinghouses, and cold-storage plants, (2) state inspection of grain and grain dockage, (3) the exemption of farm improvements from taxation, (4) state hail insurance, and (5) state rural credit banks. Ably led by Arthur C. Townley, the organization by 1920 had all but gained its first objective in North Dakota, but its efforts to go too far too fast led to a reaction, beginning in 1921, when the governor and attorney general it had elected lost office in a recall election. Thereafter it continued to exist, and to promote its program throughout the graingrowing area, but its influence was on the wane.[32]

This was not the case, however, with the American Farm Bureau Federation, most important of all the farm orders of the period. The roots of this organization went somewhat deeper, but its more important beginnings dated back only to the Smith-Lever Act of May 8, 1914, by which Congress appropriated $5 million for work in agricultural extension, with the understanding that the various states would match the sums allocated from national funds for use within their borders. The idea back of the law was to make more generally available for farm use the rapid advances then being scored by scientific agriculture. For the implementation of the program, principal dependence rested with the extension departments of the land-grant colleges, and with the numerous county agents whose duty it was to explain to the farmers, by demonstration if necessary, what the scientists had learned. As a speedy and natural development came the organization within each county of a Farm Bureau to facilitate the work of the county agent.

[32] *Ibid.*, 111–148, 219–254; Robert L. Morlan, *Political Prairie Fire, The Nonpartisan League, 1915–1922* (Minneapolis, 1955).

During the First World War the Farm Bureau movement spread like wildfire all over the country, and led inexorably to another development. In November, 1919, at Chicago, representatives of a thousand farm bureaus, drawn from thirty-six states, formed a new national organization, the American Farm Bureau Federation, an ideal pressure group for the effective promotion of the nation's entire agricultural interest. Soon a Farm Bureau lobby, amply backed by farmers' dues and headed by a paid director, Gray Silver of West Virginia, appeared in Washington, together with similar lobbies in nearly every state capital. The Farm Bureau now no longer restricted itself to the task of increasing agricultural production, but sought also to promote all the wider interests of agriculture, in particular the better marketing of farm produce. The expanded activities of the Farm Bureau, reasonable as they might seem to their promoters, met firm objections from two opposite extremes: (1) the other farm orders, who resented the Bureau's access to public funds they could not hope to tap and denounced its readiness to co-operate with the farmers' enemies, and (2) the more conservative business interests, who saw in the adoption by a farm organization of the same type of pressure methods that businessmen had long used to advantage only a conscienceless effort to serve the selfish purposes of a single class.[33]

As a matter of fact, industry as well as agriculture soon had its troubles. Just as the farmers had expanded their output during and after the war beyond their ability to sell at profitable prices, so also the industrialists had optimistically overproduced. Speculative business was hit hard by the advance of rediscount rates which the Federal Reserve Board began late in 1919 and continued over into 1920. "The expansion of credit set in motion by the war," said the Board, "must be checked. Credit must be brought under control." The farmers, who were among those hardest hit by credit deflation, were no longer in the market for farm machinery and other industrial products, and other American consumers were also running short of funds. As for the European market, the demand was still there, but the United States government was no longer supplying the money with which to finance it. Confessing its inability to "assume the burdens of all the earth," the United States discontinued, early in 1920, its policy of foreign loans

[33] Ralph H. Gabriel, "The Farmer in the Commonwealth," *North American Review*, CCXIII (May, 1921), 577–586; Saloutos and Hicks, *Agricultural Discontent*, pp. 255–285.

for reconstruction purposes. The results of this decision on foreign exchange were so catastrophic as to amount almost to the creation of an embargo against purchases from the United States. The pound sterling fell to $3.19, the franc to under 8 cents, and the mark to 2½ cents.[34]

Hard hit by these various blows, business fell off steadily during the last quarter of 1920, and hit bottom in early 1921. Wholesale prices dropped by as much as one-third during the latter year. Many bankruptcies occurred, in business as well as in agriculture, but the manufacturers, unlike the farmers, who kept right on producing in spite of diminishing returns, could and did seriously curtail production. This meant that employees had to be laid off, and before the year was over an estimated 4,754,000 men were out of work—another blow at consumers' demands. Thus at last the economic consequences of the war caught up with the nation. For industry the depression was severe, but soon over; for agriculture, it lasted for two full decades.[35]

[34] Frieda Baird and C. L. Benner, *Ten Years of Federal Intermediate Credits* (Washington, 1933), pp. 30–31; Carter Glass to Homer L. Ferguson, *Congressional Record*, 66th Cong., 2nd Sess., LIX (Feb. 6, 1920), 2545; *The New York Times*, Feb. 5, 1920, p. 19.

[35] Soule, *Prosperity Decade*, p. 96; E. J. Howenstine, Jr., "Lessons of World War I," *Annals of the American Academy of Political and Social Science*, CCXXXVIII (Mar., 1945), 180–187.

CHAPTER 2

The Retreat to Isolation

NEWTON'S third law, that for every action there must be an equal and contrary reaction, was not without a certain applicability to American political history during the first three decades of the twentieth century. Before the involvement of the United States in the First World War, the American people had for well over a decade shown a remarkable interest in reform. Municipalities experimented with the commission form of government and even turned over the administration of their affairs to city managers. States curbed party bosses with the direct primary; disciplined irresponsible legislatures with the initiative and referendum; threatened unworthy elective officials with the recall. In the national field, aspiring politicians recognized that the time had come to supplant the existing ascendancy of business over government with a roughly equivalent ascendancy of government over business. Beginning with Theodore Roosevelt and culminating during Woodrow Wilson's first term, the reform spirit effected a series of domestic innovations that gladdened the hearts of forward-looking citizens; then, as a logical projection of the same spirit into international affairs, came the crusade "to make the world safe for democracy," which to many liberals meant also to make the whole world democratic. But immediately after the war the reaction set in, and the pendulum that had swung so far to the left headed backward toward the right.[1]

[1] Richard Hofstadter, *The Age of Reform, From Bryan to F.D.R.* (New York, 1955), pp. 273–274.

Warren Gamaliel Harding, twenty-ninth President of the United States, well represented the reactionary trend; indeed, his fondness for comparing himself to William McKinley correctly classified his views with those of nineteenth-century conservatives. In his youth he had tried to study law, but found the strain too great and turned first to salesmanship, then to journalism, in which he succeeded moderately as owner and editor of the Marion (Ohio) *Star*. He was tall and handsome, wrote and spoke with impressive pomposity, drifted naturally into politics. Early in his career he made friends with Harry Micajah Daugherty, a small-time lawyer who had also turned politician, and who helped Harding graduate from a seat in the state senate to the lieutenant governorship. Harding carried the Republican banner as candidate for governor of Ohio in 1910, and lost. He presented Taft's name to the Republican convention of 1912, and stood steadfastly by Taft throughout the ensuing campaign, in which Taft also lost. But in 1914, when the war in Europe had produced a business slump that hurt the Democrats, Harding's luck changed. Even his standpat Republicanism was then insufficient to prevent his nomination and election to the United States Senate. As senator he was consistently conservative and partisan; keynoted the Republican National Convention of 1916 with a strongly anti-Wilson speech; stood firmly with the reservationists in the fight on the Treaty and the League.[2]

This regular but undistinguished record had an irresistible appeal for the men who made Harding President. After the frustrations they had suffered from Theodore Roosevelt and Woodrow Wilson, they were tired to death of presidential leadership, and wanted someone in the White House who would take advice instead of giving orders. Furthermore, Harding had already provided the party with a slogan that was to outlive the election—"back to normalcy." What the country needed, he had told a Boston audience the May before his nomination, was "not heroism but healing, not nostrums but normalcy, not revolution but restoration, not agitation but adjustment, not surgery but serenity, not the dramatic but the dispassionate, not experiment but equipoise, not submergence in internationality but sustainment in triumphant nationality."

Periods such as these led William Gibbs McAdoo to observe that

[2] Joe Mitchell Chapple, *Life and Times of Warren G. Harding* (Boston, 1924), pp. 7–198; Harry M. Daugherty, *The Inside Story of the Harding Tragedy* (New York, 1932), pp. 1–40.

Harding, with his "big bow-wow style of oratory," left "the impression of an army of pompous phrases moving over the landscape in search of an idea," but the word "normalcy" became the best known and most effective of the Republican battlecries. As a candidate, there was little reason to fear that Harding might take a too clear stand on some controversial issue. Harding's genius lay not so much in his ability to conceal his thought as in the absence of any serious thought to reveal. The election of 1920 still stands as one of the greatest affronts to the democratic process that the American record affords. The voters gave Harding, whose unfitness for the Presidency could hardly have been more obvious, the highest percentage of the popular vote achieved by any presidential candidate since well before the Civil War.[3]

It is by no means certain that the voters meant the election of Harding to be interpreted as a verdict against the League of Nations, but the President-elect in his first postelection statement declared that the Versailles League of Nations "is now deceased." The new administration, he said, would ask for the nations of the world to be "associated together in justice, but it will be an association which surrenders nothing of American freedom." In his inaugural address four months later, he made himself clearer on this subject than his own far from limpid English would ordinarily have permitted. He lauded the traditional American policy of noninvolvement, and promised to continue it: "Confident of our ability to work out our own destiny and jealously guarding our right to do so, we seek no part in directing the destinies of the Old World. We do not mean to be entangled. We will accept no responsibility except as our own conscience and judgment may determine." The new President, it was said, had hesitated about making so outspokenly an isolationist statement in his inaugural, but had been influenced by Mrs. Harding and Daugherty. No doubt he also sought to placate such bitter-enders as Johnson of California, who commented happily, "This is the end of the League of Nations."[4]

Much of his time between election and inauguration Harding had spent in Cabinetmaking. Evidently he had expected to rely mainly

[3] Samuel Hopkins Adams, *Incredible Era; The Life and Times of Warren Gamaliel Harding* (Boston, 1939), pp. 117, 136, 176; Mark Sullivan, *Our Times; The United States, 1900–1925*, VI, *The Twenties* (New York, 1935), 31–39; Frederic L. Paxson, *Postwar Years; Normalcy, 1918–1923* (Berkeley, Calif., 1948), pp. 152–153.

[4] *The New York Times*, Nov. 5, 1920, p. 1; Mar. 5, 1921, p. 4; Apr. 5, 1921, p. 4; Daugherty, *Inside Story*, pp. 173–176.

upon his own judgment about the "best minds" with which to surround himself, but the party leaders soon made him understand that he must listen to their advice even on such a subject as this. Even so, in a few instances he stood his ground stubbornly. Daugherty, his valued friend, went into the Cabinet as Attorney General, although his legal attainments no less than his political background proclaimed eloquently his unfitness for the post. Senator Albert B. Fall of New Mexico, whom Harding would have preferred for the Department of State, became Secretary of the Interior, although Fall's opposition to conservation was open and notorious. These were Harding's personal selections; the others, which varied from excellent to worse than mediocre, included Charles Evans Hughes, Secretary of State; Herbert Hoover, Secretary of Commerce; Andrew W. Mellon, Secretary of the Treasury; H. C. Wallace, Secretary of Agriculture; Will H. Hays, Postmaster General; John W. Weeks, Secretary of War; J. J. Davis, Secretary of Labor; Edwin Denby, Secretary of the Navy. With but few exceptions it was a Cabinet of rich men, men whose selection the business world stood ready to applaud. According to one estimate the ten Cabinet members collectively were worth, or could control, more than $600 million. Mellon was an aluminum magnate, reputed to be the second richest man in the United States. Certainly the Cabinet represented with great accuracy the Mellon point of view.[5]

Harding's other appointments were sometimes better, sometimes worse. During the two and one-half years of his Presidency he had the opportunity to choose four new members for the Supreme Court, although Wilson in eight years had filled only three vacancies. Harding's choice of William Howard Taft for Chief Justice could be criticized, perhaps, on the ground of Taft's conservatism, but Taft's legal stature well justified the selection. The other appointments fell also to men of ability, albeit in each case to an extreme conservative. Appointments to the lower federal courts, of which Harding made an unusually large number, were likewise of conservatives, but were better than might have been expected, considering the fact that each name had to run the gantlet of the Attorney General's office. The selection of General Leonard Wood to be Governor General of the Philippines was regarded with disfavor by the proponents of home rule

[5] *Ibid.*, pp. 68–91; Adams, *Incredible Era,* pp. 196–208; Sullivan, *Our Times,* VI, 144–153; Harvey O'Connor, *Mellon's Millions* (New York, 1933), pp. 117–123; Paxson, *Postwar Years,* pp. 192–196.

for the Islands, but his ability and integrity were not open to question. Colonel Harvey, whose "smoke-filled room" had turned the Republican nomination at Chicago to Harding, became ambassador to Great Britain, a position he filled with better grace than his critics had feared. Quite appropriately, Pershing became Chief of Staff of the United States Army. Harding's worst mistakes were made when he selected his old cronies for positions of high responsibility. Many of them came from Ohio, and had not outgrown the political morality of the "courthouse ring," all too frequently in evidence in almost any county seat.[6]

Whatever others may have thought, Harding did not regard himself as miscast in the role of President. Kindly and well-intentioned, unembarrassed by any overweening devotion to principle, he was by habit and instinct a harmonizer. He truly hoped that with the help of the "best minds" in his party he could chart a sure, if somewhat synthetic, course. But he soon found that too many prominent Republicans, not only in his Cabinet but also in Congress, in the individual states, and in the business world, felt that they had a right to be consulted. The "best minds" turned out in fact not to be a single responsible group, but rather a variety of separate pressure groups, each interested in a particular set of problems, and not too deeply concerned about any others. To achieve a well-co-ordinated program out of the various pressures brought to bear upon him would have required far greater talent than Harding possessed. Nor were these pressure groups particularly interested in working through the President if they could better accomplish their ends by working directly on Congress. Harding soon found that he could not count for a certainty on anybody's loyalty. His experiment with a government of "best minds" served only to demonstrate that a man of ordinary abilities had no business in the Presidency; that the office, as it had developed through the years, required exactly the kind of "superman" that the party leaders had sought to avoid.[7]

The saying "To the victors belong the oils" probably was meant to apply to the domestic policies of the Harding administration, but it had a certain pertinence in foreign affairs also. The First World War marked the nearly complete change-over from coal to oil in naval fuel-

[6] *Ibid.,* pp. 198–201; Daugherty, *Inside Story,* pp. 112, 321–323; Sullivan, *Our Times,* VI, 138–144.
[7] *Ibid.,* 180–182: Paxson, *Postwar Years,* pp. 191–192.

ing, and, with talk rife that the oil resources of the world were close
to exhaustion, assurance of an adequate oil supply became a matter
of first concern to all naval powers. The seriousness of this problem
for Great Britain, with no oil deposits whatever in the British Isles,
was greater than for the United States, which was actually far richer
in oil than scientists then knew. But even American oil men were concerned. The British government, regarding it as normal to give diplomatic support to British capital engaged in foreign ventures,
enthusiastically backed the expansionist activities of the Anglo-Persian
and the Dutch Shell oil interests, in the first of which the government
actually owned stock. American oil companies, on the other hand, were
obliged in the main to go it alone, a state of affairs that they thought
should be brought to an end. Led by the Standard companies, whose
interest in foreign expansion was outstanding, American oil men began
to voice a firm demand that their government give them the same kind
of diplomatic assistance that the British government gave British oil
interests. This they believed to be particularly their due in Latin
America, where the Monroe Doctrine could be interpreted as a kind of
warning against any excess of European zeal.[8]

It was in response to such a demand that President Harding made
it his first concern after his inauguration to promote the ratification of
the long-delayed Thompson-Urrutia treaty with Colombia, an action
admittedly designed to ease the way for United States oil interests in
the South American republic. Four days after he took office he
broached the subject at his first Cabinet meeting, and on the same day
he made public through the press his determination to seek immediate ratification of the treaty by the Senate, which was then in
session primarily to consider his nominees for administrative posts. Next
day the Senate received the President's request, but despite the earnest
support of Senator Lodge and Secretary Fall, the best the administration forces could do was to obtain agreement that the treaty would be
taken up early in the special session of Congress, to be called for the
following month.[9]

The treaty that thus engaged the President's attention—well ahead

[8] Sister Gertrude Mary (Gray), "Oil in Anglo-American Diplomatic Relations, 1920–28," unpublished doctoral dissertation, 1950, University of California, Berkeley, pp. 66–79; Ludwell Denny, *We Fight for Oil* (New York,
1928), pp. 95–109.

[9] *The New York Times,* Mar. 9, 1921, pp. 1, 3; Mar. 11, 1921, p. 3.

of his peace program—was designed to make amends to Colombia for
the deeply resented tactics by which Theodore Roosevelt in 1903 had
made possible the independence of Panama. Roosevelt's own verdict,
"I took the Isthmus," was in itself a kind of confession of wrong-
doing, although he consistently refused to concede this point. Repeated efforts on the part of the State Department failed to allay the
resentment felt in Colombia toward the United States. Taft's Secretary
of State, Philander C. Knox, even suggested an expression of regret
on the part of the American government, together with a money payment of $25 million, but his overtures were rejected. The Wilson ad-
ministration revived the subject, and actually obtained ratification by
Colombia in 1914 of the Thompson-Urrutia treaty, a document which
embodied the gist of the Knox proposals, but with a more forthright
apology. These negotiations, however, led to such frantic protests from
ex-President Roosevelt and his defenders that the United States Senate
took no action on the treaty. Twice later on, once in 1916 and once in
1917, the same treaty was before the Senate, with similar results. According to a statement by Senator Lodge and four other Republican
members of the Senate Committee on Foreign Relations, the conduct
of the United States in the Panama affair had been just and proper
in every respect, whereas the proposed treaty was an outright admission
that a wrong had been committed against Colombia. But on January
6, 1919, Theodore Roosevelt died, and with oil pressure mounting
steadily the Senate, now under Republican control, at once took a
more favorable view of the matter. It was agreed all around that the
"sincere regrets" clause might as well be stricken out, but with this and
a few other minor amendments the Senate Committee on Foreign Relations reported the treaty favorably, July 29, 1919.[10]

Just as ratification seemed assured, the government of Colombia,
with a bad sense of timing, showed signs of asserting an imprescriptible
national right to all subsurface oil. Eventually the United States received assurance that no such idea would be implemented, but the

[10] Charter Day Address, University of California, Berkeley, March 23, 1911,
quoted in A. B. Hart and H. R. Ferleger (eds.), *Theodore Roosevelt Cyclopedia*
(New York, 1941), p. 407; E. Taylor Parks, *Colombia and the United States,
1765–1934* (Durham, 1935), pp. 432–441; *The New York Times,* July 25, 1914,
p. 2; Watt Stewart, "The Ratification of the Thompson-Urrutia Treaty,"
South-western Political and Social Science Quarterly, X (1910), 427–428. The
text of this treaty is printed in *Senate Document 64,* 66th Cong., 1st Sess., pp.
1–7.

Senate did not again consider the treaty until January, 1921. Even then Roosevelt's friends had not all deserted him. Senator Kellogg of Minnesota, in particular, bitterly assailed the implied reflections on the character of Theodore Roosevelt, whose action in making possible the Panama Canal, he insisted, was "one of the great acts of a great President in a great era of American history." Again nothing was done.[11]

With Harding in the Presidency, and with the Republican majority in the Senate greatly augmented, the treaty obtained a higher priority than it had ever known before. Senator Lodge, untroubled by any qualms of conscience, led the fight for ratification. Secretary Fall, who as senator had also signed the minority protest in 1917, lent every possible assistance. There was the frankest possible admission of the fact that oil necessities required the good will of Colombia at whatever cost. Lodge pointed out that "the question of oil is one that is vital to every great maritime nation," and that the United States must stand firmly behind its overseas investors. He noted the rivalry for Colombian favors between American and British oil interests, and insisted that only the treaty could save the day. Of the five who had signed Lodge's minority report in 1917, only Borah refused to change sides. To the Senator from Idaho, the purchase of oil concessions at the price of "a great wrong to at least two great American characters" was indefensible. Nor was Borah alone in this opinion. To Senator Kenyon, the treaty was "a fine imposed after a plea of guilty"; to Senator Kellogg it was "an acknowledgment of guilt"; to Senator Watson of Georgia it was only "an indirect subsidy to the oil interests." But the proponents of ratification were undismayed, and on April 20, by a vote of 69 to 19, they had their way. Ratification by Colombia came in due time, and on March 1, 1922, the treaty was proclaimed in force. The success of American diplomacy in Colombia, judged by business results, was phenomenal. Investments of capital from the United States had stood at only about $2 million in 1912, and not much more in 1920. But by 1925, according to Department of Commerce estimates, they were up to $17 million, and by 1929 to $124 million.

Aid to American oil interests in their competition, especially with the British, for a greater share in the world's oil supply became for the next decade a kind of cornerstone of American foreign policy. While the

[11] *Congressional Record*, 66th Cong., 3rd Sess., LX (Jan. 3, 1921), 887; J. Fred Rippy, *The Capitalists and Colombia* (New York, 1931), pp. 441–451.

American government was unwilling, at least outside the Western Hemisphere, to back up oil expansion with force, it did not hesitate to use vigorous diplomatic pressure. Partly due to State Department representations, British producers cut American oil companies in on their rich holding in the Middle East, conceded them an equal chance of access to Russian oil, and retreated discreetly both in Mexico and in South America.[12]

Confident that it had done its best to promote the well-being of the nation's oil interests, the next move of the Harding administration in foreign policy was to make formal peace with Germany. After the defeat of the Treaty of Versailles, Congress had sought to declare the war at an end by joint resolution, but Wilson had interposed his veto on the ground that such an act would be "an ineffaceable stain upon the gallantry and honor of the United States." The Harding administration had no such qualms, so on July 2 the President affixed his signature to just such a resolution as Wilson had spurned. The resolution took pains to claim for the United States all the advantages that might have come to it had it signed the treaties with Germany, Austria, and Hungary, while at the same time rejecting all responsibilities that the Allies had incurred by those treaties. It also held on to such property as the government had seized from enemy aliens until "suitable provision" could be made for the satisfaction of claims which Americans held against the former enemy governments.

Secretary Hughes, when he took office, had had in mind leaving to the "Wilson" League the enforcement of the Treaty of Versailles, and establishing a new parallel League with broader purposes; also, he had hoped for changes in the Treaty of Versailles rather than a separate peace with Germany. But the irreconcilables in the Senate served notice on the President that they would wreck his administration if the old issues of the Treaty and the League were revived. The only alternative was to negotiate separate treaties with the defeated powers,

[12] *Congressional Record*, 67th Cong., 1st Sess., LXI (Apr. 12, 1921), 161; (Apr. 13, 1921), 191; (Apr. 15, 1921), 314; (Apr. 20, 1921), 477, 487; Department of State, *Papers Relating to the Foreign Relations of the United States, 1921* (Washington, 1936), I, 638–645; *ibid., 1922* (Washington, 1938), I, 974–979. See also Claudius O. Johnson, *Borah of Idaho* (New York, 1936), pp. 192–193; United States Department of Commerce, Office of Business Economics, *Foreign Investments of the United States* (Washington, 1953), p. 48; Ludwell Denny, *America Conquers Britain: A Record of Economic War* (New York, 1930), pp. 263–273.

and by the end of August this task had been accomplished. These treaties followed the formula of the joint resolution; the United States claimed all the "rights and advantages" obtained by the Allies, but assumed no obligations whatever. Claims against the Central Powers arising out of their alleged violations of neutrality before the United States entered the war, together with various claims for compensation by nationals of both sides, were settled later by amicable arbitration.[13]

The letdown from Wilsonian idealism implicit in every move of the Harding administration was not without its political hazards. Many Americans who had voted the Republican ticket had expected something quite different. During the campaign, for example, Secretary Hoover had told an Indianapolis audience: "The Republican party has pledged itself by its platform, by the actions of its majority in the Senate, by the repeated statements of Senator Harding, that they undertake the fundamental mission to put into living being the principle of an organized association of nations for the preservation of peace. The carrying out of this promise is the test of the entire sincerity, integrity, and statesmanship of the Republican party." Those who had shared Hoover's sentiments had a right to feel aggrieved. It cannot be said that the matter of good faith bothered many of Harding's intimates, but the matter of votes was something else. How were those voters who felt that they had been betrayed to be appeased?[14]

The answer was forced on Harding by Senator Borah, whose opposition to Wilson's League had been far more straightforward than the new President's. But Borah, strict nationalist though he was, convinced himself that the United States owed the world some kind of leadership in the direction of peace. As early as December 14, 1920, the Idaho senator had introduced a resolution requesting the President to invite the governments of Great Britain and Japan to send representatives to a conference on the reduction of "naval expenditures and building programs." The resolution did not come to a vote, but throughout the remaining months of the Wilson administration Borah and other believers in naval limitation kept the idea behind it vigorously alive.

---

[13] *Congressional Record,* 66th Cong., 2nd Sess., LIX (May 27, 1920), 7747; 67th Cong., 1st Sess. LXI (Apr. 13, 1921), 188–189; *United States Statutes at Large* (Washington, 1923), XLII, 105–107, 1939–1954; Henry C. Beeritz memo, pp. 16–18, 30, Hughes Papers, Box 172, Folder 25, Manuscripts Division, Library of Congress.

[14] Hoover's speech at Indianapolis, October 9, 1920, quoted in Ruhl J. Bartlett (ed.), *The Record of American Diplomacy* (New York, 1947), p. 481.

Obviously, their objective was to influence the incoming rather than the outgoing administration. Wilson, they knew, would never consider disarmament without a preliminary acceptance of the League or its equivalent, while the Navy Department, in line with Wilson's views, was advocating a rapid extension of the existing building program. The Sixty-sixth Congress seemed far more interested in naval limitation than in naval expansion, and even failed to make any naval appropriation whatever, leaving that task to its successor.[15]

Borah's course of action found high favor in certain Republican circles; indeed, peace by disarmament might serve as a satisfactory Republican alternative to the Democratic program of peace by world organization. The public generally, regardless of party, also thought well of the idea. After all, why should the United States, Great Britain, and Japan, recent partners in a common cause, be engaged in a frantic arms race with each other? Was this not a sinister plot to increase the profits of certain big businesses? On the other hand, many hardheaded businessmen saw in the high cost of naval construction one of the greatest obstacles to the reduction of taxes, an objective that for most of them had an irresistible appeal. Then, too, there were those who said that the day of the oversized battleship was done anyway. Why waste money in building obsolete weapons of warfare?[16]

When on Harding's call the Sixty-seventh Congress convened in special session the following April, Borah promptly reintroduced his resolution. It was soon apparent, however, that the President, despite his friendly attitude toward the idea during the campaign, was in no mood to be hurried. He let it be known that he favored not only the retention of the full naval building program authorized in 1916, but also the postponement until after its completion of any actual agreements on limitation. This might mean a delay of as much as three years. But the public reaction to the President's attitude was so unfavorable that he was finally obliged to make terms with the opposition. Eventually he withdrew his objection to the Borah resolution, while in return Congress allowed the naval appropriations to stand at figures well below those asked, but still fairly acceptable to the administration. By a vote of 74 to 0 in the Senate, and 332 to 4 in the House, the

[15] *Ibid.*, p. 484; Harold and Margaret Sprout, *Toward a New Order in Sea Power* (Princeton, 1946), pp. 114–121; Johnson, *Borah of Idaho*, pp. 262–266.
[16] *Ibid.*, 267–269; Sprout, *Toward a New Order,* pp. 116–117; Paxson, *Postwar Years*, p. 234.

Borah resolution became a part of the naval appropriation bill, which passed both houses, and on July 12 received the President's signature.[17]

Meantime the British government had been working earnestly toward the same end that the Borah resolution envisaged. Distress that Great Britain might soon have to confess that she no longer had the "largest navy afloat," coupled with the fear that the naval rivalry between the United States and Japan might eventually culminate in war, made some agreement on naval limitation seem essential. British diplomacy also found in the Anglo-Japanese alliance, which was due either to expire or to be renewed, a growing source of embarrassment. As long as this alliance existed, the United States could hardly be expected to renounce its building program, while the overseas Dominions, particularly Canada, disliked heartily the tie with Japan. From the British point of view it seemed evident that the problems of naval limitation and of the Far East were closely intertwined, and must both be given consideration. On the very day, July 8, 1921, that Harding let the British government know that he was ready to call a conference on the limitation of armaments, he was confronted with a British proposal that he call a conference on the problems of the Pacific and the Far East. The British would have preferred a preliminary session in London on the latter subjects, but they agreed eventually that both sets of problems should be included in the agenda of a single conference to be held in Washington.[18]

Before this expansion of the conference program was agreed upon, it was assumed that the only participants would be the "big five" naval powers: the United States, Great Britain, Japan, France, and Italy. For the discussion of Pacific and Far Eastern affairs, however, it was eventually decided to add four other powers, each with an Asiatic interest: China, the Netherlands, Portugal, and Belgium. Russia, in the bad graces of the Allies after the Bolshevik revolution, was left to protest heatedly against being left out. Germany, omitted for even more obvious reasons, was in no position even to protest. When the American State Department sought through preliminary inquiries to make sure that all the powers to be invited would be willing to send delegations, Japan alone seemed reluctant. Her leaders had little ob-

---

[17] *Congressional Record*, 67th Cong., 1st Sess., LXI (Apr. 13, 1921), 188; (Apr. 15, 1921), 357; (May 25, 1921), 1758; (June 29, 1921), 3226.

[18] *Foreign Relations, 1921*, I, 18–40; Sprout, *Toward a New Order*, pp. 126–135.

jection to the idea of a proportional reduction in naval armament, for such a procedure might possibly relieve their fears of British and American competition in the Far East; but they were by no means eager to have their imperialistic ambitions closely scrutinized, and for good reason they feared that the Anglo-Japanese alliance, on which they set great store, might become a casualty of the conference. After debating the matter for two weeks, they agreed to participate only on condition that "problems such as are of sole concern to certain powers or such matters that may be regarded [as] accomplished facts should be scrupulously avoided." These preliminaries over, Harding issued his invitation to the Great Powers and China on August 11, 1921, and to the others on October 4. The conference was called to meet in Washington on Armistice Day, November 11, 1921.[19]

There were few to deny that the time was ripe for such a conference as Harding had called. The United States and Great Britain were in many respects commercial rivals, but except for the competition over oil there was little or no animosity between them, and on both sides a general conviction that they could not possibly become antagonists in a war. Why, then, the great navies? As for the United States and Japan, there was much more than mere naval rivalry to be considered. Differences between the two countries over the Open Door policy, over American discriminations against Japanese immigrants, over Japanese wartime operations in Shantung and Siberia, over Japanese occupation of the former German islands in the North Pacific, over the whole program of Japanese expansion, were too obvious to be ignored.[20]

Trouble between the United States and Japan meant trouble for the British Empire, and some of the Dominions had particularly good

[19] The calling of the conference is set forth with authoritative detail in a Beeritz memo, "The Washington Conference," Hughes Papers, Box 169, Folder 3, Library of Congress, Manuscripts Division. See also *Conference on the Limitation of Armament*, Senate Document 126, 67th Cong., 2nd Sess. (Washington, 1922), pp. 4–9; *Foreign Relations, 1921,* I, 41–87; Tatsuji Takeuchi, *War and Diplomacy in the Japanese Empire* (Garden City, 1935), ch. 8.

[20] A. Whitney Griswold, *The Far Eastern Policy of the United States* (New York, 1938), pp. 121–132, 238–239, 245–246, 252–255, 264–266. On Siberia, see *Foreign Relations, 1921,* II, 702–705. Harding told Senator Hiram Johnson that "he had been advised by Intelligence officers, and officers in the Navy that war with Japan was imminent . . . that we probably would have had war with Japan ere this, but for the calling of the Disarmament Conference." Johnson to Hiram Johnson, Jr., and A. M. Johnson, Johnson Papers, Oct. 21, 1921, in Bancroft Library of the University of California.

reason to be concerned. Both Canada and Australia shared the attitude of the United States toward Japanese immigration, and Canada, as a near neighbor of the United States, feared the consequences that might result from a continuation of the Anglo-Japanese alliance. Suppose war should come between the United States and Japan, and suppose Great Britain, under the terms of the alliance, should be obliged to aid Japan in the war. Then Canada would have to choose between loyalty to the mother country and the danger of invasion from the United States. The possibility of such a war might be remote, but it was strong enough to make the Canadian Prime Minister, Arthur Meighan, take the lead in demanding, at an Imperial Conference held in London during June, 1921, that the Anglo-Japanese alliance should be scrapped. Canadian insistence, indeed, lay back of the British suggestion that Harding should call a conference on Pacific and Far Eastern affairs, a suggestion that won ready acceptance by the United States because of the uneasiness that Americans shared with Canadians over the alliance.[21]

As the time for the Washington Conference approached, the Harding administration, with able newspaper support, made every effort to impress the American people with the importance of the impending negotiations. The term "Peace Conference," in part no doubt because it was so familiar and so easy to say, but in part possibly with an intent to mislead, was regularly used, rather than the more accurate term, "Conference on the Limitation of Armament." The impression was cultivated that this was to be the correct and truly American substitute for the blundering Wilsonian activities in Paris. In the first place, the conference was to be held in the United States, where its proceedings could be watched, and not in some foreign capital, where scheming European diplomats could control it. In the second place, the American delegation contrasted sharply, and was meant to contrast, with the delegation Wilson had taken to Paris. The President himself was not to be a delegate; instead, the Secretary of State, Charles Evans Hughes, was to represent the United States, assisted by elder statesman Elihu Root and two members of the Senate Committee on Foreign Relations, Henry Cabot Lodge, a Republican, and Oscar W. Underwood, a Democrat. Had Wilson shown equally good judgment, people were

[21] J. B. Brebner, "Canada, the Anglo-Japanese Alliance and the Washington Conference," *Political Science Quarterly*, L (Mar., 1935), 45–58; Merlo J. Pusey, *Charles Evans Hughes* (2 vols., New York, 1951), II, 452–465.

expected to infer, how different the results at Paris might have been.[22]

The delegates to the conference were received with tremendous fanfare. Their first session was to have taken place on Armistice Day, November 11, 1921, but this was postponed until November 12 so that they might attend the ceremonious interment at Arlington Memorial Cemetery of an unknown American soldier who had died on a battlefield in France. At eleven o'clock, the armistice hour, men paused for a moment at their work all over the United States, or attended one of the innumerable memorial meetings scheduled for the occasion. The setting for the conference could hardly have been more impressive or dramatic.[23]

Other nations and peoples may not have been so starry-eyed as Americans in their optimism, but they were fully aware of the crushing burden of armament, and they took the opportunity presented by the Washington Conference with deadly seriousness. The British, although accenting naval expertness in a way the United States had sought to avoid, sent the best they had. Arthur Balfour, brilliant of mind, experienced in every detail of politics and diplomacy, full of good will toward the United States, headed their delegation. At first Premier Aristide Briand, then later former-Premier René Viviani, led the French delegation; Baron Tomosaburo Kato, who as Minister of Marine was directly responsible only to the Emperor, was the actual if not the technical head of the Japanese delegation; the Italians sent Senator Carlos Schanzer; the Chinese, two outstanding diplomats, Alfred Sze and Wellington Koo; and so on down the list.[24]

The conference was opened by President Harding with a dignified but highly emotional address, which was well received. Then Secretary Hughes, who on nomination of Balfour had been made permanent presiding officer of the conference, instead of confining his acceptance speech to the expected generalities, set forth with specific and accurate detail the precise reductions in naval strength that he wished the three leading powers to make. Altogether he marked for the scrap heap no less than sixty-six capital ships, built, building, or planned, with an aggregate displacement of over 1,878,000 tons (United States, 845,740;

[22] See, for example, Lyman Abbott, "The Washington Conference," in *Outlook*, CXXIX (Oct. 26, 1921), 283–284.

[23] *Ibid.* (Nov. 23, 1921), 462–465; H. G. Wells, *Washington and the Riddle of Peace* (New York, 1922), pp. 59–67.

[24] *Outlook*, CXXIX (Nov. 9, 1921), 377; *Conference on the Limitation of Armament*, pp. 18, 24, 30, 34, 38, 40.

Great Britain, 583,375; Japan, 448,928). The United States was to
scrap fifteen ships under construction, and fifteen old ships; the British
were to give up their far-advanced plans for four new *"Hoods,"* and
to destroy nineteen older craft; the Japanese were to scrap seven ships
planned or building, and ten older ships. Furthermore, no new capital
ships were to be laid down for a ten-year period. As for auxiliary
surface craft, submarines, and aircraft carriers, a supplementary
proposal, not included in the address, was "ready for submission to
the delegates."[25]

By the time the Secretary had finished reading his manuscript the
perturbation felt by members of the British and Japanese delegations
was beyond concealment. They had expected a prolonged series of
behind-the-scenes negotiations, but here in one public statement the
American Secretary of State had sunk more British battleships "than
all the admirals of the world had destroyed in a cycle of centuries,"
and plenty of other ships besides. They were amazed, too, at the inti-
mate knowledge he possessed of the British and Japanese navies, and
of their construction plans. In making these suggestions Hughes and
the three individuals with whom he had consulted most closely,
Assistant Secretary of the Navy Theodore Roosevelt, Jr., Admiral
Robert E. Coontz, and Captain William V. Pratt, had in mind to
retain the roughly 5:5:3 ratio that in their opinions then existed between the three navies concerned, taking due account of the difference
between ships merely planned or partly built and ships actually in
service. To secure secrecy and surprise, Hughes had not even made
known the precise details of his proposals to the other members of the
American delegation.[26]

The unexpected candor of Hughes's speech could be pointed to as
the kind of open diplomacy Wilson had advocated in the first of his
Fourteen Points, but had forsworn at Paris. From the galleries and from
the American press the response was almost ecstatic, and the overseas
reaction, while more restrained, augured well for the success of the

[25] Hughes's speech is printed in full, *ibid.,* 50–66. See also O. G. Villard
in *The Nation,* CXIII (Nov. 23, 1921), 589–591; Mark Sullivan, *The Great
Adventure at Washington* (Garden City, 1922), pp. 1–34; Pusey, *Hughes,* II,
466–473. According to Arthur Brisbane, Harding was puzzled, disgruntled, and
sore that he was not the chief recipient of the acclaim that went instead to
Hughes. Hiram Johnson to A. M. Johnson and Hiram Johnson, Jr., Nov. 19,
1921, Johnson Papers, Bancroft Library of the University of California.
[26] Sullivan, *The Great Adventure,* pp. 35–49; Sprout, *Toward a New Order,*
pp. 147, 155.

conference. But both the British and the Japanese bargained skillfully.[27] The British made it clear that they would brook no serious rivalry in European waters, while the Japanese refused point-blank to destroy their newest, largest, and virtually completed battleship, the *Mutsu,* which was on Hughes's proscribed list, and asked equality with the United States and Great Britain in aircraft carriers. Crucial in Japanese thinking was the fear that rival powers might construct fortifications and naval bases in too easy reach of Japan. American naval experts, professionally conscious of the possibility of war with Japan, as they had to be, insisted that without a strongly fortified base in Guam and a secondary base in the Philippines the United States could not hope to defend its Pacific empire. But the Japanese, intent not only on the security of their home islands but also on full freedom to expand their influence in easten Asia, saw in the proposed American program a serious threat. If these menacing gestures had to be faced, the only safety for Japan lay in a ratio of not less than $10:10:7$.[28]

It is by no means certain that Hughes, in revealing at the outset exactly what the United States was willing to do and exactly what he wanted from the British and the Japanese, had played his diplomatic cards in the most advantageous way. Patient and prolonged negotiations were necessary to obtain final agreement, and what the United States had at last to accept was substantially different from what Hughes had at first had in mind. The Japanese finally made a negotiable proposal. If they could keep the *Mutsu* and obtain a pledge that the *status quo* as to naval bases and fortifications in the Pacific would not be altered, they were prepared to accept the $5:5:3$ ratio. American cryptographers had broken the Japanese diplomatic code, so that Hughes was in a position to know that this was as far as the Japanese government would be willing to go; he must either accept these demands or face the prospect of failure. So accept them he did. As for the *Mutsu,* it was eventually arranged that the United States by way of compensation should retain two of its ships farthest advanced toward construction and scrap two older ships, while the British, who for several years had refrained from building capital ships, should lay down two new ships and scrap four older ones.[29]

[27] Balfour's reply to Hughes is printed in *Conference on the Limitation of Armament,* pp. 96–104. See also Chaput, *Disarmament,* pp. 110–113.

[28] *Conference on the Limitation of Armament,* pp. 106, 140; *Foreign Relations, 1922,* I, pp. 76–83; Pusey, *Hughes,* II, 476–479.

[29] Herbert O. Yardley, *The American Black Chamber* (Indianapolis, 1931),

The problem of the Pacific bases and fortifications was much harder to solve. The General Board of the United States Navy was known to be adamant in its opposition to any commitments on the subject, and had earnestly advised against its consideration by the conference. Yet in the end Japan got almost exactly what she wanted. As finally adopted, the Treaty for the Limitation of Armament included as Article XIX provisions which pledged the United States, the British Empire, and Japan to abstain from new fortifications or the construction of naval bases in their western Pacific island possessions. This meant that Great Britain was barred from the further strengthening of Hong Kong, while the United States must do nothing to improve the naval defenses of the Philippine Islands, Guam, or the Aleutians, and must be content with the Alaska-Hawaiian Islands-Canal Zone defense triangle. In return, Japan agreed to maintain the *status quo* in fortifications for the islands adjacent to her homeland, and for any other Pacific islands she might acquire. The net result was that the British and American possessions in the western Pacific were left at the mercy of Japanese attack—hostages, so to speak, that the Japanese might take at will should they decide that either nation threatened their Far Eastern policy. In reaching this agreement Secretary Hughes had the support of the other members of the American delegation, who were sure that Congress could never be persuaded anyway to appropriate funds for additional fortifications and new naval bases in Guam and the Philippines. But apparently he did not, possibly he dared not, consult his naval advisers at all.[30]

The decision to maintain the *status quo* in the Pacific islands was actually part of a much larger deal. As a substitute for the Anglo-Japanese alliance, which even the Japanese now knew that they could not retain, first the British and then the Japanese delegations had proposed a tripartite agreement dealing with both eastern Asia and the Pacific Ocean, and containing pledges of mutual nonaggression. But

---

pp. 308–313; *Foreign Relations, 1922*, I, 84–86, 90–106, 127–130; Sprout, *Toward a New Order*, pp. 176–180; Yamato Ichihashi, *The Washington Conference and After* (Stanford, Calif., 1928), pp. 46–59; Pusey, *Hughes*, II, 479–482.

[30] *Conference on the Limitation of Armament*, pp. 1581–1582; Sprout, *Toward a New Order*, pp. 175–176. Beeritz says Hughes used former Senator George Sutherland and Theodore Roosevelt, Jr., as go-betweens with the Navy, which had "no solution to the problem." Beeritz memo, Hughes Papers, Box 170, Folder 10, Library of Congress, Manuscripts Division.

such an agreement would have involved recognition by the United States of the Japanese conquests in Asia, and would have made it virtually impossible for the American government to oppose further Japanese expansion of the same kind. Hughes therefore countered with the idea of narrowing the area of the proposed pact to the islands of the Pacific, and this was done. Thus, instead of the United States acquiescing in the Japanese program of aggression, Hughes obtained recognition by Japan of American sovereignty over the Philippines. At Hughes's suggestion, also, France was included in what became a four-power instead of a three-power treaty. This was done in part to please France, whose Far Eastern holdings were not inconsiderable, and in part to avoid the risk that two of three signatory powers might join forces against a third. With France a member, as Secretary Hughes observed later, there would be four votes to cast instead of three, "and no one could say that England and Japan could combine against us."[31]

The Four Power Pact that at length materialized was adopted separately from the treaty for the limitation of armaments. By it the four powers agreed "as between themselves to respect their rights in relation to their insular possessions and insular dominions in the region of the Pacific Ocean." They agreed also to consult in case of any "controversy arising out of any Pacific question," and to "communicate with each other" on how to "meet the exigencies" of any "particular situation." This was a weak and watery substitute for the Anglo-Japanese alliance, and the Japanese were not unaware of the fact. But at least it saved face, and they were keenly aware of the important pledges they had obtained in Article XIX. They had not made a bad bargain, as the events of the Second World War were presently to prove.[32]

The one-sided character of the agreement with Japan was lost on the American public, which took little interest in western Pacific and eastern Asiatic problems, and had no faintest notion that the United States would ever have to fight about them. But the Washington decisions, as they began to leak out even before the end of the conference, filled most American naval experts with dismay. In an address delivered shortly after the naval treaty was concluded, Rear Admiral Harry S. Knapp summarized the opinion of the Navy on the outcome.

[31] Sprout, pp. 170–176; *Foreign Relations, 1922*, I, 74–75; Ichihashi, *Washington Conference,* pp. 112–134; Pusey, *Hughes,* II, 491–500.

[32] This treaty was presented to the Fourth Plenary Session of the conference in a speech by Senator Lodge, *Conference on the Limitation of Armament,* pp. 158–166. It was reprinted as adopted, *ibid.,* pp. 1614–1616.

In giving up the right to naval bases in Guam and Manila, he maintained, the United States had rendered virtually hopeless the task of defending American possessions in the Far East. Japan, on the other hand, in addition to the advantage of proximity, had already strongly fortified northern Formosa, and was believed to have a well-equipped base in the Pescadores. In actual fact the Japanese had obtained, as the Admiral pointed out, at "practically no cost to themselves," all that they had been straining their finances to the utmost to achieve.[33] A similar opinion was expressed by Captain D. W. Knox in a treatise he wrote on the conference, *The Eclipse of American Sea Power*. The treaty, he concluded, had so strengthened the relative position of Japan as to leave her "entirely free from the possibility of interference by America in the Orient."[34]

The agreement between the United States, Great Britain, and Japan on naval limitation left unsolved the problem of French and Italian naval strength. The British were determined that their quota must not be less than the combined strength of the French and Japanese navies, while the Italians were equally determined that their quota must not be less than that of the French. The ultimate outcome was a 5:5:3: 1.75:1.75 ratio, but this was achieved only after much acrimonious discussion. The French came to Washington with the expectation that the conference would concern itself with land as well as naval armament; indeed, the agenda circulated by the United States, shortly before the conference opened, definitely included this subject. For France the primary consideration was protection against a resurgent Germany. She had agreed to an unsatisfactory boundary in the Treaty of Versailles only on condition that the United States and Great Britain would join her against Germany in case Germany should again attack France. But the United States Senate had refused to ratify this agreement. French strategy at the Washington Conference called for a revival of the discarded military guarantees in return for a token reduction in the size of the French army, but Hughes chose to ignore totally the question of land armament, since on this score the United States had so little with which to bargain. In the end the French were obliged to accept the proposed naval ratio, but they did so only on condition

[33] Rear Admiral Harry S. Knapp, U.S.N., Ret., "The Limitation of Armament at the Conference of Washington," *Proceedings of the American Society of International Law, 1922* (Washington, 1922), pp. 12–19.

[34] Quoted in Sprout, *Toward a New Order*, pp. 268–270.

that, as far as they were concerned, it could not be extended beyond capital ships to such "defensive" craft as light cruisers, torpedo boats, and submarines. This meant in effect that the Washington reductions would be limited only to capital ships, the subject Hughes had chosen to spotlight in his initial address.[35]

Expressed in terms of tonnage limitations eventually to be achieved, rather than in terms of fighting efficiency, the capital-ship limitations agreed upon at Washington stood as follows: Great Britain, 558,950 tons; the United States, 525,850 tons; Japan, 301,320 tons; France, 221,170 tons; Italy, 182,800 tons. Certain new tonnage, however, was permitted to France and Italy, and neither nation was required to scrap any of its ships. It was further provided that the displacement of capital ships should be limited to 35,000 tons, and that the caliber of guns carried should not exceed sixteen inches. The treaty was to last until 1936, and new capital ships, with a few specified exceptions, might not be laid down for a ten-year period. To achieve these results the American delegation had made far and away the heaviest sacrifices, and had also consented to a maximum capital-ship tonnage much lower than its naval advisers had recommended. The United States, so most Navy men believed, had lost whatever chance it might otherwise have had to compete with Japan in the western Pacific, while in fighting efficiency it had dropped from a position of primacy to a position definitely second to that of Great Britain.[36]

Considered separately from capital ships in the discussions and in the final agreement on limitation was the problem of aircraft carriers. While such ships had existed experimentally from the war years, their potentialities were not as yet fully realized. That land-based planes could do terrible execution on ships at sea was proved during the summer of 1921, when in tests held one hundred miles off the Virginia coast General "Billy" Mitchell's American bombers sank a number of outmoded naval craft and the *Ostfriesland,* a surrendered German battleship only ten years old. Under these circumstances it was painfully apparent that carrier-based planes, even if less effective than land-based planes, could greatly project the fighting range of a fleet. There

[35] *Conference on the Limitation of Armament,* pp. 116–133, 452–468, 568–586; Sullivan, *The Great Adventure,* 198–201; Ichihashi, *The Washington Conference,* pp. 94–96; Sprout, *Toward a New Order,* pp. 181–189.

[36] The treaty is printed in *Conference for the Limitation of Armament,* pp. 1573–1604. American naval opinion on the treaty is summarized in Sprout, *Toward a New Order,* pp. 266–271.

were indeed those heretics who saw in the carrier the successor to the
battleship, and even the most orthodox of capital-ship defenders were
obliged to concede that the possibilities of the new craft were great.
After much haggling, the conference set the carrier strength of Great
Britain and the United States at 135,000 tons each; Japan, 81,000
tons; France and Italy, 60,000 tons each. It further agreed that a
carrier should ordinarily not exceed 27,000 tons displacement; but,
mainly because the United States wished to convert two battle cruisers,
the *Lexington* and the *Saratoga*, into carriers, the treaty also permitted
any of the powers to construct "not more than two air-craft carriers,
each of a tonnage of not more than 33,000 tons," provided that in so
doing it kept within its maximum quota. These oversized aircraft
carriers might not carry guns of above six-inch caliber, although those
of 27,000 tons and under might carry eight-inch guns.[37]

The limitations that the conference placed on the building of carriers
served to restrict somewhat the use of air power at sea, but this was
the only action it took to impede in any way full freedom in the
construction and use of aircraft. The growing war potential of air
power was too obvious to be overlooked; for the United States, the
proddings of General Mitchell and the sinking of the *Ostfriesland* had
made it crystal clear. But air power on the sea and air power on the
land were difficult to divorce, and the American delegation was unwilling to force consideration of a subject that might lead to a fruitless
discussion over land armament. Furthermore, there was no insistent
public demand for the limitation of air power, and any such efforts
might discourage the development of commercial aviation, still in its
infancy. Despite considerable anxiety on the part of the British, who
were in easy reach of military planes from the Continent, the conference took little note of what was to become the future's most potent
weapon of warfare.[38]

It was almost equally futile on the subject of the submarine. The
British, who had suffered much from submarine warfare, revived a
proposal they had made to the Paris Peace Conference that the submarine be abolished altogether, and all existing submarines scrapped.

[37] *Ibid.*, pp. 217–240.
[38] *Conference on Limitation of Armament,* pp. 750–806; Isaac Don Levine,
Mitchell, Pioneer of Air Power (New York, 1943), pp. 250–256; Sprout,
Toward a New Order, pp. 228–231, 239–240.

If this should not be deemed feasible, they favored rigorous limitations on submarine tonnage, and on the construction of large submarines designed for offensive rather than defensive action. But to the other delegations the British stand seemed far from desirable. American naval experts valued the submarine as a means of defending the coastlines and outlying possessions of the United States, while the French and all the lesser sea powers saw in the submarine their one most potent weapon against a stronger antagonist. In the end the conference did nothing about submarines except to draw up a set of unenforceable rules as to their use in wartime. This somewhat appeased public opinion, which strongly favored submarine limitations, but to compound the futility of the gesture the proposed rules were embodied in a separate five-power treaty which the French government refused to ratify, and which therefore never went into force. On the question of submarines the conference thus achieved exactly nothing.[39]

British failure to bring about submarine limitation led inevitably to failure in the limitation of the lesser surface craft with which to fight the submarine. The Americans had hoped to extend the ratio for capital ships and carriers to smaller craft, and, but for the submarine impasse, the British might have gone along. Unable to make headway with quantitative reductions, Hughes sought and obtained a qualitative limitation that accorded with current practice. Light cruisers, it was decided, might not exceed 10,000 tons displacement, or carry guns of greater than eight-inch caliber. At the moment these limitations excited little comment, but later on, as naval architects sought feverishly to cram into 10,000-ton ships greater and ever greater speed, maneuverability, fighting capacity, and cruising range, they caused anxious concern.

As finally adopted, the Treaty for the Limitation of Armament was to remain in force until December 31, 1936, but any power wishing to terminate the agreement must serve notice of intention (as Japan did eventually) two years in advance of that time. The treaty certainly did not end naval rivalry, for it left the way wide open for competition in cruisers, submarines, and aircraft, but it did set substantial limits on the construction of battleships. A few cynical observers, noting that battleships were rapidly becoming outmoded anyway, argued that the

[39] *Ibid.*, pp. 190–216, 311–312; *Conference on the Limitation of Armament*, pp. 102, 474–589, 604–626, 1605–1611; Pusey, *Hughes*, II, 484–485.

principal success of the conference lay in the reductions it had made possible in naval expenditures.[40]

The limitations set by the conference on the naval power of Great Britain and the United States in the Far East were real enough, however, to make it seem essential that the Japanese should give some guarantees of good behavior with reference to China. Naturally no other nation was more interested in this than China herself, whose delegates came prepared to insist on the elimination of "all special rights, privileges, immunities or commitments . . . claimed by any of the powers in or relating to China."[41] Under combined British and American leadership a Nine Power Treaty eventually emerged which went about as far as words could go toward substituting multilateral support of the Open Door policy for the more or less unilateral support it had received previously from the United States. The contracting nations other than China also agreed "to respect China's rights as a neutral in time of war to which China is not a party." China on her part agreed that she would not permit discriminations of any kind on her railroads, and that, whenever she was a neutral, she would "observe the obligations of neutrality."[42] But all these agreements were only words, and provided no means of enforcement other than the good faith of the nations concerned. No doubt the American delegation realized that in securing the verbal endorsement of the Open Door policy it had gone as far as public sentiment in the United States was willing to approve. Americans liked the idea of the Open Door, but they were wholly unwilling to fight for it.[43]

For all its high-sounding phrases, the Nine Power Treaty left intact many limitations on Chinese sovereignty. The protests of the Chinese delegates against such matters as extraterritoriality, and the presence of foreign troops, post offices, and radio stations in China, made little impression on the conference. On extraterritoriality, it decided to set up an investigating commission, but each power was left free to accept or reject the commission's findings, as it might see fit. The ruling on post offices was to abolish all *except* those operating with China's consent or in leased territories; and, on radio, to limit legation stations, except in emergencies, to strictly governmental communications. As for

[40] *Conference on Limitation of Armament,* pp. 88–93, 568–586; Sprout, *Toward a New Order,* pp. 208–216.
[41] *Foreign Relations, 1922,* I, 272–274.
[42] *Conference on Limitation of Armament,* pp. 1624–1625.
[43] The Nine Power Treaty is printed, *ibid.,* pp. 1621–1629.

the withdrawal of foreign troops, that would happen only when China could assure the nations concerned of her ability to protect "the lives and property of foreigners" within her borders. China's earnest effort to rid herself of the infamous Twenty-one Demands, which in 1915 had, among other things, laid the basis for Japan's expanding Manchurian claims, were even less successful. The Japanese did, indeed, withdraw Group V of these demands, many of which, however, they had found to be virtually unenforceable. The conference thus left Japan, and for that matter the other nations also, with practically the same concessions in China that they had had before.[44]

Several agreements not included in the Nine Power Treaty were also designed to reduce tensions in the Far East. During the conference, Japan and China were persuaded to negotiate a separate treaty which provided for the return to China of sovereignty over Shantung, but left Japan with some of the economic advantages she had obtained from the occupation. The British, in a burst of generosity, also announced that they would return their Weihaiwei leasehold along the Shantung coast to China, and the powers conceded, in a separate treaty on the subject, a certain amount of tariff autonomy to China, although far less than the Chinese had hoped for, and demanded. The United States and Japan ended their vexatious dispute over Yap by a treaty which left the island in the hands of Japan, but gave the two countries equal rights with respect to cable facilities; and Japan promised formally, although not as a part of any treaty, to withdraw her forces from Siberia, an action she took in October, 1922.[45]

Whatever the verdict of time was to be on the Washington Conference, the contemporary verdict was on the whole favorable. In America, in Europe, in Asia, the general assumption was that the conference had taken a long step toward world peace. Each of the three great naval powers had in effect renounced the possibility of waging aggressive war in return for security within the waters adjacent to its homelands. This meant incontestably the end of British supremacy

---

[44] *Foreign Relations, 1922,* II, 339–345; Ichihashi, *Washington Conference,* pp. 192–229, 265–288, 398–402; Griswold, *Far Eastern Policy,* pp. 327–328. A Beeritz memo, "The Far Eastern Question," covers this subject fully. Hughes Papers, Box 171, Folder 19.

[45] *Foreign Relations, 1922,* II, 363–375; Ichihashi, *Washington Conference,* pp. 306–339; Sprout, *Toward a New Order,* p. 252. Another Beeritz memo, "The Mandate Controversy," explains the Hughes position on Yap. Hughes claimed an equal voice with the Allies in the disposal of enemy colonial possessions. Hughes Papers, Box 171, Folder 16.

on the high seas, and possibly the temporary end of any American ambitions to be the successor of Great Britain in such a role. But Americans could congratulate themselves that the Anglo-Japanese alliance was at an end, and that the spirit of co-operation between the two great English-speaking nations had never been stronger. They had long stood together with reference to Atlantic affairs; now they had extended the area of agreement to include the Pacific. National rivalries, augmented by Great Britain's pride in her historic position of leadership and America's devotion to isolationism, were strong enough to prevent an Anglo-American alliance, but the danger of war between the two powers had all but vanished. There was much rejoicing also in the prospective reductions in naval expenditures; regardless of what the experts might think or fear, the conference had gone far toward insuring lower taxes and balanced budgets. As for Japan, there were some hurt feelings, particularly over the cancellation of the Anglo-Japanese alliance, but the Japanese people believed that the conference had lessened the danger of war, and the experts, despite their protestations of disappointment, knew that the conference had left little for Japan to fear. The severest criticism of the conference, and in the light of subsequent events possibly the fairest, came from France, where it was noted regretfully that the delegates, in dodging the subject of land armament, had avoided doing anything to promote the security of France in Europe, while, by holding down French naval strength to a parity with Italian, they had left France vulnerable to attack in the vital Mediterranean area.[46]

Ratification of the treaties by the United States Senate was not achieved without a struggle. Except for the Hearst press, the newspapers of the country were almost unanimous in their approval of the work done by the conference, and the public agreed with the newspapers. But the Democrats in the Senate were still smarting from the defeat they had received on the Treaty of Versailles, and some of them were unwilling to accept without a fight the Republican substitute for Wilson's peace program. Criticism tended to center on the Four Power Treaty. Did it not provide for an alliance quite as much at variance with the American tradition of noninvolvement as ever was the League of Nations? Did it not put the United States on record as guaranteeing Japan's ill-gotten imperialistic gains? Why, in particular, must the

---

[46] Sprout, pp. 255–281; *Brassey's Naval and Shipping Annual, 1923* (London, 1923), pp. 1–5, 68–84; Griswold, *Far Eastern Policy*, pp. 331–332.

United States approve the retention by Japan, under a League of Nations mandate, of the Pacific islands she had taken from Germany? And was there not some concealed understanding between the United States and Great Britain that ought to be revealed? But in the end the Four Power Treaty won out, 67 to 27; twelve Democrats joined fifty-five Republicans to provide the majority, and four Republicans voted with twenty-three Democrats in the minority. One reservation was adopted, to the effect that under the terms of the treaty the United States recognized "no commitment to armed force, no alliance, no obligation to join in any defense." The other treaties went more easily. One dissenting vote was cast against the treaty for the limitation of armament and the Chinese tariff treaty. The others were adopted unanimously.[47]

Once ratification had been achieved, American politicians of both political parties seemed so content with the agreements reached that they ignored Hughes's warning to "maintain the relative naval strength of the United States," and all but discontinued naval building. Between 1922 and 1929, the United States built or provided for the building of only eleven ships, while the comparable figure for Great Britain during this same period was 74; for Japan, 125; for France, 119; and for Italy, 82. The eagerness of the United States to abdicate its position of world leadership, and to focus attention primarily upon domestic affairs, could hardly have been more eloquently expressed.[48]

[47] *Congressional Record,* 67th Cong., 2nd Sess., LXII (Mar. 24, 1922), 4497; (Mar. 29, 1922), 4718–4719, 4730; (Mar. 30, 1922), 4784, 4791. The treaty with Japan over Yap was ratified 67 to 22, *ibid.* (Mar. 1, 1922), p. 3194. For the text of this treaty, see *United States Statutes at Large,* XLII, 2149–2153. Hiram Johnson was among the most ardent critics of the treaties, particularly the Four Power Treaty. The President, he reported, argued with him for two hours on the subject, but in Johnson's opinion Harding knew nothing whatever about the treaties. Johnson to Hiram Johnson, Jr., March 5, 1922, Johnson Papers.

[48] Pusey, *Hughes,* II, 511. Statistics on American naval building may be variously interpreted. Bemis lists eight cruisers, five submarines, and six river gunboats, all built between 1925 and 1929. Samuel Flagg Bemis, *A Diplomatic History of the United States* (New York, 1942), p. 703.

CHAPTER 3

What Price Normalcy?

O F ALL the pressure groups that operated upon the Harding administration, those which represented business suffered least from opposition. Other groups, labor, farmer, veteran, prohibition, and the like, scored occasional victories; but as nearly as a leaderless administration could be said to have had a policy, the policy of the Harding administration was to do with alacrity whatever business wanted to have done. Shorn of complexities, business demanded only a few fundamentals from government, but these were important and it demanded them with great insistence. First of all, it wanted economy and efficiency in government, in part to make possible its second great goal the lowering of taxes, particularly on business incomes. Business also, although not without some intelligent dissent, still gave its adherence to the protective tariff system, with higher duties whenever it deemed them necessary to restrain foreign competition. And, even more stridently, business called for a return to free enterprise. This meant the complete withdrawal of government from any kind of participation in business, and the virtual elimination of governmental restrictions on the full freedom of business to do exactly as it pleased; but it did not mean that government was to be discouraged from giving such aid and encouragement to business as government could. Finally, business wanted the help of government in the disciplining of labor, the growing power of which it feared and meant to curb.[1]

[1] James Warren Prothro, *The Dollar Decade, Business Ideas in the 1920's* (Baton Rouge, 1954), pp. 111–206.

The Sixty-seventh Congress which met in special session on April 11, 1921, was quick to demonstrate its responsiveness to business pressures. Among the first of the laws it enacted was a Budget and Accounting Act, which Harding signed on June 10, 1921. Few politicians who voted for this measure had any real enthusiasm for it; most of them, in fact, favored the old system, which required each bureau and department of the government to come to Congress each year, hat in hand, asking for what it wanted. But the trouble with the traditional process was that it made no provision for an adequate over-all study of proposed expenditures and receipts; Congress tended to vote appropriations and revenues quite independently of each other, trusting that somehow what came in and what went out would about balance. After years of talk, Congress finally, in the last half of Wilson's second term, passed a budget act, but with one stipulation that Wilson, who otherwise favored the measure, was unwilling to accept. The act provided for two new officials, a Director of the Budget who should advise the President in the preparation of an annual budget, and a Comptroller General who should audit all accounts to insure that expenditures were being made in accordance with the law. Both officials were to be appointed by the President, but Congress set the term of office for the Comptroller General at fifteen years and, perhaps as a slap at Wilson, gave Congress rather than the President the right to remove him. Wilson believed this provision to be both unconstitutional and unwise, and because of it he vetoed the bill.[2]

The act that Harding signed was substantially the one that Wilson had vetoed. For Comptroller General Harding selected a politician, John Raymond McCarl of McCook, Nebraska, who had once been Senator Norris's private secretary, but had deserted Norris on the eve of his campaign for re-election in 1918 to become executive secretary of the Republican Congressional Committee. While McCarl had little background for his new duties, the same could not be said of Harding's choice for Director of the Budget, Charles Gates ("Hell 'n' Maria") Dawes, the Chicago banker who had won renown as Purchasing Agent for the A.E.F. in France. Dawes took vigorous command of the new office, and by December, 1921, when Harding submitted his first estimate of needs to Congress, had worked out a notable program of economy. The budget Harding recommended for 1922–23 called for

[2] Frederick L. Paxson, *Postwar Years, Normalcy, 1918–1923* (Berkeley, Calif., 1948), pp. 224–225.

appropriations of only $3.5 billion, and despite considerable congressional tampering it made possible the desired goal of an annual surplus rather than a deficit.[3]

This development, so gratifying to the business community, by no means pleased the veterans' lobby, which, under the leadership of the American Legion, was demanding "adjusted compensation" for all servicemen. Military personnel, the argument ran, had drawn low pay from the government while the stay-at-homes had fattened off the high wartime wages and profits. With farm returns down from 1920 on, and business slackening, the drive for back pay grew ever more insistent; Congress, always sensitive to the strength of the soldier vote, was in a mood to yield to it. The Senate had under consideration a bill that gave veterans one of two options, either an extra dollar (a dollar and a quarter if overseas) for each day spent in service or a paid-up twenty-year insurance policy of equivalent value. To head off passage of any such measure, Harding, for once, used the full power of the Presidency, even to the extent of appearing in person before the Senate to record his protest. As a result the Senate voted to recommit the bill, 47 to 29, and this particular threat to economy was averted. But not for long. Next year, with the mid-term elections of 1922 in sight and signatures available by the million on petitions asking Congress to yield to the veterans' demands, a "Bonus" bill based on the paid-up insurance principle passed both houses of Congress, only to be vetoed by the President. Disappointed but undismayed, the veterans' lobby continued its work, and in May, 1924, an Adjusted Compensation Act finally became law over President Coolidge's veto. Cash payments were avoided, but in its final form the Act permitted holders of insurance policies to borrow on them up to about one-fourth of their face value.[4]

Harding and the Republican stalwarts in Congress, by holding the line as long as they did against the "Bonus," won the undying gratitude of the business community, which hoped almost above all else to translate economies in government into lower taxes. In Harding's

[3] Ibid., 225–227; Charles Gates Dawes, The First Year of Budget of the United States (New York, 1923), pp. 3, 173; Alfred Lief, Democracy's Norris; The Biography of a Lonely Crusade (New York, 1939), pp. 212, 236.

[4] Paxson, Postwar Years, pp. 228–229, 306–307; Congressional Record, 67th Cong., 1st Sess., LXI (July 12, 1921), 3597–3598; (July 15, 1924), 3874; 68th Cong., 1st Sess., LXV (May 15, 1924), 8660–8661; (May 17, 1924), 8813; (May 19, 1924), 8871.

Secretary of the Treasury, Andrew W. Mellon, the business leaders had a spokesman on whose judgment they knew they could depend; in order to qualify for the Treasury post Mellon had had to resign directorships in sixty corporations with an aggregate capital of $2 billion. One of Mellon's first acts on taking office was to urge upon Congress (1) the outright repeal of the excess profits tax, which still endured as a legacy of the war, and (2) an immediate reduction of the maximum surtax rate from 65 per cent to 40 per cent, with an ultimate goal of only 33 per cent. This would leave unchanged the taxes on incomes below $66,000, but to reimburse the Treasury for losses due to the high-bracket reductions he suggested a doubling of the stamp tax on documents, a two-cent tax on every bank check, two-cent postal cards, and a federal license tax on automobiles. Confronted with the argument that his program would serve merely to transfer from the rich to the people generally a large share of the tax burden, he contended that the higher surtax rates had "already passed the point where they can be collected." Or, as Senator La Follette freely translated this statement, "Wealth will not and cannot be made to bear its full share of taxation." As if to provide proof of this contention the Treasury Department was soon handing out generous refunds, mainly to large corporations. During his first eight years as Secretary of the Treasury, Mellon's refunds reached the total of $3.5 billion, including several million dollars returned to the various Mellon interests.[5]

The reduction of taxation for the rich and the transfer of as much of the burden as possible to the middle and lower incomes was a matter of principle with Mellon, and not merely of self-interest. He later wrote a book on the subject in which he contended earnestly against burdensome taxes on "wealth in the making." The result of such a system, he argued, was to drive money that should be put to better use into "safe but unproductive forms of investment." If the wealth producers were only left alone, he reasoned, they would create more jobs for more people, and add to the country's prosperity. But if the government continued to take away so large a share of their profits, they would

[5] Philip H. Love, *Andrew W. Mellon; The Man and His Work* (Baltimore, 1929), pp. 34–50; Harvey O'Connor, *Mellon's Millions; The Biography of a Fortune* (New York, 1933), pp. 124–129; A. M. Schlesinger, Jr., *The Age of Roosevelt; The Crisis of the Old Order, 1919–1933* (Boston, 1957), pp. 62–63; *Congressional Record*, 71st Cong., 2nd Sess., LXXII (Mar. 14, 1930), 5529; 71st Cong., 3rd Sess. (Dec. 16, 1930), 873–876.

refuse to take the chances necessary to the proper expansion of business, and so everyone would suffer. Despite the vigorous opposition of La Follette and other progressive-minded members of Congress, Mellon got a substantial reduction of taxes on the rich. In the Revenue Act of 1921, which Harding signed on November 23, the excess profits tax disappeared, and the maximum surtax was reduced to 50 per cent. As a sop to the low-bracket taxpayers, the exemption for heads of families with incomes of $5,000 or less was raised from $2,000 to $2,500, the exemption for each dependent from $200 to $400, and many "nuisance" taxes were omitted entirely. Quite undesired by business, but a political necessity, the tax on net profits of corporations was set at 12½ per cent instead of 10 per cent.[6]

The failure of the business interests to obtain in full the changes Mellon had urged was due largely to the activities of the Agricultural Bloc, or, as it was more commonly called, the Farm Bloc. This was a more or less informal group of about twenty senators and a somewhat larger number of representatives, nearly all from the agricultural states of the Middle West or the South. Members of the Bloc insisted not only that favors to business should be strictly limited but also that farm relief should take priority over every other subject; in particular, they demanded that the farmers have whatever benefits they could obtain from a protective tariff on farm products. An Emergency Agricultural Tariff bill along these lines had passed Congress late in the Wilson administration, only to be vetoed by the President, who pointed out that it "would not furnish in any substantial degree the relief sought." What the farmer really needed, Wilson argued, was "a better system of domestic marketing and credit," and "larger foreign markets for his surplus products."[7]

After Harding's inauguration a similar measure, with the Bloc behind it, received the President's signature, May 27, 1921. It placed nearly prohibitive charges on twenty-eight agricultural items; but as Wilson had predicted, the new imposts proved to be notably ineffective in raising farm prices. Only in the case of wool, sugar, and a few

[6] Andrew W. Mellon, *Taxation: The People's Business* (New York, 1924), pp. 93–94; Paxson, *Postwar Years*, pp. 260–262; Belle Case La Follette and Fola La Follette, *Robert M. La Follette* (2 vols., New York, 1953), II, 1033–1036; *United States Statutes at Large* (Washington, 1923), XLII, 237, 252.

[7] *New Republic*, XXVI (Mar. 9, 1921), 2; Arthur Capper, *The Agricultural Bloc* (New York, 1922), pp. 3–12, 105–117; *Congressional Record*, 66th Cong., 3rd Sess., LX (Mar. 3, 1921), 4498–4499.

relatively unimportant items did they make any real difference. They did, however, commit the Farm Bloc irretrievably to the high-tariff program, so that when the time came for an all-out tariff revision its members could stage no such protest as had preceded the passage of the Payne-Aldrich Tariff in 1909. As an earnest of what was yet to come, the Emergency Act itself placed an embargo, aimed mainly at German producers, on dyestuffs and chemicals, and prohibited the dumping (that is, "sale at less than its fair value") of foreign goods on the American market. The Emergency Act was to last for six months only, except for the dye and chemical clauses, which were for three months only, but in practice its rates were extended until replaced by the Fordney-McCumber Act of 1922.[8]

Other measures forced on Congress by the Farm Bloc were less futile than the agricultural tariffs. Farm Bloc pressure resulted in the voting of a billion dollars to the War Finance Corporation (which Congress had revived over Wilson's veto shortly before he retired) to aid in the transportation and exportation of agricultural commodities; a Future Trading Act designed to restrict speculation in wheat on the grain exchanges; and a Packers and Stockyards Act which supplemented the regulatory authority of the Federal Trade Commission by giving the Department of Agriculture substantial powers over the inspection and control of the meat-packing industries. The Farm Bloc won these victories in spite of vigorous opposition from more conservative Republicans, who reflected accurately the business point of view, but whatever the regulars might think of the other measures the Farm Bloc had forced upon them, they were not unduly alarmed over the emergency tariff on agricultural products. They still believed in the pre-Wilson protective tariff as it applied to manufactured goods, and they accepted the higher rates on farm produce as a means toward the greater end of restoring the general increases they desired.[9]

Since constitutionally all money bills must originate in the House, it fell to Chairman Joseph W. Fordney of the House Ways and Means Committee to take the lead in the formation of the new general tariff.

[8] *United States Statutes at Large* (Washington, 1923), XLII, 9–10, 191, 220; Frank W. Taussig, *The Tariff History of the United States* (8th ed., New York, 1931), p. 452; *New Republic*, XXVI (Mar. 9, 1921), 32.

[9] Paxson, *Postwar Years*, pp. 255–256; *Industry*, III (Oct. 15, 1921), 2. This magazine was published in Washington, 1919–22, and edited by Henry Harrison Lewis. Beginning with Vol. V (1922), it became a monthly. It was strongly proindustry and antilabor.

This he did in the way custom had long decreed, first by open hearings, then by secret sessions of the majority members only, with the Democrats excluded. By the end of June, 1921, the bill was ready for the House, where debate was held to a minimum by a special "gag" rule that limited amendments from the floor and required a final vote on July 21. On that date the bill passed the House, 288 to 177, with the Republicans furnishing most of the ayes and the Democrats the noes. Everyone knew that this was only a starter, for the bill was certain to be rewritten in the Senate.[10]

In contrast with the House, the Senate took its time; not until April 11, 1922, did the Senate Committee on Finance even report out a bill. By that date Penrose was dead, and Porter J. McCumber of North Dakota was in charge of the measure. The bill he presented to the Senate proposed some 2,082 amendments to the House bill, most of them designed to revive and reinvigorate still further the protective system. The debate in the Senate was long and acrimonious. The Farm Bloc, now occasionally called the "tariff bloc," objected among other things to the retention of the embargo on dyestuffs and chemicals. Some of its members charged that the new American chemical industry had come into existence only by what amounted to an outright theft of German patents seized during the war, then sold at bargain rates to an American syndicate. For an industry so created to protest against foreign competition was more than many western Senators could condone. But in the end the Farm Bloc voted for the bill, embargo and all, since it included, like the Emergency Act, the desired schedules on farm products. Senator Hiram Johnson, for example, fought valiantly and successfully for higher duties on California nuts and citrus fruits, and, having obtained what he wanted, felt that he could not in good conscience oppose the rest of the bill. The only Republican senators to vote with the opposition were Borah and La Follette, although Norris was prevented from joining them only by being absent. The Democrats lined up solidly against the bill, but even so it passed, 48 to 25.[11]

[10] *Congressional Record,* LXI, 67th Cong., 1st Sess. (July 21, 1921), p. 4127; Paxson, *Postwar Years,* pp. 288–292.

[11] *Ibid.,* pp. 293–294; *Congressional Record,* 67th Cong., 2nd Sess., LXII (Aug. 19, 1922), 11627. The Senate vote on the report of the Conference Committee was slightly different, 43 to 28, *ibid.* (Sept. 19, 1922), p. 12907. See also Taussig, *Tariff History,* pp. 472–477; and Hiram Johnson to A. M. Johnson and Hiram Johnson, Jr., in Johnson Papers, July 8, 15, 1922, Bancroft Library of the University of California.

While a few Democrats undoubtedly cast their negative votes on principle, many of them were in fact almost as protectionist in their sympathies as the Republicans. During the war, industry had made rapid headway both in the South and the West, and with this development low-tariff views in those sections tended to decline and almost to disappear. Among Republicans and Democrats alike, the details of schedules were well worth arguing about, but the necessity of protection was hardly challenged. The dominant sentiment, both in Congress and throughout the country, held that the American producer must at all costs be given the advantage in the American market. When, after two lively encounters with conference committees, the Fordney-McCumber Act finally passed both houses of Congress and on September 21, 1922, received the President's signature, it achieved the distinction of setting the highest tariff rates ever known up to that time in all American history. In the final version the embargo on dyestuffs and chemicals lost out, but duties designed to accomplish the same purpose were written in. Silk and rayon textiles, china, cutlery, toys, and other products of Germany and Japan drew similarly prohibitive rates. The Act gave lip service to the principle of equalizing the cost of production at home and abroad, but it lowered tariffs only in rare instances, and tended to follow the high Payne-Aldrich schedules of 1907 as a norm rather than the lower rates of the Underwood-Simmons Act of 1913. In deference to the Farm Bloc, the duty on wheat was set at 30 cents a pound, an empty gesture, except for keeping out a little Canadian wheat, and no real help to the American price. Other agricultural tariffs remained at about where they had been in the Emergency Act, with about the same results.[12]

Whatever the shortcomings of the Fordney-McCumber Act, its administrative provisions were a distinct improvement over those previously in force. This was due in large part to the work of the bipartisan Tariff Commission which Woodrow Wilson had obtained from Congress in 1916, partly as a concession to business demands. By the time the Fordney-McCumber Act was formed, the Commission had much technical information at its command, and could suggest rearrangements and reclassifications that would help greatly in administering whatever rates Congress chose to charge. Extreme protectionists, for example, had talked loudly of an "American valuation," that is,

[12] *United States Statutes at Large*, XLII, 858–868; Taussig, *Tariff History*, pp. 465–471.

assessing the value of imports at whatever their selling price would have been if they had been produced in the United States. The discovery that the Commission had alternative and more reasonable suggestions on this and other administrative matters led to the careful scrutiny of its recommendations, and their general acceptance.[13]

The Fordney-McCumber Act gave the Commission the new burden of helping the President determine differences in cost of production at home and abroad. On the Commission's recommendation the President might raise or decrease any duty by as much as 50 per cent, if he deemed the change necessary to wipe out the margin between American and foreign costs; indeed, if the customary rule did not permit an adequate increase (but not decrease) in rates, he might even impose the American valuation as the basis for his calculations. This involved procedure, it was hoped, would provide a sliding tariff scale; duties would go up without an act of Congress when extra protection was needed, and down when the rates were found to be too high. But in practice the flexible schedules did not work out well. During the next six years of the Harding-Coolidge regime the Tariff Commission, despite the requirement of bipartisan membership, grew steadily more protectionist in sentiment and made few recommendations of consequence. Harding and Coolidge together instituted only thirty-seven changes, thirty-two of which called for higher rates. The five items on which they lowered the duties were millfeeds, bobwhite quail, paintbrush handles, cresylic acid, and phenol. A recommendation of the Commission in 1924 that the President should lower the duty on sugar—an important consumer item—was pigeonholed.[14]

The Fordney-McCumber Act did about all that tariff protection could do for American manufacturers. Despite duty increases on raw wool from 15 to (in effect) 111 per cent, it compensated woolens manufacturers by rates high enough to keep out all but the very finest grades of foreign fabrics. Cotton goods, also, carried duties that were virtually prohibitive on all the cheaper grades. As for aluminum, the new tariff was set at 5 cents a pound, instead of 2 cents, as formerly. Within a few days after the bill received Harding's signature, the

---

[13] *United States Statutes at Large* (Washington, 1917), XXXIX, 795; Taussig, *Tariff History*, pp. 481–486.

[14] *United States Statutes at Large*, XLII, 941–943; Louis M. Hacker, *American Problems of Today; A History of the United States Since the World War* (New York, 1938), p. 25.

price of aluminum to Americans rose from 20 cents a pound to 22 cents, then shortly after that to 23 cents, then to 26 cents, then to 28 cents. In 1924 the Democratic candidate, John W. Davis, asserted that certain Mellon interests, on a capitalization of $18 million, were making an annual profit of $10 million. This was denied, but there seemed little reason to doubt that, as far as aluminum was concerned, the tariff amounted primarily to a license to overcharge.[15]

The Fordney-McCumber Tariff served not only to build up monopoly in the United States but it served also as a severe brake on American foreign trade. To a very great extent international trade is only barter; in general, a nation can buy only to the extent that it can sell. The high rates, therefore, tended not only to prevent Europeans from selling freely to America, as Congress intended, but also placed obstacles in the way of American sales to Europe. In particular, the American farmers, whose greatest need was to export, were hurt rather than helped. Further, the new tariff made much more difficult the payment of debts owed by European nations to the United States. Only by selling more goods across the Atlantic than they bought in return could they hope to pile up the surpluses necessary to enable them to reduce their debts. Naturally the nations that saw their export markets threatened showed their resentment in heated protests, and some governments attempted reprisals. The situation was considerably eased when American investors began to buy European securities in great volume, but this only added dangerously to the problem of debt collection.[16]

Along with economy in government, lower taxes, and a protective tariff, the business leadership, which so completely dominated the Harding regime, demanded the speedy liquidation of all governmental projects that might in any way compete with private enterprise. During the last year of the Wilson administration Congress, already under Republican control, had made a beginning on this program with the passage of the Transportation Act of 1920. It was soon apparent that the return to private ownership, for which the Act provided, was by no means the complete answer to their problems that the railroads had expected. They had hoped for high, government-guaranteed profits,

[15] Taussig, *Tariff History*, pp. 458–467; James C. Malin, *The United States After the World War* (Boston, 1930), pp. 108–109; O'Connor, *Mellon's Millions*, pp. 182–183.
[16] *The New York Times*, Sept. 21, 1922, p. 2, Sept. 22, 1922, p. 1; Mark Sullivan, *Our Times*, VI, *The Twenties* (New York, 1935), 200–203; Joseph M. Jones, *Tariff Retaliation* (Philadelphia, 1934), pp. 10, 39.

and thought that they had obtained this objective in the Act of 1920. But railroad earnings in 1922 amounted to only about 3.3 per cent, in 1922 to 4.05 per cent, and in 1923 to 5.1 per cent. Throughout the decade they failed to rise to the 5¾ per cent that the Interstate Commerce Commission had set as a fair return.[17] The stronger railroads also resented being obliged, as the law required, to contribute to a revolving fund from which the weaker roads might borrow, but the Supreme Court decision in the O'Fallon case (1929) served virtually to eliminate this difficulty. Nor did the stronger roads take kindly to any plans that proposed to combine or consolidate them with roads that were less prosperous, and accomplishments along this line were negligible.[18]

Remembering still their earlier and greater days, the railroads adjusted themselves with difficulty to the new competition they had to meet in the 1920's. Bus lines and private automobiles interfered with their monopoly on passenger traffic; truck lines took much of their freight away; pipe lines carried great quantities of oil; the Panama Canal provided a cheap water route between the Atlantic and the Pacific; coastal and inland waterways began to revive and multiply. Faced by these changed conditions, the railroads tended to blame their troubles upon government operation during the war, together with public expenditures for the building of highways and the improvement of waterways. The answer to their problems, or so they learned later, lay more in modernizing their equipment and improving their relations with the public than in querulous complaints to the government. But not until the 1930's, under the stimulus of the depression, did they begin the transformations that the times demanded.[19]

The return of the railroads to the corporations that had owned and operated them before the war offered less difficulty than the equally determined effort to free the United States from its wartime involve-

[17] *The New International Yearbook, 1921* (New York, 1922), p. 606; *ibid., 1922* (New York, 1923), p. 613; *ibid., 1923* (New York, 1924), p. 636; *ibid., 1924* (New York, 1925), p. 629; Malin, *United States After the World War,* p. 136.

[18] *Ibid.,* pp. 133–137; St. Louis and O'Fallon Railway Co. *v.* United States, 279 U.S., 461 (1929); D. P. Locklin, *Railroad Regulation Since 1920* (Chicago, 1928), pp. 164–170.

[19] Hacker, *American Problems,* pp. 31–32; President's Conference on Unemployment, *Recent Economic Changes* (2 vols., New York, 1929), I, 272–274, 303–308; George Soule, *Prosperity Decade; From War to Depression: 1917–1929* (New York, 1947), pp. 158–162.

ment in the shipping business. During the Wilson administration little had been done to implement the Merchant Marine Act of 1920, since Wilson's appointees to the new Shipping Board had failed of confirmation. Only after June, 1921, with a Harding appointee, Albert D. Lasker of Chicago, at its head could the Board really begin to function as the law intended. But the times were inauspicious; foreign trade continued to fall off alarmingly; few purchasers came forward to buy government ships; and the outlays necessary to maintain thousands of unused vessels mounted ominously. The President, strongly backed in his contention by Lasker and the shipping interests, eventually made up his mind that only a generous ship subsidy would serve to accomplish the objectives of the Merchant Marine Act. The outlay necessary for this purpose, it was estimated, would amount to about $52 million a year for an indefinite period. The debate in Congress on the subject was heated, involving those who thought the private shipping companies ought to be able to go it alone unaided, those who favored governmental operation, and those who were ready to pay whatever price was necessary to get the merchant marine out of government hands. In the end the House passed the bill, November 29, 1922, about as the President wanted it; but the Senate, with the help of a filibuster on a quite irrelevant antilynching bill, avoided the necessity of taking a vote.[20]

Thus denied the assistance of a subsidy, the Shipping Board found it difficult indeed to replace the existing government-owned ships and services with a privately owned merchant marine. Its first concern was to get rid of its laid-up ships, which it chose to regard merely as an undesirable surplus rather than as a strategic reserve. It began by setting its prices too high, but when the ships did not sell fast enough to satisfy Harding's successor, Calvin Coolidge, he changed the Board's personnel, and with drastically lowered prices it achieved better results. No one worried much that the returns to the government were meager; 104 ships, for example, that had cost originally $258 million sold during the years 1925–30 for $23 million. Nor was it easy to find purchasers for the steamship lines that the Board had laid out and felt obliged to maintain. Not until 1925 was there any substantial progress

[20] Herbert Hoover, *The Memoirs of Herbert Hoover*, II, *The Cabinet and the Presidencey, 1920–1933* (New York, 1952), 135–138; Paxson, *Postwar Years*, pp. 351–359; Charles Muller to A. D. Lasker, June 16, 1922, U.S. Shipping Board, RG 32, File 580–2707, Pt. 3, National Archives, Washington.

toward this end, and the returns on all sales were devastatingly small. The Merchant Marine Act of 1928 offered many new favors to shipowners, including generous mail subsidies at the expense of the Post Office Department, but the Board was unable to extricate itself entirely from the shipping business. Nor was the other objective of American shipping policy, an up-to-date merchant marine, fully achieved. Foreign ships tended to outclass American ships in speed, tonnage, and service; while during the depression years following 1929, many American shipping companies collapsed altogether.[21]

The determination of the Republican administration to free itself as completely as possible from the slightest taint of competition with business was further strikingly manifest in its attitude toward the Muscle Shoals development. During the First World War the pressing need for nitrogen to be used in the manufacture of explosives led the government to build two plants at Muscle Shoals in the Tennessee Valley, both designed for the purpose of extracting nitrogen from the air by the cyanamide process. One of these plants was completed before the armistice was signed, the other shortly after. To obtain power for their operation Congress had also authorized the construction of a series of dams along the Tennessee River, the first of which, the Wilson Dam, was well advanced, although by no means finished, when the fighting ended. One of the earliest actions taken by the Harding administration in April, 1921, was to terminate all work on the Wilson Dam, a decision, incidentally, that, by destroying the existing organization for its construction, made the later resumption of building unnecessarily expensive.[22]

What the administration had in mind was to turn the whole Muscle Shoals development over to private enterprise, so it not only stopped construction on the dam but also, through the Secretary of War, John W. Weeks, invited bids from prospective purchasers. In response, Henry Ford, the well-known manufacturer of automobiles, made the only offer worth considering, an offer that according to the Secretary of Commerce, Herbert Hoover, displayed real business "courage," but, according to Senator George W. Norris of Nebraska, revealed rather the normal interest of the business entrepreneur in getting as much as

[21] John G. B. Hutchins, "The American Shipping Industry Since 1914," *The Business History Review,* XXVIII (June, 1954), 112–115.

[22] Lief, *Democracy's Norris,* p. 244; George W. Norris, *Fighting Liberal; The Autobiography of George W. Norris* (New York, 1945), pp. 249–259.

possible for as little as possible. Ford's offer went through many modifications, but it never proposed the payment of more than a tiny fraction of what the government had already expended, and it contemplated such additional favors as a loan of government funds at 4 per cent or less to enable the purchaser to finance the project, the complete exemption of his operating company from the customary regulatory authority of the Federal Power Commission, and a one-hundred-year lease with right of renewal. Ford's intention, he explained, was to use the nitrate plants for the manufacture of low-priced fertilizer for the benefit of the American farmer, and also to supply the government with such nitrates as it might need for explosives, in time of peace or war. Whatever additional power remained, he would sell or use in his manufacturing business. His agents predicted great developments for the Tennessee Valley under the Ford aegis, and managed to generate much local enthusiasm for acceptance of the offer. Farmers the whole country over tended to have a high opinion of Ford, took quite literally his promise of low-priced fertilizer, and urged Congress to give him what he wanted.[23]

That the sale was never made was due primarily to the opposition of Senator Norris, chairman of the Senate Committee on Agriculture, to which Ford's offer was referred. Norris had caught the vision of what cheap public power could do "for the homes and factories of the nation"; he even dreamed of the time when the government should harness all the rivers of the country into a great national network designed to furnish cheap electricity for every section. Thus inspired, he fought tirelessly to prevent handing over the power resources of the Tennessee River to private exploitation. What he proposed instead was the creation of a governmental corporation to develop Muscle Shoals and keep it "for the people" of the Tennessee Valley. Norris went along with the idea of completing the Wilson Dam, and that was voted, but he successfully blocked every effort to sell out the government's stake in the project to Henry Ford. Ford complained bitterly against the political chicanery that had wrecked his plans. It was a "simple affair of business," he said, "which should have been decided by anyone within a week."[24]

[23] *Ibid.*, pp. 244–245; *The New York Times,* July 26, 1921, p. 13; Lief, *Democracy's Norris,* p. 257; Keith Sward, *The Legend of Henry Ford* (New York, 1948), pp. 127–131.
[24] Norris, *Fighting Liberal,* pp. 245–249; Henry Ford, *Today and Tomorrow*

But if Norris was able to prevent handing over Muscle Shoals to Henry Ford, he was quite unable to carry both Congress and the President with him on his plan for a government-operated Tennessee Valley project. Twice, by the sheer force of his personality, he got such a measure through Congress, once in 1928, when Coolidge gave it a pocket veto, and once in 1929, when Hoover denounced the idea in a veto message of unparalleled severity. After the completion of the Wilson Dam in 1925, the United States Corps of Engineers took over its operation and sold the current it generated to the Alabama Power Company for private distribution. In return the government received little more than a million dollars a year; but as events proved, Norris's fight had served a useful purpose. With the Muscle Shoals development still the property of the United States, it was possible during the Roosevelt administration for the Tennessee Valley Authority to make some of Norris's dreams come true.[25]

Conservative business opinion demanded much more of the government than its mere retirement from business; it must also free private enterprise from any unpleasant aspects of governmental regulation. Businessmen believed firmly that they knew best what was good for the country, and that any governmental interference by officials in restraint of full business freedom needed to be curtailed. This view ran counter to one of the most basic developments of the Progressive era. From the turn of the century to the time of American entrance into the First World War, with roots as deep as the Granger period, the idea had grown that a principal duty of government was to regulate and restrain business in the interest of the people as a whole. To this end the Hepburn Act of 1906 and other legislation had accorded the Interstate Commerce Commission greatly expanded powers; the Federal Reserve Act of 1913 had created a Federal Reserve Board to watch over the activities of banks and bankers; and the Federal Trade Commission Act of 1914 had set up a similar body to regulate other types of business. These groups possessed very real power, and business was genuinely fearful of what they might do in case they should fall into unco-operative hands.[26]

(New York, 1926), p. 169; George W. Norris in *The Nation*, CVIII (Apr. 23, 1924), 466.

[25] Hoover's veto message is in the *Congressional Record*, 71st Cong., 3rd Sess., LXXIV (Mar. 3, 1931), 7047–7048. See also Norris, *Fighting Liberal*, p. 267; Hacker, *American Problems*, pp. 39–40.

[26] Prothero, *Dollar Decade*, pp. 141–142.

With the Republicans back in control, the personnel of the commissions veered rapidly in the conservative direction. John J. Esch of Wisconsin, coauthor of the Esch-Cummins Transportation Act of 1920, was one of Harding's first appointees to the Interstate Commerce Commission. This to Senator Robert M. La Follette of Wisconsin seemed a travesty on justice, for Esch as commissioner would "pass upon the propriety of acts to which he had already given his consent as legislator." Even worse, from the Progressive point of view, was the fact that he replaced Robert W. Wooley, a Wilson appointee, whose attitude as commissioner the railroads had found most annoying. Harding's other appointments were similarly conservative, rewards in the main for political services, but Coolidge's appointment in 1925 of Thomas F. Woodlock, a well-known protagonist of Wall Street opinion, brought outraged cries of alarm from liberal circles. To put him on the Commission, said *The Nation*, was only to take another step toward turning it over to those whom it was meant to curb.[27]

Appointments to the Federal Reserve Board and the Federal Trade Commission showed a similar trend. As ex-officio members of the Board, Andrew Mellon, the new Secretary of the Treasury, and D. R. Crissinger, a small-caliber lawyer and banker from Marion, Ohio, whom Harding had made Comptroller of the Currency, succeeded Wilson's appointees and tipped the scales powerfully in the conservative direction. Thereafter vacancies were ordinarily filled by members of the banking fraternity, although, to limit somewhat the exclusive dominance of the banking interest in the making of Federal Reserve policies, Congress in 1922 increased the size of the Board from seven to eight, and required the appointment of a farmer member. Harding's friend Crissinger, although extremely short of competence for the post, presently became governor of the reconstituted Board, and the new farmer member, E. H. Cunningham of Iowa, was balanced by a Memphis banker and merchant, G. R. James. As for the Federal Trade Commission, Harding's first appointment was of V. W. Van Fleet, an Indiana Republican wheelhorse who had been special assistant to Attorney General Daugherty, and his second went to another Iowa farmer, C. W. Hunt. It remained for Coolidge to make even clearer the direction in which the Commission was going by the selection of William E. Humphrey, a long-time congressman and corporation

[27] La Follette and La Follette, *La Follette,* II, 1025; *The Nation,* CXX (Feb. 25, 1925), 202.

counsel, whose record, according to Senator Norris, branded him as "a fearless advocate of big business in all lines."[28]

The Tariff Commission, while not exactly comparable to the regulatory bodies, suffered a similar fate. T. O. Marvin, the first new member after the Republicans took over, was a long-time secretary of the Home Market Club of Boston, Massachusetts, and editor of a journal known as *The Protectionist*. Low-tariff holdovers had no chance of reappointment. Coolidge got rid of one of them, W. S. Culbertson, by giving him a diplomatic post. "It seems to be the idea of those in control," wrote Senator Norris, "that the Tariff Commission should be composed of men whose whole lives disclose the fact that they have always advocated an exorbitantly high tariff."[29]

As for the Federal Power Commission, set up in 1920 to deal with the ever-expanding activities of the producers of electric current, it was composed of the Secretaries of War, Agriculture, and the Interior; hence, it succumbed immediately to the administration's point of view. This Commission had authority to grant licenses for the erection of new plants, to require uniformity in systems of accounting, to rule on the issuance of new securities, and to regulate rates when state regulation did not exist, or where companies were selling current across interstate boundaries. But its members were too busy with other duties to give its work adequate attention, and the already numerous state utility commissions greatly limited its authority. Finally in 1930 Congress changed the composition of the Commission to five members appointed by the President, but it remained of little consequence until after the Republicans lost office in 1933.[30]

Ruminating the wreckage of the regulatory system, Senator Norris wrote an article which both *The Forum* and *Collier's Weekly* refused to print. But *The Nation* published it with delight. The effect of the Harding-Coolidge appointments, Norris argued, was "to set the country back more than twenty-five years."

It is an indirect but positive repeal of Congressional enactments, which no administration, however powerful, would dare to bring about by any direct means. It is the nullification of federal law by a process of boring from within. If trusts, combinations, and big business are to run the government,

28 *Ibid.*, CXXI (Sept. 16, 1925), 297–298.
29 *Ibid.*
30 Harold U. Faulkner, *From Versailles to the New Deal* (New Haven, 1951), pp. 245–249; Hoover, *Memoirs,* II, 302–306.

why not permit them to do it directly rather than through this expensive machinery which was originally honestly established for the protection of the people of the country against monopoly and control?[31]

However adamant the business world might be in its opposition to the regulation of private enterprise by the government, it had no slightest scruple against accepting, or even soliciting, government aid of any sort or kind. Protective tariff and taxation favors, important as they were, proved not to be enough. In Herbert Hoover, Secretary of Commerce, business had an understanding friend at court. He decided at once to make a governmental attack on waste in business, and marshaled effectively the resources of the Bureau of Standards and the Bureau of Foreign and Domestic Commerce to this end. It was obviously "not the function of government to manage business," he pointed out, but it was entirely legitimate "for it to recruit and distribute economic information; to investigate economic and scientific problems; to point out the remedy for economic failure or the road to progress; to inspire and assist in cooperative action." There can be no doubt that Hoover and his lieutenants made many valuable contributions to the efficiency of American business. When the Committee on Economic Trends, which Hoover had sponsored, reported in 1928 that the nation's per capita productivity had increased in eight years by 35 per cent, Hoover commented: "I do not claim the credit for this, but certainly the Department helped."[32]

There were other ways in which the government revealed its solicitude for business. Hoover's Bureau of Foreign and Domestic Commerce multiplied its services to exporters and importers, pointing out opportunities for the sale of American produce abroad and for the purchase of raw materials and noncompetitive commodities in return. The actual increases in sales abroad, Hoover reported, "ran into hundreds of millions of dollars." To redress the balance of trade, which tended to run heavily against the United States, American investors provided most of the funds. The Department of State undertook to advise them upon the "political desirability" of such loans; in addition, the Department of Commerce reported on their "security and reproductive character." Investment houses more "interested in the flotation of loans than in their soundness" sometimes objected to this procedure, but

[31] *The Nation,* CXXI (Sept. 16, 1925), 299; Lief, *Democracy's Norris,* pp. 281–282.
[32] Hoover, *Memoirs,* II, 61–78.

events were soon to prove that the restraints imposed by the government were quite inadequate. Of the $7 billion lent abroad by American investors during the 1920's, $2 billion, according to Hoover's own calculations, were in default at late as 1936, while these sums would have been much greater, he claimed, except for the services provided by the government. The Department of Commerce also did all it could to help along the development of American aviation.[33]

A government so solicitous of the welfare of business could hardly disregard one of the foremost of the obstacles that confronted business leaders, the "cold-blooded, hard-bitten, and supremely selfish" determination with which labor clung to the advantages it had won during the war. Not even the sobering effects of labor losses in the strikes of 1919 seemed sufficient; labor, or so the industrialists thought, still stood in need of discipline. During the short but sharp postwar depression of 1921–23, with business on the downgrade, many employers felt obliged to lower costs by cutting wages and increasing hours; some, hoping also to promote the so-called "American plan," made unrelenting war upon unions and the very idea of unionization. According to *Industry,* an open-shop magazine, if union organizations, when faced by "the blight of business inertia," refused to accept the lowered wage scale and longer hours that the economy demanded, "the nation should stand firm and force the concessions." Would the national government help business with this problem or would it unsympathetically permit employers to work out their destinies unaided?[34]

Early experiences were not wholly reassuring. When the textile workers of Massachusetts, New Hampshire, and Rhode Island received notice in January, 1922, that they must accept a 20 per cent wage cut, and with the exception of Massachusetts, where the hours were fixed by law, a lengthening of the work week from forty-eight to fifty-four hours in addition, they staged a general walkout. Only the year before they had absorbed a 22½ per cent reduction, and the new scale, which meant for many of them wages of not more than $14 a week, the workers regarded as totally intolerable. The New England mills were only 5 or 10 per cent unionized, if that; but the strikers appealed to the United Textile Workers of America for leadership, and resisted valiantly attacks on their picket lines and all other efforts to force them back to work. Altogether, from 85,000 to 100,000 workers walked out.

[33] *Ibid.,* II, 79–91, 132–134.
[34] *Industry,* III (Apr. 1, 1921), 4; (May 15, 1921), 14; (Sept. 15, 1921), 3.

The mill owners excused themselves for the action they had taken on the ground that their southern competitors charged impossibly low prices, but the workers insisted that the employers' real purpose was to keep up profits and dividends. In the end the strikers won a rather remarkable victory, particularly in Massachusetts and Rhode Island, where the employers, after six months of conflict, rescinded their offensive orders and took the strikers back on the old terms.[35]

There was trouble also in the coal fields. Unlike the textile workers, the coal miners were for the times well organized, and along industrial lines at that. In the anthracite fields, organization was nearly 100 per cent; in the bituminous fields, considerably less so; but about 69 per cent of all the coal miners east of the Mississippi owed allegiance to the United Mine Workers of America, the largest single union in the country, which after 1920 was headed by John L. Lewis. The chief problem of the coal industry was overdevelopment; war demands and high prices had led to the opening of far more mines, particularly in the bituminous fields, than the nation needed. In consequence, even when times were good, miners could count on only three or four days' work out of a week, while when times were bad they were lucky to get as much as two or three days. The mine workers wanted steady employment, with a six-hour day and a five-day week as the norm; the operators wanted to cut costs, and wage cuts seemed the easiest way out; the public at large wanted cheaper coal.[36]

The almost inevitable strike began on April 1, 1922, when operators in the bituminous fields refused to renew the existing wage agreement, and called for drastic wage reductions—in the South Ohio fields, for example, from 31 to 46⅔ per cent. As a result about 500,000 bituminous miners went out, to be followed a little later by 150,000 from the anthracite fields. The main issue was not really wages, since the miners for the most part were reconciled to the idea of a reduction in pay. But many mine workers felt that the principal objective of the operators was to "bust the union," whereas from their own point of

[35] Selig Perlman and Philip Taft, *Labor Movements,* in John R. Commons and Associates, *History of Labor in the United States, 1896–1932* (New York, 1935), IV, 511–514; *New International Yearbook, 1922,* p. 697; Thomas F. McMahon to Ethel M. Smith, June 6, 1922, Thomas F. McMahon to Rose Yates Forester, June 8, 1922, Borah Papers, Box 213, Library of Congress, Manuscripts Division.

[36] *New International Yearbook, 1922,* pp. 698–699; Perlman and Taft, *Labor Movements,* pp. 482–488.

view the unionization of all the mines was the correct ultimate goal. There was bitter disagreement, too, on the "checkoff," which would require the operators to collect union dues and pay it into union treasuries. The operators were also outraged at John L. Lewis's demand for negotiations on a national basis instead of district by district, or at most state by state.[37]

As the strike dragged on, week after week, and month after month, violence became inevitable. The worst outbreak came at Herrin, in Williamson County, Illinois, when a rash superintendent, C. K. McDowell, mobilized members of the Steam Shovelmen's Union and strikebreakers from Chicago in an armed attempt to resume strip mining. To the strongly prounion miners of the area this amounted to a declaration of war, and they responded accordingly. Accounts of how the fighting started varied greatly, but soon "everyone from New York to California knew that on June 21 southern Illinois erupted, and in Williamson County all hell broke loose. . . . It was war in its rawest and most primitive form, for here there was to be no quarter and no prisoners." When the fighting died down next day a score of strikebreakers, outnumbered and outfought, were dead and many others injured, all, according to the magazine *Industrial Progress,* for "exercising only their inviolate right to work." The operators blamed the labor union for what had happened, and Lewis blamed the Communists, but the coroner's jury of Williamson County held that "the deaths were due to acts direct and indirect of officials of the Southern Illinois Coal Company," and declared "that C. K. McDowell, slain superintendent of Lester Mines, had killed a union miner." There were no convictions.[38]

Before this time President Harding had pursued a hands-off policy, but he now felt obliged to act, particularly in view of the fact that coal stocks were running dangerously low. At a July conference in the White House he found the operators ready to accept arbitration and, pending a final settlement, the reopening of the mines on the terms in

[37] Freeman T. Eagleson to William E. Borah, Aug. 4, 1922, William E. Franklin to President Harding, June 26, 1922, Borah Papers, Box 213, Library of Congress. See also Chamber of Commerce of the United States, *Coal Situation* (1922), pamphlet, *ibid.*

[38] Saul Alinsky, *John L. Lewis; An Unauthorized Biography* (New York, 1949), pp. 42–50; Cecil Carnes, *John L. Lewis; Leader of Labor* (New York, 1936), pp. 90–95. See also Paul M. Angle, *Bloody Williamson* (New York, 1952), pp. 3–71.

force before the walkout. When the miners demurred, Harding ordered that the mines be opened anyway, telegraphed governors of the states concerned to protect all who wished to work, and promised further aid from the federal government if necessary. As a result, state troops patrolled the mines in Pennsylvania and Ohio, but work resumption did not follow immediately. Finally, Lewis and some of the bituminous operators agreed to continue the old wage scale and working conditions on the understanding that a federal commission of inquiry would investigate every aspect of the coal industry, and a similar agreement, separately negotiated, reopened the anthracite fields.[39]

In accordance with these settlements Congress on September 22, 1922, created a Coal Commission, composed of seven members appointed by the President, to study the problems of the industry and to make recommendations. Headed by the able John Hays Hammond, the Commission made a long and expensive investigation, which revealed clearly the almost intolerable plight of the miners. Recognizing the need of firm governmental control, the Commission reported in favor of a Coal Division in the Interstate Commerce Commission, and additional regulation at the state and local level. But it offended the unions by failing to recommend the checkoff and complete unionization, and it displeased the operators by ignoring their insistence on compulsory arbitration. Its report was ignored by Congress, which had created the Commission only in support of the agreement for a return to work, and after that was accomplished had lost interest in the subject. During the rest of the decade the plight of the coal miner, whether anthracite or bituminous, tended to become worse rather than better. Torn by internal strife, the United Mine Workers declined steadily in membership and influence.[40]

Concurrent with the coal strike of 1922 in its later phases was a railroad shopman's strike that for a time involved some 400,000 workers. The Transportation Act of 1920 had created a Railway Labor Board of nine members, three each representing labor, management, and the public, but all to be appointed by the President. Among the duties of the Board was the right to rule on wage scales and working

[39] Perlman and Taft, *Labor Movements,* pp. 484–489.

[40] *Ibid.;* John L. Lewis to candidates for Congress, Oct. 6, 1928, in Norris Papers, Tray 1, Box 6, Library of Congress, Manuscripts Division; *Industrial Progress,* V (Sept., 1922), 12–13; *New International Yearbook, 1922,* p. 700; Hoover, Memoirs, II, 70–71.

conditions among railroad employees. Before Harding took office, the Board had granted wage increases which, for the shopman, amounted to 22 per cent. But as business fell off during the next two years, the operators began to voice a demand for wage reductions. The response of the Board to such demands was cordial, and with respect to the shopmen amounted to a cut of 12 per cent, which the workers concerned, after a ballot, refused to take. On July 1, 1922, they walked out, but they were not joined by the four great railroad brotherhoods or by any other railway employees, all of whom made terms with their employers. Standing alone, the shopmen had hardly a chance to win, but for two months their inactivity interfered seriously with the efficiency of railroad operation.[41]

Finally, after all efforts at agreement had failed, Attorney General Daugherty asked Federal Judge James Wilkerson of Chicago, a Harding appointee, to grant an injunction against the strikers. "There comes a time in the history of all nations," Daugherty pontificated, "when a people must be advised whether they have a government or not." Already the Supreme Court had ruled that the Clayton Act did not prevent the issuance of injunctions in labor disputes, and Wilkerson took full advantage of this interpretation. In one of the most sweeping injunctions ever written, he forbade the officers of unions from "picketing or in any manner by letters, circulars, telephone messages, word of mouth, or interviews encouraging any person to leave the employ of a railroad." This injunction, according to the strikers, was in flagrant violation of the constitutional rights of American citizens, but it left them virtually powerless, and within a few weeks most of them were back at work. Some of the shopmen secured separate agreements with individual roads; others returned to their jobs without any agreement; nearly all of them took substantial wage cuts. Organized labor in general, if it had not known it before, knew now where the administration stood. It was clear enough, from the Wilkerson injunction and from the President's order to the state governors during the coal strike, that during industrial disputes the government would neither assist labor nor remain neutral; rather, it would throw its influence firmly

[41] *New Republic*, XXVI (March 23, 1921), 90; *United States Statutes at Large* (Washington, 1921), XLI, 470–473; Press release, Jan. 31, 1921, from President Railway Employees A.F. of L., RG 13, Railroad Labor Board, II, in National Archives; *Industrial Progress*, V (Aug., 1922), 3.

on the employer's side. And it could trust the courts to rule accordingly.[42]

Indeed, the climate of opinion on the subject of labor could hardly have been chillier. "Yellow dog" contracts, upheld by the United States Supreme Court in 1917, still retained legal sanction, and the right of strikers to maintain picket lines was seriously questioned. Evidence existed, despite denials, that the exploitation of child labor in the coal mines, the glass factories, the cotton mills, and the "street trades" was all too common, but in 1922 the Supreme Court ruled for the second time (once before in 1918) against the pre-Harding efforts of Congress to legislate on the subject. Further, a constitutional amendment designed to give Congress the authority over child labor that it had sought to assert, although submitted in 1924, failed of adoption for lack of sufficient state ratifications. The need for better legislation to protect women in industry seemed obvious to many women's organizations, but attempts to achieve it usually ran into difficulties, as, for example, when the Supreme Court in 1923 declared unconstitutional a District of Columbia minimum-wage law for women. Proposals for social-security legislation brought expressions of horror. A Massachusetts study branded old-age pensions as "a counsel of depair. If such a scheme be defensible or excusable in this country, then the whole economic and social system is a failure."[43]

In a sense, the slanting of government during the 1920's to support whatever stand the dominant business interests wanted was far more scandalous than the merely political depravity for which the Harding regime was noted. But in choosing the pliable Harding to carry out their program the ultraconservatives in the Republican party had overshot the mark. Harding's code of morality, such as it was, called for loyalty to his friends. He enjoyed being President; tremendously valued the high status to which it had raised him, and meant to deport himself as a President should. Apparently he assumed that the men he

[42] *The New York Times,* Sept. 14, 1922, p. 1; Harry M. Daugherty and Thomas Dixon, *The Inside Story of the Harding Tragedy* (New York, 1932), pp. 139–153; Felix Frankfurter and Nathan Green, *The Labor Injunction* (New York, 1930), pp. 253–263; Duplex Printing Press Co. *v.* Deering, 254 U.S., 443 (1921).

[43] Hacker, *American Problems,* pp. 90–94; *Industry,* III (May 1, 1921), 9–12; "Transcript, 1922," I, 159, in League of Women Voters Papers, Series I, Box 100, Library of Congress, Manuscripts Division; *Open Shop Association,* II (Feb., 1923), 2.

liked and trusted would share his new sense of responsibility and do nothing that might in any way discredit him. But they somehow failed to get the point. Certainly when they visited the White House they saw nothing to suggest that the old familiar pattern of behavior had suffered a change. Prohibition might be the law, but in the White House, as elsewhere in the country, it was not the fact. There Alice Roosevelt Longworth among others reported that in the upstairs rooms "trays with bottles containing every imaginable brand of whiskey stood about" in "a general atmosphere of waistcoat unbuttoned, feet on the desk, and spittoon alongside."[44]

Actually, the scandals of the Harding administration did not become public until after the President's death, but he knew of some of them, and his uneasiness over what the future held in store may have hastened his passing. Harding had taken pleasure in appointing as head of the Veterans' Bureau one Charles R. Forbes, whom he had met on a vacation in Hawaii. Forbes was a cheerful extrovert with abounding energy; Harding liked the way he got hospitals built and put to work the money appropriated for his use. But early in 1923 Daugherty, who was in no way responsible for the Forbes appointment, felt obliged to report that there was crooked work going on in the Veterans' Bureau. A little investigation revealed that Daugherty knew what he was talking about, and Harding promptly arranged for Forbes to turn in his resignation. But with a Senate investigation pending, Charles F. Cramer, Forbes's second in command, committed suicide, an ominous warning of what eventually was to come out. Some time later, after Harding's death, Forbes was sent to the Federal Penitentiary at Leavenworth for defrauding the government of fantastic sums.[45]

Another suicide, with similar implications, occurred before Harding's death in 1923. "Jess" Smith was the "faithful retainer" of Attorney General Daugherty; he held no governmental appointment of any kind, but he had an office in the Department of Justice, and his close connection with Daugherty gave him standing. Soon his services as a fixer and lobbyist were known among insiders to be for sale. But Smith lacked the fortitude necessary to carry on big-time graft, and in a fright committed suicide. After his death it came to light that he was deeply involved in a deal with the Alien Property Custodian, Thomas W. Miller, a Harding appointee, whereby some $6.5 million in Liberty

---

[44] Alice Roosevelt Longworth, *Crowded Hours* (New York, 1933), p. 324.
[45] Sullivan, *Our Times,* VI, 143, 238–242, 362.

bonds were for a consideration handed over to alien claimants. The government had obtained this huge sum by the seizure and sale of American Metal Company property on the theory that the owners were German nationals. But a certain Richard Merton, representing that the owners were in reality Swiss, not German, sought to get the money released. As his attorney, he employed John T. King, Republican National Chairman from Connecticut. King introduced Merton to Smith and to Miller, seemingly his only legal service, and eventually the bonds were restored to their alien owners. King's fee was a substantial $441,000, mostly paid in identifiable Liberty bonds. Of these bonds $200,000 worth were turned over to Jess Smith for expediting the claim, while $50,000 worth went to Miller, who was tried, convicted, and given an eighteen-month sentence for accepting a bribe. Smith gave another block of bonds to his Ohio banker, Mal S. Daugherty, brother of the Attorney General, who sold them and promptly deposited $49,165 to a "political" account from which Smith drew checks, but which Harry M. Daugherty managed. The Attorney General, who was eventually dismissed by Coolidge and brought to trial for fraud, refused to testify on the ground that he might incriminate himself, and implied that his silence was necessary to shield others, presumably President and Mrs. Harding, from unpleasant revelations. Daugherty was tried twice, but in each case the jury failed to agree on a verdict.[46]

Harding would have suffered many blows had he lived long enough, but none would have hurt him more than the utter humiliation that befell his Secretary of the Interior, Albert B. Fall. Soon after taking office Fall had approached the Secretary of the Navy, Edwin N. Denby, with the proposition that administration of the great oil reserves held in trust to meet the future needs of the Navy should be transferred from the Department of the Navy to the Department of the Interior. Denby, unsuspecting and pitifully incompetent, acquiesced, although there were strong protests from high-ranking Navy personnel, coupled with doubts about the legality of the procedure. The President also agreed, albeit not without misgivings; "I guess there will be hell to pay," he remarked to a friend. Promptly on receiving the authority he coveted, Fall leased the great Elk Hills reserve in California to Edward L. Doheny of the Pan American Petroleum Company, and the great

[46] *Ibid.*, VI, 226–238, 350–357; Frederick Lewis Allen, *Only Yesterday* (New York, 1931), pp. 149–154; Daugherty, *Inside Story,* pp. 242–260.

Teapot Dome reserves in Wyoming to Harry F. Sinclair, representing the Continental Trading Company, a Canadian corporation of dubious reputation. Coincident with these deals Doheny made a "loan" of $100,000 to Fall. Oddly enough, this was not a bank transaction; instead, Doheny's son delivered to Fall in person a little black bag containing currency to the amount of the "loan." Equally unusual was the delivery to Fall's son-in-law of well over $200,000 in Liberty bonds owned by the Continental Trading Company, bonds which somehow found their way into Fall's possession. Later Sinclair also made Fall a present of some blooded stock and, after Fall had resigned from office, about $85,000 in cash.[47]

All this might have gone unnoted but for the fact that Fall's ranch in New Mexico, which had been badly run down, and on which the taxes had not been paid since 1912, suddenly began to prosper. Fall had reputedly been broke, but now, on a Cabinet officer's salary of $12,000 a year, he was able to pay up all back taxes, make extensive improvements, and even buy more land. Prying senators, such as Kendrick of Wyoming and La Follette of Wisconsin, were easily alerted, and insisted on an explanation of the oil leases; nor were they willing to take Fall's word for it that what he had done was designed merely to protect the Navy oil pools from being drained by adjacent drilling. Eventually, a full-fledged investigation conducted by Senator Thomas J. Walsh of Montana laid bare the facts, and the courts took over. Criminal actions against the millionaire principals proved singularly disappointing. Sinclair refused to testify to a Senate committee, and was eventually fined $1,000 and sent to jail for three months for contempt of the Senate. When on trial for conspiracy to defraud the government, it was shown that his detectives were shadowing the jury, and that netted him another six months in jail for contempt of court. But on the main charges of bribery and conspiracy, both Sinclair and Doheny escaped convictions: "You can't convict a million dollars," the cynical were wont to say. Fall, on the other hand, was convicted of accepting a bribe, fined $100,000, and sent to jail for a year. In the civil cases, the prosecutions fared better. Suits to annul the leases were carried to the Supreme Court, which adjudged the defendants in the

[47] M. E. Ravage, *The Story of Teapot Dome* (New York, 1924), pp. 1–194; Samuel Hopkins Adams, *Incredible Era; The Life and Times of Warren Gamaliel Harding* (Boston, 1939), pp. 341–355; Allen, *Only Yesterday,* pp. 136–145; Sullivan, *Our Times,* VI, 321–323.

Teapot Dome case to be guilty of "collusion and conspiracy," and in the Elk Hills case to be guilty of "fraud and corruption." Not only were the leases canceled, but the leaseholders were required to make complete restitution for their illegal use of government property.[48]

The oil investigation bared another gigantic fraud, not directly connected, however, with any faithless governmental official. The Continental Trading Company, Ltd., was the Canadian corporation through which Sinclair and three others, each the representative of a great American oil company, bought oil from a certain producer at $1.50 a barrel for resale to their own companies at $1.75 a barrel. The substantial profits of this transaction were then turned over in Liberty bonds to the four individuals concerned. Of the approximately $750,000 that fell to Sinclair, $185,000 went to the Republican National Committee as a loan (of which only $100,000 was repaid), another $75,000 as a gift, and the sum already noted to Fall.[49]

Judged by any standards, the Harding administration was badly tainted with corruption. Insofar as this involved venality on the part of public officials, the people disapproved heartily and were ashamed. On the other hand, had there been no bribery, no one would have cared very much. The abysmally low ethical standards of the businessmen who took part in the deals were seemingly accepted with little resentment, both by the juries that refused to convict them and by the public at large. Sinclair and Doheny each testified that their respective bargains should have made for their companies profits of approximately $100 million each. These profits were to be attained at the expense of the government, from government-owned land, and at the risk of the national safety. But apparently free enterprise covered all that. Nor was there much excitement about such inside business frauds as the Continental Trading Company, Ltd. When discovered, the principals who had profited from the chicanery were obliged to make an accounting of one kind or another, and their conduct cost some of them dear. At the insistence of John D. Rockefeller, Jr., for example, Colonel Robert W. Stewart, one of the conspirators, lost his position as chairman of the board of the Standard Oil Company of Indiana. But the obvious inference that similar but undisclosed transactions were probably a

[48] *Ibid.*, VI, 302–349; Burl Noggle, "The Origins of the Teapot Dome Investigation," *Mississippi Valley Historical Review*, XLIV (Sept., 1957), 237–266.
[49] Daugherty, *Inside Story*, p. 81; Allen, *Only Yesterday*, pp. 139–140.

commonplace of big business worried only the liberal journals and other professional worriers. For the average American all this was taken for granted as just another aspect of "normalcy."[50]

[50] *Ibid.*, pp. 154–158; Raymond B. Fosdick, *John D. Rockefeller, Jr., A Portrait* (New York, 1956), pp. 229–247.

CHAPTER 4

The Progressive Protest

FEW WITNESSES who reported on the inauguration ceremonies of March, 1921, could forbear to contrast the broken physical condition of the outgoing President with the radiant good health of his successor. But Wilson, despite his infirmities, was to outlive Harding by over six months. There is no particular reason to believe that the exhaustive duties of the Presidency killed Harding, although undoubtedly he was worried almost to the point of illness by the growing evidence of misconduct on the part of his cronies. Possibly, also, he had begun to realize that as President he was beyond his depth. Partly to get away from Washington and its problems, and partly to bolster up the waning popularity of his administration, he decided on a speaking tour during the summer of 1923 that would take him across the continent and to Alaska. And so, with a trainload of newspaper reporters, Secret Service men, administrative assistants, and friends, he and Mrs. Harding set out on June 20 to meet the people. He had with him his personal physician, Dr. Charles E. Sawyer, a homeopath from Marion, Ohio, for whom he had obtained the rank of brigadier-general; also Dr. Joel T. Boone, a naval medical officer of more orthodox training. Just before leaving Washington the President took the precaution of making his will.[1]

Harding found the trip more wearing than he had anticipated, and the response to his speeches unsatisfying; as the trip progressed he grew

[1] Mark Sullivan, *Our Times*, VI, *The Twenties* (New York, 1935), 140, 244–245; Harry M. Daugherty and Thomas Dixon, *The Inside Story of the Harding Tragedy* (New York, 1932), p. 262.

more "nervous and distraught" all the while. He played bridge incessantly, and as a result Herbert Hoover, who was drawn reluctantly into the presidential game, "developed a distaste for bridge on this journey and never played it again." The trip continued to Fairbanks, but at Seattle, on the way back, the President had difficulty in finishing his address. That night he was in great pain, from eating tainted crabs, Dr. Sawyer insisted, but Dr. Boone privately told Hoover that in his judgment the President's illness was "something worse than a digestive upset." The party went on to San Francisco, where Harding was scheduled to speak on July 31. At Boone's insistence, Hoover arranged for some heart specialists to examine Harding on his arrival in San Francisco, and this was done. Contrary to Sawyer's opinion they decided that the President was suffering from a heart attack, and must have at least two months' rest; seemingly he also developed bronchopneumonia. On the evening of August 2, with a nurse and Dr. Sawyer also present, Mrs. Harding was reading to her husband in his room at the Palace Hotel. Suddenly he gave a convulsive shudder and died; according to Dr. Ray Lyman Wilbur, one of his attendant physicians, because a blood vessel had "burst in the vital centers of the brain." The various stories that there was something strange about the President's passing are totally without foundation. There is nothing strange about the death from apoplexy of a man Harding's age who had long overeaten, overdrunk, and overworried.[2]

The death of Harding made the Vice-President, Calvin Coolidge of Massachusetts, thirtieth President of the United States. Coolidge's name on the ticket with Harding in 1920 was a kind of political accident, for the party leaders who had engineered the nomination of Harding at the Republican convention had decided on Senator Irvine Lenroot of Wisconsin for second place. The delegates received the nomination of Lenroot without enthusiasm; then, when a loud-voiced delegate from Oregon, acting on his own responsibility, nominated Coolidge, they mustered a hearty cheer. In the voting Coolidge won

[2] Herbert Hoover, *The Memoirs of Herbert Hoover,* II, *The Cabinet and the Presidency, 1920–1933* (New York, 1952), 47–53; Sullivan, *Our Times,* VI, 245–250; George Christian, "Why Presidents Break," *Saturday Evening Post,* CXCVI (Oct. 13, 1923), 3–4, 165–170; Ray Lyman Wilbur, "The Last Illness of a Calm Man," *ibid.,* p. 64; Gaston Means, *The Strange Death of President Harding* (New York, 1930), pp. 255–279; Daugherty and Dixon, *Inside Story,* pp. 266–276; William Allen White, *A Puritan in Babylon; The Story of Calvin Coolidge* (New York, 1938), p. 239.

by 674½ to Lenroot's 146, and the nomination was made unanimous. The convention thus presented to the nation a ticket of two conservatives, rather than the customary conservative-liberal, or liberal-conservative, combination. On the fundamental question of his attitude toward business, Coolidge saw eye to eye with Harding. "The business of America is business," he later proclaimed; and the business of government, he might have added, was to help business in every possible way.[3]

If Harding and Coolidge had identical views on the relation of government to business, they were in many other respects worlds apart. Harding was genial and friendly; Coolidge was aloof and austere. Harding could understand and tolerate the low ethical standards of the ordinary politician; Coolidge made a fetish of honesty and propriety. Harding liked people and people liked him; Coolidge held himself aloof from the crowd, and made friends with difficulty. Harding was big and handsome; Coolidge was wizened and unimpressive. Nevertheless for the Republican party, with a nauseating set of scandals about to break, the succession to the Presidency of such a man as Coolidge was a matter of the greatest good fortune. What the country needed was a "Puritan in Babylon," and the claim that it had such a man in Coolidge was easy to promote.[4]

And yet, if what the country needed even more was leadership, as many people thought, there was little in the Coolidge record to justify high hopes. Coolidge's career in politics was a shining example of what inertia could do for a man of patience; he had mounted the first step of the political escalator when he was very young, and had risen almost effortlessly to the top. Graduating from Amherst College in 1885, he had located in Northampton, Massachusetts, studied law, and won admission to the bar in 1897. Elected to the city council in 1899, he was thereafter seldom out of office, serving successively as city solicitor, clerk of the courts, member of the Massachusetts lower house, mayor of Northampton, member of the state senate, lieutenant governor, and governor. He first broke into national news with the ill-starred Boston police strike in 1919, in which the policemen, with greater desperation than judgment, sought by direct methods to raise their wages above

[3] *Ibid.,* pp. 212–215; Sullivan, *Our Times,* VI, 77–84; Samuel Hopkins Adams, *Incredible Era; The Life and Times of Warren Gamaliel Harding* (Boston, 1939), pp. 163–167.
[4] White, *Puritan in Babylon,* p. 222.

prewar levels. When the city fell into disorder, Mayor Andrew Peters, a Democrat, called out the Boston companies of state troops, as was his legal right. This action proved sufficient to restore order, although the strike was not yet broken. Finally, on the third day of the strike, Coolidge called out additional state troops from outside Boston, and asked for federal troops in case a general strike should occur. When, with the strike broken, Samuel Gompers urged Coolidge to help the strikers get their jobs back, the governor refused in ringing words: "There is no right to strike against the public safety, by anybody, anywhere, anytime." Actually, Coolidge had played an insignificant part in ending the strike, but this statement won him the congratulations of President Wilson, and opened for him the road to the Vice-Presidency and the Presidency.[5]

Coolidge's record as Vice-President was in line with his previous career. He was not without a flair for melodrama; Cal Coolidge, the son of a small-town Vermont storekeeper, had come a long way, and he wished the world to know it. He was visiting his father when the news came of Harding's death, and he took care to be sworn in at once as President, "the oath of office being administered by his father, a notary public." As Vice-President he took silent satisfaction in presiding over the Senate, in attending Cabinet meetings (a Harding innovation), and in ranking next to the President in all ceremonial functions. He made speeches—longer speeches than previously had been his wont; he kept the wise cracks that came so easily to his lips at a minimum, lest he give offense; he wrote a few innocuous articles for magazines, including a series for the *Delineator* on "Enemies of the Republic," from one of which the reader learned that there were dangerous "Reds in our Women's Colleges." He played the game safe, and waited for what might come next.[6]

As President, it fell to Coolidge to liquidate the Harding scandals, a task he discharged competently, but without casting himself in the role of avenging angel; he had no desire to make unnecessary enemies.

[5] *Ibid.*, pp. 154–167; Selig Perlman and Philip Taft, *Labor Movements*, in John R. Commons and associates, *History of Labor in the United States, 1896–1932* (New York, 1935), IV, 447–449; Arthur Warner, "The End of Boston's Police Strike," *The Nation*, CIX (Dec. 20, 1919), 790–792; editorial, "Calvin Coolidge, Made by a Myth," *ibid.*, CXVII (Aug. 15, 1923), 153.

[6] *Who's Who in America* (Chicago, 1924), XIII, 801; C. M. Fuess, *Calvin Coolidge: The Man from Vermont* (Boston, 1940), pp. 285–312; *Delineator*, XCVIII (June, 1921), 4–5; (July, 1921), 10–11; XCIX (Aug., 1921), 10–11.

A Senate investigation of the Fall leases, obtained by Senator Robert M. La Follette in April, 1922, and carried forward thereafter under the able direction of Senator Thomas J. Walsh of Montana, brought out the gruesome facts, so Coolidge chose two prominent lawyers, Owen J. Roberts of Pennsylvania and Atlee Pomerene of Ohio, to act as government prosecutors. In thus by-passing the Department of Justice, he tacitly admitted that Attorney General Daugherty, whom he had retained in office along with the rest of Harding's Cabinet, was under suspicion; but not until March 27, 1924, did he request Daugherty's resignation; even then he chose not to question Daugherty's "fairness or integrity." He selected as his personal secretary C. Bascom Slemp of Virginia, a former congressman who knew his way about in party circles, and was notably broad-minded on the niceties of political behavior. But when Daugherty's place had to be filled, Coolidge chose as the new Attorney General Harlan Fiske Stone, formerly dean of the Columbia University School of Law, who at once began a regime of irreproachable integrity. In the White House itself, where the President's wife, Grace Coolidge, presided with charm and dignity, the fumigation was complete; every trace of the Harding atmosphere was ruthlessly eradicated. But Coolidge accomplished the transition from obscenity in government to relative decency with a minimum of fanfare; if he had any slightest desire to capitalize on his record as renovator, he concealed the fact with skill.[7]

However much the Republican party may have profited from the presence of a virtuous man in the White House, it profited even more from the return of prosperity. By the end of 1922 the setback to business of the preceding year had run its course, so that when Coolidge became President the economic skies seemed fairly clear. There is reason to suppose that, at least as far as industry was concerned, things had not really been as bad as they had seemed. Prices had indeed declined, and both manufacturers and distributors had taken losses on whatever excess of high-priced goods they had had on hand. But once the process of liquidating their surplus inventories had come to an end, they found that they could still produce and sell profitably at the new price levels. Workers' wages might have declined in terms of dollars, but in terms of purchasing power they actually had tended to rise; by 1922, consumers were buying an even larger volume of goods and

[7] White, *Puritan in Babylon,* pp. 251, 269–277.

services than they had bought when the postwar boom was at its peak. With prices a little lower and mortgage money abundant, the demand for housing grew in vigor, and gave further impetus to the upswing. Unemployment, which had reached a peak of 5,735,000 in 1921, began to drop, and a steadily growing volume of workers' wages began to find its way into the channels of trade.[8]

To Republican politicians the best explanation for this return of prosperity lay in the businessman's program that Congress and the Executive had recently adopted. As party spokesmen saw it, governmental economies, a balanced budget, lower taxes, a reliable protective tariff, and the restoration of free enterprise had accomplished the desired end. In actual fact, the business revival occurred more in spite of these policies than because of them. Governmental measures were essentially deflationary in character, and acted as a brake on business expansion. Federal spending was declining, and the Treasury was now taking in each year more money than it paid out. Bond flotation had given way to repayments on the national debt, thus providing an automatic curb on the expansion of credit. The cessation of loans to foreign powers, the pressure for collection of principal and interest on debts due, and the operation of the high protective tariff, all tended to diminish foreign purchasing power in the United States. But politicians can rarely afford to look below the surface when surface facts are satisfying. For them it was enough to be able to say that the recession was over and business was beginning to boom; party decisions obviously must be responsible. And most of the people, easily impressed by a *post hoc, ergo propter hoc* argument, tended to agree.[9]

Those who did not share fully in the return of prosperity naturally held other opinions. Among the dissenters were great numbers of farmers who found that by any reasonable system of computation their costs of production tended to exceed the prices they were able to obtain for their products. Within the ranks of labor there was a comparable spirit of unrest. Unemployment continued for perhaps two and one-half millions, and the threat of unemployment hovered over many

[8] George Soule, *Prosperity Decade; From War to Depression: 1917–1919* (New York, 1947), pp. 111–113; statement of Secretary J. J. Davis, Sept., 1921, RG 174, Department of Labor, File 20–145, National Archives.

[9] Calvin Coolidge, *The Autobiography of Calvin Coolidge* (New York, 1929), pp. 165–166; Soule, *Prosperity Decade,* pp. 110–111; President's Conference on Unemployment, *Recent Economic Changes in the United States* (2 vols., New York, 1929), II, 899.

more. In certain unhealthy industries, such as coal and textiles, the future looked dark indeed. In addition to the discontented farmers and workers, many liberal intellectuals, although personally often well-to-do, found good reason for joining in the chorus of protests. Why should there be want and misery in the midst of plenty? How trustworthy was an economic system that seemed primarily designed to bring its greatest benefits to only a favored few?[10]

The voice of protest reached the people in a variety of ways. Organized labor presented its point of view through the *American Federationist,* official organ of the A.F. of L; through *Labor,* a paper issued by the railway brotherhoods; and through a host of minor periodicals, almost one each for every union of consequence. Farm grievances got a thorough airing in a *Weekly News Letter* circulated by the American Farm Bureau Federation; in the newspapers of other farm orders, such, for example, as the *Non-partisan Leader;* and in the innumerable farm journals which tended to sympathize, in one degree or another, with the farmers' woes. Some of the latter, such as *Wallace's Farmer,* an Iowa publication, were essentially conservative, but they found it quite impossible to overlook the discontent of their rural patrons. Dearest to the hearts of the liberal intellectuals were *The Nation,* and *The New Republic.* The former had a record of continuous protest from the end of the Civil War on down, and under the able editorship of Oswald Garrison Villard was as vehement as ever in its espousal of worthy causes. *The New Republic* dated back only to 1914, when Willard and Dorothy Straight, inspired by Herbert Croly's *The Promise of American Life* (1909), backed the new liberal weekly with their very considerable wealth, and made Croly its editor. Less emotional than Villard, and considerably more philosophic in his approach to public problems, Croly was equally dedicated to the idea of reform.[11] In addition to the liberal journals there were many Socialist and Communist publications, but the public disliked their doctrinaire concepts, and for that reason tended to discount their caustic criticisms of the established order. Many Americans were open to conviction on the subject of reform, but only a few were ready to flirt with the idea of revolution.

The reform movement did not lack for leaders. Outstanding among

[10] Fred E. Haynes, *Social Politics in the United States* (Boston, 1924), pp. 332–334, 395–397.

[11] Bruce Bliven, "The First Forty Years," *New Republic,* Fortieth Anniversary Issue, 1914–1954, CXXXI (Nov. 22, 1954), 6–10.

them was Robert M. La Follette, senior United States senator from Wisconsin, and consistent enemy of the monopolistic privileges sought by big business. His votes against American involvement in World War I had cost him many friends for a time, but by the 1920's his war record tended to be forgotten, or forgiven, or even approved. Through *La Follette's Magazine*, a weekly publication he had started back in 1909, his point of view reached a small but influential section of the American public, while his frequent speeches in the Senate and throughout the country were always news. Next in influence to La Follette came another senator, George W. Norris of Nebraska, the indefatigable advocate of public power, and in consequence the favorite enemy of the power trust. Two other senators, Hiram Johnson of California and William E. Borah of Idaho, were less dependable in their irregularity, but for good reason were regarded by the conservatives with great suspicion. As early as 1921, agricultural discontent had placed Dr. Edwin F. Ladd of North Dakota in the United States Senate, and after the elections of 1922 he was joined by such other "sons of the wild jackass"[12] as Lynn J. Frazier, also of North Dakota, Burton K. Wheeler of Montana, Magnus Johnson and Henrik Shipstead of Minnesota, and Smith W. Brookhart of Iowa. Fiorello La Guardia of New York, whether in or out of office, John R. Commons of the University of Wisconsin, Felix Frankfurter of the Harvard Law School, William Allen White of the Emporia (Kansas) *Gazette,* and Chester H. Rowell of the San Francisco *Chronicle* were among the many others who provided leadership in thought or deed for the forces of reform.

Efforts of the independents to organize politically centered mainly in the activities of three quite divergent groups. The first of these groups drew its strength from militant trade unionists who believed that labor had more to gain from separate political action than from the bipartisan tactics of the A.F. of L. Delegates so minded met in Chicago, November 22, 1919, and launched what they called the American Labor party. The second group, known as the Committee of Forty-eight, stemmed from the old Bull Moose Progressives who had

[12] The term is attributed to Senator George H. Moses of New Hampshire. Comments on these independents may be found in Ray Tucker and Frederick R. Barkley, *Sons of the Wild Jackass* (Boston, 1932), pp. 1–20. See also Robert S. Allen and Drew Pearson, *Washington Merry-Go-Round* (New York, 1931), pp. 184–216.

followed Theodore Roosevelt in 1912. Their leader was J. A. H. Hopkins of New Jersey, a well-to-do insurance broker who had served as national treasurer of the Progressive party, and after 1916 claimed authority to turn over all its "assets and names" to the next organization of similar principles to be formed. Late in the summer of 1919, Hopkins and other members of a self-styled Committee of Forty-eight launched a movement for the union of farmer and labor forces in the campaign of 1920, with La Follette as its candidate for President. But labor extremists, although consenting to a new name, the Farmer-Labor party, blocked all efforts at any real union, and La Follette refused to consider a meaningless nomination. The Farmer-Labor candidate finally chosen, Parley P. Christensen of Utah, received in the election only about a quarter of a million votes.[13]

The third, and most important, group to participate in the organization of protest was the Conference for Progressive Political Action. The C.P.P.A., as it was generally called, originated with the railroad brotherhoods, where the feeling was strong that management ought not to monopolize control of the railroads, but should somehow share its responsibilities with the workers, as proposed, for example, in the Plumb Plan. Hoping to unite all dissident elements in support of some such program, the brotherhood chiefs called a conference to meet in Chicago, February 20, 1922. The response was excellent; only the extreme radicals stayed away. The important thing, at least to a majority of the delegates, was to promote the election of as many progressives as possible in November, regardless of the political party to which any particular individual happened to belong. A second conference, to be held in December, after the elections, would chart the C.P.P.A. course for the future.[14]

Under the active leadership of a Committee of Fifteen, the C.P.P.A. went earnestly to work. Existing economic conditions greatly aided its efforts. Two years of low farm prices left the western farmers full of

[13] Nathan Fine, *Labor and Farmer Parties in the United States, 1828–1928* (New York, 1928), pp. 382–386, 395; Belle Case La Follette and Fola La Follette, *Robert M. La Follette* (2 vols., New York, 1953), II, 998, 1010; Lincoln Colcord, "The Committee of Forty-eight," *The Nation,* CIX (Dec. 27, 1919), 821–822; Kenneth C. McKay, *The Progressive Movement of 1924* (New York, 1947), pp. 56–58.

[14] Fine, *Labor and Farmer Parties,* pp. 400–402; Russel B. Nye, *Midwestern Progressive Politics* (East Lansing, Mich., 1951), p. 326; MacKay, *Progressive Movement,* pp. 60–67.

resentment against the administration, while a similar period of deflated wages, liberally interlarded with unemployment, produced in eastern workers an equally critical mood. Furthermore, the open alliance of the Harding regime with the employers in all industrial crises, culminating in Daugherty's use of the injunction, gave labor little promise of better things to come. The high tariff rates, the high taxes on low incomes, the high freight rates, and the high cost of living in general, all offended great numbers of voters. Prohibition enforcement displeased one section of the public because it was too effective, and another because it was not effective enough. Rumors of scandals in high places, although still unproved, did the administration no good, and the overfree use of money by some Republicans to influence elections—"Newberryism"—aroused deep resentment.[15]

Election results, according to one pleased observer, if not a complete victory for the reformers, at least amounted to "a great political upheaval." In the new Senate the division was 51 Republicans to 43 Democrats and two Farmer-Laborites; in the House, 225 Republicans, 205 Democrats, and one Socialist. But the issues of the election crossed party lines, and the blow that the conservative Harding administration had suffered was far more serious than the surface facts seemed to indicate. Many close friends of the President lost office; the percentage of casualties among those responsible for the Fordney-McCumber Act was phenomenally high; and the western antiadministration bloc won heavy reinforcements. Conservative reversals extended also to the states, where twelve out of sixteen gubernatorial candidates supported by the C.P.P.A. won election; in New York, for example, Alfred E. Smith, the liberal Democrat who had lost the governorship to a Republican in 1920, came back with a sweeping victory, while in Pennsylvania, Gifford Pinchot, the Roosevelt Progressive, won nomination and election as a Republican.[16] Summarizing the results, *Labor* insisted

[15] In the Michigan election of 1918, Truman H. Newberry, running as a Republican, had defeated Henry Ford, running as a Democrat, for a vacant Senate seat. Newberry's victory was achieved by such heavy expenditures that he became "a symbol of money in politics," and resigned before his term ended. Sullivan, *Our Times*, VI, 521–523. On the activities of the C.P.P.A. in the 1922 campaign, see Vincent P. Carosso, "The Conference for Progressive Political Action, 1922–1925," unpublished master's thesis, University of California, 1944.

[16] Gavin McNab to T. J. Walsh, Nov. 21, 1922, in Walsh Papers, Box 373, Library of Congress, Manuscripts Division; La Follette and La Follette, *La Follette*, II, 1064; *Official Congressional Directory*, 68th Cong., 1st Sess.

with pardonable exaggeration that the election "wasn't a 'Democratic landslide,' but it was a Progressive triumph, such a victory as the Progressives have not won in this country in many a day. It was gloriously non-partisan. Party lines were smashed and labor displayed its strength in a manner unparalleled in the history of the country. . . . La Follette was the outstanding winner and Washington is already talking of him as a most formidable presidential possibility in 1924."[17]

La Follette was by no means unconscious of his responsibilities as leader of the progressive forces in Congress. When the President, hoping to push through his ship-subsidy bill and perhaps other conservative measures, called a special session of the "lame duck" Congress for November 20, 1922, La Follette countered by inviting progressives from all over the country to meet with him in a conference at Washington, December 1–2, 1922. As a result, thirteen senators and "more than twenty-three" representatives, including Norris, Borah, Wheeler, and La Guardia, joined with such outstanding nonpolitical leaders as Gompers, Croly, and Villard in a program designed "to drive special privilege out of the control of the government and restore it to the people." There was talk that the "Progressive Bloc," most of whom were nominally Republican, might co-operate with the Democrats in taking formal control of Congress, but such an alliance was discreetly shunned in order to leave the way open for independent political action. Ten days after the Washington Conference, the C.P.P.A. met in St. Louis, fought off a Communist effort at infiltration, and postponed further its decision on the formation of a third party.[18]

Republican politicians, somewhat shaken by the results of the 1922 elections, were soon relieved by Harding's death of the necessity for renominating him in 1924. For a time they hesitated about according Coolidge the nomination, but the new President was determined to

(Dec., 1933), pp. 129, 131. The results of the election are carefully analyzed in James H. Shideler, "The Neo-Progressives: Reform Politics in the United States, 1920–1925," unpublished Ph.D. dissertation, University of California, Berkeley, 1945, p. 110. See also James H. Shideler, *Farm Crisis, 1919–1923* (Berkeley, Calif., 1957), pp. 221–230.

[17] *Labor,* IV, Nov. 11, 1922.

[18] La Follette and La Follette, *La Follette,* II, 1066–1067; Nye, *Midwestern Progressive Politics,* p. 327; Mackay, *Progressive Movement,* pp. 66–67; Fine, *Labor and Farmer Parties,* pp. 402–405; Hiram Johnson to Hiram Johnson, Jr., Dec. 9, 1922, Johnson Papers, Bancroft Library of the University of California.

have it, and laid his plans well. He depended upon his secretary, C. Bascom Slemp, to round up the southern delegates, and he used his New England connection to such good advantage that Senator George Moses of New Hampshire was soon calling upon "all New England to stand behind President Coolidge for a second term." The President also conferred unexpected courtesies upon certain Republican irregulars, and Borah repaid handsomely by saying publicly, "Give him a chance to make good. I think he is an able man."[19]

Behind the scenes the President began to shift control of the party away from the politicians and directly into the hands of the businessmen to whom they and he owed allegiance. The business world liked Coolidge; the things he said and did were exactly right. And the canny Coolidge knew whom to trust. In the Cabinet Mellon's importance grew steadily; in Massachusetts a Boston industrialist, William M. Butler, supplanted Henry Cabot Lodge as party leader. Not only did Butler head the Massachusetts delegation to the nominating convention; on White House orders, he became the new National Chairman, while Lodge was not even permitted to address the convention.[20]

When the Republican convention met in Cleveland on June 10, Coolidge's nomination was assured. Hiram Johnson, in what he characterized as "the most terrible and heart-breaking experience" of his life, had announced his candidacy late in 1923, and had attempted to head off Coolidge in the western primaries. But after an initial victory in South Dakota, Johnson's campaign fizzled out. "Money is king of politics again," he wrote, "as it probably has not been in our generation, and of course, it looks askance at me."[21] The Wisconsin delegation, except for one vote, stood steadfastly by La Follette, who received also six votes from North Dakota. On the first and only ballot the record showed 1,065 for Coolidge, 34 for La Follette, and 10 for Johnson. The platform urged governmental economies and further tax cuts, extolled the protective tariff policy, and favored a strong merchant marine, immigration restriction, liberal treatment of the veterans, and measures to give agriculture economic equality with other interests. On international affairs it opposed the League of Nations and the cancellation of war debts, but recommended United States adherence to

[19] White, *Puritan in Babylon,* p. 295.
[20] *Ibid.,* pp. 296–300.
[21] Johnson to Hiram Johnson, Jr., and A. M. Johnson, Mar. 30, 1924; Apr. 15, 1924, Johnson Papers.

the World Court. Efforts of the Wisconsin delegation to substitute a more liberal platform failed, as expected; except for a few face-saving gestures in the direction of labor and social legislation, the Republican platform was exactly what the nation's business leaders wanted it to be.[22]

The choice of a vice-presidential candidate entailed considerable confusion. Early in May Coolidge had sounded out Governor Frank O. Lowden of Illinois for second place, but Lowden had refused. The President also considered Senator Borah, and apparently hoped even after the convention was in session that Borah would accept. But Borah, too, refused even to permit the presentation of his name. Left to its own devices, the convention first nominated Lowden; then when he declined, as predicted, chose Charles Gates Dawes, the able ex-Director of the Budget. It is not without significance that Lowden was more the businessman than the politician, while Dawes was definitely a banker, and not a politician at all.[23] "I think Coolidge will be able to buy the election," Hiram Johnson observed. "The amount of money behind him will be greater than in all previous campaigns during our lives."[24]

It was true enough that the Republican party had the business interests of the country predominantly behind it. Business executives, particularly in the Northeast, which was the home of the great corporations, tended to be Republicans. The propertied classes everywhere expected favors from the government, and under Republican rule generally got them—lower taxes, higher tariffs, a minimum of governmental interference. So, always excepting the South, the property-minded voter was usually a Republican. But the Republican party, like its Democratic adversary, was essentially a coalition of diverse elements. It regularly drew to its standard many voters throughout the North who still thought of it as the party that had saved the Union and freed the slaves; ever since the Civil War there had been a more or less

[22] *Official Reports of the Proceedings of the Eighteenth Republican National Convention* (New York, 1924), pp. 114, 163–164; New York *Herald Tribune*, June 8–14, 1924; *The New York Times*, June 8–14, 1924; Kirk H. Porter, *National Party Platforms* (New York, 1924), pp. 497–513.

[23] White, *Puritan in Babylon*, pp. 301–305; Clinton W. Gilbert, *You Takes Your Choice* (New York, 1924), pp. 44–47; William T. Hutchinson, *Lowden of Illinois* (2 vols., Chicago, 1957), II, 534–535.

[24] Johnson to Hiram Johnson, Jr., and A. M. Johnson, June 13, 1924, Johnson Papers.

solid Republican North to oppose the solid Democratic South. Partly on this account, and partly because most men of wealth were Republicans, the Republican party tended also to be a status party; it was more respectable to be a Republican than to be a Democrat. And yet the Republican party could count on a certain amount of support from western radicals; only rarely did the discontented farmers who so heatedly denounced eastern control of the party and demanded measures of relief and reform actually go over to the Democrats. The party even numbered among its supporters many workers who identified their own interests with those of their employers, and voted as the boss voted. Last, and certainly least in voting strength, the southern Negroes, before the advent of the New Deal, remained loyal to the party that, in their judgment, had freed the slaves. Even the Negroes who had moved to the North usually thought of themselves as Republicans.[25]

Among the Democrats there was even less cohesion than among the Republicans; as the saying had it, "a Democrat would rather fight another Democrat than a Republican any day." In the deep South the whites were Democrats almost without exception, whatever their economic status. But the "solid South" was not as solid as it seemed; within southern Democratic ranks there was a clearly defined line of cleavage. The townspeople, the business and professional classes, the descendants of the reconstruction Bourbons, all lined up rigidly against the rural underprivileged whites—the "crackers," the "hillbillies," the "wool-hat boys," and the "woodpeckers," as they were variously called in derision. Contests between these warring groups in the southern Democratic primaries were among the bitterest in the nation; but the primary was decisive. Most of the time the conservatives won, but occasionally some such demagogic leader as Huey P. Long of Louisiana might achieve a majority. But by a generally accepted code, whichever faction won the primary also won the election; only in this way could the danger of Negro voting be averted. Labor in the South was still inarticulate, and usually voted as the industrialists voted, if it voted at all.

Eastern Democrats of the Grover Cleveland type, conservative and respectable, continued to exist, but their numbers were small, and the real leadership of the Democratic party in the East lay with the city machines. Best known of these was the Tammany organization in New

[25] André Siegfried, *America Comes of Age* (New York, 1927), pp. 275–284.

York, which for generations had traded a rough sort of social security for votes. Local party leaders helped the sick and jobless and aged through emergencies, and collected their reward on election day. Most of the city workers who followed machine direction in their voting were immigrants, or the descendants of immigrants. Frequently they were also Roman Catholic or Jewish, and they were rarely well seasoned in the American democratic tradition. In the West the Democratic party was strongly tinged with Bryan radicalism. Like the analogous western group in the Republican party, western Democrats wanted greater restrictions on industry and more effective aids to agriculture, lower prices for manufactured goods and higher prices for what the farmers had to sell.[26]

Despite the confusion it produced, there was much to be said for the two-party system, as it had worked itself out in the United States. The nation was far too large and its interests far too varied for two parties to represent every point of view. If political parties were to be based primarily on principle, or on economic interest, then the United States would need a dozen or so of them, some representing strictly sectional demands such as those of the midwestern farmers, and others pleading the cause of a special group such as organized labor. But a major political party must have wide appeal; it must cut across sectional and class lines; it must somehow draw within its ranks voters of nearly every political persuasion.[27] How to achieve a semblance of unity out of such varied elements was the continuing problem of both Republican and Democratic party leaders. The official policy of Gompers and the labor chiefs made matters even worse, for they had long sought to play off the two parties against each other, and to throw the influence of organized labor to whichever party and whichever candidates at a given time were willing to give labor the better deal. But the net result was that there always existed in the United States two political parties, each ready to take over the responsibility of running the government. When the time came to "throw the rascals out," there was always an alternative organization to which the voters could turn.[28]

[26] *Ibid.*, pp. 256–274; Wilfred E. Binkley, *American Political Parties; Their Natural History* (New York, 1951), pp. 372–373.

[27] Siegfried, *America Comes of Age,* pp. 247–255.

[28] Fine, *Labor and Farmer Parties,* p. 254; Herbert Agar, *The Price of Union* (Boston, 1950), pp. xiv–xvii, 688–691.

Senator Thomas J. Walsh, who became permanent chairman of the 1924 Democratic National Convention, suggested in advance of that meeting that there were four questions of prime importance on which real differences between the parties existed: (1) clean government, (2) taxation, (3) the tariff, and (4) the policy of isolation. A campaign waged by the Democrats on these issues, he believed, had a chance to succeed.[29] But Walsh was oversanguine in hoping that the Democrats would ignore their internal controversies and concentrate on the areas in which they could agree. Indeed, on two of the four issues Walsh mentioned, they were already in deep trouble. Their delight in condemning Republican scandals was tempered by the fact that, several months before their convention was scheduled to meet, the man in the lead for the presidential nomination, William Gibbs McAdoo, had admitted accepting a $25,000 annual retainer from the same Edward L. Doheny who had bribed Secretary Fall. McAdoo had not known of Doheny's "loan" to Fall, and he promptly canceled his contract with the oil man when he heard of it; but the "smear," however unjustified, was hard to explain away. Doheny also claimed that he had had three other former members of Wilson's Cabinet in his employ. Were the Democrats, under these circumstances, in a position to force the fighting on the subject of clean government? As for isolationism versus the League of Nations, public opinion had veered so far from the internationalist attitudes of the war years that many Democrats were ready to forget the subject entirely.[30]

The issue that destroyed all hope of Democratic unity in 1924 was the Ku Klux Klan. This organization, founded in 1915 by a Georgia colonel, William J. Simmons, was in its earlier years an inconsequential echo of the old Reconstruction Klan. But in 1920 an efficient super-salesman and organizer named Edward Y. Clarke took over its promotion. Sensing the money-making possibilities of an order based on the principle of intolerance, Clarke not only appealed to Southerners who wished to keep the Negro in his place but also drew into his net ardent nativists who resented the presence in the United States of recent immigrants; religious bigots among the Protestants who cherished an un-Christlike hatred of Catholics and Jews; political reactionaries who

[29] "The Issues of the Campaign," undated manuscript in Walsh Papers, Box 374.
[30] Mark Sullivan, *Our Times*, VI, 335–337; Hiram Johnson to Hiram Johnson, Jr., and A. M. Johnson, June 9, 1924, Johnson Papers.

were out to get liberals and radicals of whatever race or creed; "drys" who were certain that all "wets" were in league with the devil himself. By appealing to everyone who held a grudge against some minority group, and by promising joiners the immunity of secrecy, Clarke and his agents sold $10 memberships throughout the South and West, and even penetrated the Northeast. There was also a brisk business in robes and masks, for the order revived the garb associated with the earlier K.K.K. and fostered an elaborate ritualism, complete with a hierarchy of Kleagles, Goblins, and Wizards, each of whom, incidentally, collected his cut of the profits. Professing the deepest devotion to Americanism, the Klan often undertook to enforce its ideas by direct action. It burned fiery crosses at night to proclaim its presence; it administered whippings to Negroes, aliens, and sinners; it made its weight felt in elections. By the end of 1924 there were perhaps four or five million Klansmen in the United States, far too many voters for politicians to disregard with impunity.[31]

Possibilities of tragedy hung heavily over the delegates to the Democratic National Convention as they assembled in New York, June 24, 1924. The choice of a meeting place was unfortunate, for the local Tammany Democrats were fanatically opposed to the Klan, and cherished the hope of nominating for President their idol, Alfred E. Smith, an Irish-Catholic wet who had risen from the sidewalks of New York to the governorship of the state. Madison Square Garden was therefore anything but neutral territory. The galleries were packed with Smith adherents. The selection of Walsh as presiding officer, however, was peculiarly fortunate. As a Catholic, he was acceptable to the eastern city Democrats; as a dry, he reflected the views of the West; and as the chief investigator of the oil scandals, he had won the respect of every section. His impartial chairmanship during the tempestuous sessions that were to follow was about all that held the convention together.[32]

As anticipated, the principal divisions came over the League and the Klan. As for the former, the platform committee decided on a dodge;

[31] Preston W. Slosson, *The Great Crusade and After, 1914–1928* (New York, 1930), pp. 307–315; Frederick Lewis Allen, *Only Yesterday* (New York, 1931), pp. 65–69; J. M. Mecklin, *The Ku Klux Klan; A Study of the American Mind* (New York, 1924), pp. 3–51.
[32] *Official Report of the Proceedings of the Democratic National Convention, 1924* (Indianapolis, 1924), pp. 7–28, 80–89; Josephine O'Keane, *Thomas J. Walsh, A Senator from Montana* (Francestown, N.H., 1955), pp. 149–162.

it would have the convention endorse the League in principle, but call for a referendum on the subject of ratification. Newton D. Baker pleaded eloquently with the delegates to accept a minority report which stood more firmly by Wilsonian principles, but they applauded him to the echo, then voted him down by a more than two-thirds majority. Thereafter, the League, as an issue, was virtually dead. As for the Klan, the platform committee sought again to compromise, this time by avoiding specific condemnation of the order, while reaffirming Democratic devotion to civil liberties and religious freedom. But a minority report, which stated the case against the Klan in forthright terms, precipitated a prolonged and vehement debate that destroyed the last vestige of harmony. The city machines were determined to brand the Klan as the unmitigated evil they felt it to be; rural delegates from the West and the South fought back with equal ardor. In the end specific mention of the Klan was defeated by so close a margin—less than five votes—as to rob the victory of all significance.[33]

Aside from the stands taken on the League and the Klan, the Democratic platform was about what anyone might have expected. It attacked the control of the Republican party by special interests and the corruption of the Harding regime; it favored lower freight rates, a lower tariff, and a lower income tax; it urged more effective aid for agriculture, and collective bargaining for labor. It denounced the Republicans for their failure to enforce prohibition, and promised, somewhat unconvincingly in view of the record of the city machines, "to respect and enforce the Constitution and all laws."[34]

It was the disagreements and dissensions of the convention, rather than the agreements, that impressed the American public. In 1924, for the first time in history, the people generally were able to listen in by radio on convention proceedings, and they were a little shocked at some of the things they heard. At times the New York police force had to detail as many as a thousand men to convention duty in order to keep delegates and spectators from doing each other bodily violence. Unseemly conduct always attracts attention; ten plays on Broadway had to close during the convention for lack of business. But if the spectacle made interesting news, it did the Democrats no good. "How

[33] *Proceedings of the Democratic National Convention, 1924,* pp. 246–309; *The New York Times,* June 20–26, 1924; New York *Herald Tribune,* June 20–26, 1924.
[34] *Proceedings of the Democratic National Convention, 1924,* pp. 227–245.

true was Grant's exclamation," wrote Hiram Johnson, "that the Democratic Party could be relied upon at the right time to do the wrong thing!" Well before the convention began its protracted search for a candidate, impartial observers were convinced that its nominee would have no faintest chance of election.[35]

The deep division in the convention might have yielded more readily to compromise had not each of the two principal factions been so firmly committed to a favorite candidate. The city democracies wanted Smith, and would listen to no other name; the rural South and West, in general, wanted McAdoo. Furthermore, both candidates were obdurate and refused to concede, far longer than was reasonable, that the nomination must go to some third person. McAdoo's highest vote came on the sixty-ninth ballot, when he achieved 530 votes, only 20 less than a majority, but 202 less than the two-thirds necessary to a nomination. Smith's highest vote was 368. Even with both leaders out of the running, the difficulty of finding anyone on whom the delegates could agree was profound. Finally, on the 103rd ballot the convention turned to John W. Davis of West Virginia, a distinguished lawyer with Wall Street connections. To balance the ticket, it named for the Vice-Presidency Governor Charles W. Bryan of Nebraska, the brother of William Jennings Bryan. But the western radicals who deplored Davis's intimacy with the House of Morgan were not appeased, while the very name of Bryan frightened and irritated eastern conservatives. If the convention had deliberately set out to displease as many voters as possible with its nominees, it could hardly have done worse.[36]

The ultraconservatism of the Republicans and the suicidal tactics of the Democrats played into the hands of the Progressives. Heartened by the course of events since 1922, the C.P.P.A. at its third session held in St. Louis, February 11–12, 1924, formally called a nominating convention to meet in Cleveland the following July 4. In response, six hundred delegates appeared, most of them as representatives of Labor unions, farmer organizations, the Committee of Forty-eight, or the Socialist party. Communists were ruthlessly excluded. La Follette him-

[35] New York *Herald Tribune,* June 29, 30, 1924; Hiram Johnson to Hiram Johnson, Jr., and A. M. Johnson, July 3, 1924, Johnson Papers; Rev. Richard Brady to T. J. Walsh, Oct. 1, 1924, Walsh Papers, Box 373.

[36] Editorial, *Herald Tribune,* June 21, 1924; Clarence Cannon to Walsh, July 18, 1924, Walsh to Daniel Colahan, Sept. 27, 1924, in Walsh Papers, Box 374; *Proceedings of the Democratic National Convention, 1924,* pp. 346, 720, 825, 974–979.

self had set the pattern for this course in a letter he had written, May 28, 1924, denouncing the objectives of the Communists as "absolutely repugnant to democratic ideals and to all American aspirations. . . . To pretend that the communists can work with the progressives who believe in democracy is deliberately to deceive the public. The communists are antagonistic to the progressive cause and their only purpose in joining such a movement is to disrupt it."[37]

Probably most of the Cleveland delegates, including especially the Socialists, would have preferred to form a third party, but La Follette took pains to head off such a course. A straight-out third-party fight, he warned, would jeopardize the seats of the many progressives in Congress who had won office as Republicans or Democrats, and who might be called upon to help choose a President should the election be thrown into the House. Far better, La Follette argued, that there be only an independent presidential ticket, with the entire progressive effort directed toward its election. The formation of a third party could come later. The convention, however reluctantly, accepted La Follette's decision against a third party, nominated him for the Presidency by acclamation, adopted the brief platform he had written, and left to the National Committee the task of choosing a vice-presidential candidate. When Democratic Senator Burton K. Wheeler of Montana announced some days later that he could not support for President "any candidate representing Wall Street," meaning Davis, his selection as La Follette's running mate became a foregone conclusion. Wheeler, as chief Senate investigator of the Department of Justice under Daugherty's regime, had won much acclaim in progressive circles, and at La Follette's suggestion he was chosen to complete the ticket.[38]

Although La Follette and Wheeler headed a progressive ticket, and the success of their candidacies would doubtless have meant the formation of a Progressive party, the platform on which they ran contained little that was new. "The great issue," it maintained, was "the control of government and industry by private monopoly," which had "crushed competition, stifled private initiative and independent enterprise," and exacted "extortionate profits." But the only remedy the progressives could agree upon, apparently, was to seek the restoration of competi-

[37] MacKay, *Progressive Movement,* p. 87; La Follette and La Follette, *La Follette,* II, 1101; Fine, *Labor and Farmer Movement,* p. 435.

[38] MacKay, *Progressive Movement,* pp. 134–135; La Follette and La Follette, *La Follette,* II, 1110–1114.

tion, to turn back the clock. This unwillingness to look the facts of the twentieth century in the face worried the Socialists, who were ready to admit the hopelessness of the competitive system, and to prescribe as a substitute governmental ownership and operation of all agencies of production and distribution. La Follette was willing to go along with them to the extent of demanding the public ownership of water power, and in due time of the railroads, but for the most part the other planks in the Progressive platform only reiterated the demands of nineteenth-century antimonopolists, Grangers, and Populists. To please labor, the Progressives urged the abolition of the use of the injunction in labor disputes and complete protection of labor's right to collective bargaining. They also advocated a constitutional amendment restricting the use of "judicial veto" by the federal courts, and providing for the election of all federal judges for ten-year terms. The last plank of their platform, a kind of afterthought on foreign affairs, denounced "the mercenary system of foreign policy under recent administrations," favored a revision of the Versailles Treaty in accordance with the terms of the armistice, opposed conscription, and called for the outlawry of war, the reduction of armaments, and a "public referendum on peace and war." But the heart of the platform lay in its antimonopoly stand. In La Follette's words, the Progressive purpose was to break "the combined power of private monopoly over the political and economic life of the American people."[39]

Whatever the shortcomings of the La Follette program, the demand for a "united front" of all reformers proved to be almost irresistible. The Socialist party, which held its national convention in Cleveland immediately following the Progressive convention, decided by a large majority to endorse La Follette, an action by which, according to *The New York Times,* it came "close to filing a petition in voluntary bankruptcy."[40] Farmer-Labor candidates nominated at St. Paul earlier in the year soon withdrew in favor of La Follette. More important still, the Executive Council of the American Federation of Labor, at a meeting held early in August, gave La Follette and Wheeler its cordial endorsement—the first time a third ticket had ever achieved such an honor. In giving its support to the Progressives, however, it still claimed that its decision was strictly nonpolitical; that it was only approving the best of three sets of candidates available. A few of the splinter parties,

[39] Porter, *National Party Platforms,* pp. 516–522.
[40] *The New York Times,* July 9, 1924, p. 18.

including the Communists, whose candidate, William Z. Foster, declared the Progressive party platform to be "the most reactionary document of the year," stood out against the general tendency of all dissenters to unite on La Follette, but the number of voters they could command was insignificant.[41]

With the conservatives divided and the progressives united, the hopes of the La Follette supporters soared far higher than the facts justified. It was true enough that both Coolidge and Davis stood for pretty much the same program. Under their leadership the difference between the two major parties, according to one cynic, was "whether the entrance to the office of J. P. Morgan and Company should be on Wall or Broad Street."[42] As if conscious of the paucity of issues between them, both the Republicans and the Democrats tended to concentrate their fire on the Progressives, and to ignore each other. Coolidge did little campaigning, but his running mate Dawes took to the stump with enthusiasm, and denounced La Follette in vigorous terms, dwelling with particular delight on the dangers of Supreme Court reform inherent in the La Follette demands, and identifying the American Progressives as completely as possible with the Russian Bolshevists. Davis, too, found fault with the court plank in the Progressive platform, and considered it the most important issue in the campaign.[43]

Against this concerted attack La Follette fought back with what vigor he could command. He was an old man, far from well, and too much depended on him personally. He had thought it sound strategy to keep his candidacy clear of all third-party implications, but the lack of local organizations based on the hope of local offices proved to be a serious handicap. Funds, too, were scarce. The Republicans had unlimited resources, and admitted to collecting over $4 million for campaign purposes. The Democrats were far less well off, but managed to obtain over $800,000 in gifts and to spend nearly $100,000 more than that. As against all this outpouring of wealth, the La Follette-Wheeler campaign cost only about $211,000. Despite this handicap La Follette made three extensive tours, two in the East, and one in the Middle West, where he spoke, as a rule, to large and responsive audiences.

[41] Shideler, "The Neo-Progressives," pp. 254–255; MacKay, *Progressive Movement*, pp. 152–156; Nye, *Midwestern Progressive Politics*, p. 336.

[42] Hiram Johnson to Hiram Johnson, Jr., and A. M. Johnson, July 3, 1924, Johnson Papers.

[43] MacKay, *Progressive Movement*, pp. 159–161; Nye, *Midwestern Progressive Politics*, pp. 339–340.

Wheeler also campaigned actively, but the La Follette forces received far less support from prominent liberals than they had expected. Brookhart of Iowa, Johnson of California, La Guardia of New York, and some others publicly endorsed La Follette, but Norris of Nebraska gave little more than sympathy to the movement, while Borah of Idaho actively supported Coolidge.[44]

For both La Follette and Davis the greatest handicap was prosperity. Except for the farmers, there was little economic distress anywhere in the nation, and even farm prices took a convenient turn upward during election year. The admonition to "Keep Cool with Coolidge" outweighed in the minds of most voters all such minor issues as the misdeeds of the Ohio gang, the dangers of monopoly, and the iniquities of the high tariff. The Republican party made much of its long record as the party of prosperity; if it were voted out of office, would prosperity go, too? Why take such a chance? With greater imagination than common sense, Republican campaigners also conjured up the spectacle of a three-way division in the electoral college, with no majority for anyone. This could be followed by a deadlock in the closely divided House of Representatives and a Progressive-Democratic combine in the Senate that might make Charles W. Bryan President of the United States. This danger, dramatized by George Harvey as "Coolidge or Chaos," no doubt seemed real enough to swing some of the politically naïve to Coolidge. As for foreign affairs, the Republican return to isolation probably offended fewer voters than Davis's mild internationalism and La Follette's unsavory war record. Besides all this, the people liked "Silent Cal." They understood his small-town, cracker-barrel philosophy, they believed in his honesty, and they tended to have the same respect he had for the big business leaders who had known how to get on in the world. Monopoly might be a very bad thing, but it could be tolerated if it meant also general prosperity.[45]

When the votes were counted, it was apparent that the Progressive protest had fallen far short of the goals its leaders had set. They had hoped for at least a good enough showing to justify the formation of a third party, but La Follette carried only one state, Wisconsin, in the

[44] MacKay, *Progressive Movement*, pp. 157, 184, 195–196; La Follette and La Follette, *La Follette*, II, 1127–1147; Norris, *Fighting Liberal*, p. 286; Claudius O. Johnson, *Borah of Idaho* (New York, 1936), p. 303.

[45] MacKay, *Progressive Movement*, pp. 204–216, 249–253.

ELECTION RETURNS, 1924

	Popular	Electoral	States Carried
Coolidge	15,275,003	382	35
Davis	8,385,586	136	12
La Follette	4,826,471	13	1
Others	160,644		
Totals	28,647,709	531	48

Electoral College, and obtained only 16.5 per cent of the popular vote. Moreover, Coolidge's popular as well as electoral majorities exceeded the combined Davis and La Follette totals, while the Coolidge landslide carried into office overwhelming Republican majorities in both the Senate and the House: in the former, 56 Republicans to 39 Democrats and 1 Farmer-Laborite; in the latter, 247 Republicans to 183 Democrats, 2 Socialists, and 2 Farmer-Laborites. The balance-of-power status that had given the irregulars so much standing in the preceding Congress was now a thing of the past, and Republican conservatives, with an occasional assist when necessary from like-minded Democrats, were in complete control.[46]

Despite this serious setback, La Follette was ready to go ahead with the work of organizing for the campaign of 1926. "We have just begun to fight," he said. But he got little support from his discouraged erstwhile followers. In accordance with a decision reached at the Cleveland nominating convention, the C.P.P.A. National Committee called a post-election convention to decide the future course of the Progressives. Responding to this call, three hundred delegates met in Chicago, February 21, 1925, and voted to adjourn *sine die*. In making this decision they had little choice, for the A.F. of L. had officially announced the preceding month that it would never again associate itself with third-party activities. Since most of the trade-union representatives in the convention agreed with the A.F. of L., only a hard corps of La Follette admirers and the Socialist contingent were ready to carry the movement further. But even between these two groups there were unresolvable differences. The Socialists favored a third party organized along class

[46] *Ibid.,* 219; *Official Congressional Directory,* 69th Cong., 1st Sess. (Dec., 1925), pp. 133, 135.

lines and committed to Socialist principles, a program that La Follette and the western agrarians could never accept.[47]

In voting the C.P.P.A. out of existence the convention softened the blow a little by suggesting that individuals who so desired might meet later in the day to form a third party, if they chose. Such a meeting took place the evening of February 21, but the delegates who participated could agree only on postponing until autumn the formation of a new party, and entrusting the future of the movement to an executive committee. The call for the new convention never came, and the executive committee gradually disintegrated. As for the Socialist party, it had already begun to decline before the election of 1924, and its participation in the united-front adventure of that year seemed to weaken it still further. Never again was it to regain the voting strength it had shown in the election of 1920. The final climax to Progressive gloom came when La Follette, overwearied by the rigors of the campaign, succumbed to a heart attack, June 18, 1925. Ironically, his son, Robert M. La Follette, Jr., who was elected the following September to fill out his father's term in the Senate, took office as a Republican.[48]

The unseemly haste with which the Progressives of 1924 liquidated their organization gives a quite incorrect impression of the results they had achieved. Actually they had made an excellent showing, considering the many obstacles they had confronted. Wiser than the discouraged politicians, William B. Colver, editor in chief of the Scripps-Howard newspapers, which had warmly supported La Follette in the campaign, wired the defeated Progressive leader: "Don't let anybody tell you it wasn't worth while nor that the net result is not a great gain in the public service." La Follette had thrown a heavy scare into the old party machines during the campaign. In the end he carried only one state, but he had run second in eleven others—California, Idaho, Iowa, Minnesota, Montana, Nevada, North Dakota, South Dakota, Oregon, Washington and Wyoming—while in thirteen states he had polled enough votes so that Coolidge won them only by pluralities rather than by majorities. But unlike Theodore Roosevelt in 1912, who had split the Republican party and made possible a Democratic victory, La

[47] La Follette and La Follette, *La Follette,* II, 1155–1157; MacKay, *Progressive Movement,* 232–235.

[48] *Ibid.,* pp. 235–242; Fine, *Labor and Farmer Parties,* pp. 423–429; David A. Shannon, *The Socialist Party of America* (New York, 1955), pp. 178–181; La Follette and La Follette, *La Follette,* II, 1168–1169.

Follette had drawn far more heavily from Democratic than from Republican ranks. The Davis showing, particularly in the Middle West and the Pacific states, was extremely dismal; in California, for example, La Follette polled 424,649 votes to 105,514 for Davis. The most obvious lesson of the campaign was that the Democrats, if they wished to win future elections, must come forward with liberal candidates and a liberal program. Independent voters in 1924 turned to La Follette to register their protest rather than to Davis, because La Follette was a liberal and Davis was not. Or, in many cases, they simply neglected to vote. The number of stay-at-homes was unusually large—about 49 per cent of the total eligibles—although in the region where La Follette was strongest, about 65 per cent of those entitled to vote actually went to the polls.[49]

The significance of a third party in American politics is not to be found in its ability to win elections. What it accomplishes, rather, is to focus the attention of the older parties on the issues it has presented. After the returns of 1924 came in, the Republicans were filled with complacency; they had won with ease. But the Democrats, if they were ever to win again, must take pains to woo the discontented voters who had supported La Follette. No one sensed this more fully than Franklin D. Roosevelt, the prominent New Yorker who had so ably presented Smith's name at the Madison Square Garden convention. Roosevelt took occasion after the election to write to all the delegates to the Democratic National Convention of 1924, urging them to stand together in defense of liberal principles:

There is room for but two parties. The Republican leadership has stood and still stands for conservatism, for the control of the social and economic structure of the nation by a small minority of handpicked associates. The Democratic party organization is made more difficult by the fact that it is made up in chief part by men and women who are unwilling to stand still but who often differ as to the methods and lines of progress. Yet we are unequivocally the party of progress and liberal thought. Only by uniting can we win.[50]

[49] *Ibid.*, II, 1148; Nye, *Midwestern Progressive Politics,* pp. 340–342; MacKay, *Progressive Movement,* p. 223.

[50] Franklin D. Roosevelt to Josephus Daniels, Dec. 5, 1924, Daniels Papers, Box 15, Library of Congress, Manuscript Division; Carroll Kilpatrick (ed.), *Roosevelt and Daniels; A Friendship in Politics* (Chapel Hill, 1952), p. 83. See also Margaret L. Coit, *Mr. Baruch* (Boston, 1957), pp. 367–372.

Among the groups that had supported La Follette in the campaign of 1924 was a "Committee of One Hundred," headed by Oswald Garrison Villard, editor of *The Nation*. In a telegram pledging their allegiance to the Progressive cause they had said: "We believe that the time has come for a new deal."[51] This was exactly what Roosevelt had in mind, but the agency through which it must be achieved was in his judgment the Democratic, not the Progressive, party. And the day of delivery might have to be postponed. "Frankly," he admitted to one correspondent, "I do not look for a Democratic president until after the 1932 election."[52]

---

[51] La Follette and La Follette, *La Follette*, II, 1117.
[52] Arthur M. Schlesinger, Jr., *The Age of Roosevelt; The Crisis of the Old Order, 1919–1933* (Boston, 1957), p. 378.

CHAPTER 5

Prosperity Plus

WITH Coolidge finally President in his own right, the spirit of governmental favoritism toward business, so earnestly cultivated during the preceding four years, began to achieve really spectacular results. Mellon's proposals on taxation, for example, which up to this time the Progressives in Congress had blocked from full acceptance, now went through with hardly a protest. Mellon's principal victories came with the reduction of the surtax and estate-tax maximums from 40 to 20 per cent each, which meant a great saving for the well-to-do. Congress also repealed the gift tax, which in practice meant a still further reduction of the estate tax, for it permitted tax-free gifts to prospective heirs. The new measure also eliminated the annoying section on income-tax publicity. The one important tax on wealth that the Act of 1926 did not reduce was the corporation tax, which Congress raised from 12 to 12½ per cent the first year and 13 the second, but the Revenue Act of 1928 restored the 12 per cent rate, while making no significant changes in the other principal schedules. According to one estimate, the amount of tax money "released for productive investment" by the Mellon schedules amounted to about $350 million annually. A man with a million-dollar annual income now paid less than $200,000 in federal taxes, instead of over $600,000 as formerly; while for the larger incomes, which would include Mellon's, the savings were still more substantial. Concessions to the small taxpayer were held at a minimum.[1]

[1] Revenue Act of 1926, *United States Statutes at Large* (Washington, 1927), XLIV, 21–29, 69, 126; Harvey O'Connor, *Mellon's Millions* (New York, 1933), p. 141.

The fact that these reductions in tax rates did not result in financial embarrassment to the federal government made Andrew Mellon, in many eyes, "the greatest Secretary of the Treasury since Alexander Hamilton." The revenue collected each year amounted to about $4 billion, while the economy-minded administration held annual expenditures down to a little over $3 billion. The Treasury surplus so produced went toward the liquidation of the national debt, which dropped from about $24 billion in 1920 to about $16 billion in 1930. The frugal-minded Coolidge expressed his pleasure with these developments in his 1928 message to Congress.

Four times we have made a drastic revision of our internal revenue system, abolishing many taxes and substantially reducing almost all others. Each time the resulting stimulation to business has so increased taxable incomes and profits that a surplus has been produced. One-third of the national debt has been paid, while much of the other two-thirds has been refunded at lower rates, and these savings of interest and constant economies have enabled us to repeat the satisfying process of more tax reductions.

No doubt Coolidge overstated the significance of tax reduction in stimulating the business boom. Other factors also contributed to this end, among them, the mounting volume of state, municipal, and private debt, which rose as precipitately as the federal debt declined.[2]

A firm believer in the dictum the less government the better, Coolidge saw only good rather than evil in breaking down as completely as possible all governmental controls over business. As already noted, he turned the great federal regulatory commissions over to the very interests they were supposed to regulate, and, at least in the eyes of the Progressives, he also sought to rig the Attorney General's office in much the same way. Early in 1925 the President named Harlan Fiske Stone, the able Attorney General he had named to clean up after Daugherty, to a vacancy on the Supreme Court. To succeed Stone he chose Charles B. Warren of Detroit, a lawyer-politician of ultraconservative views whose efforts to extend the monopolistic holdings of the sugar trust were well remembered. The Progressives in the Senate, although reduced in influence after the election of 1924, pounced on the Warren record with glee, and with Democratic assistance were able to refuse confirmation by a tie vote, 40 to 40, Vice-President Dawes being absent

[2] *Congressional Record*, 70th Cong., 2nd Sess., LXX (Dec. 4, 1928), 20; George Soule, *Prosperity Decade* (New York, 1947), pp. 132–133, 323.

at the time for his noonday nap at the Willard Hotel. Stubbornly
Coolidge, who saw nothing wrong in the sugar transaction and had
openly defended it, resubmitted Warren's name, only to have it rejected the second time by a more decisive vote, 39 to 46. The President
then, in some petulance, nominated for the vacant post a virtually
unknown Vermont lawyer, John Garibaldi Sargent, whom the Senate
promptly confirmed.[3]

By a strange coincidence it happened that Attorney General Stone,
shortly before his promotion to the Supreme Court, had discovered that
the Aluminum Company of America was openly continuing illegal
practices from which the Federal Trade Commission had ordered it to
desist. But the evidence at hand was based on the company's behavior
prior to 1922, and needed to be brought down to date; also, a one-year
statute of limitations made necessary the accumulation of new evidence.
At Stone's request the Commission then resumed its investigations, but
in the meantime Coolidge's new appointees had changed its temper
completely. The Coolidge majority now refused to tell the Attorney
General's office the results of its new investigation; furthermore, neither
Attorney General Sargent nor his assistant, William J. Donovan, showed
much interest in the case. In due time the Department of Justice reported that the company was entirely innocent of all the charges lodged
against it. This did not satisfy Senators Norris and Walsh, who tried
to obtain a Senate investigation of the Aluminum trust, only to fail by
a vote of 36 to 33.[4]

Small wonder that the business world came to regard Coolidge as the
ideal President. He in turn liked the men who had achieved prominence
in American business, and invited them often to the White House.
Under their spell he lent the weight of his office to the expansion of
credit they believed desirable, and so gave incalculable aid to the business boom. No doubt the President assumed that in approving such a
course he was merely heading off the danger of depression; prosperity,
his Wall Street advisers told him, could be maintained indefinitely if

[3] *Congressional Record,* 69th Cong., Special Sess., LXVII (Mar. 10, 1925),
92–101; (Mar. 16, 1925), 274–275; William Allen White, *A Puritan in
Babylon* (New York, 1938), pp. 319–322.

[4] *Congressional Record,* 69th Cong., 1st Sess., LXVII, (Feb. 26, 1926),
4607–4622; O'Connor, *Mellon's Millions,* pp. 171–184; Soule, *Prosperity
Decade,* pp. 137–138; Thomas C. Blaisdell, Jr., *The Federal Trade Commission* (New York, 1932), pp. 89–91, 236–243; *Annual Report of the Federal
Trade Commission, June 30, 1930* (Washington, 1930), p. 175.

only the country were given the easier credit it needed whenever an emergency threatened. And they knew exactly how this could be done. The Federal Reserve Board could help to some extent by keeping the rediscount rate low, while the various Federal Reserve Banks could help even more by making discreet purchases of government securities. When they bought these investments, it was a matter of common knowledge that they made more credit available for member banks; when they sold them, credit tightened up. So, assured of the President's backing, they bought. According to Herbert Hoover, foreign pressure also, particularly in 1925 and 1927, played a leading role in inducing the Coolidge administration to favor an easy money policy. Undoubtedly European nations had need of conserving their gold supply, and were fearful of what might happen to their finances if American credit should tighten up. But the pressure to which the American authorities yielded was no less American than European.[5]

What were the banks to do with all the money they had on hand? They loaded up freely with government securities, and so added still more to the credit they could make available. They lent to investors in stocks and bonds, which they took as collateral, with much the same result; they provided the necessary backing for installment financing, another principal means of promoting the boom; and they underwrote long-term real estate investments to an alarming degree. Easy credit also contributed to heavy purchases by American investors of European securities—over a billion dollars a year during the Coolidge ascendancy. Americans thus furnished Europeans the extra money they needed to buy American goods; in so doing they contributed greatly to both the European and the American booms, but they also added dangerously to the imposing volume of uncollectable debts.[6]

Whatever index of prosperity one cares to choose, the evidence is overwhelming that during the Coolidge era the country was experiencing a business boom of unprecedented proportions. The nation's total

[5] *Tenth Annual Report of the Federal Reserve Board, 1923* (Washington, 1924), pp. 3–16; *Eleventh Annual Report of the Federal Reserve Board, 1924* (Washington, 1925), pp. 2–12; White, *Puritan in Babylon*, p. 289; Soule, *Prosperity Decade*, p. 154; Lionel Robbins, *The Great Depression* (London, 1934), p. 53; Herbert Hoover, *The Memoirs of Herbert Hoover* (New York, 1952), III, 6–11; H. G. Warren, *Herbert Hoover and the Great Depression* (New York, 1959), pp. 98–103.

[6] President's Conference on Unemployment, *Recent Economic Changes in the United States* (New York, 1929), II, 696–700; Soule, *Prosperity Decade*, pp. 155–156; White, *Puritan in Babylon*, pp. 290–291.

realized income, which included all such items as payrolls, pensions, rents, and profits, climbed from $74.3 billion in 1923 to $89 billion in 1928. During the same period the annual net income of corporations rose from $8.3 billion to $10.6 billion, savings and time deposits from $19.7 billion to $28.4 billion, life insurance assets from $9.4 billion to $15.9 billion, building and loan assets from $3.9 billion to $8 billion. In most instances the 1929 figures exceeded those of 1928. Even with allowances made for the shrinking value of the dollar, the net increases during the Coolidge years were phenomenal. Workers in industry fared particularly well while the boom lasted. During the decade 1919–29, they experienced a rise in real wages of about 26 per cent, while in the lush years 1923–29 their average real earnings increased by 8 per cent and their average work week decreased from 47.3 to 45.7 hours. The total labor force for the period showed remarkably little fluctuation, the number actually employed varying from about 40 to about 43 million persons.[7]

It would be quite unreasonable to assume that the Coolidge policies alone accounted for the business boom that characterized the middle and later 1920's. Undoubtedly the government sometimes provided stimulants when restraints would have served far better, but the principal ingredients of the boom came from nongovernmental sources. The First World War, with its labor shortages and its insistent demand for speed in production, greatly accelerated technical changes that were already on the way, but that in time of peace might have come more slowly. Increasingly machines did work once done by men, and did it better. Scientific management introduced also a degree of efficiency unknown in earlier years. After the war, with the value of the new methods amply attested, prudent operators poured millions of dollars into industrial research, hoping, rarely in vain, to improve their procedures. As a result, output per worker soared steadily during the 1920's, and total production soared with it, although many workers suffered at least temporarily from technological unemployment—machines had taken over their jobs.[8]

[7] *Recent Economic Changes,* II, 468, 673, 763; *Statistical Abstract of the United States, 1931,* pp. 191, 275, 279, 308; Robert F. Martin, *National Income in the United States* (New York, 1939), pp. 6–7.

[8] *Recent Economic Changes,* I, 88–91, II, 459; Stuart Chase, *Prosperity, Fact or Myth* (New York, 1930), pp. 135–151; Soule, *Prosperity Decade,* 31; Henry Ford, *My Life and Work* (New York, 1922), pp. 77–90; Thomas C. Cochran and William Miller, *The Age of Enterprise* (New York, 1942), pp. 184–185.

. PRESIDENT HARDING throwing out
the ball in 1921.

Wide World

2. CALVIN COOLIDGE dips a hook in a Vermont trout stream.

Wide World

3. The American delegation to the Washington Armament Conference in 1921—Elihu Root, Henry Cabot Lodge, Charles Evans Hughes, and Oscar Underwood.

4. SENATOR BORAH, leading American advocate of the Conference, but conspicuously not a delegate.

Wide World

5. **CALVIN COOLIDGE** and **CHARLES G. DAWES**, successful candidates for President and Vice-President, respectively, in 1924.

6. **ROBERT M. LA FOLLETTE** of Wisconsin, defeated Progressive candidate for President in 1924, and his son, Robert M. La Follette, Jr., who succeeded to his father's seat in the Senate in 1925.

Wide World

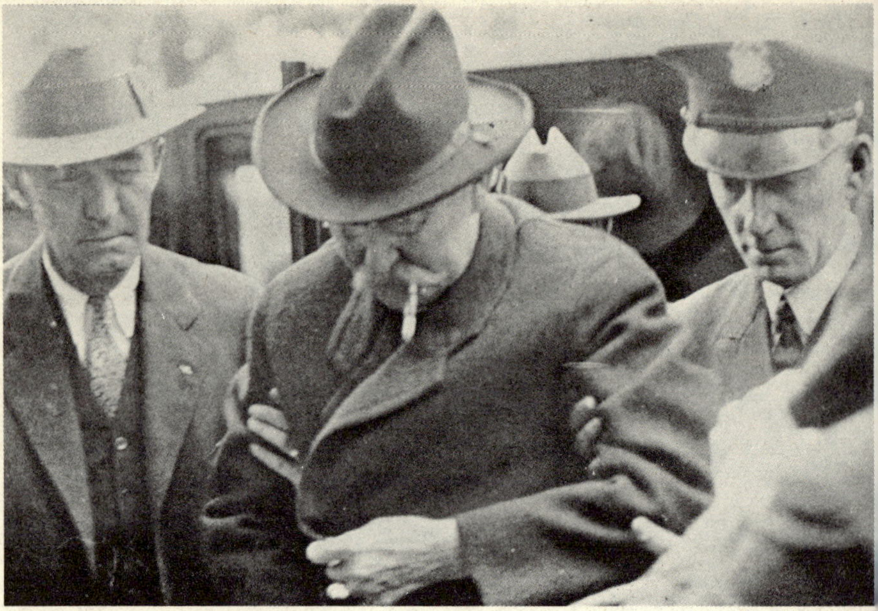

United Press International

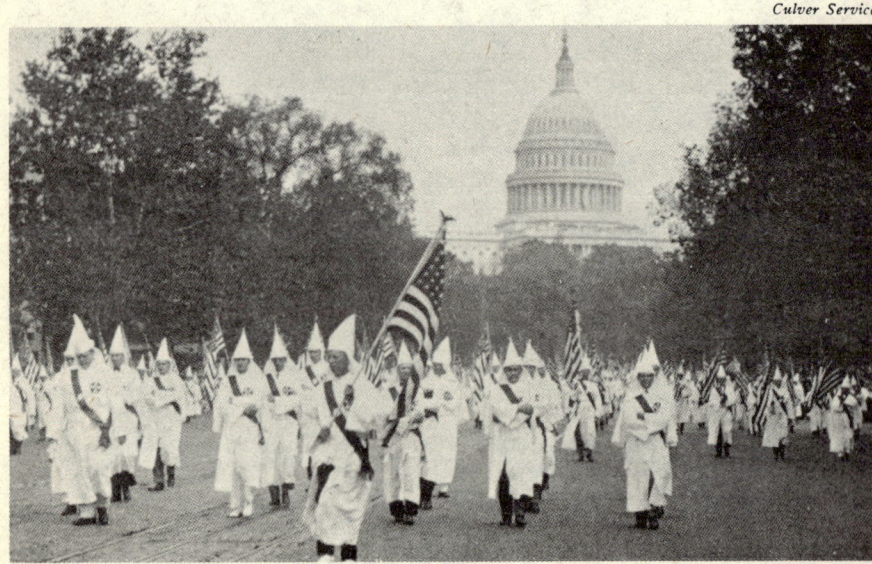

7. ALBERT B. FALL, former Secretary of the Interior, being assisted into the courtroom to stand trial for fraud and corruption in 1927.

8. A Ku Klux Klan parade in the national capital.

Culver Service

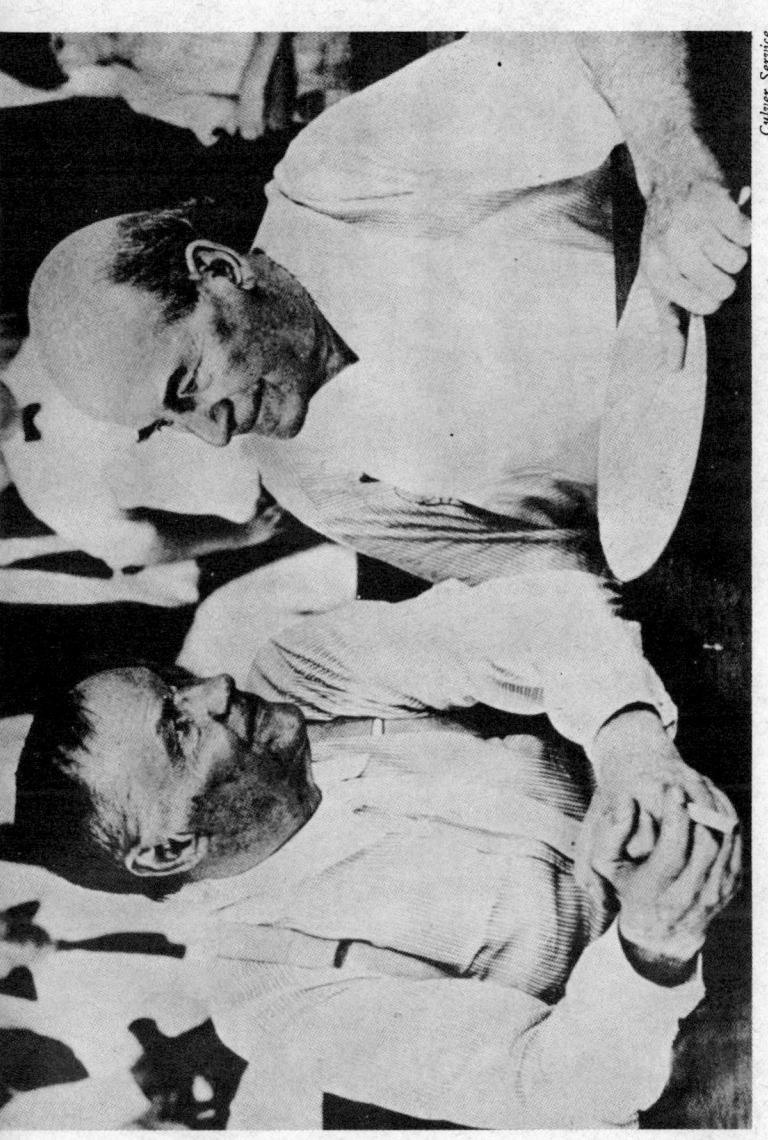

Culver Service

9. CLARENCE DARROW and WILLIAM JENNINGS BRYAN, opposing counsel at the Scopes trial in Dayton, Tennessee, 1925.

10. CHARLES A. LINDBERGH and the monoplane, *Spirit of St. Louis,* with which he
flew the Atlantic, May 20-21, 1927.

11. GENERAL "BILLY" MITCHELL, whose protests against the neglect of air power in national defense led to his court-martial in
October, 1925.

12. Wreck of the *Shenandoah* near Ava, Ohio, September 3, 1925.

13. Three motion picture stars of the "silent drama" era—Douglas Fairbanks, Mary Pickford, and Charlie Chaplin.

Brown Brothers

14. AL CAPONE in Florida during his heyday.

Brown Brothers

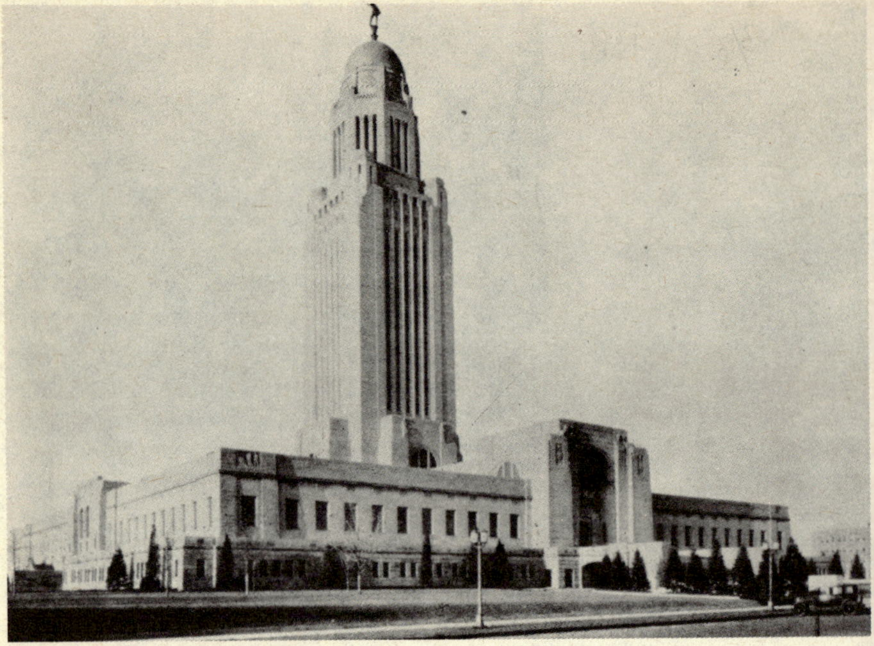

Wide World

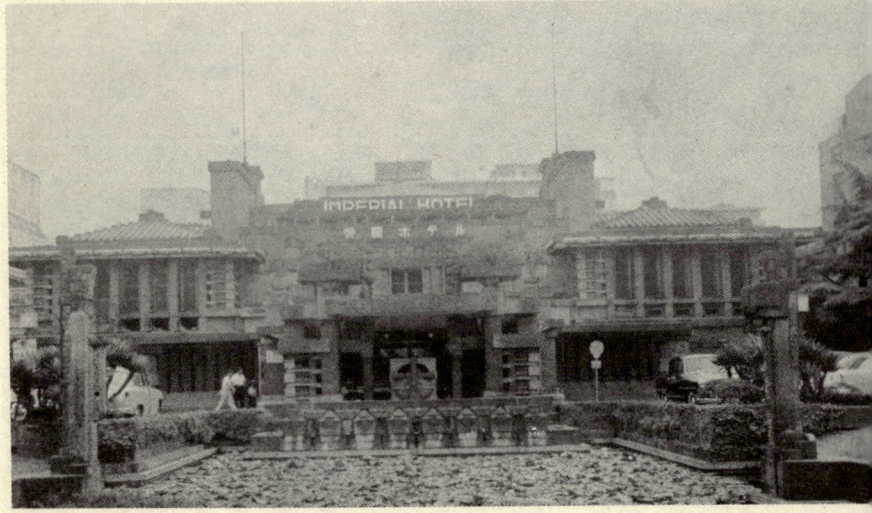

15. The Nebraska State Capitol, completed in the 1920's.

16. Imperial Hotel, Tokyo, Japan, designed by Frank Lloyd Wright, which withstood the earthquake of 1923.

Wide World

Brown Brothers

17. An early radio and radio equipment store.

18. HENRY and EDSEL FORD, with every model produced by the Ford plant from its founding to 1932.

Wide World

Culver Service

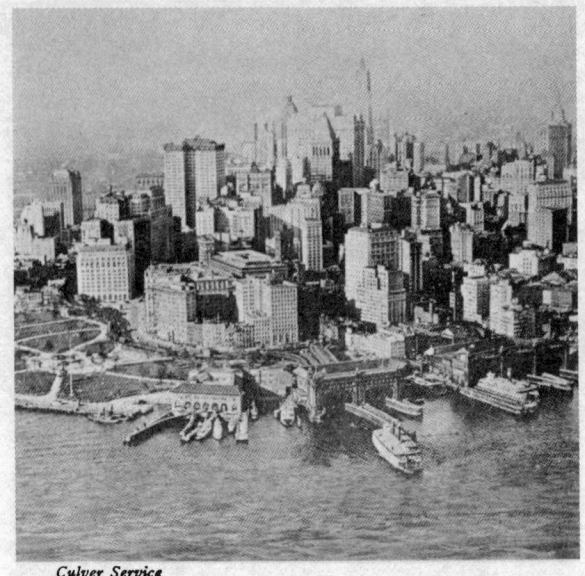

19. The New York skyline when the Woolworth Building was the tallest building in the world.

20. Forty-second Street in New York, 1929.

Wide World

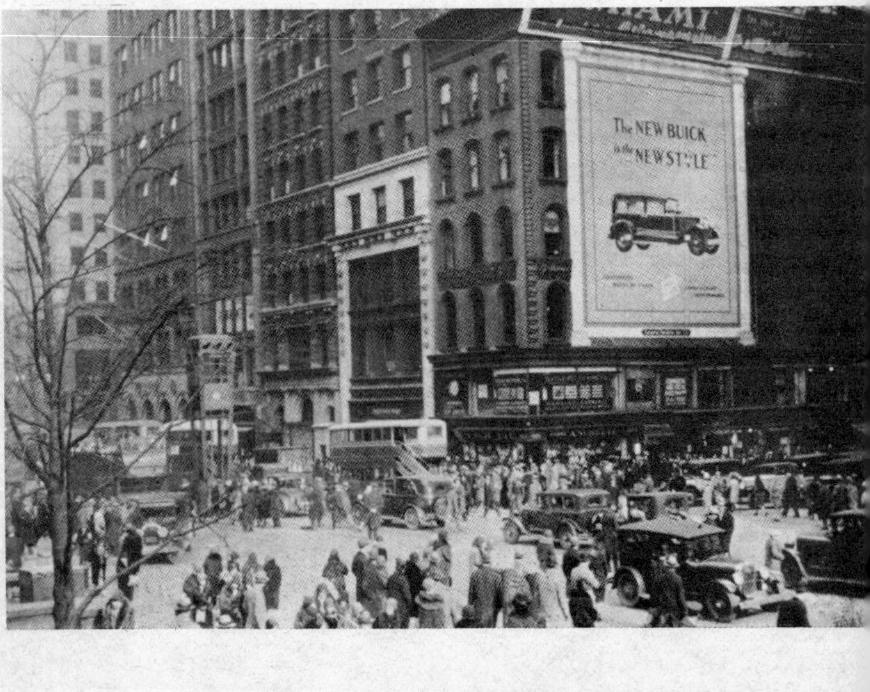

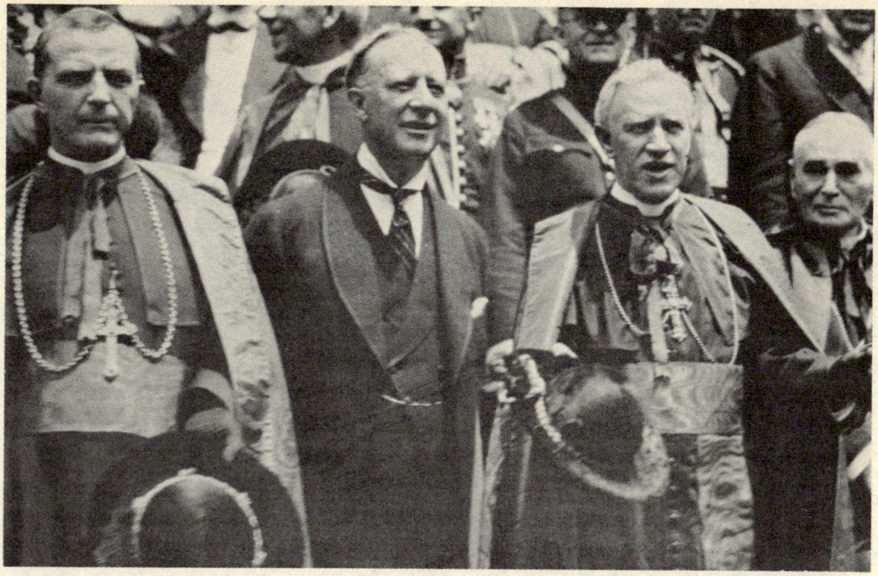

Culver Service

21. ALFRED E. SMITH (center), whose devout Catholicism became an issue in the election of 1928.

22. President-elect Herbert Hoover with Henry Ford, Thomas A. Edison, and Harvey Firestone on a Florida vacation, February, 1929.

Wide World

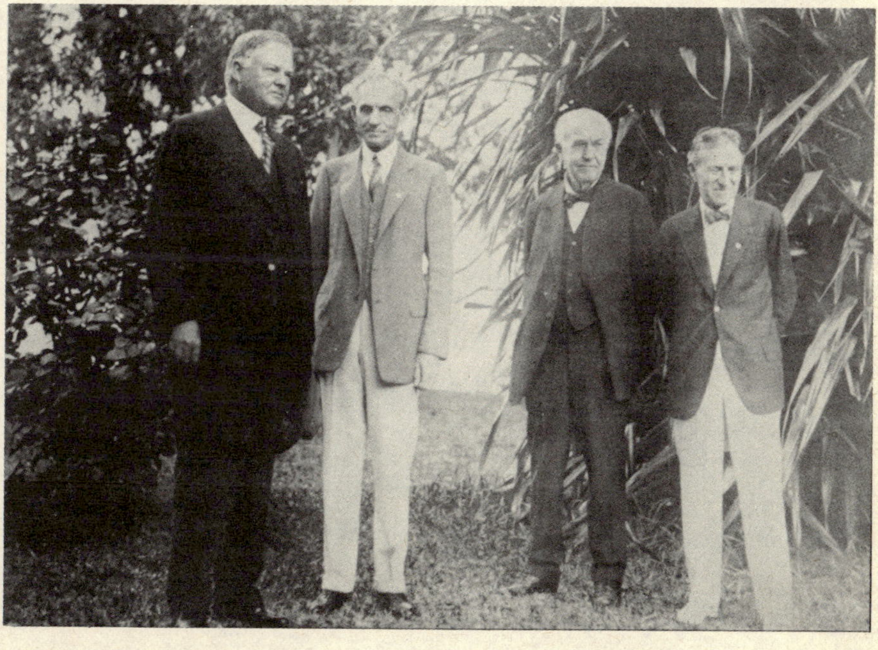

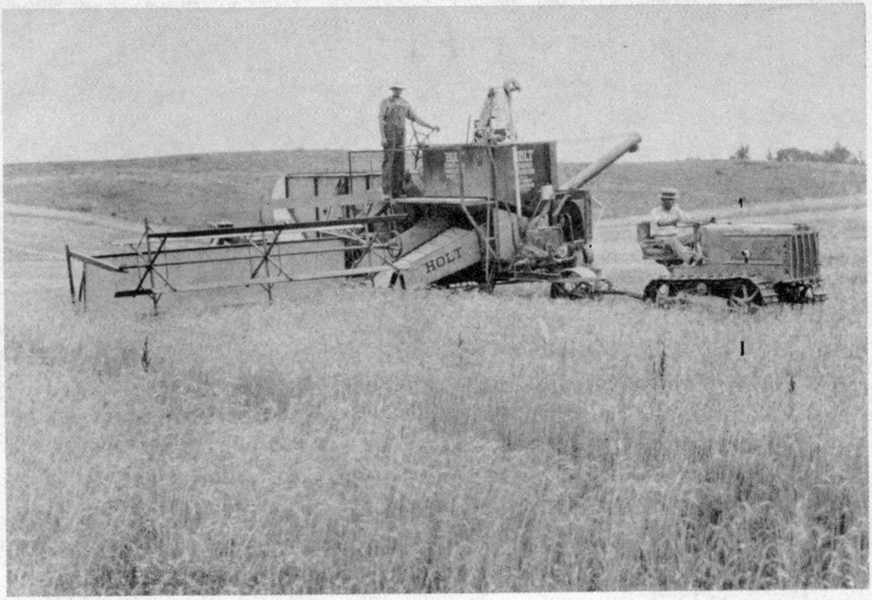

Brown Brothers

23. Combination harvester-thresher cuts and threshes thirty-five acres per day.

24. Caterpillar-drawn cultivator-seeder capable of seeding nine acres per hour.

Brown Brothers

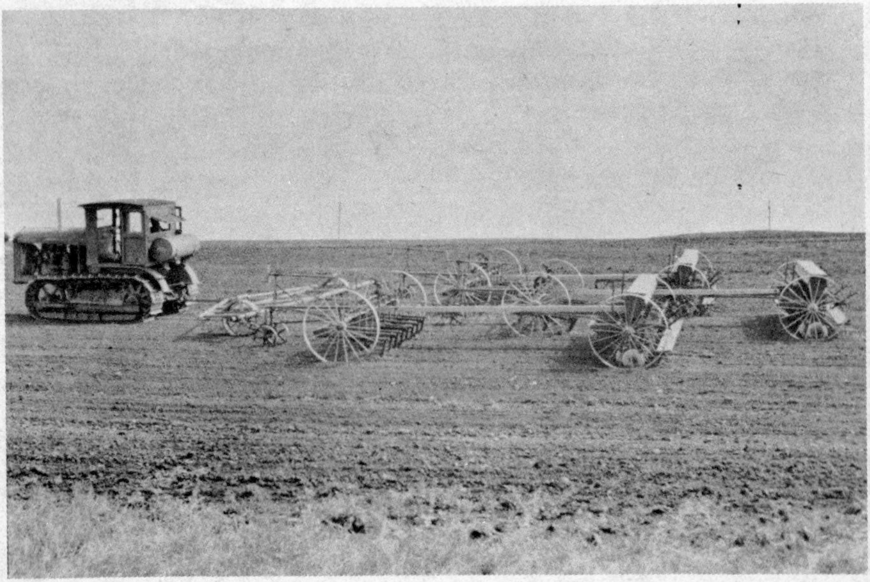

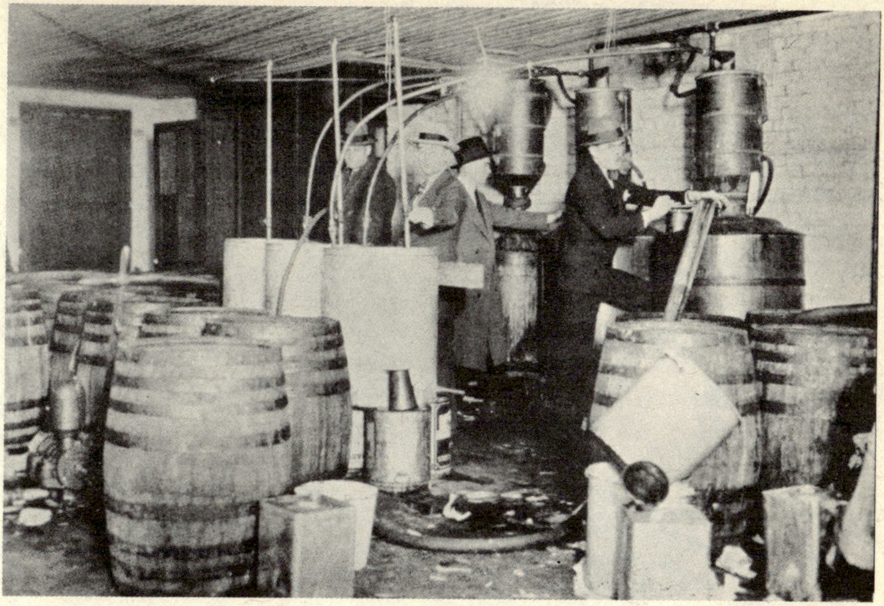

Brown Brothers

25. Prohibition agents make a find.

26. The St. Valentine's Day massacre of 1929, in which gangsters mowed down with machine guns seven members of an opposing outfit in a Chicago garage.

Brown Brothers

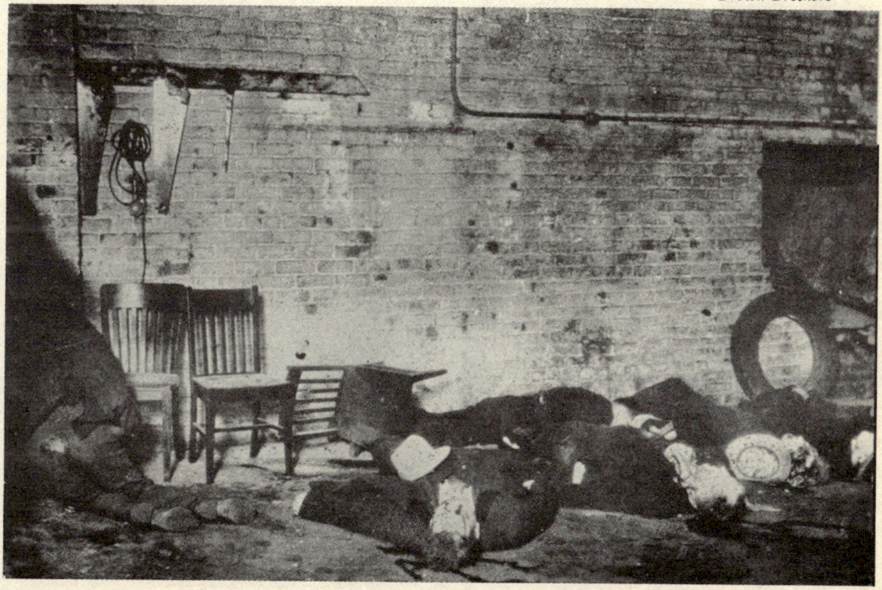

Wide World

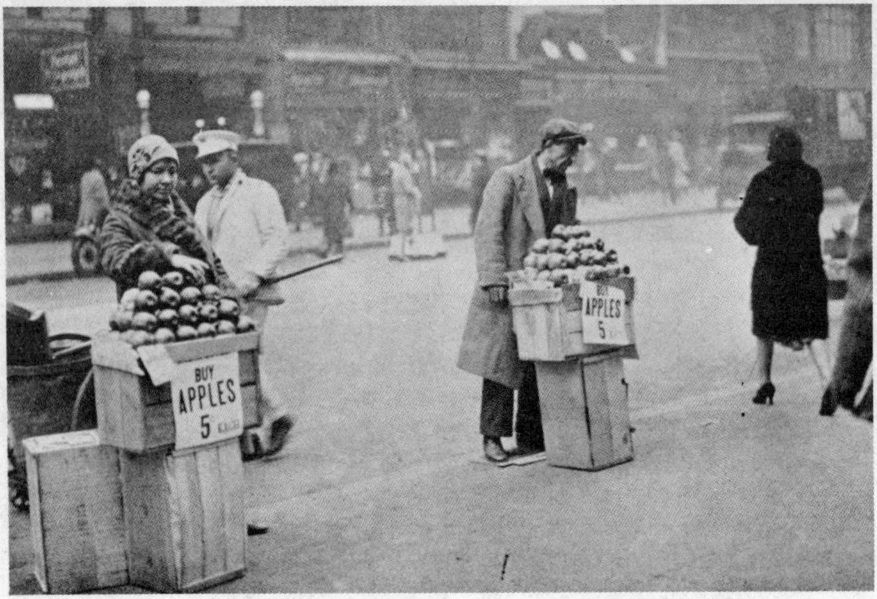

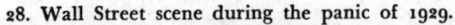

27. Apple vending by the unemployed, November, 1930.

28. Wall Street scene during the panic of 1929.

Brown Brothers

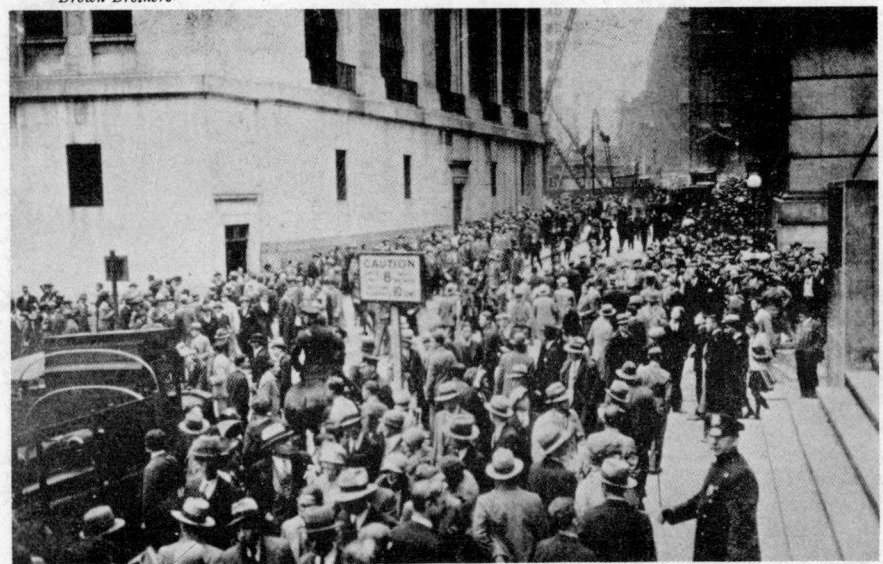

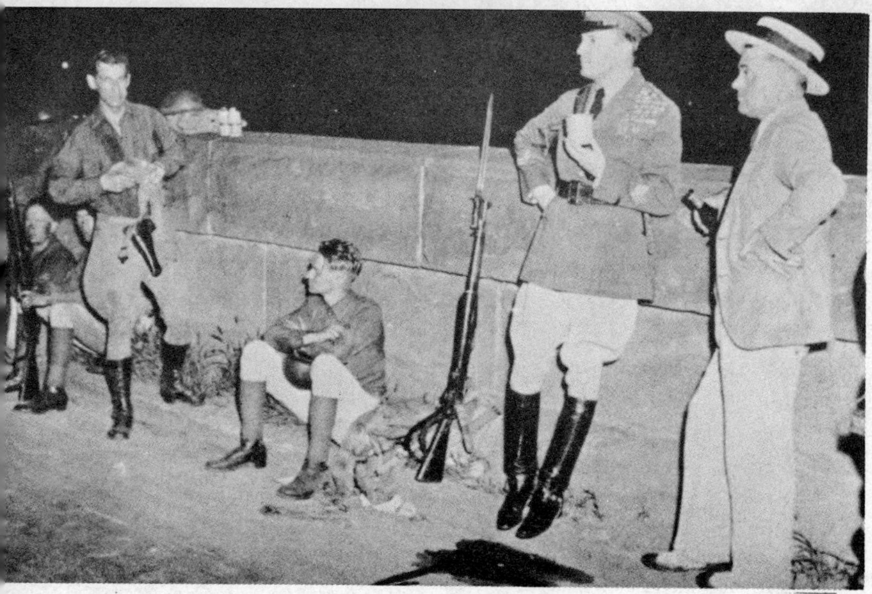

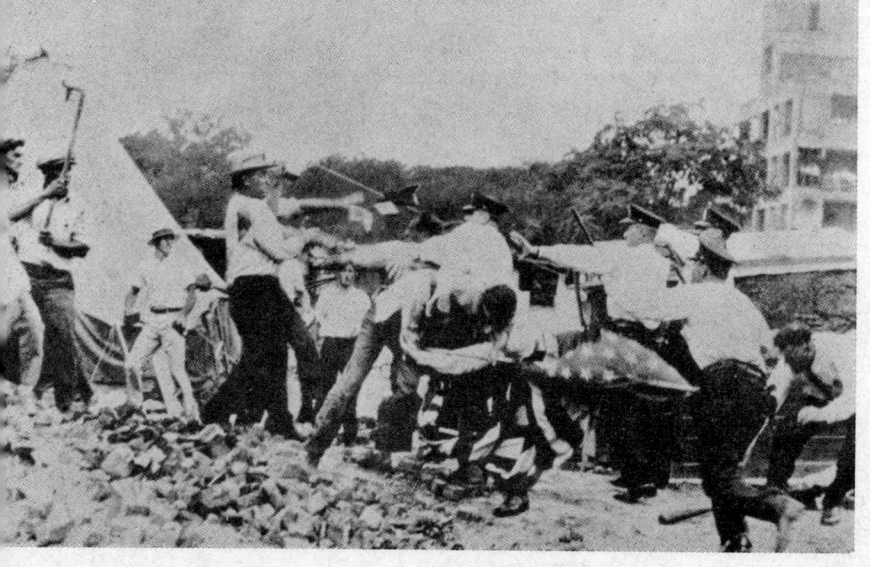

Wide World

). GENERAL DOUGLAS MACARTHUR, then Chief of Staff, during a break in the A my's bat-
e to oust the bonus marchers.

). Police and veterans fight a fierce battle on a Washington, D.C., lot in 1932.

Wide World

Oh Yeah?

Irving Fisher—CONTINUED   OCTOBER 16, 1929.

Stock prices have reached what looks like a permanently high plateau. I do not feel that there will soon, if ever, be a fifty or sixty point break below present levels, such as Mr. Babson has predicted.

I expect to see the stock market a good deal higher than it is today within a few months.

THE PERMANENTLY HIGH PLATEAU

THE NEW YORK TIMES 25 INDUSTRIALS BY CALENDAR WEEKS

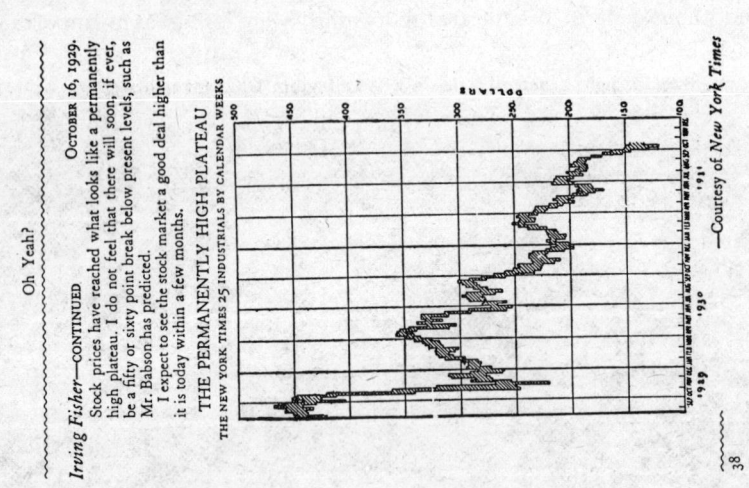

—*Courtesy of New York Times*

38

Oh Yeah?

OCTOBER 22, 1929.

I believe the breaks of the last few days have driven stocks down to hard rock. I believe that we will have a ragged market for a few weeks and then the beginning of a mild bull movement that will gain momentum next year. . . .
—*New York Herald Tribune*

OCTOBER 24, 1929.

If it is true that 15 billions in stock quotation losses have been suffered in the present break I have no hesitation in saying values are too low.   —*New York Herald Tribune*

OCTOBER 25, 1929.

WORST STOCK CRASH

12,894,650 Share Day

Swamps Markets   —*New York Times*

NOVEMBER 3, 1929.

OVEREAGER 'SHOESTRING' TRADERS CAUSED CRASH IN MARKET, SAYS FISHER

Holds Prices Still Are 'Absurdly Low'

—*New York Herald Tribune*

NOVEMBER 13, 1929.

WIDE BREAK IN STOCK LIST

'Big Board' and Curb Show 491 New Lows

—*New York Herald Tribune*

39

31. Two pages from *Oh Yeah?*, edited by Edward Angly and published in 1931. (Courtesy the Viking Press)

Of themselves the new techniques were not enough to create a business boom; they must be applied to the production of goods for which there was a demand, and the people must have the means with which to buy. A number of new industries, nonexistent or relatively unimportant before the war, helped immeasurably to supply these needs. Linked most closely with the past was the electric power industry, which was inconsequential at the turn of the century, but by the end of the 1920's was furnishing most of the power used by the nation's manufacturers, and was lighting most of the nation's homes. The existence of cheap power nearly everywhere also stimulated the production of electric appliances and machinery both for household use and for farm and factory. Similarly the radio, which was little more than a toy before the war, became a major item of production in the 1920's with the Radio Corporation of America, a General Electric-Westinghouse subsidiary, leading the way. Also among the new industries was motion pictures, which not only created an exciting new way of life in Hollywood, but stimulated the building and operation of appropriate theaters throughout the nation. Aviation, too, was new, and made substantial progress during the decade, although the large-scale manufacture of airplanes, and their general use in transportation, were of greater importance later on. Most revolutionary of all the new products was the automobile, which not only served to underwrite heavily the business boom but also promoted far-reaching changes in the American way of life. The wages paid to workers in these and other industries provided in considerable part the purchasing power that made business prosper, and the extended use of installment buying, particularly in the case of automobiles, greatly accelerated the demand.[9]

The saga of the motor car cannot be dissociated from the life of Henry Ford, who built his first successful automobile in the 1890's, and founded the Ford Motor Company in 1903. His famous Model T, a car cheap enough to attract many purchasers and sturdy enough to battle the strenuous roads of the times, dated back only to 1909. Ford's business methods interested the public hardly less than the ugly little black cars he built. By mass production he was able to lower the price of his product steadily; a car that would have cost $1,500 in 1913, or $760 in 1920, was selling by 1929 at $600, or even less. Quite correctly he preferred a large volume of sales at a small profit to a small volume at a

[9] *Recent Economic Changes,* I, 56–58, 126–127, 322–324; H. S. Raushenbush and Harry W. Laidler, *Power Control* (New York, 1928), p. 12.

large profit. "Get the costs down by better management," he argued. "Get the prices down to the buying power." Another policy that endeared Ford to the public was his determination to keep clear of the Wall Street bankers, no mean feat considering the magnitude of his operations. But somehow, without surrendering any of his cherished independence, he was always able to raise the money he needed. He also paid his men well, a minimum of $5 or $6 a day when that wage was decidedly above the going rate. But he never compromised on his right to hire and fire at will, he would have nothing to do with labor unions, and he was ruthless, too, in the sales allotments he assigned to local dealers. Nevertheless, he became a folk hero to thousands of satisfied customers, and some of them even urged him to go into politics. Senator Walsh of Montana wrote to candidate McAdoo in 1923 that the farmers and laboring men were leaning to Ford for the Democratic nomination for President, and McAdoo wrote back in great relief when Ford "clarified the situation . . . by his confession of his Republican affiliations."[10]

Ford's was not the only great name in automobile production; at least two others deserve mention, William C. Durant and Walter P. Chrysler. The former was a carriage manufacturer of Flint, Michigan, who in the horse-and-buggy days had "developed a business reaching 150,000 carriages a year." While others scoffed, Durant saw the possibilities of the automobile, and in 1905 took over and reconditioned the failing Buick Motor Car Company. But Durant was a dreamer with visions of far greater things to come. When New York bankers refused him the financial backing he sought, he managed to interest Pierre du Pont, who, unlike the bankers but like Durant, saw a future in automobiles. In 1908, with the aid of du Pont capital, he organized the General Motors Company, which drew together under one management the manufacture of numerous automobiles and automobile accessories, and in its first year accounted for one-fifth of the national output of cars. Due to darkening economic skies Durant in 1920 was obliged to resign the presidency of what was already called "the greatest industrial corporation in the world," but General Motors survived the

[10] Chase, *Prosperity, Fact or Myth,* p. 74; Ford, *My Life and Work,* pp. 136–140; Keith Sward, *The Legend of Henry Ford* (New York, 1948), pp. 185–194; T. J. Walsh to W. G. McAdoo, Aug. 1, 1923; W. G. McAdoo to T. J. Walsh, Dec. 24, 1923, Walsh Papers, Box 373, Library of Congress, Manuscripts Division.

depression, and by building more comfortable and more attractive cars presently forced Ford to abandon his famous Model T. For eighteen months, beginning in 1927, Ford closed his plant in order to make ready for the production of his equally famous Model A; during this period General Motors manufactured 40 per cent of the total number of cars that the American market absorbed.[11]

Walter P. Chrysler, unlike Durant but like Ford, rose from the mechanical rather than from the promotional side of the business. Born in western Kansas, he got his initial training in the Union Pacific shops of Ellis, Kansas; became at only thirty-three years of age a Great Western superintendent of motive power and machinery; went on to head the Pittsburgh works of the American Locomotive Company. In 1911 he turned from steam to gasoline engines when he took over the management of the Buick plant in Flint, Michigan. So spectacular was his success here that Durant soon placed him in charge of all General Motors production. In 1919 he resigned to devote himself to the rejuvenation of ailing automobile companies, and four years later gave one of them, the Maxwell Motor Corporation, a new name, the Chrysler Corporation, and a new car, the Chrysler. Within a few years the Chrysler stood third in the list of best sellers. In 1928 the Chrysler Corporation took over Dodge Brothers, to create "a new colossus of the automotive industry," outranked only by the Ford Company and General Motors. By the end of the decade the Chrysler line, which in 1929 added the Plymouth, was as varied as that of General Motors, and Chrysler sales accounted for one-fourth of the new cars marketed in the United States. As a symbol of success, the Chrysler Building, completed in 1929, gave the New York skyline its tallest building up to that date.[12]

The great rise in the volume of automobile sales began about 1922–23, when for the first time closed cars came on the market at popular prices. Every American family now wanted an automobile, and before the end of the decade nearly every American family had one. The success of the "big three," which by 1929 produced 83 per cent of the cars manufactured in the United States, accounted in considerable part for

[11] *Who's Who in America* (Chicago, 1940), XXI, 821; F. W. Parsons, "Everybody's Business," *Saturday Evening Post*, CXCII (Feb. 7, 1920), 34–37; Soule, *Prosperity Decade*, p. 166; Allan Nevins and F. E. Hill, *Ford, Expansion and Challenge, 1915–1933* (New York, 1957), pp. 459–478.
[12] W. A. P. John, "Chrysler Punches In," *Everybody's*, LIV (Jan., 1926), 19–25; *Review of Reviews*, LVIII (July, 1928), 108; *Literary Digest* XCVII (June 16, 1928), 12.

the failure of many lesser companies, although a few of the latter survived, notably Studebaker, Nash, Packard, and Hudson. Competition, especially in the low-priced fields, served less to keep prices down, for on that necessity there was general agreement, than to bring quality up. In 1919 there was only one automobile for every sixteen Americans, and the market for the expensive and uncomfortable cars then produced seemed about satiated. But by 1928 there was one car for every six Americans; with a little crowding the entire population of the nation could have been on the highways at the same time. In the year 1922 the annual production of passenger cars exceeded three million vehicles, but by 1928 it was four million. Trucks and buses ran the totals still higher, and made the manufacture of automobiles the first industry in the nation. In value automobiles by 1929 accounted for 12.7 per cent of the annual total for all American manufacturers; the industry employed 7.1 per cent of all factory workers, and it paid 8.7 per cent of the wages earned by factory employees.[13]

AUTOMOBILE REGISTRATIONS

Year	Passenger Cars	Trucks
1919	6,771,074	794,372
1920	8,225,859	1,006,082
1921	9,346,195	1,118,520
1922	10,864,128	1,135,725
1923	13,479,608	1,612,569
1924	15,460,649	2,134,724
1925	17,512,638	2,441,709
1926	19,237,171	2,764,222
1927	20,230,429	2,896,886
1928	21,630,000	3,120,000
1929	23,122,000	3,380,000

These totals fail to reveal the full effect of the automobile upon the national economy. The materials that went into the manufacture of automobiles greatly stimulated the steel industry, which sold about 15 per cent of its product to the builders of automobiles. The producers of nickel, lead, and other metals profited similarly. The popularity of the closed car gave aid and comfort to the glass, leather, and textile industries. The manufacture of rubber tires and inner tubes expanded even more rapidly than the manufacture of automobiles; for each car during

[13] Soule, *Prosperity Decade*, pp. 164–170; Ralph C. Epstein, *The Automobile Industry* (Chicago, 1928), pp. 162–174, 213–225.

its life time wore out several sets of both. The refining of gasoline increased consistently from 1914 onward, with "no flattening of the curve" until 1925, and not much thereafter. The rapid multiplication of sales agencies (usually equipped to sell both new and used cars), of filling stations and garages, of hot-dog stands and "tourist homes," defied statistical analysis. Perhaps most important of all was the encouragement that automobiles gave to the building of good roads; during the 1920's the American people spent more than a billion dollars annually on the construction and maintenance of rural highways, and at least another $400 million each year on city streets. Thanks alike to the passenger cars and the good roads, country clubs, golf courses, and road houses mushroomed in every section, suburbanization brought a building boom to every sizable city, and tourism became a national obsession.[14]

The construction industry, toward which the automobile contributed so directly, included much else besides roadbuilding, and was another key factor in producing the abundant prosperity of the 1920's. The new urbanization involved a pressing need for expansion in housing; in office, store, and factory space; in hotel accommodations, schools, hospitals, churches, public buildings of every sort and kind. The demand for dwelling houses and apartments set in immediately after the First World War, when returning veterans found great difficulty in obtaining adequate living quarters, and after 1922 accounted each year for more than 40 per cent of the building that went on, creating in the process new suburbs for every sizable city. Industrial and commercial construction, spectacular as it was, actually accounted for only about half as much expenditure as went into residential building. But during these years the skyscraper soared to new heights; with the completion of the Empire State Building in 1931 the skyline of New York City rose to an unbelievable 1,248 feet and provided a rental area of over 2 million square feet. The lure of the tall building proved to be contagious, and the skyscraper invaded many small cities that were not seriously cramped for space. Cost estimates on all construction of every sort and kind showed a rise from over $12 billion in 1919 to over $17 billion in 1928 and over $16 billion in 1929.[15]

[14] *Recent Economic Changes*, I, 59, 149–150, 246; *Statistical Abstract of the United States, 1931*, p. 403 (for 1929 figures); Soule, *Prosperity Decade*, pp. 168–169.

[15] *Ibid.*, 170–171; *Recent Economic Changes*, I, 222, 236.

Any given industry, however great, could not live to itself alone. Just as the manufacture of automobiles contributed extensively to the prosperity of other business enterprises, so also the effect of construction reached into many different channels. Construction demands accounted almost exclusively for the production of such items as brick, stone, tile, cement, lumber, hardware, and plumbing supplies. Likewise, builders absorbed much of the nation's output of steel, glass, and electrical equipment. Transportation profited from the task of getting these various materials from the place of production to the place of use. Financial profits accrued to the banks and other moneylenders, which often had more funds at their disposal than they knew what to do with. Indeed, by the end of the decade the flow of bank credit into the financing of commercial building had reached the speculative stage. Builders sometimes had money pressed upon them, and built far beyond any real demand. Residential construction reached its peak in the middle 1920's, and thereafter, as the number of persons who could afford to buy or to pay higher rent declined, tended to taper off. But the speculation in commercial building continued on into the year 1929.[16]

The borders between real estate and construction activities were not always clear; each shaded into the other. Every building rested on a spot of land, large or small, and the business of providing the land usually fell to the real estate dealers, or, as they refined the term, the realtors. But real estate men themselves often opened up new housing developments; laid them out in lots suitable for building; induced city councils and public utilities to put in the necessary pavements, as well as water, light, gas, telephone, and sewer systems; engaged contractors and subcontractors to build the houses; then offered them for sale to individuals, who for a small down payment, and many monthly installments thereafter, could escape the difficult problems that confronted individual builders, and would eventually "own their own homes." Real estate adventurers who had, or could raise, the capital for such developments often made spectacular profits.[17]

Through the buying and selling they carried on, real estate operators also helped determine new land values—the "unearned increment" that came about presumably as the result of more profitable use of the land.

[16] Soule, *Prosperity Decade,* pp. 171–174; Homer Hoyt, *One Hundred Years of Land Values in Chicago* (Chicago, 1933), pp. 240–261.
[17] *Ibid.,* pp. 255–257; Soule, *Prosperity Decade,* pp. 172–173.

During the 1920's some extraordinary changes in land values occurred. Estimates placed upon the value of all land in American cities of more than 30,000 population ran to only $25 billion in 1920, but by 1926 to $50 billion, in striking contrast to farm land values, which in the same period had dropped from $55 billion to $37 billion. Although the total area of the land in these cities amounted to only one-fifth of 1 per cent of the land in the United States, the value of these city lots was held to be 33 per cent greater than the value of all the farm lands in the nation. As the city land values went up, rentals and sales prices rose correspondingly. Here was a fabulous opportunity for profit, and realtors sought to make the most of it, both for themselves and for those whose money they invested. Land speculation was nothing new to American history, and it had served all too often as a prelude to economic distress. Investors should have been forewarned, but they were not.[18]

The real estate boom reached its crest during the middle twenties, oddly enough in Florida, where an unusual set of circumstances combined to trap the unwary. The automobile, as with so much that happened during this decade, was in large part to blame. Tourists in search of escape from the rigors of winter found the climate they wanted only a few days' drive from the most heavily populated eastern centers. They flocked to Florida in unprecedented numbers; paid high rentals for cheap accommodations along its fabulous beaches; told tall tales when they returned home that brought other visitors in. Florida realtors saw and seized the opportunity; why not induce the newcomers to buy and build? Land prices, at least to begin with, were not high; even people of moderate means could aspire to own a winter home below the ice belt. Or, if they could not raise the money to build, they could buy a lot or two, and sell for a neat profit when prices went up, as was inevitable. And if they could put up only a part of the purchase money, easy monthly payments would do the rest. For only token sums they might even buy options, or "binders," to use the local term. Whipped up by unrestrained salesmanship and advertising, the madness grew. Miami, a town of 30,000 in 1920, had 75,000 inhabitants by 1925, and during tourist season probably twice that many. The city needed everything by way of buildings, skyscrapers, luxury hotels, apartments, and in particular beach developments. City lots were platted far into

[18] Hoyt, *One Hundred Years,* pp. 234–235.

the interior, and sold to avid purchasers who saw only the blueprints.[19]

What went on in Miami was duplicated in various places up and down both the east and the west coasts of the state, not to mention many beachless villages in between. According to one estimate the number of lots platted and offered for sale reached 20 million. Prices, once low, rose to fantastic heights. A New Yorker who had bought a stretch of land in West Palm Beach for a reasonable price before the craze struck sold it in 1923 for $800,000. It was then turned into city lots which sold for $1.5 million. By 1925 it was valued at $4 million. Lots fronting on the sea were most in demand and might bring as much as $15,000 to $25,000 each. Prices grew more moderate farther inland, as well they might, for sometimes the plats extended into swamps and thickets ten, twenty, or even thirty miles from the shore. Throughout most of 1925 the boom continued unabated, but by January, 1926, it was apparent that something had gone wrong; the visitors were not coming in the numbers expected, installment collections were beginning to fall off, new purchasers grew harder and harder to find. It was all over even before nature took a hand, but a vicious hurricane that struck the state on September 18, 1926, and turned the jerry-built developments into ruins, sobered up even the most ardent enthusiasts. Miami bank clearings, over a billion dollars in 1925, were down to $143 million by 1928; an epidemic of bank failures set in; and eventually dozens of the cities that had overexpanded their indebtedness began to default on their obligations. As for the individual speculators who had bought or built, most of them lost every penny they had invested.[20]

What happened in Florida differed mainly in degree from what happened in the rest of urban America; in Florida the boom merely went to a greater and more ridiculous extreme than elsewhere. Overexpansion in southern California, particularly in the Los Angeles area, came dangerously near reaching Florida proportions. But most California investors had come to the Pacific Coast to stay, and possibly a smaller proportion of them pulled up stakes and left when times grew hard. As already noted, by the year 1927 the housing boom had begun

[19] F. L. Allen, *Only Yesterday* (New York, 1931), pp. 270–282; Mark Sullivan, *Our Times*, VI, *The Twenties* (New York, 1935), 647–648.

[20] Homer Vauderblue, "The Florida Land Boom," *Journal of Land and Public Utility Economics*, III (May, 1927), 113–131; *ibid.*, (Aug., 1927), 252–269; Gertrude Mathews Shelby, "Florida Frenzy," *Harper's Magazine*, CLII (Jan. 1926), 177–186.

to subside almost everywhere. Investors who hoped for big profits now began to turn away from real estate, and to put their money into the stock market. So obvious was this tendency that some real estate operators regarded the stock-market crash of October, 1929, with considerable satisfaction, believing, no doubt, that stock purchasers who had learned their lesson would now go back to the solid security of real estate. As a matter of fact, American cities in general had not so much overbuilt as they had built too expensively and beyond their means. The time would come when they could make use of all the space they had created, and more. Even Florida had a bright enough future, given the patience necessary to produce it.[21]

Not only in real estate but in every aspect of business the techniques of advertising and salesmanship changed markedly during the 1920's. Mass production required mass consumption; for every item placed on the market there must be a purchaser. How to reach and persuade the people to buy became a business of vast proportions. Advertising agencies took on "clients" who had something to sell, and for a consideration forced an acute awareness of their products on the public. Slick-paper magazines, rural and metropolitan newspapers, billboards along every highway, intermission pictures in the movies, and constant commercials on the radio bombarded the prospective customer with the virtues of whatever anyone who chose to advertise had to sell. The radio and the movies destroyed such immunity as nonreaders had possessed before; there was no escape from the insistent demand to buy now and, if necessary, pay later. Every medium of mass communication drew so much of its support from the advertisers that it dared not offend them—the radio least of all, for the radio had no subscription list to fall back upon and depended on the advertisers for its sole support. Haunting slogans became from endless repetition as familiar as Mother Goose rhymes.[22]

The advertisers claimed that they did society a great service by making the people aware of new and better products, products that would contribute to their happiness. In this the President of the United States concurred. Advertising "makes new thoughts, new desires and new actions," he said. "It is the most potent influence in adopting and changing the habits and modes of life, affecting what we eat, what we

[21] Allen, *Only Yesterday*, pp. 286–287; Hoyt, *One Hundred Years*, pp. 265–266; Chase, *Prosperity, Fact or Myth*, pp. 52–63.

[22] J. T. Adams, *Our Business Civilization* (New York, 1929), p. 58; Stuart Chase and F. J. Schlink, *Your Money's Worth* (New York, 1927), pp. 13–15.

wear, and the work and play of a whole nation." To the business world it became a necessity; adequately advertised, almost any product of even a little merit would catch on; unadvertised, however great its merits, it might die unknown. Producers who cut down on advertising found that their sales fell off correspondingly. Small wonder that the national bill for advertising doubled during the decade, rising to $1.5 billion by 1927, for advertising provided the only sure way to enlarge markets and to meet competition. Temptation to overstatement was great, and so rarely resisted that associations were formed to promote "Truth in Advertising," and "Better Business Bureaus" to provide a degree of self-regulation.[23]

Advertising shaded off into salesmanship; it was hard to say where one left off and the other began. The individual who could induce "prospects" to buy automobiles, or houses, or household equipment, or radio sets, or city lots, or stocks and bonds, or aluminumware, or encyclopedias, or any of the other items on the market, need not long be without a job. Although high-pressure salesmen were more often born than made, the new colleges of business administration in the universities offered courses on advertising and salesmanship that students took hopefully, while the number of books written on these subjects was legion. Installment buying, always a valuable talking point in sales promotion, increased greatly in volume throughout the 1920's; students of the subject estimated that in the middle 1920's it accounted for sales amounting to nearly $5 billion annually.[24]

There was abundant opportunity for advertisers and salesmen in the electric power industry, which, along with automobiles and construction, contributed mightily to the mounting business boom. From 1922 to 1930 the capacity of electric generating stations in the United States grew from 22 million horsepower to 43 million, a rate of increase made possible by revolutionary technological changes. Among the new developments were (1) improvements in design that greatly reduced the cost of generating power, (2) the installment of cheaper and more effective means for long-distance transmission of power; and (3) the interconnection of stations serving local regions in order to facilitate an evener distribution of loads. The cost of these changes was great, on

[23] Cochran and Miller, *Age of Enterprise,* pp. 310–312; P. W. Slosson, *The Great Crusade and After* (New York, 1930), pp. 363–365; *Recent Economic Changes,* I, 401–421.
[24] *Ibid.,* I, 390–402.

an average about $750 million a year during the middle 1920's, and only the stronger companies could afford the heavy investment. The advantages of combination were almost irresistible, and led to more than a thousand mergers in the field of public utilities during the year 1926 alone. Many of these consolidations involved municipally owned plants which sold out to private companies; the expressed objective of some of the utility magnates was to eliminate public ownership altogether. By the end of the decade ten "groups of systems" controlled three-fourths of the electric power generated in the nation. Most of their product they sold to industry at prices well under those charged domestic consumers; without the reduced rates, utility managers contended, industrialists would provide their own plants and generate their own power. But retail prices also went down, and the consumption of current by domestic users went up.[25]

For the promotion of concentration in the public utilities field the holding company proved to be an ideal instrument. Sometimes this device was used to bring a number of connectable plants under unified control, and also to build up great regional systems. But this latter objective was by no means the rule, for many of the holding companies acquired control over operating companies distributed throughout a widely scattered field, and seemingly with no slightest concern about maintaining a recognizable geographic pattern; the Insull interests, for example, had haphazard holdings that spread through no less than twenty-one states. Apologists for the holding companies claimed that they provided many useful services for their subsidiaries, including advice on management and engineering, the supervision of new construction, centralized purchasing, and the marketing of securities. For each such service the holding company made a charge and in return there were certainly instances in which the operating company got its money's worth, or more.

There also were instances, as unfriendly critics pointed out, in which holding companies used their voting rights in subsidiaries to collect fantastically high service charges, and to siphon off profits for the benefit of the favored few. Ordinarily each local utility had monopolistic privileges in the locality it served, with earnings set by the local authorities at about 7 or 8 per cent. Out of these practically guaranteed profits,

[25] *Ibid.*, I, 187–250; Charles O. Hardy, *Recent Growth of the Electric Light and Power Industry* (Washington, 1929), pp. 1–53; Soule, *Prosperity Decade,* pp. 182–184.

the holders of bonds and preferred stock collected about 6 per cent on their investments, but the rest went to the owners of the common or voting stock, which the holding companies made it their business to own or control. The insiders thus received far more than the legal 8 per cent, often as high as from 15 to 40 per cent. It was easy, also, to pyramid one holding company upon another and, by multiplying in each instance the fixed charges at low interest rates, to build up almost at will the take of the promoters who held the voting stock. Holding companies five deep were not unknown, with returns for the lucky few of from as high as 50 or 60 per cent, which was quite ordinary, to 2,000 or 3,000 per cent in exceptional cases. For the hierarchy of officers there were also high salaries and bonuses.[26]

The shrewd manipulators who amassed fortunes in the public utility field embraced every opportunity to expand their profits. They denied vehemently the charge of "stock watering," but they accomplished the same end in other ways. The most commonly used device was the "write up." By reappraising the value of the company's holdings on the basis of new earning capacity, appreciation, stock dividends, and the like, the original capital investment could be multiplied many times over. One western power company, for example, started in 1909 with $50,000 in capital stock; nineteen years later, with only such additions to its investment as it could make from customer receipts, it claimed to be worth over $500,000, and fixed its charges accordingly. Companies could also increase their capital accounts by stock splitting, that is, by issuing two, or more (sometimes as high as fifteen) shares of stock for each share held. Despite claims by the companies that these inflations did not affect the rates they charged, the exact reverse seems to have been true. There were fine profits, too, in the marketing of new securities whenever a consolidation occurred or a new holding company appeared on the scene; banks, insurance companies, and indeed the whole investing public greedily absorbed the new issues, and so became deeply involved in the predatory practices of the "power trust."[27]

[26] Raushenbush and Laidler, *Power Control* (New York, 1928), p. 51; Carl D. Thompson, *Confessions of the Power Trust* (New York, 1932), pp. 67, 84–97, 98–102, 178–189; James C. Bonbright and Gardiner C. Means, *The Holding Company* (New York, 1932), pp. 90–187.

[27] Thompson, *Confessions of the Power Trust,* pp. 61–62, 118–130, 149–158; William Z. Ripley, "From Main Street to Wall Street," *Atlantic Monthly,* CXXXVII (Jan., 1926), 94–108; Louis D. Brandeis, *Other People's Money* (new ed., New York, 1932), pp. xxxviii–xl, 146–147, 155–160.

Easily the outstanding figure in the public utility field was Samuel Insull of Chicago, whom Edison had brought over from England in 1881. Insull was the son of an indigent preacher whose strong temperance views led him to spend much of his life trying to uplift the fallen on the streets of London. For good reason young Insull went to work at an early age; learned stenography; eventually, by answering a London *Times* want ad, got a job with Edison's London representative; wrote some reports that impressed Edison; became as a result the inventor's private secretary. Shuttling back and forth between Edison's office at 65 Fifth Avenue in New York and his laboratories at Menlo Park, New Jersey, Insull during the next eleven years learned the secrets of science and invention that were to make possible his subsequent career. Soon he became Edison's assistant, then general manager in charge of all his employer's far-flung affairs, then, after 1892, head of the Edison activities in Chicago. By 1908 the Commonwealth Edison Company, a $30-million corporation with Insull as president, had consolidated the Chicago field, and was spreading its influence throughout the surrounding area. Insull was at his best in promoting the combination of smaller companies into larger units with better generating and distributing facilities. He was at his worst when he turned to finance and began to pile holding companies on top of one another in endless confusion, failing to see that a reduction of profits at the operating level could topple the unstable structures that he had devised. When the Insull empire finally crashed in 1932, trusting investors lost a billion dollars, "the largest corporate failure in American business history."[28]

The need for a curb on the practices of Insull and his kind was obvious, and state commissions for the purpose did exist. The monopolistic character of most public utilities, and the fact that they were so clearly "affected with a public interest," resolved all doubts about the constitutional right of the states to regulate them. The great trouble with state utility commissions was that, like the railroad commissions before them, they tended to fall under the domination of the corporations they were supposed to regulate. Even when the commissioners tried to do their duty, they were often so bewildered by the intricate

[28] *The Nation,* CXXXIV (May 25, 1932), 584; John T. Flynn, "Up and Down with Sam Insull," *Colliers,* XC (Dec. 3, 1932), 10–11, 32–33; (Dec. 10, 1932), 18–19, 35–36; (Dec. 17, 1932), 20–21, 41–43; (Dec. 24, 1932), 27–29, 40. Samuel Insull died in 1938. He is not to be confused with his son of the same name.

corporate organization of the utilities that they found it almost impossible to determine what a just rate would be. Fully aware of power company practice in his own state, Governor Gifford Pinchot of Pennsylvania worked out a plan for real, rather than sham, state regulation that won the approval of reformers everywhere, but that greatly angered the power trust. In general, however, the Pinchot proposals and all similar changes of consequence failed to become law.[29]

In addition to better regulation at the state level, critics of utility practices also wanted more effective national regulation than the existing Federal Power Commission was able or willing to supply. Again, the constitutional basis for such action was abundantly clear. The power trust had become almost a national monopoly, its transmission lines crossed state borders with the utmost indifference, and it was making increasing use of water power for the production of current. Since the building of dams at almost any site might affect the interstate navigation of rivers, the right of the federal government to a voice in the proceedings was incontestable. But throughout the Republican ascendancy, the power trust had little to fear from national regulation.[30]

With regulation so inconsequential the proponents of an effective curb on the power trust turned for a remedy to government ownership, not only at the municipal level where it still saved the people money, but primarily at the national level. While most of the energy for generating power came from the use of coal, oil, and gas, by the 1920's about one-third of the total came from water power. Many of the best sites for dams were still unused, partly because of the great cost involved in the building of the larger projects, and partly because of the extensive legal complications. The national government had both the money and the constitutional right to proceed with construction. The dams were needed for both flood control and irrigation, and could generate low-priced current as a by-product. In addition, if the generating plants were owned and operated by a governmental agency, they might serve a useful regulatory end, for the price of the current they sold would provide a yardstick against which to measure the rates that private companies might reasonably charge.

Every section of the country stood to profit from the development of

[29] Thompson, *Confessions of the Power Trust,* pp. 613–626; Gifford Pinchot, *The Power Monopoly; Its Make-up and Menace* (Milford, Pa., 1928), pp. 1–16.

[30] Raushenbush and Laidler, *Power Control,* pp. 116–157.

hydroelectric power: the Northeast from the harnessing of the St. Lawrence; the Southeast, the Tennessee; the Northwest, the Columbia; and the Southwest, the Colorado, to mention only the most outstanding opportunities. The St. Lawrence project involved, besides water power, the construction of a ship canal from the Atlantic to the Great Lakes, a proposal that required agreement with Canada, and that led to interminable delays. The Tennessee Valley development, as already noted, met the opposition of Presidents Coolidge and Hoover, and came to full fruition only with the advent of the New Deal. But both the other projects won preliminary authorization during the 1920's, and work on the taming of the Colorado actually began while Hoover was President.[31]

Before the actual impounding of the Colorado's waters could begin, an intricate network of legal complications had to be untangled. The river and its tributaries bordered on or crossed the territory of no less than seven states, Arizona, California, Colorado, Nevada, New Mexico, Utah, and Wyoming, and the claims of each to the water involved had somehow to be adjusted. To add to the difficulty, these seven states, although equal in constitutional rights and at least comparable in territorial extent, were otherwise quite unequal; California far exceeded its neighbors in wealth, population, and the need for water. Well aware of all this, Congress took the first step on August 19, 1921, when it authorized the seven states concerned to negotiate a compact for the division among themselves of the waters involved. With Secretary Hoover representing the federal government, they were able to decide that 7.5 million acre-feet should be reserved for the upper basin states, Utah, New Mexico, Colorado, and Wyoming; and 8.5 million acre-feet for the lower states, California, Arizona, and Nevada, leaving to each group the further working out of details. Differences between Arizona and California remained unresolved until 1928, when six of the seven states, by agreeing that a six-to-one vote should be binding on all, voted Arizona down. Thereupon Congress, on December 21, 1928, passed the Boulder Canyon Project Act, which allotted 4.4 million acre-feet to California, 2.8 million to Arizona, and 300,000 to Nevada, with one-half of all surplus waters to go to California, and one-fourth each to Arizona and Nevada. The Act provided

[31] *Ibid.*, 193–259; Hiram Johnson, "The Boulder Canyon Project," *Annals of the American Academy of Political and Social Science,* CXXXV (Jan., 1928), 150–156.

further for the construction of (1) a dam that would impound 20 million acre-feet of water, (2) a 75-mile-long canal to divert water from the Colorado River to the Imperial and Coachella valleys in California, and (3) a power plant to develop electric current from falling water. The cost of the dam, which would exceed $100 million, was to be repaid out of revenues, and the cost of the canal, over $38 million, by the water users it benefited. The dam was to be 726 feet high and 1,244 feet long, the largest such construction in the world.[32]

The Boulder Dam bill, as this measure was popularly called, was sponsored in the Senate by Hiram Johnson of California, who fought valiantly for it and deserved much credit for its passage. The preceding year the Senate had filibustered the bill to death. Opposition came from the power trust, which, according to Johnson, reached "into every State and almost every community," and from the Coolidge administration, which, "while pretending to be for it," conspired to delay its passage through the House long enough to insure its failure in the Senate. "The only enthusiastic advocacy we have," Johnson complained, "is from the insurgent group, whose philosophy of government naturally makes them for the Bill." Johnson even doubted the sincerity of Hoover, who professed to be for the bill, since "every individual connected with him is against us." Only by compromises that Johnson regretted was final passage achieved. In deference to the power interests, the law left open the decision whether the construction and operation of the power plant should be in the hands of the government or of private interests. Eventually, with Hoover in the Presidency, the power interests got about all they wanted, and the President took credit for having "kept the Federal Government out of the business of generating and distributing power."[33]

When such individuals as Johnson and Norris spoke of the "power trust," they had in mind not only the interlocking interests that bound all the nation's great power companies together, but also the well-

[32] Boulder Canyon Project Act, *United States Statutes at Large* (Washington, 1929), XLV, 1057–1066. See also Jerome W. Williams, "The History, Organization and Economic Problems of the Metropolitan Water District of Southern California," unpublished Ph.D. dissertation, University of California, Los Angeles, 1956.

[33] Hiram Johnson to Hiram Johnson, Jr., and A. M. Johnson, March 3, 11, 1927, Apr. 30, 1928, May 8, 12, 1928, Johnson Papers, Bancroft Library of the University of California; Thompson, *Confessions of the Power Trust*, pp. 554–562; Hoover, *Memoirs* II, 228.

co-ordinated system that these companies had developed for lobbying and for the molding of public opinion. Through a "Joint Committee of the National Utilities Association" and its subsidiaries, representing about 90 per cent of the nation's electrical industry, power company representatives dispensed millions of dollars each year to accomplish the ends their sponsors desired. Private power propaganda reached practically every lawmaker on every level throughout the nation, and every official who might in any way serve the cause. The power interests controlled the press, by direct persuasion if possible, by the granting or withholding of advertising if necessary, and by the actual purchase and publication of newspapers when other means failed. They hired as consultants professors who were willing to recite their line, brought pressure to bear upon others who were not, even took care that school-books must conform with the private utility point of view. They made unceasing war on every variety of public ownership, whether local, state, or national; they pretended to favor regulation, but in effect they favored it only when they could control the regulatory agencies; they defended with enthusiasm the unsound holding-company system of corporate organization.[34]

Whatever the sins of the power trust, the people, in their general enthusiasm for prosperous times, paid little attention to anything else. Prosperity at whatever cost was the goal that gripped the nation throughout the 1920's. It was a fact, however, that numerous in-equalities existed in the pattern of prosperity; many people and many sections shared far less fully than others in the good times. A book by Stuart Chase, *Prosperity, Fact or Myth* (1929), pointed out this situa-tion in words and tables that the ordinary reader could understand. The share in the new prosperity of the unemployed, always a con-siderable number, was nil. The share of the farmer was disproportion-ately small. The share of labor, while increasing steadily, could not keep pace with the new essentials—an automobile, a radio, a telephone, a well-appointed bathroom, and the latest kitchen equipment. As a result, in many working-class families the wife and the older children got jobs to supplement the family income. Similarly, the share of the "white-collar workers," the storekeepers, and the professional classes

---

[34] Thompson, *Confessions of the Power Trust,* pp. 33–42, 49–51, 269–286, 295–553; Jack Levin, *Power Ethics* (New York, 1931), pp. 3–174. The com-plete F.T.C. report is printed in 70th Cong., 1st Sess., Senate Document 92, *Utility Corporations,* Pts. 1–84 (Washington, 1929–37).

lagged far behind the demands necessary to keep up with the "implacable Joneses." Prosperity favored some sections far more than others. Most prosperous were the Middle Atlantic, the East North Central, and the Pacific states. Least prosperous were the agricultural West North Central states and the South. New England suffered from the shift of various types of textile manufacturing to the South. Even when prosperity existed it was spotty, for there were many ailing industries, including, besides those that were moving out of New England, coal, leather, shipbuilding, and railroad equipment—all serious "soft spots," according to Chase, in the prevailing prosperity.[35]

On balance, no doubt, the nation was prosperous, despite these irregularities, and those who shared generously in the flush times liked what they had achieved very much—Coolidge prosperity, the politically minded called it. Claiming full credit for all that had turned out well, the party in power meant to make the most of the prosperity issue in the mid-term elections of 1926. According to the President himself, prosperity was the only issue of consequence, of far greater importance than prohibition or any of the other side issues that might confuse the voters' thinking. Republican spokesmen claimed that they had kept wages up and prices down; that their high protective-tariff rates had not only helped the farmer and the manufacturer, but had also helped foreign trade. In reply the Democrats attacked the administration as "morally and intellectually bankrupt," subservient to big business, indifferent to the farmers' woes, unfair in the overtaxing of small incomes. Actually, about the only effective party issue was prosperity. Contests between wets and drys, while extremely important in many local elections, cut through both parties; tax reductions won universal favor, although the Democrats wanted immediate action to relieve small incomes, while the Republicans preferred to wait a while and make reductions on the eve of the election of 1928. Both parties promised to do something to help the farmer, but neither knew quite what action to take. The K.K.K. was on the way out, and Democrats vied with Republicans in ignoring it. Apathy worried both parties, but the Republicans more than the Democrats. With all going well, why even bother to vote?[36]

In the end probably the pattern of prosperity determined the results

[35] Chase, *Prosperity, Fact or Myth*, pp. 35, 92–97, 120–121, 173–174.
[36] Washington *Post*, Sept. 1, 5, 7, 13, Oct. 13, 20, 27, 1926; *The New York Times*, Oct. 13, 1926, p. 22; Oct. 30, 1926, p. 16.

more than anything else. It soon developed that Republican control of the Senate was actually in doubt; too many of the contests for the upper house lay in the Middle West, where the percentage of discontent was highest. When the next Congress convened, the Republicans could muster in the Senate only forty-eight members, barely half the voting strength, to forty-seven Democrats and one Farmer-Laborite. And among the Republicans whose votes were necessary to organize the Senate were such sturdy Sons of the Wild Jackass as Smith W. Brookhart of Iowa, whom the Senate had unseated the preceding year in a contested election, Gerald P. Nye of North Dakota, and John J. Blaine of Wisconsin, both belligerent foes of the Old Guard, to say nothing of such more permanent irregulars as Norris, Johnson, Borah, and the junior La Follette. Henrik Shipstead of Minnesota was the Senate's sole Farmer-Laborite. There were also some galling Republican losses to the Democrats. In Massachusetts Senator William M. Butler, Republican National Chairman in 1924, and the "principal Coolidge man in the nation," was defeated by the Irish Catholic David I. Walsh, while in New York the able and personable Senator James W. Wadsworth, Jr., lost out to the social-welfare-minded Robert F. Wagner. Nor did that tell the whole story. Two victorious Republican candidates for the Senate, William S. Vare of Pennsylvania and Frank L. Smith of Illinois, were under attack for excessive campaign expenditures, and might even lose their seats; Smith's list of contributors included the utility magnate Samuel Insull, whose gift amounted to $125,000. The Republicans, however, still had a good working majority in the House of Representatives, 237 to 195, with two Farmer-Laborites and one Socialist; while in the states they still had twenty-six governorships to twenty-two for the Democrats. Perhaps the losses they had suffered reflected only the customary midterm slump; or, perhaps again, the undercurrents of discontent were stronger than the contented wished to think.[37]

[37] Washington *Post*, Oct. 17, Nov. 6, 1926; *The New York Times,* Nov. 3, 1926, pp. 1, 22; Johnson to Hiram Johnson, Jr., and A. M. Johnson, Oct. 26, Nov. 13, 1926, Johnson Papers; *Official Congressional Directory* (Dec., 1927), pp. 31, 135, 137; Lloyd Wendt and Herman Kogan, *Big Bill of Chicago* (New York, 1953), pp. 230–231; Robert Hunt Lyman (ed.), *The World Almanac an⸝ Book of Facts for 1927* (New York, 1927), p. 241.

CHAPTER 6

The Diplomacy of Isolation

COOLIDGE prosperity and American isolationism were in a sense two sides of the same coin. Whatever the American people might have thought about the subject during the debate on the Treaty of Versailles, most of them as the years wore on tended to accept as right and proper a minimum of American involvement in foreign affairs. American prosperity seemed to vindicate Harding's decision to turn his back on the League and the world, and Coolidge was not the man to embark upon any dangerous changes of direction.

There is reason to believe that Secretary Hughes accepted the return to isolation with considerable misgivings, but he was wise enough to know that the President, whatever his shortcomings, makes American foreign policy, not the Secretary of State.[1] At first Hughes even failed to acknowledge the communications the United States received from the League of Nations, but when he saw that this gave offense, he corrected the error. Also he arranged that the United States, through unofficial observers, should keep in touch with League affairs. When the American Bar Association met in London in July, 1924, as guests of the British bar, Hughes, who attended as president of the visiting group, took advantage of the opportunity to spell out American foreign policy, as he saw it, in precise detail. The United States, he said in a public address, was a nonaggressor nation devoted to peace; it would

---

[1] Dexter Perkins, *Charles Evans Hughes and American Democratic Statesmanship* (Boston, 1956), p. 96; Beeritz memo, "The Separate Peace with Germany," pp. 16–18, 30, Hughes Papers, Box 172, Folder 25, Manuscripts Division, Library of Congress.

co-operate fully with other nations in the promotion of public health and other humanitarian enterprises, such as checking the trade of narcotics; it would give its support to institutions of international justice; and it would help with the economic rehabilitation of Europe, but by means other than direct governmental aid. Hughes's efforts to maintain international good manners worried some of the extreme isolationists, among them Senator Hiram Johnson of California, who privately questioned the Secretary's good faith, and as a member of the Senate Committee on Foreign Relations gloomily expressed his hope to delay, even if he could not prevent, "our going into Europe in one form or another."[2]

The new immigration policy of the postwar years served to emphasize the wish of the American people to cut as completely as possible the ties that bound them to the Old World. During the war the double loyalties of certain "hyphenate" groups had aroused much criticism, and after the war the "red hysteria" undoubtedly contributed further to the conviction that the American nation had taken in about as many foreigners as it could digest. Organized labor had long expressed disapproval of letting in immigrants to compete in the American job market, and industry, with a steady backlog of unemployed from which to draw, offered little more than token objection to restriction. One of the first acts of the Harding administration was the Emergency Quota Act, signed May 19, 1921, which limited the number of aliens of any nationality who might be admitted in any fiscal year "to 3 per centum of the number of foreign-born persons of such nationality resident in the United States as determined by the United States census of 1910." The Act was originally designed to last for one year only, but it was later extended until 1924.[3]

By that time experience had shown that the assigned quotas were permitting far more immigrants to enter the United States than Congress had intended—the total for 1924 exceeded 700,000; also, the law failed to discriminate as much as its proponents had hoped against

[2] *Ibid.*, pp. 26–27; Beeritz memo, "European Trip," pp. 5, 17, Hughes Papers, Box 173, Folder 54; Hiram Johnson to sons, Sept. 23, 1921, Jan. 13, 1925, Johnson Papers, Bancroft Library of the University of California.

[3] *United States Statutes at Large* (Washington, 1923), XLII, 5; Robert DeC. Ward, "Our New Immigration Policy," *Foreign Affairs*, III (Sept. 15, 1924), pp. 99–111. Opposition to restriction did exist. An editorial in *Industrial Progress*, V (July, 1922), p. 6, argued "we shall, regardless of all machinery and improvements, need a far greater force of unskilled labor."

immigrants from southern and eastern Europe. The Immigration Act of 1924, therefore, reduced the annual quota of each nationality to 2 per cent, and for the next three years shifted the computation of quotas to the census of 1890. The law stated that after 1927, however, the annual quota for each nationality was no longer to be computed from the number of foreign-born in the United States at any given time, but from "the number of inhabitants in 1920 whose origin by birth *or ancestry*" could be attributed to a given national area. And the annual quota of any nationality was to be a number which would bear "the same relationship to 150,000 as the number of inhabitants in continental United States in 1920 having that national origin" bore to the total number of inhabitants for the same year. To the Secretaries of State, Commerce, and Labor fell the thankless task of fixing quotas, but they found "national origins" so difficult to determine that the application of this aspect of the law was postponed from 1927 to 1929. The effect of the Act of 1924 was to hold immigration from 1925 to 1930 down to an annual average of about 300,000; and for the next ten years after that, with the help of the depression, to an annual average of about 50,000. The new Immigration Act thus marked the end of an era. The United States was no longer the refuge of the world's poor and oppressed; the Statue of Liberty now lifted her lamp only for a favored few.[4]

The Act of 1924 made certain other innovations. Quotas established under the Act of 1921 applied only to Europe, the Near East, Africa, and Australia; for the Western Hemisphere there were no restrictions, and for certain Asiatic countries, notably Japan, other and special arrangements provided for virtual exclusion. The new law still permitted free access to the United States for immigrants from Canada, Newfoundland, and all the independent American republics, but it extended the quota system to the rest of the world, allowing to each nation a minimum of 100 immigrants, with this notable exception, that "No alien ineligible to citizenship shall be admitted to the United States." It was obvious that this clause was aimed directly at Japan, although the Gentlemen's Agreement of Theodore Roosevelt's administration was accomplishing the same end without a direct prohibition. But anti-Japanese sentiment on the Pacific Coast was strong,

[4] *United States Statutes at Large* (Washington, 1925), XLIII, 159–160; John Kieran (ed.), *Information Please Almanac, 1947* (New York, 1947), p. 175.

and Congress yielded to it the more readily when the Japanese ambassador announced that such a direct affront would have grave consequences. Japan, some congressmen implied, was threatening the United States. Secretary Hughes did his best to persuade Congress that this wanton insult to a supersensitive nation would destroy much of the good will achieved by the Washington Conference and by the generous American response to Japan's needs after the great earthquake of 1923. But Congress was not to be deterred, and Coolidge weakly signed the bill into law. Since the Supreme Court in *Ozawa* v. *the United States* (1922) had already decided that persons of Japanese birth were ineligible for naturalization, the effect of the law was crystal clear, and the reaction in Japan was extremely unfavorable. Congress by its thoughtless action had handled another weapon—popular hatred of the United States—to the Japanese militarists who plotted expansion in the Far East, even at the cost of war.[5]

The Immigration Act of 1924 aroused much resentment also in Europe, particularly in Italy, where under the new quotas emigration to the United States dropped off by about nine-tenths. Because of the increased population pressure from which Italy suffered, Mussolini, whose attainment of power showed how unsafe the world was becoming for democracy, felt the freer to proceed with his program of colonial empire. Not only in Italy, but in many other countries also, the United States lost friends as the cruelties implicit in the law began to make themselves felt—wives denied permission to join their husbands in America, children separated from their parents, long quota waits for those who could go, detention and return for the ill-advised. Furthermore, the void left by the drop in European immigration tended to be filled in part by entrance into the United States of equally alien peoples from the Western Hemisphere, especially from Mexico, French Canada, and Puerto Rico. Also, there was a serious problem of enforcement, and the "bootlegging" of ineligibles into the United States, together with their occasional enforced return to their own country, added further to the international strain. Yet for the great majority of Americans there was no sign of regret over the policy of exclusion; the inequities in the law, most people agreed, should be ironed out, but the

[5] *Annual Report of the Commissioner General of Immigration, 1924* (Washington, 1924), pp. 24–30; Beeritz memo, "Japan and the Immigration Act of 1924," Hughes Papers, Box 173, Folder 50; R. W. Paul, *The Abrogation of the Gentlemen's Agreement* (Cambridge, Mass., 1936), pp. 58–103; R. L. Garis, *Immigration Restriction* (New York, 1927), pp. 169–202.

United States must never again open its portals to the Old World's "huddled masses yearning to breathe free."[6]

There was something of this same spirit in the refusal of the United States to recognize the new government of Soviet Russia; if the actions of a given nation varied too much from what Americans regarded as proper, then its existence could simply be ignored. This policy, which the Harding administration inherited from its predecessor, was by no means universally approved in the United States. Two senators, William E. Borah of Idaho and Joseph I. France of Maryland, took a particularly firm stand in favor of recognition. Borah was much influenced by Raymond Robins and other outstanding liberals, who believed that as long as the Russian problem remained unsettled the peace of Europe would remain unsettled, while France had visited Russia in the summer of 1921, had met the Bolshevik leaders, and had returned to the United States convinced that American recognition would help advance the conservative trend he thought he had seen in the Soviet Union. But Borah's Senate resolution favoring recognition was merely laid on the table, while France was ridiculed in the press as an "innocent abroad," or worse. On behalf of the administration, Secretary Hughes denied that the form of government adopted by Soviet Russia had anything to do with the official American attitude. The trouble, he said, was that the Soviet government had refused in three ways to accept its international obligations: (1) it had repudiated the debt it owed to the government of the United States, (2) it had confiscated the private property of American nationals, and (3) it had promoted propaganda in the United States that had as its object the overthrow of the American government. Borah, France, and others returned to the attack time after time, but Russian recognition was delayed until after the Roosevelt administration took office in 1933.[7]

Nor was the American government disposed to promote in any way

[6] R. L. Garis, "Lest Immigration Restriction Fail," *Saturday Evening Post,* CXCVIII (Oct. 10, 1925), 41, 229–233; Beckles Wilson, "Italy's Vital Insurgence," *Nineteenth Century,* XCVIII (Dec., 1925), 858–864; "Italy's Emigration Worries," *Literary Digest,* XL (July 3, 1926), 17; Edward Corsi, *In the Shadow of Liberty; The Chronicle of Ellis Island* (New York, 1935), pp. 129–148.

[7] Claudius O. Johnson, *Borah of Idaho* (New York, 1936), pp. 356–357; clippings in France Scrapbooks, 1921, in possession of Horace S. Merrill, University of Maryland, especially Baltimore *Sun,* Aug. 8, 28, 1921; Beeritz memo, "Relations with Soviet Russia," p. 8, Hughes Papers, Box 172, Folder 33.

the resumption of normal trade relations between the United States and Soviet Russia. It had no objection to the mobilizing of American charity to help battle starvation during the Russian famine of 1921; according to Secretary Hoover the American Relief Administration spent $50 million for this purpose, and for the purchase of seed to be used in the 1922 planting. Nor was there any prohibition against individuals risking their property in trade with Russia, or even lending money to Russia if they so desired. But all Russian overtures for assistance from the United States government in reviving trade between the two nations were sternly discountenanced. The power of Russia to buy, Hughes maintained, depended on its ability to produce something to sell, and both he and Secretary Hoover implied in public statements that Russia could not hope to revive production until the Soviet government was ready to recognize the rights of private property.

Senator France argued for an American loan to Russia, the proceeds of which would enable the Soviets to pay claims against them and to buy American goods. But Hughes was adamant in his insistence that the Soviet government must demonstrate its willingness to guarantee within its borders the safety of life and property, the sanctity of contracts, and the rights of free labor before the United States would negotiate. The Russians made some effort to satisfy these conditions. At the Genoa Conference, which the nations of Europe held in the spring of 1922, a Russian representative told the American ambassador to Italy that, while Russia was unwilling to admit any such obligations as Hughes stipulated, it would in fact observe them with reference to Americans, if only the United States would recognize Russia. But again the United States was unresponsive. Whatever else the Department of State may have had in mind, it is obvious that it had no intention of doing anything that might in any way serve to perpetuate the Soviet system of government.[8]

The United States also pursued an uncompromising policy, as long as it could, in its attempt to collect the intergovernmental debts due it

[8] *Congressional Record,* 67th Cong., 2nd Sess., LXII (May 31, 1922), 7911; Herbert Hoover, *Memoirs,* II, 182; St. Louis *Post-Dispatch,* Aug. 30, 1921, clipping in France Scrapbooks, 1921; Beeritz memo, "Relations with Soviet Russia," pp. 2–3. Hughes Papers, Box 172, Folder 33; *Papers Relating to the Foreign Relations of the United States, 1922* (Washington, 1938), II, 812–814; J. Saxon Mills, *The Genoa Conference* (London, 1922), pp. 9–13; E. C. Buehler and others (eds.), *Selected Articles on Recognition of Soviet Russia* (New York, 1931), pp. 141–147.

from its former associates in the war, and from the succession states that the Peace of Paris had created in central and eastern Europe. Of the more than $10.3 billion so lent, only about $7 billion net was actually borrowed during the war, and not less than nine-tenths of this sum was used to pay for American goods purchased in the United States by the Allies. After the war was over the American government lent the war-torn nations of Europe an additional $3.3 billion in money and supplies for use in rehabilitation and relief. The American public should have distinguished between the war debts and these "peace debts," but it seldom did so; most Americans assumed that the European nations had borrowed the entire $10.3 billion for war purposes, and that ultimately they would repay these sums with interest—the rate, pending a postwar settlement, being set at 5 per cent.[9]

The war was not long over before European nations began to take a very different view of debt repayment. To Americans the problem seemed simple: the United States had lent vast sums; the nations that had borrowed the money should pay back their loans. In Coolidge's words, "They hired the money, didn't they?" But to Europeans it was not that easy. In their view the war was fought for a common objective, and the victory was as essential for the safety of the United States as for their own. The United States had entered the struggle late, and had poured forth no such contribution in lives and losses as the Allies had made. It had paid in dollars, not in death and destruction, and now it wanted its dollars back—Uncle Shylock. Many Americans saw in this attitude only an attempt to defraud. A correspondent who had toured Europe wrote to Senator Johnson: "All of the peoples abroad look upon us as an international sucker from whom should be obtained by wheedling or otherwise part of our ill-gotten gains, but whom, during the process of relieving us of our funds, they regard with contempt, and about whom they laugh among themselves."[10]

The real trouble was that the European nations had not the means with which to pay. Their gold had flowed in great quantity to the United States during the period of neutrality in payment for American goods; they could not send more without completely wrecking their

[9] S. F. Bemis, *A Diplomatic History of the United States* (New York, 1942), p. 715, tabulates the war debts in detail. See also H. E. Fisk, *The Inter-Ally Debts* (New York, 1924), pp. 348–349.

[10] William Allen White, *A Puritan in Babylon* (New York, 1938), p. 324; Hiram Johnson to sons, April 28, 1922, Johnson Papers.

currencies. Equally distressing was the American tariff policy; European nations could never hope to sell enough to the United States over its high tariff wall to enable them to build up the American balances they would need to liquidate their debts. The problem was further complicated by the debts that European nations owed each other, debts mainly due to loans the stronger Allies had made to the weaker before the United States became the chief banker for them all. Indeed, the British government had made loans comparable in face value to those made by the United States, and had actually lent more to the other Allies by many billions of dollars than it had borrowed from the United States. Protected by these mitigating circumstances, Great Britain took the lead as early as February, 1920, in broaching to the American government the subject of a general cancellation of war debts, pointing out the political and economic advantages that the adoption of such a policy would ensure.[11]

Whatever the merits of the case, the American government showed no slightest disposition to accept the British overtures. Nor would it ever concede that the capacity of the Allies to repay the United States depended upon their ability to collect corresponding reparations from Germany. During the campaign of 1920, the Republicans denounced the Wilson administration for its failure to begin collections, and promised that as soon as they took office they would do better. When Secretary Mellon attempted to deliver on this promise, he found existing legislation inadequate to authorize the funding policy he had in mind, and asked Congress for plenary powers to deal with the problem. But Congress thought the matter too important for the Secretary of the Treasury to handle alone, and by an act of February 9, 1922, set up instead a World War Debt Funding Commission, consisting at first of five and by a later amendment of eight members, with the Secretary of the Treasury as chairman and the other members to be appointed by the President and confirmed by the Senate. (Among the appointive members, Harding chose Secretaries Hughes and Hoover.) The law also stipulated that loans should be repaid in twenty-five years, that the rate of interest charged should not be less than 4.25 per cent, and that there should be no cancellation of debts "except through payment thereof."[12]

[11] Harold G. Moulton and Leo Pasvolsky, *War Debts and World Prosperity* (Washington, 1932), pp. 48–70.

[12] *Ibid.*, pp. 71–80; Johnson to sons, June 20, 1921; July 2, 1921, Johnson Papers.

Smarting under the necessity, but consoled by the hope of collecting reparations from Germany, all the major debtors and most of the others—thirteen in all—eventually negotiated agreements with the Commission. In the negotiations the American representatives departed considerably from the instructions Congress had given them. While in each case they required ultimate payment in full of the principal, they spread the amortization over a period of sixty-two years instead of twenty-five, and they disregarded at will the high interest rate set by Congress. This policy meant that each agreement would have to be submitted to Congress for approval, but the commissioners realized, even if Congress did not, that the alternative would be no agreements at all. Throughout the negotiations the commissioners kept one eye on the capacity of each debtor nation to pay and the other on what minimum terms Congress would be willing to accept. They reached their first settlement with Great Britain in July, 1923, after six months of negotiation. The British representatives were shocked at the interest rates the American negotiators demanded, for the prewar borrowing rates in England had been much lower, and the American ambassador to Great Britain, Colonel George Harvey, had given them reason to expect a 2 per cent rate instead of the 3.3 per cent that the American commissioners demanded. Eventually the British government accepted the sixty-two year, 3.3 per cent terms as the best it could get.[13]

The British agreement served as a model for the others, but Great Britain was the only wartime borrower to be charged so high a rate of interest. The other nations that agreed to pay 3.3 per cent on their loans were Czechoslovakia, Estonia, Finland, Hungary, Latvia, Lithuania, Poland, and Rumania, none of whom had borrowed from the United States until after the signing of the armistice, and all of whom owed comparatively small sums. For the remaining borrowers there were greatly reduced interest rates, for Belgium 1.8 per cent, for France 1.6 per cent, for Italy 0.4 per cent, and for Yugoslavia 1 per cent. The terms of payment also differed considerably from country to country—Belgium, for example, was charged no interest on her pre-armistice debt, while France and Italy were not required to pay interest for the first five years of their indebtedness. But had the debts been

[13] Beeritz memo, "The Separate Peace with Germany," pp. 16–18, 30, and "Funding the Allied Debts," p. 4, Hughes Papers, Box 172, Folders 25, 29; Harold G. Moulton and Leo Pasvolsky, *World War Debt Settlements* (New York, 1926), pp. 225–240.

paid in accordance with the agreements, the interest rates would have averaged out about as indicated. The life of the Commission expired by law on February 9, 1927; thereafter the Treasury Department worked out such agreements with other borrowers as were deemed necessary and possible. Among the impossible was the settlement of the Russian debt to the United States, which, however, was only $192 million, a small sum in comparison with Russia's debt to Great Britain of $4.3 billion.[14]

Whatever the United States chose to pretend regarding the divorcement of war debts and reparations, in actual practice the two subjects were closely intertwined. By the much-debated war guilt clause, the Treaty of Versailles had required Germany to accept for herself and her allies the responsibility "for causing all the loss and damage to which the Allied and Associated Governments and their nationals have been subjected as a consequence of the war imposed upon them by the aggression of Germany and her allies." This clause in itself aroused great resentment, for few Germans believed that the Central Powers alone were responsible for the outbreak of war in 1914. Allied reliance upon the war-guilt thesis as the sole reason for demanding reparations made matters even worse. Had the victors merely assumed that they had the right to make the vanquished pay because they had lost the war, there would have been less room for argument. As it was, Germans could maintain with reason that the demand for reparations had no more validity than the charge of war guilt. Partly on this account neither the German government nor the German people ever really accepted the obligation of reparations payments; lacking any will to pay, their goal became instead the avoidance of payment. As Germans saw it, the Treaty of Versailles, by trimming Germany's borders at many vital spots, and by dividing her colonies among the victors, had gone far enough; the demand for reparations in addition was both unjust and unrealistic. Some Americans agreed. "I should like to see the 'sole guilt' fallacy rejected once and for all," wrote Senator Borah a few years later. "It is to the benefit of no one to maintain a false contention which serves only to keep alive resentment and retard the good faith and amity which we ought in every way seek to foster and maintain. There was no 'sole guilt' as to that war."[15]

[14] Moulton and Pasvolsky, *War Debts and World Prosperity*, pp. 80–108.
[15] Raymond Leslie Buell, *Europe: A History of Ten Years* (New York, 1928),

Since the negotiators at Paris were unable to agree upon the total reparations bill, they put off for a period of two years the determination of the final figure; during this interval, however, they required Germany to pay nearly $5 billion in cash or in goods. The rest of the debt was to be determined by a Reparations Commission consisting of representatives from Great Britain, the United States, France, Italy, and, in alternation, Japan and Belgium. Failure of the United States to ratify the treaty cost Germany its only possible friend on the Commission; the other members differed only as to how much they thought they could get. When the Commission reported in the spring of 1921, it proposed the colossal sum of $33 billion to be paid during a period of still undetermined length, but with an expectation of about $375 million each year from 1921 to 1925, and about $900 million each year thereafter. The Commission might reduce either the debt or the interest charges, but the Allied governments could punish by the armed invasion of German territory any willful defaults. Efforts to collect the huge sums expected proved to be singularly fruitless, but such payments as were made, together with the disruptions that the war had bequeathed to the German economy, led to a runaway inflation in Germany that virtually destroyed the middle class and undermined the authority of the new Weimar Republic. In January, 1923, over the opposition of Great Britain, the Reparations Commission declared Germany in willful default, and the troops of France and Belgium occupied the Ruhr Valley, the greatest industrial district left to Germany. But the military demonstration solved no problems, and made more; passive resistance in the Ruhr cut down on German production, while in France inflation began to mount ominously.[16]

However much the United States might wish to remain isolated from Europe, there was no escaping the fact that the economic collapse of Germany would be a matter of almost as grave concern to Americans as to Europeans. Not only were the problems of war debts and reparations involved but also the economic health of Europe as a whole. American trade with Europe was vital to American prosperity; with the reparations problem unsolved that trade could not follow its

pp. 394–397; press release, Dec. 31, 1926, in Borah Papers, Box 285, Manuscripts Division, Library of Congress.

[16] Moulton and Pasvolsky, *War Debts and World Prosperity,* pp. 144–160; Buell, *Europe,* pp. 40–59; George Soule, *Prosperity Decade* (New York, 1947), pp. 259–264.

natural lines. Secretary Hughes, who well understood that American isolation was a myth, began even before the invasion of the Ruhr to take a hand in the diplomatic game. Speaking before the American Historical Association in New Haven, Connecticut, he suggested on December 29, 1922, the creation of an international commission of experts to determine how much Germany was able to pay, and how the payments were to be made. "I have no doubt," he added, "that distinguished Americans would be willing to serve in such a commission." But the French were unwilling to accept this arrangement until the fall of 1923, when it became evident that the Ruhr invasion would accomplish nothing. They then joined with the other Allies in devising a plan whereby the Reparations Commission should appoint two committees, one to concentrate principally on problems of the German currency and budget, and the other on the recovery of German holdings from abroad. To head the first committee the choice fell upon an American, Charles Gates Dawes, and the agreements the committees reached became known as the Dawes Plan. Most Americans acquiesced readily in this limited degree of American participation in European affairs, but to a few extreme isolationists anything of the kind remained a base betrayal.[17]

Whether Hughes was "the real author and spiritual father of the Dawes Plan," as a German journalist claimed, or Dawes himself, the program that the experts devised seemed to make sense. It recognized that there were two separate problems involved, (1) the attainment of solvency by the German government, with an annual excess of receipts over expenditures, and (2) the actual transfer to the Allies of surplus sums so accumulated. First of all Germany had to have a stable currency. To this end the Dawes Plan proposed an international loan of $200 million in gold, the reorganization of the Reichsbank under Allied supervision, and the issuance of a new monetary unit, the reichsmark, with a gold value of 23.8 U.S. cents. As for reparations, the plan set no precise figure, but, on the basis of careful study of Germany's capacity to pay, it proposed a graduated schedule of annuities, beginning at $250 million the first year and rising over a period of five years to a normal expectation of $625 million; this sum, however, could be

[17] Beeritz memo, "The Dawes Plan," pp. 4–20, Hughes Papers, Box 172, Folder 27; Hiram Johnson to Hiram Johnson, Jr., Jan. 20, 1923, Johnson Papers; Bascom N. Timmons, Portrait of an American; Charles G. Dawes (New York, 1953), pp. 215–226.

increased or reduced as German prosperity rose or fell. During the first two years the German government might meet its obligations in part from the international loan, but it was also required to bond and mortgage its railways and principal industries, and to use the proceeds along with taxes to make the stipulated payments. The Dawes Plan also provided safeguards to prevent reparations payments from "threatening the stability of the German currency." While the German government must make all payments as scheduled, these funds would remain in Germany until such a time as the exchange market justified their transfer. An Agent General for Reparations Payments, to be appointed by the Reparations Commission, was to co-ordinate and supervise these activities.[18]

The Dawes Plan, after acceptance by both Germany and the Allies, went into effect September 1, 1924, and for a time seemed to work reasonably well. It carried with it a separate agreement for the withdrawal of foreign troops from the Ruhr, a process that began at once and ended on July 31, 1925. The international loan was readily subscribed, with over half the money coming from American investors, and the other measures that the Plan called for were gradually effected. For a time the revival of the German economy seemed assured. The choice of S. Parker Gilbert of Morgan and Company as Agent General proved to be singularly felicitous, and the German government profited greatly from his advice. It was Gilbert's opinion, however, that Germany must eventually be left "to perform on her own responsibility," while with the fulfillment of the German disarmament program it also seemed reasonable that the foreign troops still stationed in the Rhineland should be removed.

Eventually another committee of experts, headed by another American, Owen D. Young, produced a new set of agreements even more favorable to Germany than those of the Dawes Plan. The representatives of fifteen nations, including Germany, signed the preliminary terms at The Hague, August 31, 1929, in the presence of an American observer. This time Germany's total liability was set definitely at a little more than $8 billion, with interest at 5.5 per cent, the payments to be distributed over a period of 58.5 years. The new plan required

---

[18] Beeritz memo, "European Trip," p. 46, Hughes Papers, Box 173, Folder 54; Charles G. Dawes, *A Journal of Reparations* (London, 1939), pp. 284–291, 343–345; Clarence P. Howland, *Survey of American Foreign Relations, 1928* (New Haven, 1928), pp. 371–379.

"unconditional" annuities of only $153 million, much less than the payments required by the Dawes Plan, but, oddly enough, about equal to the total sums the Allied nations had agreed to pay each year on their war debts to the United States. "Conditional" payments, which depended on German prosperity, and ran much higher, were secured by a mortgage on the German railways. The problem of turning German marks into foreign currencies now became the responsibility of the German government, which would work through a new Bank of International Settlements set up by the Allies at Basel, Switzerland. Whereas the Dawes Plan was meant to be merely temporary, the Young Plan was regarded as "final and definitive." As further evidence that the Allies now regarded Germany as trustworthy, they withdrew the rest of their troops from German soil.[19]

During the five years of the Dawes Plan and the first two of the Young Plan the German government met its reparations payments regularly, although it was usually forced to borrow in order to balance its budget. But confidence in German recovery was high, and there were plenty of investors who were ready to purchase German securities, both within and without Germany. It was the outside borrowing that enabled Germany to keep up with its reparations payments. Not only the various German governmental units, federal state and municipal, borrowed heavily from foreign investors, but German business firms, banks, and public utilities also followed this course. Precise figures on the amount of outside capital that flowed into Germany during these years are hard to get, but undoubtedly the American loans alone were not less than the $2.6 billion that the United States collected from the Allies prior to July 1, 1931, on their war debts. The direct relation between German reparations and Allied payments to the United States on war debts could hardly have been more obvious. What happened in effect was that Germany used the credits provided by outside investors, at least in part, to pay its reparations bills, while the Allies used that portion of these credits furnished by American investors to meet their war-debt payments to the United States. Thus the sums that the American Treasury collected from European debtor nations came in reality from the American people. More than that, the export of American capital to foreign borrowers, regardless of nationality, did

[19] *Ibid.*, pp. 379–401; Moulton and Pasvolsky, *War Debts and World Prosperity*, pp. 187–231.

much to support the business boom of the 1920's in the United States. Few people seemed to realize that the American nation was not only sending American goods abroad in gratifying volume, but that it was also sending along the money with which to pay for them. When finally American investors cut down on their foreign loans, the resulting decline in foreign purchases added materially to the economic gloom that settled down over the United States in the early 1930's.[20]

American participation in the settlement with Germany indicated that the involvement of the United States in world affairs ran far deeper than many Americans realized. The United States, try as it might, could not simply concentrate on its own prosperity, and let the rest of the world "stew in its own juice"; it could not even permit Germany to collapse. Above all, the American nation must somehow share in the task of preserving world peace, for war anywhere in the world was certain to affect the United States, however determined its neutrality. A convinced minority of the American people still adhered to the conviction that the United States should have entered the League of Nations, and hoped that eventually this end might be achieved.

Numerous societies made this their goal, among them the League of Nations Non-Partisan Association, headed by John H. Clarke, a former Justice of the United States Supreme Court, whose book on *America and World Power* (1925) well summarized the pro-League position. The World Peace Foundation, generously endowed many years before by Edwin Ginn, the Boston publisher; the Carnegie Endowment for International Peace, headed by the indefatigable Nicholas Murray Butler; and the Institute of International Relations, operating from Geneva with both British and American backing, all undertook the wide distribution of pro-League literature.

Such prominent individuals as Walter Lippmann, William Allen White, Hamilton Holt, Manley O. Hudson, and Raymond B. Fosdick gave the cause their earnest support. The Woodrow Wilson Foundation presented in 1924 the first of a series of $2,500 awards to individuals who had in some outstanding way contributed to world peace; Elihu Root, recipient of the second such award, rebuked the United States in his acceptance statement for its faithlessness in failing to enter the League. But the implacable opposition of the Republican party to the League, coupled with the indifference toward it of too many leading Democrats, foredoomed the pro-League advocates to failure. By the

[20] *Ibid.,* pp. 265, 283–300.

end of the 1920's they tacitly accepted as a substitute goal the greater co-operation of the United States with the League, pointed with pride to the important parts that American observers took in League meetings, and noted pleasurably the numerous League agreements that the United States had accepted. According to Charles A. Beard, the United States was in actual fact a member of the League, whatever its pretenses.[21]

But Beard was wrong; the United States was not only not a member of the League, it refused so much as to give its adherence to the World Court, although during the Roosevelt and Taft administrations Republicans and Democrats alike had regarded the creation of such a body as a matter of primary importance. In accordance with Article 14 of the League Covenant, plans for the establishment of a Permanent Court of International Justice began to take form as early as June, 1920, and by January, 1922, the Court was able to hold its first session. Among the distinguished jurists who had framed the protocol under which it was to operate was Elihu Root, elder statesman of the Republican party, and during the deliberations he had had as his legal adviser James Brown Scott, a distinguished American authority on international law. The protocol left the way open for American adherence to the World Court, as it was commonly called, and undoubtedly the overwhelming majority of the American people favored such a course. But the extreme isolationists in the Senate had driven themselves into such a frenzy of opposition to anything that savored of "Wilsonism" or the League that the Harding administration moved cautiously on the subject. Finally Hughes, who strongly favored American adherence, persuaded the President to advocate such a course in a message to the Senate, February 24, 1923. Four reservations drawn by Hughes were designed to protect the United States against any slightest League involvement. But the Senate Committee on Foreign Relations was still dominated by the intransigents, Harding's support proved to be only lukewarm, and the Senate failed to act.[22]

[21] Robert H. Ferrell, *Peace in Their Time; The Origins of the Kellogg-Briand Pact* (New Haven, 1952), pp. 21–26; C. A. Beard, "Prospects for Peace," *Harper's Magazine,* CLVIII (Feb., 1929), pp. 320–330; Irving Fisher, *League or War* (New York, 1923), pp. 202–211. *The New York Times,* Dec. 29, 1926, p. 1, reports Root's condemnation of the United States for its failure to enter the League.

[22] Beeritz memo, "Separate Peace with Germany," pp. 33–38, Hughes Papers, Box 172, Folder 25; D. F. Fleming, *The United States and the World Court* (New York, 1945), pp. 40–44.

President Coolidge in his first annual message, December, 1923, also commended the Court to the favorable consideration of the Senate, and the evidence that public opinion still favored adherence could hardly have been stronger. The Senate obstructionists, lacking any real arguments to justify their position, finally hit upon the right of the Court to give "advisory opinions" as somehow dangerous to the independence of signatory powers. The result, arrived at after a maximum of delay and debate, was a fifth reservation, insisting that the Court should not render any such opinion without giving due notice in advance to all interested states and providing them an opportunity for public hearings if they so desired; also, that it should not, "without the consent of the United States, entertain any request for an advisory opinion touching any dispute or question in which the United States has an interest." Finally on January 27, 1926, nearly three years after Harding's original message on the subject, the Senate voted for adherence to the Court, 76 to 17, conditioned upon acceptance of the reservations it had adopted. But the end was not yet. When the Council of the League of Nations sought to clarify the meaning of the American reservations, President Coolidge took the position that they had been rejected. Under the circumstances, he said, he could see "no prospect of this country adhering to the Court." Twice later, once during Hoover's administration and once during Roosevelt's, the Senate had a chance to ratify the World Court protocol on terms carefully drawn to meet American objections, but twice more the Senate failed to approve.[23]

If the World Court had to be ruled out as the official answer to Americans who were praying for action or peace, what substitute could there be? Early in 1927 the Coolidge administration decided to give the Harding formula of peace by disarmament another try. The famous 5:5:3 ratio of the Washington Conference had applied only to battleships and aircraft carriers—capital ships—and had ignored such smaller craft as cruisers, submarines, and destroyers. Would the great powers consent to an extension of the Washington ratio to these auxiliary units also? Such an agreement would somewhat redeem the sagging reputation of the Republican administration in foreign affairs, and would at the same time serve to preserve the budget from the

[23] *Ibid.*, pp. 44–81, 102–109, 133; *Congressional Record*, 69th Cong., 1st Sess., LXVII (Jan. 27, 1926), 2824–2825; League of Nations, *Ten Years of World Cooperation* (London, 1930), pp. 125–126, 135–138.

expenditures advocated by most naval experts. For the United States, sure that it had turned its back on war forever, had not only lived up to the terms of the Washington agreement, but had also practically ceased new naval construction of every sort and kind. To maintain its parity with Great Britain and its lead over Japan, either the American nation must begin to build, as the naval experts demanded, or it must induce its international rivals not to build.[24]

Ignoring the need for advance diplomatic preparation, President Coolidge on February 10, 1927, asked the five powers that had signed the Washington Treaty to meet at Geneva later in the summer for a conference on additional naval limitations. The place designated was significant. Geneva was the seat of the League of Nations, and there a "Preparatory Commission" had long been at work under League auspices on the general problem of disarmament. The United States was not a member of the League, but League facilities and League co-operation might help to promote accord on the limited area Coolidge had singled out for consideration. Furthermore, there was some reason to hope that at least the European powers were in the proper mood to negotiate. Late in 1925, at the little Swiss town of Locarno, they had signed a series of agreements that augured well for peace. Most important of these was a treaty between Great Britain, France, Belgium, Italy, and Germany which guaranteed the western boundaries of Germany and the demilitarization of the Rhineland. The three powers most directly concerned, France, Belgium, and Germany, also promised never "to attack or to invade each other or to resort to war against each other," except for flagrant violation of the agreement or on League authorization. Also, Germany signed a series of arbitration treaties with Poland, Czechoslovakia, Belgium, and France, while France, as additional security, signed mutual-assistance pacts with Poland and Czechoslovakia. The effect of the Locarno Pact, as this elaborate series of agreements was generally called, was greatly to reduce European tensions, and the "spirit of Locarno" was still very much in evidence when Coolidge called the Geneva Conference. With the Dawes plan working well, Germany in 1926 won admission to the League of Nations and a permanent seat on its Council. Europe seemed at last to be settling down.[25]

[24] Merze Tate, *The United States and Armaments* (Cambridge, Mass., 1948), pp. 141–142.
[25] *Ibid.,* pp. 73–82; League of Nations, *Ten Years,* pp. 97–104; Leopold

But the Geneva negotiations proved to be a great disappointment. In the first place, both France and Italy refused to participate, except as observers, on the ground that to do so would be inconsistent with their commitment to the disarmament program of the League. The real reasons were no doubt somewhat different. France had always regarded the outcome of the Washington Conference as humiliating, had resented deeply being paired as an equal with Italy, and had even refused to ratify the Conference agreement on the use of submarines and noxious gases. French naval experts, moreover, considered that submarines provided the only effective means of protecting France against the maritime superiority of her near neighbor Great Britain, and objected strenuously to the idea of limiting their production. Italy, under the spell of Mussolini's expansionist dreams, was even less willing to consider the curtailments Coolidge proposed. So the Geneva Conference turned out to be a three-power affair, with only Great Britain, Japan, and the United States as participants.[26]

Lack of political preparation turned the Geneva Conference over to the naval experts, from whom agreement should never have been expected. Coolidge had hoped that former Secretary Hughes would head the American delegation, but Hughes declined, and the choice fell on Hugh Gibson, American ambassador to Belgium, assisted by Admiral Hilary P. Jones and eight naval advisers. The British and Japanese delegations were quite as completely overshadowed by naval and military personnel. The civilian delegates, particularly Ambassador Gibson and Viscount Cecil of Great Britain, made a good try, but they were at the mercy of the experts, whose wrangling, particularly on the size and armament of cruisers, soon wrecked all hope of agreement. The Japanese delegates kept smugly quiet while their two adversaries fought each other to a standstill. An uninvited lobbyist, William Baldwin Shearer, claiming to represent three American firms, the New York Shipbuilding Company, the Bethlehem Steel Company, and the Newport News Shipbuilding Company, was also present at Geneva during the Conference, and gave what encouragement he could to American

---

Schwarzchild, *World in Trance; From Versailles to Pearl Harbor* (New York, 1942), pp. 231–247; H. S. Quigley, *From Versailles to Locarno* (Minneapolis, 1927), pp. 7–20; Buell, *Europe*, pp. 98–118. Hiram Johnson thought that Coolidge had no expectation of favorable results from the conference. Johnson to sons, Feb. 11, 1927, Johnson Papers.

[26] Tate, *United States and Armaments*, pp. 142–143; Harold and Margaret Sprout, *Toward a New Order of Sea Power* (Princeton, N.J., 1946), p. 311.

intransigence. But the claim that Shearer was "the man who broke up the conference" cannot be substantiated. Probably the Geneva discussions would have failed had he not been present.[27]

In the end all the conference could do was to agree to disagree. Its failure was not the fault merely of the participants, who tried hard to reach agreements, nor perhaps even to the inadequacy of preliminary negotiations. The great trouble, as Senator Borah pointed out, was the lack of a sufficiently "aroused and sustained public sentiment" throughout the world. For without "the driving, compelling power of public opinion," the conference had little chance to succeed. As far as the United States was concerned, the most obvious result of the Geneva Conference was a recommendation by President Coolidge to Congress the following December of a five-year billion-dollar naval building program, which included twenty-six cruisers of 10,000 tons each, three aircraft carriers, eighteen destroyers, and five submarines. This program Congress began to implement by an Act of February 13, 1929, which authorized the construction of fifteen light cruisers and one aircraft carrier, but provided also that the President might suspend the Act, in whole or in part, in the event of an international agreement limiting naval armament. In short, if the nation could not obtain peace by disarmament, it was ready to revert to the old formula of peace by preparedness.[28]

Before his term of office ended, Coolidge consented to one more effort on behalf of world peace. Two Americans, a Chicago lawyer named Salmon O. Levinson and a Columbia University professor, James T. Shotwell, had for several years advocated, quite separately from each other, that the true approach to world peace was through an international agreement that would officially condemn war. As matters stood, international law accepted war as legal; why should war not be made to bear instead the stigma of illegality? Levinson believed that if the nations of the world would only outlaw war formally, that might be enough, but Shotwell regarded sanctions as a necessity; there must be force behind the agreement. Among the many Americans who took up with the "outlawry of war" idea, as the concept came generally to

[27] Beeritz memo, "Activities," p. 28, Hughes Papers, Box 180, Folder 28; H. C. Englebrecht and F. C. Hanighen, *Merchants of Death* (New York, 1934), pp. 205–217; Jonathan Mitchell, *Goose Steps to Peace* (New York, 1931), pp. 160–163; Tate, *United States and Armaments*, pp. 143–160.
[28] *Ibid.*, p. 161; press release, Sept. 21, 1927, Borah Papers, Box 285; *United States Statutes at Large* (Washington, 1929), XLV, 1165.

be called, was William E. Borah, chairman of the Senate Committee on Foreign Relations. The notion that some positive action should be taken toward the abolition of war also crossed the Atlantic, where it was deliberately planted in the mind of Aristide Briand, French Foreign Minister, by Professor Shotwell himself. And Briand, a master politician, used it in an address to the American people, April 6, 1927, which announced that "France would be ready publicly to subscribe, with the United States, to any mutual engagement tending, as between those two countries, to outlaw war." Since France did not see eye to eye with the United States on such important matters as the Geneva Conference and war debts, Briand perhaps thought this gesture of good will might not be amiss. Secretary Frank B. Kellogg, who had succeeded Hughes in 1925, was at first annoyed at Briand's move, while President Coolidge was piqued that the French Foreign Minister had gone over the head of the American government to the American people directly. Just at this juncture Charles A. Lindbergh flew the Atlantic in his *Spirit of St. Louis* and landed at Paris; the general enthusiasm that this exploit awakened seemed somehow to call for appropriate action. Both the Levinson and the Shotwell groups made the most of this situation, public opinion soon began to veer strongly their way, and Kellogg at length invited Briand to submit his proposal through normal diplomatic channels, which was done.[29]

Both Borah and the American State Department were quick to see the hazards of the Briand proposal in its original form. It would not do for the United States to sign a special treaty outlawing war between the United States and France without signing similar treaties with many other powers. A bilateral treaty might, by itself, even imply an alliance; for if France went to war with some other nation, then the United States would be bound in advance not to fight against France, come what might. The only tolerable procedure would be to expand the Briand proposal into a general agreement. Finally on December 28, 1927, Kellogg wrote Briand that the United States would favor, instead of the two-power treaty, "an effort to obtain the adherence of all the principal powers of the world to a declaration renouncing war as an

---

[29] Ferrell, *Peace in Their Time*, pp. 70–71, 78–83, 105; James T. Shotwell, *War as an Instrument of National Policy* (New York, 1929), pp. 41–52, and *On the Rim of the Abyss* (New York, 1937), pp. 105–136; John E. Stoner, *S. O. Levinson and the Pact of Paris: A Study in the Techniques of Influence* (Chicago, 1942), pp. 184–211; Johnson, *Borah of Idaho*, pp. 386–407.

instrument of national policy." This was more than Briand had bargained on, and for a time he stalled. Could such a treaty, he questioned, be reconciled with the commitments to other powers that France had already made? But Kellogg's enthusiasm for the idea grew; he even circulated a draft agreement among the great powers that was accepted without hesitation by Germany, Italy, and Japan. Great Britain and France, after the best American tradition, insisted on wordy reservations, but at length they also agreed. Kellogg would have preferred to sign the treaty in Washington, but as part of the price necessary to win French approval, he yielded to Briand's desire that it be signed in Paris.[30] There on August 27, 1928, fifteen nations affixed their signatures to a pact renouncing war "as an instrument of national policy," and promising to solve all disputes of "whatever nature or whatever origin" by "pacific means." Thereafter the pact remained open "for adherence by all the other powers of the world." The first such adherent was the Soviet Union, whose presence at Paris the United States had not desired, lest it might imply recognition.[31]

By the time the Pact of Paris reached the United States Senate, public opinion throughout the nation had so firmly endorsed the document that ratification came easily. Instead of the customary reservations, the Committee on Foreign Relations provided the Senate with an interpretative report. The pact, declared the committee, did not in any way curtail the right of the United States to self-defense, of which the Monroe Doctrine was an essential part; nor did it provide for sanctions, either express or implied, which would in any way oblige the United States to take action against a violator of the pact; nor did it in any respect change or qualify "our present position or relation to any pact or treaty existing between other nations or governments." So interpreted, the Pact of Paris received the approval of the Senate by a vote of 85 to 1, the lone objector being Senator John J. Blaine of Wisconsin. Not every senator who voted for it, however, believed in its value. Senator Carter Glass of Virginia, for example, pointed out that unless the signatory powers stood behind the treaty with force it could

[30] The documentary history of the Pact is given in *Foreign Relations, 1927* (Washington, 1942), II, 611–630; *1928* (Washington, 1942), I, 1–235. See also Drew Pearson and Constantine Brown, *The American Diplomatic Game* (New York, 1935), pp. 25–37; Kellogg to Borah, July 27, 1928, Borah Papers, Box 542; Ferrell, *Peace in Their Time*, pp. 230–231.

[31] *Foreign Relations, 1928*, I, pp. 155–156.

never amount to anything, and voted for it as "worthless, but perfectly harmless." Senator Hiram Johnson of California asserted that, like the characters in a Henry James novel, it had been "analyzed by its proponents practically into disintegration." "The explanations and interpretations," he wrote to his sons, "have made its nothingness complete." But Borah noted in rebuttal that treaties with sanctions had usually only led to war, and that the mobilization of world opinion against war was in itself a considerable victory. By the time the treaty was officially declared in force at Washington, July 24, 1929, thirty-one nations, in addition to the original fifteen, had adhered to it, and they were later followed by eighteen others, a total of sixty-four. Only four nations, all Latin American (Argentina, Bolivia, El Salvador, and Uruguay), failed to adhere. Mere gesture that it was, the Kellogg-Briand Peace Pact expressed eloquently the earnest hope of the world for peace.[32]

[32] *Congressional Record,* 70th Cong., 2nd Sess., LXX (Jan. 15, 1929), 1728–1731; Hiram Johnson to sons, Jan. 19, 1929, Johnson Papers; Ferrell, *Peace in Their Time,* pp. 231–239, 258–259; Frank H. Simonds, *Can America Stay at Home?* (New York, 1932), pp. 200–210; W. E. Rappard, *The Quest for Peace* (Cambridge, Mass., 1940), pp. 168–174.

CHAPTER 7

The Other Americas

THE RELATIONS of the United States during the 1920's with the other Americas, while less in the limelight than Old World involvements, were far from unimportant. After the First World War, the menace of German imperialism, whatever it may have been, was gone; no longer did the danger of direct European intervention in any American republic seem plausible. European nations could even view with considerable equanimity the Roosevelt Corollary to the Monroe Doctrine. If the United States stood ready unilaterally, and without exacting special favors in return, to guarantee order and stability in Latin America, that was a very good bargain indeed; neither European traders and investors nor their governments need ask for more. But most citizens of the United States took a quite different view of the matter. They had no more desire to play a large part in the internal affairs of the other American nations than in the internal affairs of European nations. It was one thing for the United States to ward off Old World attacks on the independence of its American neighbors, but quite another to keep order within their borders; the less of the latter, the better. With the reduction in transatlantic tensions that followed the war and the lessened danger to the Panama Canal, the time seemed ripe for the United States to retreat from the imperialistic policies of Roosevelt, Taft, and Wilson, and to make friends with the other nations of the New World.[1]

[1] S. F. Bemis, *The Latin American Policy of the United States* (New York, 1943), p. 202.

Difficulties with Mexico were chronic in American history, and the decade of the 1920's afforded no exception to the rule. Article 27 of the new Mexican Constitution, which President Venustiano Carranza had proclaimed in 1917, contained clauses that were almost certain to promote trouble with the United States. It asserted the right of eminent domain over all lands and waters within the nation, and sanctioned the breakup of great landed estates, subject to indemnification. It authorized the villages, which the Díaz dictatorship had ruthlessly stripped of their communal holdings, to regain the lands they had lost, or to acquire new tracts. It provided for the nationalization of all subsoil deposits, including petroleum. It placed curbs on the acquisition of property by foreigners, particularly for agricultural purposes. And it took over for the nation the possessions of all "religious institutions known as churches." Some of these provisions merely echoed legislation already in force, while others looked well toward the future, but together they embodied the essentials of the Mexican Revolution. Under Carranza enough was done by way of enforcement to arouse vigorous protests from the American government, but not enough, particularly on the all-important matter of who owned the oil deposits, to prevent the achievement of a tolerable *modus vivendi.* Carranza's inadequacy, together with his laxity in enforcing the Constitution of 1917, led to his downfall and death in 1920.[2]

Carranza's successor, following a brief interregnum, was General Alvaro Obregón, who took office as President of Mexico shortly before Harding became President of the United States. Secretary Hughes, eager to achieve a more permanent settlement, now tried to obtain, in return for the recognition of Obregón, a treaty that would cover all outstanding disputes. In this objective he was not wholly successful, but in 1923, after prolonged negotiations, commissioners representing the two governments met in Mexico City, and worked out a program which committed the Mexican government to respect the pre-1917 subsoil privileges of foreign operators, provided they had before that date performed some "positive act," and to grant them drilling permits subject to Mexican regulations and taxes. The Mexican government also agreed to pay for expropriated surface property, and to submit

[2] *Ibid.,* pp. 214–215; Charles W. Hackett, *The Mexican Revolution and the United States, 1910–1926,* World Peace Foundation, Pamphlets (Boston, 1926), IX, pp. 346–351, 407–412; Beeritz memo, "Relations with Mexico," pp. 1–4, Box 172, Folder 37, Library of Congress, Manuscripts Division.

American claims for damages, both pre- and post-Revolutionary, to claims commissions. All this Obregón implemented by executive agreement, rather than by treaty, but Hughes was sufficiently satisfied that he went along with the plan and accorded Obregón the recognition he craved. So content was the American government with Obregón's behavior that it furnished him on credit, from the United States arsenals, the arms and munitions he needed to put down a revolt which theatened to interfere with the orderly choice of his successor. This action drew vigorous criticism, for it amounted to an act of intervention in Mexican affairs more forthright even than the Wilson policy of permitting sales by private American firms to whichever faction the United States favored.[3]

The trouble with an executive agreement was that it could be as easily abrogated as made. Obregón's successor, Plutarco Elías Calles, was a true disciple of the Revolution who refused to continue the temporizing policies of Carranza and Obregón. Late in 1925 the Mexican Congress enacted two pieces of legislation that greatly disturbed the American State Department. One was an alien lands law which, in conformity with the Constitution of 1917, permitted foreigners to acquire land in Mexico only on condition that for this purpose they consider themselves Mexicans and renounce all rights of protection by their own governments. The other, generally called the petroleum law, insisted that subsoil deposits such as oil were the "inalienable and imprescribable" property of the nation, and laid down strict regulations for concessionaires. Oil companies were told that by January 1, 1927, they must apply for the renewal of their concessions under the terms of the new law, or have their rights revert to the state. According to Calles some 380 companies, representing 26,835,000 acres, complied with the law, while only 22 companies, representing 1,661,000 acres, refused to comply. But among those refusing were certain Doheny, Sinclair, Standard, and Gulf interests of great power and importance. Demands for military intervention by the United States to arrest the spread of bolshevism in Mexico began to appear in the American press. Mexico, representatives of the oil interests claimed, was going the way of Soviet Russia, and if not restrained would be-

[3] *Ibid.*, pp. 7–12; Bemis, *Latin American Policy,* pp. 216–217; *Congressional Record,* 68th Cong., 1st Sess., LXV (Jan. 24, 1924), 1406–1408; *ibid.* (Apr. 1, 1924), 5323. See also Hiram Johnson to sons, Jan. 17, 1927, Johnson Papers, Bancroft Library of the University of California.

come a steppingstone to Communist revolution throughout the Western Hemisphere. "The truth is," said Borah, "that effort is being made to get this country into a shameless, cowardly little war with Mexico. . . . They talk communism and bolshevism, but what they mean is war."[4]

Catholics in the United States had a grievance against the Mexican government that further imperiled the good relations between the two countries. Until Calles became President the anti-Catholic provisions of the Constitution of 1917 had been largely ignored, but the Calles regime nationalized church property; expelled foreign monks, nuns, and priests; prohibited religious instruction in private primary schools; and severely limited the number of priests permitted to exercise religious functions within the various states. With the sanction of the Pope, the Mexican hierarchy struck back with an interdict, July 30, 1926, which restrained the clergy from performing public religious rites and handed over the care of the churches to selected lay groups. Also, armed bands known as "Cristeros" began a campaign of terror designed to force the government into a moderation of its policy. The government, in return, fought the Cristeros with every weapon at its command, took reprisals against their families and property, and expelled an archbishop who asserted the right of Catholics to defend themselves by arms if necessary. Not until 1929 were these repressive measures entirely successful. Meantime, American Catholics, unhappy with what they regarded as an unwarranted persecution of their coreligionists below the border, urged that the American government aid the oppressed churchmen in every possible peaceful way. On the other hand, some Americans, among them Senator Norris of Nebraska, openly defended Calles for what they regarded as an effort to separate Church and State in Mexico.[5]

Neither Secretary Kellogg nor the American ambassador to Mexico, James R. Sheffield, displayed much ingenuity in dealing with the

[4] Hackett, *Mexican Revolution,* pp. 375–380; Harold Nicolson, *Dwight Morrow* (New York, 1935), pp. 329–333; Borah press release, Dec. 24, 1926; Calles to Borah, Jan. 24, 1927; MS. of speech by Borah, May 9, 1927; all in Borah Papers, Box 285, Library of Congress, Manuscripts Division.

[5] P. H. Callahan to O. S. Villard, Feb. 5, 1927, Borah Papers, Box 276; George W. Norris to John F. Cordeal, Jan. 6, 1929, Norris Papers, Tray 1, Box 6, Library of Congress, Manuscripts Division; Washington *Post,* Sept. 2, 1926; J. F. Bannon, S.J., and P. M. Dunne, S.J., *Latin America* (Milwaukee, 1947), pp. 706–707.

Mexican situation, but whatever danger of intervention existed was rather effectively blocked when Senator Borah carried through the United States Senate by a unanimous vote, January 25, 1927, a resolution demanding the settlement of all outstanding disputes with Mexico by arbitration, if necessary. Eventually, at the suggestion of Secretary Kellogg, President Coolidge sent as ambassador to Mexico an old friend of his, Dwight W. Morrow of J. P. Morgan and Company, with only one directive, "to keep us out of war with Mexico." Morrow, arriving in the fall of 1927, proved to be an ideal man for the task. He cultivated good relations with both the Mexican people and with Calles; he cleverly induced Lindbergh to fly his celebrated *Spirit of St. Louis* to Mexico City, where the aviator received a magnificent popular ovation; and he figured out face-saving formulas whereby Calles could retreat far enough from the extreme positions he had taken to satisfy American demands. On the crucial question of subsurface oil rights, Morrow, a lawyer, noted precedents in the Mexican lower courts which would enable the Mexican Supreme Court to declare unconstitutional the more objectionable provisions of the Mexican law. This was done. He urged a more conciliatory attitude toward American landowners in Mexico, and obtained the mitigation of some harsh actions and the postponement of others. He induced Calles to discuss with a prominent American cleric, Father John J. Burke, the problem of a new accord between the Mexican government and the Mexican Church. Out of this and subsequent meetings came an agreement, implemented in 1929 after Calles had left office, whereby the Mexican Church would call off its interdict in return for a governmental promise not to seek the destruction of the Church as such. And so, after three years, the church bells rang again. Actually, Morrow had achieved no really permanent solutions to the problems that confronted him, but he had demonstrated that with tact and patience the peace could be kept.[6]

In Nicaragua, the course of events during these same years followed a similar pattern. There the policies of the Taft and Wilson administrations had culminated in the Bryan-Chamorro Treaty of 1916, by which Nicaragua, in return for $3 million, granted the United States the right

[6] Claudius O. Johnson, *Borah of Idaho* (New York, 1936), p. 337; David Bryn Jones, *Frank B. Kellogg* (New York, 1937), p. 183; Nicolson, *Morrow*, pp. 309–314, 334–335, 338–347; Hewitt H. Howland, *Dwight Whitney Morrow* (New York, 1930), pp. 52–61.

to construct a canal across Nicaragua; also, to fortify the Corn Islands on the Atlantic side, and to build a naval base on the Pacific side. The finances of the country, in practice if not in theory, were under American supervision, payments were regularly required on foreign obligations, and a token force of American marines remained in Managua, the capital, to keep order. In 1925, with debts owing to outside bankers either paid or in a satisfactory state of amoritization, the Coolidge administration undertook to remove the last of the marines from Managua. This action, as events proved, was a mistake, for Nicaragua reverted almost immediately to the same kind of anarchy that had led to American intervention in 1912, and the marines had to be returned, this time in far greater numbers, ultimately 5,000, rather than the 100 legation guards that Coolidge had withdrawn. Worse still, the United States soon found itself backing a Conservative faction in control of the government, headed by Adolfo Díaz, while Mexico under Calles was backing a Liberal rebel faction, headed by Juan B. Sacasa. To carry on the war the Díaz government imported arms from the United States, and paid for them with money supplied by American bankers, while the Sacasa faction got the arms it needed from Mexico. Blood flowed freely, although the marines did what they could to restrict the fighting area and to protect foreign property.[7]

In the spring of 1927 (shortly after the State Department had announced a direct sale of arms by the United States to Díaz) President Coolidge commissioned Henry L. Stimson, once Taft's Secretary of War, as his personal representative to restore peace in Nicaragua. Stimson reached Managua by the end of April, conferred at once with the leaders of both factions, and found that they were ready for a settlement if only they could be assured of a fair election without danger of a new outbreak. Stimson insisted that Díaz must remain as President temporarily, but he was able to induce nearly all of the combatants, both government and rebel, to disband and turn their arms over to American custody, on condition that the United States would do its best to give the country a fair election in 1928. One small rebel band under the command of General Augusto Sandino held out until its leader's death in 1934, but the promised election was duly held, and as a result General José María Moncada, military commander of the

[7] I. J. Cox, *Nicaragua and the United States, 1909–1927* (Boston, 1927), pp. 722–728, 783–797; G. H. Stuart, *Latin-America and the United States* (New York, 1955), pp. 366–376.

rebel forces, was chosen President. Subsequent elections, in 1930 and in 1932, took place under American supervision, but in 1933 the American marines again withdrew.[8]

Speaking in 1922 at Rio, as the representative of the American government during the centennial celebrations of Brazilian independence, Secretary Hughes had vigorously denied the existence of imperialistic sentiment in the United States. "We covet no territory," he said; "we seek no conquest; the liberty we cherish for ourselves we desire for others; and we accept no rights for ourselves that we do not accord to others." This new attitude bore fruit in the repeated acceptance of the good offices of the United States in the settlement of boundary disputes between Latin-American nations. The Tacna-Arica wrangle between Chile and Peru, referred to the President of the United States in 1922, dragged on throughout the Harding-Coolidge administrations, but reached a compromise settlement in 1929, following Hoover's post-election tour of South America. On Secretary Hughes's last day in office, Brazil, Colombia, and Peru accepted his suggestions for the settlement of their long-standing triangular boundary controversy. A similar dispute between Guatemala and Honduras was finally arbitrated by Chief Justice Hughes and two eminent Latin-American jurists in 1930. By way of contrast, the United States early in the Harding administration forced its protégé, Panama, to permit the occupation by Costa Rica, in accordance with an arbitral award, of a district that Panama was determined to hold. According to Secretary Hughes, the honor and prestige of the United States, no less than of Panama, were at stake. Hughes also induced Panama to accept a boundary line that the United States had worked out with Colombia in 1914.[9]

What the Latin Americans resented most about "Yanqui imperialism" was the continued claim of the United States to the right of intervention, as stated in the Roosevelt Corollary. "Our interest," Secretary

[8] Henry L. Stimson and McGeorge Bundy, *On Active Service in Peace and War* (New York, 1947), pp. 111–116; Henry L. Stimson, *American Policy in Nicaragua* (New York, 1927), pp. 42–89; Bemis, *Latin American Policy*, pp. 211–213.

[9] Beeritz memo, "The Brazilian Trip of 1922," p. 9, Hughes Papers, Box 172, Folder 39; "Latin-American Boundary Disputes," pp. 2–21, *ibid.*, Box 180, Folder 12; W. J. Dennis, *Tacna and Arica* (New Haven, 1931), pp. 260–289; Charles E. Hughes, *Our Relations to the Nations of the Western Hemisphere* (Princeton, N.J., 1928), pp. 85–91.

Hughes maintained, "does not lie in controlling foreign peoples; that would be a policy of mischief and disaster. Our interest is in having prosperous, peaceful, and law abiding neighbors with whom we can cooperate to mutual advantage." But as long as American troops remained on Latin-American soil all such words carried a heavy discount. Seeking to match words with deeds, Secretary Hughes, ably assisted by Sumner Welles, did manage to get the marines out of the Dominican Republic by 1924, but they stayed on in Haiti, where in Hughes's opinion their removal would have been merely an "invitation to bloodshed," until 1934.

Knowing full well that trouble anywhere in the Panama Canal area would almost certainly lead to other interventions, Hughes sought to forestall the danger by inducing the five Central American republics to accept, at a conference in Washington held from December 4, 1922, to February 7, 1923, an elaborate set of treaties designed to keep the peace. One of the agreements, which bound the adherents not to recognize a government that had come to power through a *coup d'état,* troubled Hughes; for in countries where elections were fully controlled by the current administration, how else could change be effected? But the need for order, not only because of the Canal but also to protect American trade and investments in the area, was so great that he accepted the embargo on revolutions as a necessary evil. Even before the Washington treaties could be ratified, a defeated presidential candidate started a revolution in Honduras, and the United States promptly sent warships and marines to the scene. This time, however, instead of acting alone, the American government joined with the four Central American neighbors of Honduras in setting up and recognizing a provisional government. Before many years the policy of nonrecognition of revolutionary governments broke down, but meantime the peace of Central America was at least less insecure than formerly.[10]

[10] Charles E. Hughes, *The Pathway of Peace* (New York, 1925), p. 137; Beeritz memo, "American Intervention and the Monroe Doctrine," p. 3, Hughes Papers, Box 173, Folder 41; "Latin American Conferences," pp. 1–9, *ibid.,* Box 180, Folder 10; Stuart, *Latin America and the United States,* pp. 26, 325; Bemis, *Latin American Policy,* pp. 202–213; Sumner Welles, *Naboth's Vineyard; The Dominican Republic, 1844–1924* (2 vols., New York, 1928), II, 836–899.

The United States, much as it desired the friendship of all Latin America, was slow to concede that the right of intervention was no longer necessary. By treaty provisions it had Platt Amendment privileges in Cuba, Panama, Haiti, and the Dominican Republic. And by the generally accepted interpretation of the Roosevelt Corollary, it could intervene elsewhere if in its opinion local conditions warranted. At the fifth Pan-American Conference, held in Santiago, Chile, in 1923, Hughes agreed to a treaty, later ratified, providing that all controversies between American nations, if not settled by diplomacy or submitted to arbitration, should be referred to a commission on inquiry before any military action should be taken. At the sixth Pan-American Conference, held in Havana five years later, Hughes again headed the American delegation, standing in for Secretary Kellogg, who was involved in the Peace Pact negotiations. Hughes had a stiff fight on his hands, for an International Commission of Jurists, meeting at Rio the preceding year, had recommended that "no American country have the right to intervene in any other American country," and the leader of the Argentinian delegation demanded that the conference take such a stand. But Hughes opposed any flat statement of the kind, and obtained its rejection. Later in the year a Conference on Conciliation and Arbitration, called by the Havana Conference, met in Washington and drew up two treaties, one on Conciliation and one on Arbitration, which eventually won ratification by the United States and most of the other American republics, although not without certain crippling reservations. Implicit in these treaties was the doctrine of the Kellogg-Briand Peace Pact, that war was no longer to be regarded as a legal instrument for the settlement of international disputes.[11]

The United States, in a final effort to reconcile its conduct with its professions, backed away from the Roosevelt Corollary. In a State Department document known as the Clark Memorandum, it took the stand that the Corollary was not "justified by the terms of the Monroe Doctrine," which "does not concern itself with purely inter-American relations," and "has nothing to do with the relationship between the United States and other American nations" except in cases "which threaten the security of the United States."

[11] Stuart, *Latin America and the United States,* p. 26; Beeritz memo, "Latin American Conferences," pp. 10–18, Hughes Papers, Box 180, Folder 10; Bemis, *Latin American Policy,* pp. 253–254.

The doctrine states a case of the United States *vs.* Europe, and not of the United States *vs.* Latin America. . . . So far as Latin America is concerned, the Doctrine is now, and always has been, not an instrument of violence and oppression, but an unbought, freely bestowed, and wholly effective guaranty of their [sic] freedom, independence, and territorial integrity against the imperialistic designs of Europe.

This memorandum was the work of Kellogg's Under Secretary of State, J. Reuben Clark, who produced it after only two months of investigation, and turned it over to his chief on December 17, 1928. Although it was not published until after Hoover became President, it clearly indicates a willingness on the part of the State Department even before that time to concede that the United States would no longer regard itself as bound to police Latin-American nations on behalf of outside residents and investors; these individuals and corporations would have to look out for themselves. But there was no retreat from the prohibition against non-American intervention. The United States still maintained that as a matter of self-defense it had the right to ward off foreign aggressors anywhere in the Western Hemisphere. Acceptance of the theory that all such action should be jointly rather than unilaterally undertaken was yet to come.[12]

Much as these peaceable protestations were appreciated in Latin America, fear and suspicion of the United States still remained. When the lion and the lamb lie down together, it is rarely the lion that disappears. Moreover, diplomatic interchanges, and even military missions, were secondary in importance to commercial relations. After the First World War, the United States supplanted Great Britain as the principal source of capital for Latin-American development; American businesses acquired Latin-American branches or affiliates; American investors bought up Latin-American bond issues; American corporations turned more and more to Latin America for markets and materials. In many ways the economies of the United States and Latin America supplemented each other. The United States exported manufactured goods such as automobiles and machinery, and bought in return such items as coffee, rubber, tin, copper, nitrates, sugar, bananas, mahogany, and even oil; indeed, some of the smaller nations, particularly the "banana republics" of Central America, traded almost

[12] J. Reuben Clark, *Memorandum on the Monroe Doctrine* (Washington, 1930), pp. xxiii; Bemis, *Latin American Policy*, pp. 220–223.

exclusively with the United States. But in many ways the intra-continental interests conflicted. The Argentine, for example, had a surplus of agricultural produce for sale, and so did the United States. Further, how could any of the lesser American nations attain the coveted goal of self-sufficiency, and depend so much on the Colossus of the North for manufactured goods? How free were they, after all, to trade as they chose? Would the United States permit European and American corporations to compete for oil concessions on equal terms? Why should the United States, as late as 1927, seek to bar all foreign air services from the Caribbean, and consider applying the Monroe Doctrine to air navigation?

Culturally, too, there were conflicts. The Latin Americans had far more in common with the peoples of southwestern Europe than with the Anglo-Americans of North America; for appreciative understanding they looked to Madrid, Lisbon, Paris, and Rome rather than to Washington. Attempts to feature the unity of the Western Hemisphere, such as emanated from the Bolton school of historians in California and the Pan-American Union in Washington, were received with some satisfaction—it was pleasant to be so recognized—but without much conviction. Finally, when the Panic of 1929 and the depression which followed it put an end to the lush prosperity, it was easy to blame the United States for all that had gone wrong. Hemispheric solidarity was long to remain a dream rather than a reality.[13]

Canada, as a part of the British Empire, occupied a somewhat anomalous position among American nations. The historic connection with Great Britain made it both ineligible and unwilling to participate in the Pan-American movement, although it was bound to the United States, by ties of language and culture, far more closely than were any of the Latin-American republics. Canadians not only clung tenaciously to their imperial loyalties but they also cherished certain deep-seated jealousies and resentments toward their nearest neighbor. They were extremely conscious of the superiority of the United States in wealth,

[13] Luis Quintanilla, *A Latin American Speaks* (New York, 1943), pp. 172–189; Gaston Nerval, *An Autopsy of the Monroe Doctrine* (New York, 1934), pp. 241–286; Max Winkler, *Investments of United States Capital in Latin America* (Boston, 1929), pp. 1–9; Clarence H. Haring, *South America Looks at the United States* (New York, 1928), pp. 80–101; Arthur P. Whitaker, *The Western Hemispheric Idea; Its Rise and Decline* (Ithaca, N.Y., 1954), pp. 113–114.

population, and resources, and deplored the many ways in which
Canada was dependent upon the immensely greater economic power
that lay across its southern borders. They viewed with a jaundiced
eye the isolationist attitudes of the Washington government—the late
entrance of the United States into the First World War, the failure of
the Senate to accept the Treaty of Versailles and the League of
Nations, the effort to collect the wartime loans to European powers.
And yet they took pride in the peaceful relations between Canada and
the United States, the long tradition of arbitration, and the thousands
of miles of undefended border. That the two nations must continue to
live together amicably was taken for granted by both.[14]

Diplomacy between the United States and Canada reflected the
rapid growth of Canadian nationalism that followed the First World
War. Formerly all Canadian negotiations with foreign powers had been
carried on through London, an awkward arrangement that Canadians
increasingly resented. But in 1923 the British government permitted
Canada to negotiate, directly with the United States, a treaty designed
to preserve the halibut fisheries of the North Pacific. Canada also
wished to establish separate legations at foreign capitals, and as early as
1920 obtained a concession on this point, one which the London Imperial Conference of 1926 fully endorsed. That conference held further
that the self-governing states within the British Empire, Great Britain
included, were equal in status, being connected only through their
"common allegiance to the Crown" and through their free association
as "members of the British Commonwealth of Nations." Next year
Canada and the United States exchanged ministers, with Vincent
Massey heading the Canadian legation in Washington and William
Phillips the American legation in Canada.

For some time two areas of conflict between the two nations were
persistently in evidence, prohibition enforcement and the tariff. American efforts to restrain rumrunning across the Canadian border and by
sea from Canadian ports resulted in numerous international complications and some heated diplomatic exchanges. But from this source of
difficulty the end of prohibition brought relief. The tariff problem
lasted longer. The high rates of the Fordney-McCumber Act of 1922

[14] Hugh L. Keenlyside and Gerald S. Brown, *Canada and the United States*
(New York, 1952), pp. 342–360; Carl Wittke, *A History of Canada* (New
York, 1941), pp. 334, 351–354, 381–382, 389.

and the Smoot-Hawley Act of 1930 hit hard at numerous Canadian exports, and led to higher Canadian tariffs in 1927 and 1930 on goods manufactured in the United States. Further, the Ottawa Conference of 1932, in which nine countries of the British Empire and Commonwealth participated, drew up a series of treaties that provided favorable tariff rates for trade within the Empire and discriminations against outsiders, which as far as Canada was concerned meant mainly the United States.[15]

On one matter, the creation of a deep-sea waterway that would connect the Great Lakes with the Atlantic, both nations apparently had much to gain. This idea was by no means new, but the problems of transportation that had harassed Middle America during the First World War made it seem to the residents of that area more desirable than ever before. The State of New York, on the other hand, opposed any such project, for it owned a Barge Canal from Lake Erie to the Hudson that might suffer from the competition, and it was eager also to protect the trade advantages of the port of New York. In spite of New York's opposition, Congress in 1919 voted to explore the possibilities of such a seaway, and next year the governments of the United States and Canada requested the International Joint Commission to make the necessary investigations. This Commission, established by a convention of 1907, consisted of three Americans and three Canadians, and was charged with a variety of duties that concerned the common boundary. It proceeded at once with the investigation, and reported in 1922 that the project was feasible, although the cost would be considerable and the returns on the investment problematic. An incidental benefit would be the generation of electric current by two great dams of 1.5-million-horse-power capacity. With American opinion outside New York State tending strongly to favor the seaway, President Harding gave it his blessing, and Secretary Hughes made the necessary diplomatic overtures to the Canadian government. But the Liberal ministry that had just come to power in Canada proved to be unexpectedly unco-operative, and the first of a long series of delays ensued. Not until 1932, under Hoover, did the two governments get together on a treaty, which in 1934 the United States Senate refused to ratify by a vote of 46 for and 42 against. By this time the New York

[15] S. F. Bemis, *A Diplomatic History of the United States* (New York, 1942), pp. 801–802; Allan Nevins, *The United States in a Chaotic World* (New Haven, 1951), p. 219.

opponents of the seaway had made converts all along the Atlantic seaboard and in the lower Mississippi Valley. Twenty years more were to elapse before the two countries would be able to reach a satisfactory agreement on the subject.[16]

[16] Congressional Record, 67th Cong., 2nd Sess., LXII (Feb. 28, 1922), 3135; 73rd Cong., 2nd Sess., LXXVIII (Mar. 14, 1934), 4475; J. G. Fechter, "Opposition of New York State to the St. Lawrence Project, 1895–1934," unpublished master's thesis, University of California, Berkeley, 1948; C. P. Wright, The St. Lawrence Deep Waterway; A Canadian Appraisal (Toronto, 1935), pp. 63–64; H. G. Moulton and others, The St. Lawrence Navigation and Power Project (Washington, 1929), pp. 204–227.

CHAPTER 8

Social Insecurity

M OST Americans accepted with satisfaction the way of life that emerged in the United States during the 1920's. They had received from the past a goodly heritage. In the Constitution the founding fathers had provided an instrument of government that fitted well the needs of a growing nation, one that adapted itself easily to changing times. Isolationism in foreign affairs, considering the disillusionments that had followed the First World War, was still sound doctrine. Freedom of religious belief, and the separation of Church and State, had worked to good advantage. Public education was worth the price. Business leadership, whatever its shortcomings, was on the whole preferable to the earlier leadership of irresponsible politicians. Although the prevailing mood was conservative, this did not mean that the people had lost faith in the idea of progress. Americans liked to think of their civilization as dynamic, not static; it was going somewhere. Progress showed itself in technological advances that made man increasingly the master rather than the servant of his environment, in the new medical knowledge that had almost defeated certain dread diseases and had greatly improved the public health, in educational opportunities for the masses no less than for the classes, in rising living standards for the people as a whole rather than for only the favored few. This was America to most Americans, and America was good.[1]

[1] Clarke A. Chambers, "The Belief in Progress in Twentieth-Century America," *Journal of the History of Ideas,* XIX (Apr., 1958), 197–224; Selig Adler, *The Isolationist Impulse; Its Twentieth Century Reaction* (New York, 1957), pp. 136–161.

While most Americans before 1929 were content to ride along com-placently on the prevailing tide of prosperity, there were others who viewed the scene with grave misgivings. At one extreme were the re-actionaries who held that America was departing too far from its tradi-tions, and must be turned back on its course, if necessary, by drastic means. Among these rightists were leaders in the movement to preserve "Nordic" supremacy; joiners of the Ku Klux Klan; participants in the Red Scare; adherents of "fundamentalism" in religion, politics, and everything else; would-be censors of books, periodicals, and movies. At the other extreme was a bewildering array of radicals who found cer-tain basic defects in American society, and deplored the changes that were taking place as inadequate or wrongly conceived. Communists and other Marxists naturally had their say, but they were less effective than the literary rebels, who might or might not profess leftist political views. Opponents of the traditional in art, architecture, and music, Freudians and Jungians with revolutionary ideas on the meaning of sex, religious iconoclasts with a complex on Puritanism, progressive educationists, and a host of splinter groups with a cause to further— all attacked whatever aspects of conventional behavior offended them most.

The lines that separated radicals and reactionaries from ordinary conformists could rarely be drawn with clarity. Every "ism" had its fellow travelers all the way from right to left; sometimes, indeed, the same person proclaimed both radical and reactionary views, depending on the subject. In a general sort of way the reactionaries hailed mainly from the country and the radicals mainly from the city. In the country tradition held on tenaciously; but in the city it tended more easily to disappear, for the country people and the immigrants who flocked to the new American cities sometimes left their old convictions behind them, and in the face of new conditions acquired startlingly different ideas. Nevertheless, there were many agrarian radicals, and even more city conservatives, especially among the well-to-do.[2]

Probably the automobile produced greater changes in the American way of life than derived from any other single source. The introduction of the horseless carriage meant far more than a mere acceleration of

[2] Henry F. May, "Shifting Perspectives on the 1920's," *Mississippi Valley Historical Review,* XLIII (Dec., 1956), 405–427; Richard Hofstadter, *The Age of Reform* (New York, 1955), pp. 280–300; Merle Curti, *The Growth of American Thought* (New York, 1943), pp. 686–716.

horse-and-buggy speed. In unnumbered ways the automobile altered the whole pattern of American behavior. Electric railway and streetcar companies disappeared as wage earners joined the business and professional classes in driving their own cars to work. New factory sites could now be located far from city centers and with little regard for public transportation. People who had once of necessity rented city apartments became "home owners" in the suburbs, joined a more fashionable church, and sometimes a more conservative political party. Country towns dwindled to insignificance as they lost out to distant cities in the competition for business. Farm families, emancipated at last from the isolation of centuries, hastily introduced city ways into the country. Vacation habits changed; the people went farther away from home on long vacations, and they went oftener on short ones. National and state park authorities hastily multiplied their facilities to accommodate the torrents of tourists who poured in upon them. With automobile mobility, residents of every section met residents of every other; local differences tended to fade away and homogeneity to intensify.

Few areas of American life were left unchanged. With school buses available, the ungraded country school, where one teacher had taught every pupil and every subject, lost ground to the consolidated school, where the grades were separated and instruction specialized. Long-established habits of churchgoing broke down as both saints and sinners took to the roads for Sunday drives and picnic lunches. The restraints that had once circumscribed courtship somehow lost their validity on and off the highways, and the chaperon disappeared. Women drivers found long skirts a dangerous anachronism, and shortened them. Criminals discovered in the automobile an easy means of escape from the scene of their crime, and often also a high degree of immunity from prosecution across state or national lines. As the highways grew more crowded the number of accidents increased; the automobile was soon to become a greater killer than any known disease, greater even than war itself. More significant still, the possession of a car did something to its owner; with all that power at his command, he was never quite the same man again. Indeed, this automobile psychology seemed almost to characterize the nation as a whole; the American people, like the drivers of many American cars, were relentlessly on their way, but not quite sure where they were going, or why.[3]

[3] President's Research Committee, *Recent Social Trends in the United States* (2 vols., New York, 1933), I, 172–180, 402, 457–465; memorandum for

Close behind the automobile in its effect upon the American way of life came the movies. By the 1920's the crudities of the earlier motion pictures had disappeared, and the "silent drama" had achieved a high degree of perfection. Its success was due not only to stars with a gift for pantomime whose every look and action conveyed a thought but also to skillful producers, among whom D. W. Griffith was perhaps most outstanding. Together with Mary Pickford, whose portrayal of girlish innocence had made her a national favorite, and Douglas Fairbanks, the epitome of courageous masculinity, and Charlie Chaplin, the shuffling little comedian who subtly satirized the bewilderment of humanity in the face of forces that were much too much for men to understand, Griffith in 1919 created the United Artists Corporation, which for a decade turned out one successful film after another. The advent of the "talkies" in 1927 presented producers with new, and for a time baffling, problems. Stars who could act but not talk lost their appeal, and new talent, sometimes borrowed from the legitimate stage, had to be found. Furthermore, it was not easy to balance action against words in a sufficiently realistic fashion to satisfy the unsophisticated audiences that flocked to the movies. But by combining the best of the silent-film techniques with those of the traditional theater, the producers eventually evolved a form of dramatic art that deserved respect, and also won its way with the multitudes.[4]

Motion pictures were not only art; they were business, big business. Production centered in and around Hollywood, California, a suburb of Los Angeles, where lavish offices and sets accounted in themselves for a considerable investment. Leading stars commanded fabulous salaries and lived in well-publicized luxury. The cost of filming a single picture, especially a spectacle production of the Cecil B. de Mille variety that required great crowds, ran far into the hundreds of thousands of dollars, often into the millions. The number of American feature films produced during the year 1930 reached about 500, with about 200 prints of each. Distribution and exhibition involved still further outlays; in 1931, according to a reliable estimate, there were 22,731 motion

---

Congressman Crompton, Records of the National Park Service, RG 79, Central Classified Files, Misc., Pt. 44, National Archives; P. W. Slosson, *The Great Crusade and After* (New York, 1930), pp. 219–250.

[4] Lewis Jacobs, *The Rise of the American Film; A Critical History* (New York, 1939), pp. 233–245, 335–372; *Recent Social Trends*, I, 208–211, II, 940–941.

picture houses in the country, many of them correctly described as palaces, with a total capacity of 11.3 million persons. Average weekly attendance grew from 40 million in 1922 to 95 million in 1929, and 115 million in 1930.

Inevitably the tastes and interests of the masses who viewed the pictures determined the character of the films that were made; box-office receipts talked. When state and local censorship threatened to eliminate some of the overfrank scenes of sex and crime that the public appetite demanded, the picture industry countered with a gesture of self-regulation. It induced Will H. Hays, Harding's first Postmaster General, to resign his seat in the Cabinet in 1922 in order to lay down rules for the entire organized picture industry, although the restraints that the "Hays office" imposed provided mainly a gloss of hypocrisy that in reality hid nothing, and often got in the way of real art. Despite the obstacles, producers of the 1920's gave the nation and the world (for American films had a great vogue abroad) many fine pictures, but it also gave the public what it wanted. Clara Bow, the "It" girl; Rudolph Valentino, the "Sheik"; Theda Bara, the "Vamp"; and their like were rarely unemployed.[5]

There is no way of measuring the effect of the movies upon the American people, but that the effect was considerable few would care to deny. The pictures were designed to produce amusement, but viewers took what they saw with deadly seriousness; sent fan mail in wholesale quantities to their favorite stars; imitated their costumes, their manner of speech, their use of cosmetics, their conduct, on and off the stage. The art of lovemaking, while by no means unknown before the days of the movies, received from film performances many rich embellishments. Children, and sometimes their elders also, reveled in the blood-and-thunder westerns, the deadly gunplay of cops and robbers, the commission and detection of crime. It was an open question whether the movies promoted juvenile delinquency more by what they portrayed than they restrained it by providing amusement for juveniles. Sunday movies were regarded as unfair competition by preachers and habitual churchgoers, and the lessons of the screen as

[5] *Ibid.*, II, 905; Jacobs, *Rise of the American Film*, pp. 287–301; Terry Ramsaye, "The Rise and Place of the Motion Picture," *Annals of the American Academy of Political and Social Science*, CCLIV (Nov., 1947), 7–9; Arthur Mayer, *Merely Colossal* (New York, 1953), pp. 70–72, 109–111, 127–128; Slosson, *Great Crusade*, pp. 393–397.

poor substitutes for those of the Sunday school. Movie magazines told the life stories of actors and actresses with exaggerated candor, and newspapers played up with zest the endless quest of the screen colony for the satisfying romances they portrayed so effectively on stage, but in private life so often failed to achieve. Newsreels and other nonfiction films undoubtedly had a certain educational value, but they were received with scant attention by audiences eager for greater thrills than "true life" could provide. Foreign viewers of American films obtained from them a weird interpretation of life in the United States. Judging from what they saw, the American people lived in the lap of luxury, accepted the morality of the bordello, fought a losing battle against city racketeers, and dressed up frequently in cowboy costumes to kill Indians and bad men along the western frontier. Seemingly foreign audiences rarely realized that for Americans no less than for non-Americans the films they were viewing provided in the main an escape from reality rather than a reflection of it.[6]

Another new and unmeasurable influence upon the pattern of American culture was the radio. During the First World War, governments restricted the use of wireless to military ends, and in Europe state control continued even after the war. But in the United States free enterprise took over. For a time the radio was little more than a mechanical toy from which bright boys with scientific bent of mind obtained amusement. But on November 2, 1920, an East Pittsburgh station known as KDKA began to broadcast regular programs, the first of which featured the election returns just received. From then on the expansion of the radio was spectacular. The earliest stations, including KDKA, were primarily outlets for radio manufacturers or electrical service agencies, but commercial broadcasting companies gradually absorbed most of the business. The first major broadcasting network, the National Broadcasting Company, appeared in 1926, and was followed closely in 1927 by the Columbia Broadcasting Company. Educational institutions, churches, and newspapers also owned stations, although by 1930 over one-third of the 612 such centers scattered throughout the country were in the hands of the commercial companies. To remedy the chaotic conditions that developed when each broadcaster was free to choose his own frequency, Congress created a

[6] Gerald M. Mayer, "American Motion Pictures in World Trade," *Annals*, CCLIV (Nov., 1947), 31–36; *Recent Social Trends*, I, 386; II, 1012–1013.

Federal Radio Commission in 1927, with authority to license broadcasting stations and to assign appropriate wave lengths to each. The manufacture, sale, and repair of radio sets graduated quickly to big-business status. The total value of radio sets and parts produced in 1921 reached only a little more than $10 million; by 1929 it was over $400 million. Retail sales ran much higher. According to the census of 1930 over 12 million American families (40 per cent of the total) owned radios, and in 1932 a reliable estimate set the figure at over 16 million. Naturally city dwellers took up with the new device in advance of country dwellers, and primarily for financial reasons Northerners purchased far more sets proportionately than Southerners.[7]

Everywhere in the United States the cost of radio broadcasting fell principally upon sponsors who purchased time on the air for its advertising value. Velvet-voiced announcers interrupted programs at frequent intervals with plugs designed to break down consumer resistance, to build up consumer acceptance, and to increase consumer demand for whatever item they were hired to sell. The chief virtue of a program thus became the number of listeners it could attract, something the experts were soon able to measure with great accuracy. News commentators early won a hearing; also, play-by play broadcasts of baseball and football games, and blow-by-blow accounts of prize fights. "Canned" music, or phonograph records, filled in time when other programs were not available, but "live" broadcasts from jazz bands, symphony orchestras, and even grand-opera companies became increasingly common. The problem of dramatic presentation without visual aid was as challenging as the reverse problem of seeing without hearing in the silent films, and was met with comparable skill. Vaude-villians crowded off stage by the movies occasionally caught on with radio, as, for example, the famous "Amos 'n' Andy" team of Freeman F. Gosden and Charles J. Correll, to which millions of Americans listened every evening at the appointed hours. Children's stories, church services, market information, dramatic readings, educational broadcasts, weather reports, everything that the ear could follow without the eye, came in over the radio; but especially music, which as late as 1927 probably accounted for about three-fourths of the programs.[8]

[7] *Ibid.*, I, 211–217, II, 941–942; Slosson, *The Great Crusade*, pp. 387–393; Paul Schubert, *The Electric Word; The Rise of the Radio* (New York, 1928), pp. 191–211; F. L. Allen, *Only Yesterday* (New York, 1931), pp. 164–167.

[8] *Ibid.*, p. 352; Schubert, *The Electric Word*, pp. 212–249.

What the radio was doing to the American people won the attention of the sociologists almost immediately. W. F. Ogburn and S. C. Gilfillan, writing for the President's Committee on Social Trends, listed 150 different effects of radio broadcasting, and admitted that "if those cited had been broken down into others, the list would have been longer." Probably the radio did a great deal toward raising the cultural level of the general public. Millions of persons listened to it at first with interest, and then with increasing appreciation. Regarded for a time as a threat to the phonograph, the radio proved eventually to be the exact opposite; with the public appetite for music whetted by the radio, the demand for records and record players grew. The radio, along with the movie, did its share toward promoting national homogeneity. The same advertising, the same interpretations of the news, the same songs, the same manner of speaking, the same clichés penetrated by air wave to every section, and to country and city dwellers alike. The educational value of the radio was also important—agricultural advice, health hints, information about international affairs, and a great variety of other subjects reached the people over the air, sometimes even through the broadcasting of classroom lectures. Campaigners in quest of political office, the advocates of causes, religious zealots—all who had the price—bought radio time to propagate their views. Censorship was more or less automatic; advertisers in search of customers and stations in search of advertisers were at great pains not to give offense. Oddly enough television, although a demonstrated possibility in the 1920's, did not become a commercial reality until after the Second World War.[9]

The airplane as an instrument of social change made less headway in the United States during the 1920's than might have been expected. One trouble was the initial unwillingness of the federal government to foster in any adequate way either military or commercial aviation. When the First World War ended there were twenty-four aircraft plants in the country capable of producing 21,000 airplanes a year, but the wholesale cancellation of contracts that followed the armistice put nearly all of them out of business. Army and Navy conservatives who discounted the airplane as a weapon of war joined with economy-minded politicians to keep air power insignificant in both services. This misjudgment was challenged by General William ("Billy")

[9] *Recent Social Trends,* I, 133, 152–157.

Mitchell of the Army Air Service, whose bombers had sunk the *Ostfreisland* in 1921. Two years later in a comprehensive report Mitchell argued that "the utility of the great surface battleships," because of their vulnerability to air attack, was drawing to a close, and described with variation only in detail what the Japanese air force would do eighteen years later at Pearl Harbor. The needless wrecking in September, 1925, of the *Shenandoah,* a Zeppelin-type lighter-than-air craft that the naval authorities, in defiance of expert opinion, ordered into a storm-swept area, incensed Mitchell into a public attack on the incompetence of both Army and Navy high commands. For this insubordination he was court-martialed, found guilty, and suspended from duty for five years. Eventually his contention that the government should create a single united air force, independent of the two traditional services, won out; but as one of his correspondents observed, "in all great reforms some fanatic has got to be crucified for the public good before people believe in his doctrines." Following Mitchell's charges, President Coolidge appointed a board of inquiry, headed by his friend Dwight W. Morrow, to investigate the use of aircraft in national defense. Morrow's board heard Mitchell out, but it was unimpressed by his pleas, and held that the United States was in no real danger of outside attack anyway.[10]

Unlike the leading European powers, which on the basis of their war experiences not only spent money to continue the development of military aviation but also subsidized commercial flying, the United States for many years after the war did little to encourage civilian efforts to build and operate aircraft; indeed, by selling warplanes as surplus commodities, the government at first placed a serious obstacle in the path of would-be plane manufacturers. Stunt flyers with made-over planes of uncertain merit thrilled county-fair audiences with their daredevil performances, took trusting passengers up into the air for a price, and by their enthusiasm did something toward keeping interest in aviation alive. Long-distance exploration by air did even more. In 1926, for

[10] Slossan, *The Great Crusade,* p. 400; Harold and Margaret Sprout, *Toward a New Order of Sea Power* (Princeton, 1946), pp. 221–223; William Mitchell, "Preliminary Report of Inspection of Air Service Activities in the Hawaiian Department," Dec. 10, 1923; clipping from San Antonio (Tex.) *Light,* Sept. 9, 1925; Charles Grey to William Mitchell, June 11, 1925; all in Mitchell Papers, Library of Congress, Manuscripts Division; Harold Nicolson, *Dwight Morrow* (New York, 1935), pp. 280–286; Herbert Hoover, *Memoirs,* II (New York, 1952), pp. 132–133.

example, Lieutenant Commander Richard E. Byrd of the American Navy, accompanied by Floyd G. Bennett, flew from Spitsbergen to the North Pole and back again in sixteen hours. But the flight that gave the public its greatest thrill took place on May 20–21, 1927, when an American solo pilot, Charles A. Lindbergh, flew his monoplane, the *Spirit of St. Louis,* from Roosevelt Air Field, New York, nonstop to Le Bourget Air Field, Paris, in thirty-three and one-half hours. Lindbergh received a hero's welcome in Europe and, by invitation of President Coolidge, returned to the United States as the nation's guest on the cruiser *Memphis.* The ovations accorded the flyer in New York, Washington, St. Louis, and elsewhere exceeded anything of the kind the nation ever had witnessed before. After Lindbergh's triumph the longer flight of Clarence D. Chamberlin and C. A. Levine to within one hundred miles of Berlin in June, 1927, won less attention than it deserved, while the news that Richard E. Byrd had reached the South Pole by air in 1929 occasioned little excitement. These, together with numerous other long-distance flights, made it evident that the conquest of the air was in sight.[11]

Meantime commercial air companies were struggling earnestly to get a start, but with indifferent success. A few of them got contracts for carrying the mail short distances, but the Post Office Department, while greatly interested in developing air-mail service, preferred at first to fly its own planes and hire its own pilots. Landing fields were scarce and inadequate, air lanes were not properly marked, safety provisions were almost totally lacking. This situation was a challenge to Secretary Hoover, who believed that the government should do all in its power to stimulate commercial aviation, including the turning over to private companies of the carrying of the mail. Finally, under Hoover's insistent hammering, Congress, on May 20, 1926, passed an Air Commerce Act which vested extensive powers over commercial aviation in Hoover's Department. Hoover promptly launched a campaign for "municipal development of air-ports," and "began building airways with radio beacons, lights, emergency landing fields, and weather services." With Hoover's encouragement commercial air lines gradually took over the carrying of all air mail, with the larger and stronger companies, according to a well-defined pattern of business growth, operating at a

[11] Mark Sullivan, *Our Times* (New York, 1935), VI, 515–519; Slosson, *Great Crusade,* pp. 401–405; Charles A. Lindbergh, *"We"* (New York, 1927), pp. 213–314, and *The Spirit of St. Louis* (New York, 1953), *passim.*

great advantage over the little companies. When Hoover reported to Congress in 1929 on the work of his Aviation Division, he claimed "25,000 miles of government-improved airways," with "regular flights of over 25,000,000 miles per annum." Meantime the output of planes by manufacturers had risen to 7,500 planes a year.[12]

Government assistance to private air enterprise went to even greater lengths after Hoover became President. Up to this time the air lines were paid primarily for carrying the mail, but Hoover and his Post-master General, Walter Folger Brown, wanted to stimulate the building of larger and better planes, both for the contribution they could make to peacetime transportation and for the aid they might give the nation in time of war. Accordingly, Brown abandoned the old "per pound" system of awarding contracts in favor of a new and costlier "space-mile" principle, which would stimulate the building of larger planes more suitable for passenger traffic. Again the weaker companies suf-fered in competition with the stronger companies, and many independ-ents went out of business, but the new policy undoubtedly achieved the desired ends. By 1931 the nation had 126 airway services covering 45,704 miles of air lanes, and the number of passengers carried each year had risen to 522,345. The prudent traveler still preferred ground transportation, but the future of commercial aviation seemed assured.[13]

During these years of adjustment to so many mechanical innovations, American society also had to deal with the baffling experiment of nation-wide prohibition. To a very considerable extent the Eighteenth Amendment was a wartime legacy. It was submitted early in the war when the expansion of national powers was at its peak. It was regarded by many who voted for it as a war measure necessary for the saving of food and man power; it was accepted by others as a means of appeasing the ever-insistent drys who, led by the Anti-Saloon League, could think and talk of nothing else. It was ratified hastily by the legis-latures of three-fourths of the states under the pressure of wartime psychology, which tended to identify prohibition and patriotism, and without opportunity in any instance for a popular referendum on the subject. Furthermore, the amendment, while forbidding the manu-facture, sale, and transportation of intoxicating beverages, conspicu-ously failed to brand their purchase or use as illegal. Full ratification

---

[12] Hoover, *Memoirs*, II, 133–134; Henry Ladd Smith, *Airways; The History of Commercial Aviation in the United States* (New York, 1942), pp. 103–104.
[13] *Ibid.*, pp. 156–186; *Recent Social Trends*, I, 183–184.

was achieved by January, 1919, but as a concession to the liquor interests, the amendment delayed the actual inauguration of prohibition for one year. Congress and the several states were given concurrent responsibility for enforcement, and Congress by the Volstead Act of 1919 defined as intoxicating all beverages of more than one-half of 1 per cent alcoholic content. The states tended to accept this definition, but particularly in the wetter areas left to the national government the principal task of enforcement.[14]

By the time Harding became President, prohibition had been the law of the land for over a year, and the difficulties it entailed were painfully apparent. People who wished to drink had no notion of being deprived of their liquor, whatever the Constitution might say on the subject; indeed, it became the smart thing to drink, and many who had been temperate in their habits before were now moved to imbibe freely as a protest against the legal invasion of their "personal liberty." Statistics as to the effect of prohibition on liquor consumption and drunkenness were manufactured freely by both wets and drys, but they were almost entirely worthless. All that is certain is that the demand for liquor still existed. And private enterprise, although in this instance unassisted by the law, never showed greater efficiency in meeting a consumer demand. The sources of supply included liquor manufactured for medicinal purposes, importations brought in by rumrunners, revitalized near beer, more or less renovated industrial alcohol, unfermented grape juice that had somehow gathered potency, and the produce of innumerable stills and breweries. Bootleggers, already experienced in their business thanks to prohibition laws in some twenty-six of the states, got the liquor around. Inevitably the enormous profits from this illicit trade led to fierce competition, in which the richer and more ruthless operators triumphed. Bootlegging became big business, and the survival of the fittest left a few successful entrepreneurs, surrounded by their private armies of gunmen and thugs, in complete control. In Chicago, for example, Al Capone, after a series of fantastic killings that were never punished, emerged supreme.[15]

[14] Charles Merz, *The Dry Decade* (New York, 1931), pp. 23–50; Herbert Asbury, *The Great Illusion; An Informal History of Prohibition* (New York, 1950), pp. 121–137; Justin Steuart, *Wayne Wheeler, Dry Boss* (New York, 1928), pp. 99–115; Peter Odegard, *Pressure Politics; The Story of the Anti-Saloon League* (New York, 1928), pp. 78–80.
[15] Merz, *Dry Decade,* pp. 54, 61–74; Asbury, *Great Illusion,* pp. 199–208;

Enforcement from beginning to end was an elaborate farce. Congressional appropriations for the purpose never amounted to over a few million dollars a year, always a hopelessly inadequate sum. The Prohibition Bureau, on which the task devolved, was for many years attached to the Treasury Department, where it had no business to be, and for over a decade every effort to transfer it to the Justice Department, where it belonged, was successfully resisted. Moreover, it was not under civil service—part of the price the drys had paid for passage of the Volstead Act—and throughout its existence was filled with incompetents or worse. Both Harding and Coolidge talked enforcement, but neither ever recommended the appropriations needed to give the law a chance. District attorneys and federal judges found the glut of prohibition cases well beyond their ability to handle. General Smedley D. Butler of the United States Marine Corps, who agreed to head the Philadelphia Police Department under a newly elected reform mayor in 1924, tried every device he could think of to enforce prohibition in that city, but gave up in less than two years with the comment that the job was a "waste of time." In many cities there was a complete understanding between the local boss of the bootleggers and the police. In Chicago, under the regime of "Big Bill" Thompson, elected to his third term as mayor in 1927, it was sometimes difficult to tell exactly where city rule left off and gangster rule began, while in New York the Seabury investigation of 1930 proved conclusively that even the decisions of judges were for sale.[16]

The profits of lawlessness tempted the gangsters to extend their operations to other fields, or "rackets," in addition to the liquor traffic. Gambling, prostitution, and the trade in narcotics fell naturally under their sway, but they frequently exacted a heavy toll also from wholly legitimate activities. They offered protection, for a price, to night clubs, restaurants, garages, laundries, cleaners and dyers, barbershops, any business with a cash intake large enough to interest them; and if neces-

Fred D. Pasley, *Al Capone; The Biography of a Self-made Man* (Garden City, 1930), pp. 7–61; Slosson, *Great Crusade,* pp. 105–129.

[16] Merz, *Dry Decade,* pp. 88, 107–108, 123–124, 144, 154; Albert E. Sawyer, "The Enforcement of National Prohibition," *Annals,* CLXIII (Sept. 1932), pp. 10–29; Mabel W. Willebrandt, *The Inside of Prohibition* (Indianapolis, 1929), pp. 94–121; Lloyd Wendt and Herman Kogan, *Big Bill of Chicago* (Indianapolis, 1953), pp. 271–277; William B. Northrop and John B. Northrop, *The Insolence of Office* (New York, 1932), pp. 12–16; Walter Chambers, *Samuel Seabury; A Challenge* (New York, 1932), pp. 227–381.

sary they dealt out death and destruction until their terms were met. Racketeers "muscled in" on labor unions, merchant associations, and other dues-collecting organizations for a cut in the receipts. The protection accorded such criminals by their allies in government, together with the shrewdness of the lawyers, or "mouthpieces," they hired, made them almost immune to punishment. They divided areas of activity among themselves at will and punished ruthlessly those who failed to keep agreements. Independent operators carried on at their peril, but usually not for long. Gang warfare, particularly in New York and Chicago, was almost continuous and resulted in numerous deaths that made spectacular headlines, but resulted in few court cases. The Federal Bureau of Investigation (F.B.I.), later so effective in dealing with crime, was itself "a national disgrace" until cleaned up by J. Edgar Hoover in the middle twenties, and even then it lacked, until after Roosevelt became President, the legal authority it needed to curb gangster activities.[17]

Syndicated criminals by no means accounted for all of the crime committed during the decade; private crime seemed also on the increase. From the notorious Halls-Mills case of 1922, in which the murderers of a preacher and his choir-leader mistress went unpunished, to the kidnaping and brutal murder of the infant son of Charles A. Lindbergh in 1932, the newspapers were rarely without some such grisly story to exploit, not to mention the countless other homicides that they did not choose to feature, or for lack of space did not even report. Automobile thefts, bank robberies, burglaries, holdups, sex crimes, felonies of every sort and kind occurred in bewildering confusion. The Hearst newspapers, still the largest chain in the country, exploited all such sensational news without restraint, and were joined in the enterprise by the new tabloids, which concentrated on sex and crime, and assisted nonreaders with gruesome illustrations. Criminologists and publicists who sought to explain the violence of the period pointed to the experience with weapons obtained by Americans in the fighting overseas, to the automobile as an easy means of escape, to the ineffectiveness of the police in the apprehending of criminals and of the courts in convicting them, to prison conditions that made

[17] John Landesco, "Prohibition and Crime," *Annals,* CLXIII (Sept., 1922), 120–129; *Recent Social Trends,* II, 1135–1136; Allen, *Only Yesterday,* pp. 265–269; Pasley, *Al Capone,* pp. 142–145; Don Whitehead, *The FBI Story* (New York, 1956), pp. 14, 56–74, 83, 102.

most penitentiaries mere schools for crime, to the spirit of lawlessness inherited from the American frontier, to the importation of crime-hardened immigrants from the Old World, to the luxury demands of the times that ordinary incomes could rarely meet, to broken homes and easy divorce, to the movies and the radio, to prohibition itself. But none really knew the answer.[18]

It was easy for hostile critics to make a case that American morality had in some fatal way broken down. The standards of right and wrong that earlier generations had accepted no longer commanded respect. Business ethics were latitudinarian in the extreme; politicians were in all too many instances venal; even in the all-American game of base-ball, after the White Sox scandal of 1919, integrity could be guaranteed only by the professionals putting their destinies in the hands of a "czar." But at no point did the breakdown in American morality seem so frightening to the conventional as in the new standards of sexual be-havior that had followed in the wake of the war. Whether the war was to blame, directly or indirectly, or the doctrines of Jung and Freud, whom most Americans had never even heard of, the fact remained that many young adults not only talked about sex with an abandon that shocked their elders, but indulged their desires freely without benefit of clergy.[19]

To a certain extent this was incidental to the emancipation of women. With the passage of the Nineteenth Amendment, feminists had achieved one of their greatest goals; throughout the United States women now had the same right to vote as men, and the militant suffragists were freed to organize the extremely useful League of Women Voters. But this was not enough. The double standard that had prescribed one code of conduct for men and another for women must also go; women must be free to do whatever men were free to do. Perversely interpreted, this meant to many women the right to imitate men at their worst rather than at their best. If men smoked, women could smoke; if men drank, women could drink; if men took sex rela-tions casually, women could do the same. With techniques of birth con-

[18] G. W. Kirchway, "What Makes Criminals," *Current History* XXVII (Dec., 1927), 315–319; Jack Black, "A Burglar Looks at Laws and Codes," *Harper's Magazine,* CLX (Feb., 1930), 306–313; Slosson, *Great Crusade,* pp. 95–104.

[19] Walter Lippmann, *A Preface to Morals* (New York, 1929), pp. 3–20; J. T. Adams, *Our Business Civilization* (New York, 1929), pp. 63–79; Sullivan, *Our Times,* VI, 543–545; Allen, *Only Yesterday,* pp. 88–103.

trol widely disseminated, the hazards of illicit intercourse were slight. Why should any thrill be renounced? And yet if women were still to be women they must not permit feminine allure to disappear entirely. Short hair, flattened breasts, dropped waistlines, and mannish styles were accompanied by a lavish use of cosmetics and a boldness of leg display formerly associated primarily with practitioners of the world's oldest profession. Indeed, the women of the streets had to look to their laurels; amateurs took much of their business away.[20]

Thunder on the right found in these departures from the puritanical tradition the basic fault in American society. To some the trouble stemmed chiefly from the wholesale way in which Americans had abandoned the fundamental teachings of Christianity, both in doctrine and in conduct. "Billy" Sunday, the evangelist, preached the old-time religion to great audiences all over the nation; what he had to say was said better by Dwight L. Moody in the 1870's, but to millions of distraught Americans this was still the way of salvation. Aimee Semple McPherson, a Los Angeles revivalist of eclectic views, exerted an almost hypnotic influence over the vast throngs she attracted to her Angelus Temple. Great numbers of the Protestant clergy, particularly among the Methodists, the Baptists, and the other evangelical sects, were as primitive in their theology as Sunday and McPherson; as fundamentalists they denounced in unmeasured terms modernists who sought to undermine in any way the sanction of holy writ, or to reconcile the teachings of science and religion.

Following a well-worn puritanical pattern, fundamentalists did not scruple to invoke the power of the state on their side. Prohibition itself was designed to make people be good whether they wanted to be or not, laws against the teaching of evolution were designed to put the modernists out of business; the youth of the land must not be corrupted. Such a law went on the statute books in Tennessee in 1925, and shortly after its passage led to the famous Scopes trial in Dayton, Tennessee, with William Jennings Bryan arguing for the fundamentalists and Clarence Darrow, a celebrated Chicago lawyer of strictly unorthodox views, for the evolutionists. Bryan's side won the case, but Bryan died shortly after from the strain of the trial, with his pitiful ignorance of elementary science fully revealed. Religious fundamentalists provided the backbone for the Ku Klux Klan; if the pleadings of the righteous

[20] *Recent Social Trends*, I, 414–423; Lippmann, *Preface to Morals*, pp. 284–299; Allen, *Only Yesterday*, pp. 103–122.

and the law of the land failed to make people do the right thing, then private force might properly be employed. It was the revelation of the immoral, dishonest, and utterly unchristian behavior on the part of many Ku Klux Klan leaders, rather than any opposition to the use of illegal force by the Klan, that made many religious zealots abandon it.[21]

Religious fundamentalism was paralleled by a demand for social and political conformity that also looked backward rather than forward. Antagonism against the Jews was based less upon their religious convictions than upon their tendency to espouse progressive ideas and to lead reform causes, particularly those with international implications. Henry Ford, whose naïveté except within the realm of business rivaled Bryan's, lent the columns of his newspaper, the *Dearborn Independent,* to charges that Jews were international conspirators who sought to gain an ascendancy over the whole Gentile world. Belief in the mission of the American public schools went to the length of bitter attacks on the Catholic system of parochial schools, and in at least one state, Oregon, the courts were obliged to declare unconstitutional a law designed to put all such schools out of business. Both Mayors John F. Hylan of New York and "Big Bill" Thompson of Chicago made unrestrained warfare on schoolbooks that neglected to praise famous Americans in an adequate way, or failed to denounce with sufficient fervor the historic enemy of the United States, Great Britain. As a part of his fight against publications "soaked through and through with British propaganda," Thompson promoted an America First Foundation (with membership fees of $10 per person) that provided a slogan around which isolationists were long to rally. The American Legion, the Daughters of the American Revolution, and other self-described "patriotic" orders likewise deplored deviations from the traditional in the teaching of American history; in response to their pleas both Oregon and Wisconsin prohibited the use in public schools of textbooks that failed to view with proper respect American exploits in the Revolution and the War of 1812. Meantime, such organizations as the Boston Watch and Ward Society and the New York Vice Society

[21] W. G. McLoughlin, *Billy Sunday Was His Real Name* (Chicago, 1955), pp. 165–170, 270–271; Nancy Barr Mavity, *Sister Aimee* (Garden City, 1931), pp. 58–66; Slosson, *Great Crusade,* pp. 311–314; Sullivan, *Our Times,* VI, 641–644; Clarence Darrow, *The Story of My Life* (New York, 1932), pp. 244–278. An anti-Catholic, pro-Klan argument is contained in Paul M. Winter, *What Price Tolerance* (Hewlitt, N.Y., 1928), pp. 331–350.

attempted with some success to keep from public sale books, periodicals, and pictures that they deemed immoral.[22]

Thunder on the left derived less from the stock criticisms of Communists and Socialists than from sources less fettered by dogma. The nation's troubles might all be due to the capitalist system, as the Marxists believed, but neither the Communist plan of substituting another system as speedily as possible, and by force if necessary, nor the Socialist plan of gradual revision toward the same general end attracted many American followers. The critics who really counted hit hard at the shallowness of American civilization, its absorption with materialistic ends, its reliance on mechanization, its unwillingness to think. For many of this group disillusionment with what Herbert Croly had once called *The Promise of American Life* (1909) began with the failure of American objectives in the First World War. Instead of a brave new world made safe for democracy and guaranteed against all future wars, the same old world had re-emerged; the suffering and death had all been in vain. The fact that American intervention had halted the German bid for world supremacy, and temporarily, at least, had made the world safe for the United States, failed to impress those who had set their minds on higher things. Of what avail to win the war and lose the peace?

Domestically, too, the nation had retrograded. The progressive ideas of the prewar years had given way to the abject conservatism of the Harding-Coolidge era, with its complete devotion to profits as the chief end and aim of man. An early blast, *Civilization in the United States* (1922), edited by Harold Stearns, contained derogatory essays on nearly every aspect of American life, many of them written with considerable distinction but all of them surcharged with pessimism. America, a believing reader might conclude, had lost its soul; there was nothing left to be saved. Among those who shared this state of mind, some took refuge in Greenwich Village, New York, or in one of its numerous imitators elsewhere, there to find solace in "a gay disorderliness of life, cheerful bad manners, and no fixed hours or sexual stand-

---

[22] Keith Sward, *The Legend of Henry Ford* (New York, 1948), pp. 146–151; Bessie L. Pierce, *Public Opinion and the Teaching of History in the United States* (New York, 1926), pp. 208–238, 280–294, and *Citizen's Organizations and the Civic Training of Youth* (New York, 1933), pp. 3–52; Allen, *Only Yesterday,* pp. 178–180.

ards." Others, "the lost generation" whose expatriate futilities Ernest
Hemingway recorded so brilliantly in *The Sun Also Rises* (1926),
sought on the Left Bank of the Seine in Paris the full freedom that
they believed their own country denied them. Still others wrote out
their thoughts, sometimes in books, sometimes for publication in such
open-minded journals as *The Nation,* the *New Republic, The New
Yorker,* the *New Masses,* the *Freeman,* and the *American Mercury;* or
if they could not write well enough to break into print, they read with
approval and repeated endlessly what more articulate critics of the
American scene had to say.[23]

Outstanding among the writers who heaped scorn upon the values
that most Americans cherished was Henry L. Mencken, founder in
1924, with George Jean Nathan, of the *American Mercury,* and editor
of that green-covered monthly for nearly a decade. Drawing heavily
upon the philosophy of Friedrich Nietzsche, Mencken had acquired an
anti-middle-class, antidemocratic bias that knew no limits. He railed
gleefully at the American "booboisie," the shallow hypocrisies of its
businessmen, the crass illiteracy of its politicians, the timidity of its
pedagogues, the rabble-rousing absurdities of its evangelical clergy,
and the moronic moral standards they preached. Most of all he loved
to berate the "Bible Belt" of the South and the Middle West for its
intellectual aridity, best exemplified by its support of prohibition, which
of all things American he regarded with greatest contempt. In no
sense a reformer, Mencken was as critical of Communists, Socialists,
and Marxists generally as of Red-baiters, Rotarians, and Methodists;
if he had in mind any other purpose in his diatribes than for the elite
of mankind to laugh derisively at all lesser men, he concealed it well.
He opened his magazine's pages to other caustic critics and to an
endless documentation of his case against the American mind, if such a
thing could be said to exist. In every issue of the *Mercury* his column
of "Americana" listed gleefully the more extravagant absurdities of
the native *homo boobiens,* as revealed in print. Mencken's weapon was
heavy-handed satire; he disdained subtleties that might be lost on his
readers, and wielded the meat ax and the bludgeon rather than the
rapier. Would-be intellectuals and pseudo-sophisticates read the
Mercury with delight, imitated its style, reiterated its charges. Its cir-

[23] Frederick J. Hoffman, *The Twenties; American Writing in the Postwar
Decade* (New York, 1955), pp. 15–36.

culation was not large—well under 100,000—but its influence extended far beyond its subscription list.[24]

Mencken's point of view, diluted and restricted to suit the individual tastes of the writers concerned, ran through much of the literature of the period. Such outstanding novelists as Theodore Dreiser, F. Scott Fitzgerald, Sinclair Lewis, Ernest Hemingway, John Dos Passos, Sherwood Anderson, and William Faulkner took a thoroughly cynical view of the nation they lived in and the people they wrote about. The poetry of Ezra Pound and T. S. Eliot, the plays of Eugene O'Neill, the short stories of Ring Lardner, not to mention a host of lesser lights, exhibited in one degree or another the same defeatist attitude. And yet the success of these men as writers, the originality and vitality of their work, contradicted flatly the message they sought to convey. Judged by any reasonable standards, theirs was one of the great ages of American literature; considering the eminence they had achieved, their insistence on the cultural bankruptcy of the nation that had produced them had a hollow and unconvincing sound. Furthermore, they failed in the main to project their belief in the hopelessness of reform; the message they really got over was that if there were defects in American civilization they must somehow be remedied. Not all the writers of the period were consumed with this same spirit of discouragement, nor was literature the only form of creative art to achieve distinction during the 1920's. In such fields as architecture, painting, sculpture, and music, American artists broke away freely from old conventions, ceased to follow slavishly European traditions, and made contributions that have stood the test of time.[25]

On the positive side also, with some qualifications, were the achievements in the field of education that characterized the postwar years. Faith in education as the cure-all for whatever ills might beset the nation still endured, and the prosperity of the 1920's permitted a persistent expansion of school facilities. With the goal of free education for all children through the elementary grades virtually achieved, the chief concentration during these years fell on secondary and higher education. State laws usually required school attendance for all children

[24] *Ibid.*, pp. 304–314; Edgar Kemler, *The Irreverent Mr. Mencken* (Boston, 1950); William Manchester, *Disturber of the Peace; The Life of H. L. Mencken* (New York, 1950); Charles Angoff, *H. L. Mencken; A Portrait from Memory* (New York, 1956).

[25] Hoffman, *The Twenties,* pp. 388–391; *Recent Social Trends,* II, 962–965; R. L. Duffus, *The American Renaissance* (New York, 1928), pp. 317–321.

up to sixteen or eighteen years of age, and public opinion in the main
supported this legislation. Since so many of the pupils had neither the
talent nor the interest necessary to enable them to pursue the traditional curriculum, the ideas of progressive educationalists who followed
the precepts of John Dewey won increasing acceptance. Children
should be taught the things necessary to make them into socially useful
adults, and for many this meant primarily manual training and vocational education. Expensive workshops and elaborate equipment designed to meet the new needs became essentials for every up-to-date
high school. In general the college preparatory courses were not
neglected; indeed, for prestige reasons pupils sometimes elected them
who had no hope of education beyond high school. But educational
leaders made every effort to respond to what they believed to be the
needs of the masses. By way of aid to the states in these new undertakings, the federal government had fortunately provided dollar-matching
funds through the Smith-Lever Act of 1914 for agricultural education,
and through the Smith-Hughes Act of 1917 for vocational training in
commercial, industrial, and domestic-science subjects; during the 1920's
a steadily increasing number of schools were able to take advantage of
these forms of federal assistance.[26]

Higher education also expanded spectacularly; each year throughout
the decade the number of students registered in colleges and universities
was approximately 50,000 greater than the year before. This meant an
increase not only in the actual numbers of college students but also in
the proportion of college students to the total population of college age.
By 1926 one out of every eight young Americans between the ages of
eighteen and twenty-one was enrolled in some institution of higher
learning—four or five times the ratio achieved by any other nation in
the world. To some extent the influx of new students was only the result
of prosperity—more people than ever before were able to send their
sons and daughters away to school. To some extent, also, it was a by-
product of the war, which demonstrated to a certainty that college
graduates had an advantage in the competition for commissions and
other preferments. But perhaps the greatest influence was the store that

[26] *Recent Social Trends,* I, 331–338; J. H. Newlon, "John Dewey's Influence
in the Schools," *School and Society,* XXX (Nov. 23, 1929), 691–700; E. C.
Moore, "John Dewey's Contribution to Educational Theory," *ibid.,* XXXI
(Jan. 11, 1930), 37–50; Robert S. Lynd and Helen M. Lynd, *Middletown*
(New York, 1929), pp. 194–196; Slosson, *Great Crusade,* pp. 320–328.

business employers were beginning to set by college degrees. Higher education, long regarded as an essential steppingstone to a professional career, became increasingly important to getting a job in business. This situation meant, for the colleges and universities, readjustments in the course of study comparable to those being made in the high schools. Colleges of letters and science found it expedient to credit many "bread-and-butter" courses toward academic degrees, and to provide whatever "service courses" the new schools of business administration, or their equivalents, chose to demand. The tendency of the various professional schools, particularly law, medicine, engineering, and education, to require one or two years, or even more, of college work in advance of professional training also placed a heavy burden on letters and science, particularly since the professional schools so frequently dictated even the content of the courses their prospective students must be taught.[27]

If there was a certain debasement of academic standards in the undergraduate program, the same could not be said of professional and graduate schools, where the requirements grew progressively stiffer. In the nonprofessional graduate schools there was some overcrowding at the master's-degree level, primarily due to the demand for secondary school teachers with higher degrees, and many of the second degrees granted were of little consequence. But candidates for the Ph.D. in all the leading universities were obliged to complete a rigorous program, and to show some evidence of capacity to do original research. Indeed, it was this emphasis on research rather than teaching that came to characterize practically all the great American universities. Promotion and recognition for faculty members depended less upon teaching ability than upon scholarly attainments as revealed in professional publications. Universities thus tended to become primarily research centers, with the advancement of knowledge and the training of new research workers as their principal goals. The colleges, with smaller resources in libraries and laboratories, were less affected by this trend, and often experimented wisely with new methods of undergraduate teaching; similar efforts in the universities were by no means lacking,

[27] *Recent Social Trends,* I, 339–340; Abraham Flexner, *Universities: American, English, German* (New York, 1930), pp. 68–72; F. J. Kelly, *The American Arts College* (New York, 1925), pp. 61, 153–154; George P. Schmidt, *The Liberal Arts College* (New Brunswick, N.J., 1957), *passim;* Slosson, *Great Crusade,* pp. 329–344.

but the press of numbers, the necessity of providing pre-professional training, and the emphasis on graduate work all acted as deterrents. One of the most ambitious of these undertakings, the Experimental College at the University of Wisconsin, headed by Alexander Meiklejohn, disappeared after a few years, leaving little but irritations in its wake.[28]

Concentration on research in the universities may have left many undergraduates to shift for themselves (not of necessity a misfortune), but the results in terms of scholarship were impressive. Thanks mainly to the work of the university professors and to the training they had supplied for those engaged in industrial and governmental research, the long lag that had separated American from European scholarship began to shorten. In the physical sciences, for example, European scholars were still well in the lead, but Americans were beginning to catch up. Albert Einstein (who did not come to the United States until 1933) and other European theorists had developed new and revolutionary concepts with respect to matter, energy, and the nature of the universe. But Americans were soon supplying significant supplementary data, among them Robert A. Millikan of the California Institute of Technology, and Arthur H. Compton of the University of Chicago, who for their efforts won Nobel prizes in 1923 and 1927, respectively. Meantime practical-minded chemists made headway in the application of scientific data to such useful ends as the substitution of synthetic for natural fabrics, and the manufacture of numerous new commodities from wood, coal, and oil. American biologists, bacteriologists, and biochemists contributed actively to progress in medical science and public health. Scientific findings were put to such effective use within the United States as practically to eliminate such filth diseases as typhoid fever, and to reduce greatly the number of deaths from tuberculosis, diphtheria, and scarlet fever. Average life expectancy, only a little over forty-nine years in 1901, had risen by 1927 to over fifty-nine years. In the field of dentistry the United States probably led the world.[29]

American historians reached a high peak of productivity during the

[28] *Recent Social Trends,* I, 341–343; Flexner, *Universities,* pp. 73–76; P. A. Schilpp (ed.), *Higher Education Faces the Future* (New York, 1930), pp. 327–337; Alexander Meiklejohn, *The Experimental College* (New York, 1930), *passim.*
[29] *Recent Social Trends,* I, 150–151; Slosson, *Great Crusade,* pp. 377–387; Richard B. Morris (ed.), *Encyclopedia of American History* (New York, 1953), pp. 545, 685–687, 697.

1920's, and much of the work they did was of enduring merit. They displayed creditable originality in the expansion of their interests to include economic, social, and intellectual aspects of their subject, as well as the political, and particularly in dealing with the American past they brought to light much new data. Arthur M. Schlesinger, in *New Viewpoints in American History* (1922), analyzed admirably the changing interpretations of the times, while Charles A. Beard and Mary R. Beard, *The Rise of American Civilization* (2 vols., 1927), brought the new concepts together in an orderly and impressive synthesis. Comprehensive series, such as *The Chronicles of America* (1918–21), *The Pageant of America* (15 vols., 1926–29), *The American Secretaries of State* (10 vols., 1927–29), the *Dictionary of American Biography* (21 vols., 1928–44), and *A History of American Life* (13 vols., 1927–48), were all begun shortly after the First World War, and some of them were completed during the 1920's. But American historians by no means confined themselves to the history of their own country. Herbert E. Bolton of the University of California, and a whole school of writers who followed his precepts, emphasized Latin-American history, and pointed to the background of continental unity in justification of a national policy of hemispheric solidarity. American writers on the history of the Old World, meantime, stood well abreast of contemporary European historians and probably displayed wider research interests than could be credited to the historians of any other single nation.[30]

American scholarship in the other social studies was also full of promise. Economists sought valiantly to understand the industrial boom that surrounded them, and to make suitable recommendations for the guidance of both government and business. Great co-operative undertakings, amply financed both by the national government and by the various foundations, were the order of the day. One of them, for example, portrayed almost every aspect of *Recent Economic Changes in the United States* (2 vols., 1929), while another dealt with *Recent Social Trends in the United States* (2 vols., 1933). A sociological study, Robert S. and Helen M. Lynd, *Middletown* (1929), revealed intimately from on-the-spot investigations the thought life and behavior patterns of a typical small American city. In psychology the ideas of

[30] Oscar Handlin and others, *Harvard Guide to American History* (Cambridge, 1954), pp. 188, 209–210; Michael Kraus, *The Writing of American History* (Norman, Okla., 1953), pp. 286–287.

John B. Watson of Johns Hopkins University, whose *Behaviorism* (1925) emphasized environment rather than heredity as the principal explanation of human behavior, were in the ascendancy, although sophisticated amateurs were more fascinated with sexual theories derived from Sigmund Freud, and speculated endlessly on the subconscious, the libido, inferiority complexes, and psychoanalysis. Anthropology, partly because of the light that the folkways of primitive man could throw on the customs of civilized society, attracted increasing attention. Indeed, in almost every field of American scholarship there was evidence of vigorous life, with little to justify the pessimistic note so prominent in the literary output of the period.[31]

Even the business world, upon which critics of the time tended to center their fire, exhibited many redeeming traits. Undoubtedly businessmen were out for profits, but in the process of acquiring them they succeeded, far better than had ever been done before, in solving the problems of the production and distribution of whatever goods the public demanded. Their eager pursuit of wealth no doubt had much to do with the overexpansion that helped bring on the crisis of 1929, but at the same time they had accustomed the public to creature comforts that it would neither forget nor give up without a struggle. They might be, and often were, union-labor baiters, but many of them took a genuine interest in the men they hired, accepted willingly the shortening of working hours, sought earnestly to guarantee the health and safety of their employees, and made numerous experiments with "welfare capitalism," including educational, profit-sharing, and insurance schemes. They provided the dividends that kept the Rockefeller, Carnegie, and other foundations in funds, created other similar, if lesser, foundations, established organizations for research, such as the Brookings Institution and the Pollack Foundation for Economic Research, and gave direct support to innumerable educational, cultural, and artistic undertakings. Outstanding among the philanthropists of the time was John D. Rockefeller, Jr., builder of the Riverside Church in New York City, heavy subscriber to the Federal Council of Churches and other religious enterprises, unadvertised supporter of numerous

[31] F. A. Ogg, *Research in the Humanistic and Social Sciences* (New York, 1928), pp. 20–25; Lucille C. Birnbaum, "Behaviorism in the 1920's," *American Quarterly*, VII (Spring, 1955), 15–30; E. W. Burgess, "The Influence of Sigmund Freud upon Sociology in the United States," *American Journal of Sociology*, XLV (Nov., 1939), 356–374; Allen, *Only Yesterday*, pp. 98–99.

public park and conservation projects, and creator of Colonial Williamsburg, "the most ambitious restoration project ever undertaken in America." The fear of "tainted money" that had afflicted many Americans in the years when Bryanism rode high had all but disappeared. Men of great wealth were expected to recognize their social responsibilities, and usually did so. To the people generally this was, at least prior to 1929, reassuring. If business leadership rested in such generous hands, the capitalist system, whatever its faults, must somehow be more good than bad.[32]

[32] L. A. Boettiger, *Employee Welfare Work* (New York, 1923), pp. 1–12; Abraham Flexner, *Funds and Foundations* (New York, 1952), pp. 24–56, 113–124; R. B. Fosdick, *John D. Rockefeller, Jr.* (New York, 1956), pp. 220, 223, 272, 302.

CHAPTER 9

Agriculture vs. Industry

TO MOST American farmers Coolidge prosperity seemed a one-sided affair. Industry pushed forward from one triumph to another, but agriculture lagged far behind. Cities grew mightily in population and city land values soared, but farm families declined in numbers, and farm lands, when they could be sold at all, brought less and less. Nor were the farmers' woes due to inadequate production, for throughout the Harding-Coolidge period weather conditions were generally favorable and crops were good. But farm prices, whatever the yield, stayed down; and despite a considerable expansion of acreage under cultivation, farm income declined. The efforts of the Farm Bloc during the early 1920's to promote relief for agriculture had on the whole produced only disappointing results. Without the new legislation farm conditions might have become worse, but even with the favorable laws the times continued to be bad enough.[1]

To business-minded legislators of the 1920's one of the least offensive types of farm relief was the extension of new credits, valueless as such measures were to farmers who had nothing to pledge by way of security. Among such provisions the most elaborate was the Agricultural Credits Act of 1923. Congress passed this measure mainly to satisfy the demands of the livestock farmers, who complained that neither the short-term loans available under Federal Reserve System policies nor the long-term loans of the Federal Land Banks met their needs. What

[1] Theodore Saloutos and John D. Hicks, *Agricultural Discontent in the Middle West, 1900–1939* (Madison, Wis., 1951), pp. 324–335; Murray R. Benedict, *Farm Policies of the United States, 1790–1950* (New York, 1953), pp. 182–187.

they wanted was credit for from six months to three years, and this the
new law undertook to provide by setting up twelve intermediate credit
banks, one in each Federal Reserve District, all under the control of
the Federal Farm Loan Board. Capital stock up to $5 million for each
bank was to be subscribed by the Secretary of the Treasury. While the
new banks might not make loans directly to the farmers, but only to
co-operative associations which would act as intermediaries, funds were
obtainable indirectly for "any agricultural purpose or for raising,
breeding, fattening or marketing livestock." The law also provided for
privately operated National Agricultural Credit Associations, but only
three such loan agencies were formed, and two of them were soon
liquidated. It was the government owned, operated, and controlled
system that endured. Undoubtedly the newly devised credits served a
useful purpose, but they met only a limited need, and did little toward
rescuing American agriculture as a whole from the ills that beset it.[2]

Probably the most significant of the Farm Bloc measures was the
Capper-Volstead Act of 1922, sometimes called the "Magna Charta of
Co-operative Marketing," which exempted agricultural co-operatives
from prosecution under the antitrust laws and defined the conditions
under which they might engage in interstate commerce. This legislation
marked a milestone in the bitter struggle of farmer co-operatives for
the right to compete on equal terms with private dealers. The co-
operative movement had a long background both in the United States
and abroad, but by the 1920's it had won the support of most of the
American farmer organizations, and had achieved the experience
necessary to make co-operative ventures less hazardous. For a co-operative to succeed, its members must agree to sell through it exclusively,
and it must be able to enforce these agreements, not an easy matter
considering the ingrained individualism of the American farmer. If a
co-operative could control a sufficiently large proportion of any given
product, it could practically dictate the prices at which it would sell,
as the California Fruit Growers Association learned to do. But even
when it represented only a small proportion of the total output, it could
save money for its members on storage, handling, and commissions.
Prominent in the leadership of the co-operative movement was Aaron

[2] Saloutos and Hicks, *Agricultural Discontent*, pp. 339–340; Claude L. Ben-
ner, *The Federal Intermediate Credit System* (New York, 1926), pp. 103–123;
Frieda Baird and Claude L. Benner, *Ten Years of Federal Intermediate Credits*
(Washington, 1933), pp. 67–82.

Sapiro, a California lawyer who after 1923 served as general council of the American Farm Bureau Federation. Sapiro had helped organize co-operatives in the Middle West and the South, as well as in the Far West, and had drafted a model co-operative measure that became the basis for the Kentucky Co-operative Act of 1922, the first of many such laws on the subject. The Capper-Volstead Act was both a fitting climax to Sapiro's program, and a further recognition of the legitimacy and respectability of co-operative marketing.[3]

No doubt the threat of a worse alternative had much to do with the change of attitude toward co-operatives on the part of American businessmen and their political representatives. If the farmer could not somehow help himself, he would almost for a certainty turn to the government for direct assistance through some such price-fixing scheme as had been in force during the war. Senator Norris had something of the sort in mind when he urged Congress to create a gigantic government-owned corporation with authority to build warehouses and buy, sell, and export farm products at will. Conservative opinion held that such socialistic measures must be headed off at all costs. Thanks to this greater danger, therefore, it was possible to rally much conservative support for the cause of co-operative marketing; even President Coolidge endorsed it warmly, and in 1926 Congress went so far as to set up a Division of Co-operative Marketing in the Bureau of Agricultural Economics.[4]

All this sympathy for institutions that the defenders of free enterprise had once regarded as anathema served strikingly to emphasize the deplorable plight into which agriculture had fallen. Nor were agricultural economists long in pointing out the basic problem that neither rural credits nor co-operative marketing nor any other of the attempted measures could hope to solve. The fundamental trouble with American agriculture was that, especially in wheat and cotton, and to a considerable extent in other commodities also, the nation produced far more than the American market could absorb. Each year, therefore,

[3] Saloutos and Hicks, *Agricultural Discontent*, pp. 275–276, 286–320, 334; Ward W. Fetrow, *Cooperative Marketing of Agricultural Products*, Farm Credit Administration, Cooperative Division, Bulletin No. 3 (Washington, 1936), pp. 1–5; Edwin A. Nourse, *Government in Relation to Agriculture* (Washington, 1940), pp. 884–889.

[4] Saloutos and Hicks, *Agricultural Discontent*, pp. 288, 385; Federal Farm Board, *Cooperative Marketing of Farm Products*, Bulletin No. 10 (Washington, 1932), pp. 20–23.

there was an exportable surplus that must be offered for sale on the world market at whatever price it would bring. Not only in the United States, but elsewhere in the world also, agricultural production during the 1920's was high, so that the market was normally glutted and prices were correspondingly low. In Liverpool, England, for example, the great central market for wheat, grain flowed in from all over the world—from Canada, Australia, Argentina, and other countries, as well as from the United States. And the price that wheat brought in Liverpool set the price of wheat throughout the world. What was true of wheat was also true in varying degrees of many other farm commodities. If the United States produced less of any given item than it consumed, then the tariff would apply and raise the American price above the world price correspondingly. But if the United States produced more of anything than it consumed, the price that the exportable surplus would bring would set the price both at home and abroad.[5]

American farmers found it difficult to follow this line of reasoning, for they knew that American manufacturers profited greatly from the protective tariff. Politicians who knew better, or should have known better, easily persuaded the farmers that they were doing something for agriculture when they raised such tariff rates as those on wheat and meat. If an increase in the tariff on pig iron and aluminum helped the prices of those products, why should not an increase in the tariff on wheat and meat do a similar service for them? What the farmers failed to realize was that manufacturers could control production, whereas farmers could not. The prudent manufacturer, well advised by his own experience and the trade association to which he belonged, took care ordinarily not to overproduce. He could, if necessary, lay off men and idle his machinery. But not so the farmers, who operated strictly as individuals and traditionally produced all they could. Lower prices, indeed, tempted them to produce more each succeeding year than the last, for only by so doing could they hope to maintain a constant level of income.[6]

From the early 1920's onward the exportable surplus received in-

[5] Frederic L. Paxson, "The Agricultural Surplus: A Problem in History," *Agricultural History,* VI (1932), 51–58; Chester C. Davis, "The Development of Agricultural Policy Since the End of the World War," in Yearbook of Agriculture, 1940 (Washington, 1940), pp. 297–306.

[6] James H. Shideler, *Farm Crisis, 1921–1923* (Berkeley, Calif., 1957), pp. 186–187; "Uncle Sam's Bumper Wheat Crop," *Literary Digest,* XCIX (Dec. 8, 1928), 10–11; Benedict, *Farm Policies,* pp. 202–205.

creasingly careful attention as the key to the farmers' ills. How could the government do for the farmers the equivalent of what it was doing through the protective tariff for the manufacturers? One practice, not uncommon among manufacturers, seemed to give a clue to the answer. This was their habit of "dumping" abroad, at whatever price it would bring, any excess they produced above what the American market could consume. Sometimes, thanks to the generosity of the protective tariff rates, the goods so dumped could be sold at a lower price abroad than in the United States, and still bring a profit. Sometimes, however, they might be sold at a loss, but at least they were disposed of, and the losses abroad were offset by the profits from the protected price at home. Why could the American farmer not contrive somehow to do the same thing? The trouble, of course, came from the difficulty in getting multitudes of farmers to work together as a unit. Probably only a governmental agency could handle such an assignment, and conservatives of both parties were dead set against putting the government into business in any way.[7]

Credit for developing a plan that would give agriculture real equality with industry in the marketing of farm produce belongs principally to George N. Peek, chief executive of the Moline Illinois Plow Company, who had served under Bernard Baruch in the War Industries Board, and knew what power the government could exercise if it chose. Peek's motivation was clear—"You can't sell a plow to a busted customer," he complained. He discussed his ideas with General Hugh S. Johnson, whom he had known in Washington and had brought to Moline as an associate. Together they worked out the details of a two-price system for agricultural commodities—a high domestic price and a low foreign price, the American price to bear the same ratio toward other commodity prices that it had borne toward these same commodities in the years before 1914. This was the original "parity" principle. The plan was of less interest to the cotton growers, who sold so large a proportion of their produce abroad that the American price was to them somewhat inconsequential, than to the wheat and meat producers of the West and Middle West, whose sales at home far exceeded their sales abroad. It was natural, therefore, that two members of Congress from the most interested sections, Senator Charles L. McNary of Oregon and Repre-

[7] Davis, "Development of Agricultural Policy," pp. 307–312; Garet Garrett, "Industry, Agriculture & Co.," *Saturday Evening Post,* CXCIX (Apr. 16, 1927), 6–7; "The Fourth Age of Agriculture," *ibid.* (Apr. 30, 1927), 12–13.

sentative Gilbert N. Haugen of Iowa, should eventually give their names to a bill embodying the Peek-Johnson proposals.[8]

The first McNary-Haugen bill was presented to Congress in 1924. It listed eight basic commodities—wheat, flour, corn, cotton, wool, cattle, sheep, and swine (together with any food-stuffs derived from the last three)—as the objectives of its provisions. The Secretaries of Agriculture and of Labor should compute the ratio price on each farm product, using for purposes of comparison an all-commodity average for the years 1905–14 to be obtained from the Bureau of Labor Statistics. An Agricultural Export Corporation, consisting of the Secretary of Agriculture and four other members to be appointed by the President, would be authorized to buy on the American market at the ratio price and to sell on the world market at whatever price it could get. To cover the loss involved, farmers were to be charged an equalization fee, or tax, on every bushel of wheat or other item that they sold. But the fees so charged, it was assumed, would be far less than the benefits obtained from the high domestic prices. Effectively publicized by Peek and Johnson, whose talents along this line were considerable, and accepted by the Secretary of Agriculture, Henry C. Wallace, the bill won much support in the Northwest, but lack of interest in the South led to the elimination of cotton as one of the items involved, while except for Wallace the weight of the administration was thrown against it. The measure suffered the first of many defeats on June 3, 1924, when a combination of eastern Republicans and southern Democrats voted it down in the House, but its protagonists were persistent, and farm sentiment in favor of it grew. Also, as time went on, many changes went into the bill to satisfy the demands of particular groups and individuals.[9]

When finally passed by Congress in 1927, the McNary-Haugen bill varied markedly from the original measure. As introduced, it listed only five basic commodities, cotton, wheat, corn, rice, and hogs. Cotton was back in on terms satisfactory to southern congressmen, who were not averse to aid in holding operations, and during the Senate debate tobacco also was added. A Federal Farm Board of twelve members, one from each Federal Land Bank District, was to administer the measure and, out of deference to the strong position attained by co-operatives,

[8] Gilbert C. Fite, *George N. Peek and the Fight for Farm Parity* (Norman, Okla., 1954), pp. 38–58.

[9] *Ibid.*, pp. 59–94.

was to work through them in the orderly disposal of surplus crops—
the Federal Farm Board might not itself buy farm products directly.
There was no reference whatever to price fixing, but the provisions for
a stabilization fund to absorb losses and the retention of the equalization fee made it clear that the two-price system was still contemplated. Certainly the Board would be free to raise domestic prices to
the extent of the tariff Congress had placed on each individual item.
The equalization fee, however, was not to be assessed directly on
producers, but rather on the transportation, processing, or sale of a
given commodity. These and other provisions made the revised Mc-
Nary-Haugen bill a far cry from what Peek and Johnson had first
proposed, but it was so constructed as to obtain the votes necessary for
passage. Even so, it failed to win the approval of President Coolidge,
who returned it to Congress with a scathing veto message. Nothing
daunted, the farm leaders pushed another McNary-Haugen bill
through Congress the following year, with modifications designed to
meet the President's objections, but still with the equalization fee.
For their pains they got only another veto, even sharper than the first,
and in neither case could they find the necessary votes to override
the veto.[10]

However it might be phrased, the McNary-Haugen bill as Coolidge
saw it, asked government to do what government had no right to do.
It called for price fixing, for an improper delegation of the taxing
power, and for the creation of a vast and cumbersome bureaucracy.
It was economically unsound, for the higher prices it contemplated
would lead to greater overproduction and larger surpluses, while the
disposal of American goods abroad at cut-rate figures would arouse
foreign resentment and promote retaliation. The government, Coolidge
thought, might legitimately help the farmers to help themselves. It
might properly lend money to co-operatives and encourage the curtailment of production. But beyond this it should not go. The President,
like his Secretary of the Treasury and his Secretary of Commerce, was
in reality a devoted partisan of industry. He saw nothing wrong with a
protective tariff—a tax designed specifically to help industry—but he
found everything wrong with the equalization fee—a tax designed to
fit the needs of agriculture. No doubt he was opposed on principle, as

[10] *Ibid.*, pp. 173–180, 190–193; Wm. R. Sutherland (ed.), *A Debate Handbook on the McNary-Haugen Agricultural Surplus Control Act* (Lexington, Ky.,
1927), pp. 43–66.

were most industrialists, to doing anything that would raise the prices of the raw materials industry had to buy, or that would raise the price of labor by increasing the cost of living. Coolidge prosperity was merely another name for industrial prosperity, and whatever might imperil that prosperity was wrong.[11]

It seems likely that Coolidge was right in objecting to the McNary-Haugen bill on economic grounds. The raising of farm prices would undoubtedly have resulted in increased agricultural production and steadily mounting surpluses. Probably also the proposed program of overseas sales would have resulted in the adoption of anti-dumping laws and other trade restrictions by the foreign nations involved. Furthermore, the foreign demand for American wheat, beef, and pork was already declining; there was no certainty whatever that foreign nations could absorb all the excess produce the United States could have offered. And, in addition, the American protective tariff stood in the way; the United States could not indefinitely sell American farm products, or anything else, to foreign nations if it continued to erect such formidable obstacles against the acceptance of foreign goods in return. On the other hand, the McNary-Haugen program need not have been final; changes and adaptations—acreage restrictions, for example—could have been made as experience directed. Its passage would have shown a determination by the Coolidge administration to do something in aid of agriculture, whereas the President's vetoes revealed instead, as Tugwell pointed out, "a stubborn determination to do nothing."[12]

Despite the failure of the McNary-Haugen bill to become law, it concentrated attention on the problem of agriculture and paved the way for later legislation on the subject. The idea of "parity prices" lived on. The prolonged struggle also drew the battle lines more clearly than before between the interests of agriculture and of industry. No one need now doubt where Coolidge stood. As one not very grammatical farm columnist pointed out, with reference to his 1927 veto:

On the day of his courageous act, he issued a proclamation increasing the tariff on pig iron 50 percent. Who says that was not an exhibition of intrepidity, when he signed it—as all the world must know—that by the signing

[11] Fite, *Peek and the Fight for Farm Parity*, pp. 193–196.
[12] *Ibid.*, pp. 196–202; Sutherland, *Debate Handbook*, pp. 298–343; John D. Black, *Agricultural Reform in the United States* (New York, 1929), pp. 232–254.

he increased the cost of every binder, every threshing machine, every tractor and farm implement; that it increased the cost of locomotives, rails, and steel cars and thus increased the freight rates to the farmer.

The next step of the farm leaders was obvious. With the election of 1928 approaching, they must attempt to influence the nomination of candidates and the adoption of platforms favorable to their cause.[13]

That Coolidge could have had the Republican nomination again if he had wanted to work for it seemed obvious, but on August 2, 1927, he had unexpectedly announced, during his summer vacation in the Black Hills of South Dakota, that he did "not choose to run for President in nineteen twenty-eight." Perhaps he really meant to take himself out of the race; perhaps he only meant that he would not personally do anything to obtain the Republican nomination. He never clarified his enigmatic statement. But other aspirants, including his Secretary of Commerce, Herbert Hoover, interpreted his words to mean complete withdrawal, and promptly became candidates. The McNary-Haugenites knew that Hoover was, as Peek put it, the "arch-enemy of a square deal for agriculture," no better, from their point of view, than Coolidge, and possibly worse. Despite an abortive interest in Norris of Nebraska, they tended, under Peek's influence, to throw their support to Frank O. Lowden of Illinois, who came out strongly for surplus-control legislation. Despite a rash of lesser contenders, it was apparent almost from the start that the decision lay between Hoover and Lowden. Even so, the contest was one-sided. Long before the Republican convention met on June 12 in Kansas City, Hoover was well in the lead, and the last minute support he received from "Boss" Vare and Secretary Mellon of Pennsylvania assured his triumph. In desperation a delegation of several hundred midwestern farmers descended on the convention city chanting "We don't want Hoover"; but when the Convention voted down a minority attempt to place a McNary-Haugen plank in its platform, Lowden knew that he was finished and withdrew. The nomination of Hoover followed on the first ballot. For Vice-President, as a sop to the outraged farmers, the convention chose Senator Curtis, once a leader of the Farm Bloc.[14]

[13] Saloutos and Hicks, *Agricultural Discontent,* pp. 399–402; Benedict, *Farm Policies,* pp. 227–238.
[14] Fite, *Peek and the Fight for Farm Parity,* pp. 203–206; Malcolm Moos, *The Republicans; A History of Their Party* (New York, 1956), pp. 371–374; William T. Hutchinson, *Lowden of Illinois* (2 vols., Chicago, 1957), II, 588–601.

The selection of Hoover well reflected the single-interest domination under which the Republican party had fallen. The leaders of business and industry were no longer content to have a politician in the White House who would do their bidding; they wanted a businessman as President, one who would instinctively reflect their every prejudice. In Hoover they had their ideal candidate, and they spent lavishly to promote his interests. Among the professional politicians there was little real enthusiasm for Hoover, an outsider who had "muscled in" on the political game, but a majority of the delegates recognized their masters' voice, and acted as they felt they must. Even if the convention had nominated Lowden, it would have chosen an ultraconservative businessman whose sole deviation consisted of having a heart for the farmer, but the Lowden rejection was emphatic. The platform on which Hoover was nominated was similarly revealing. It sang the praises of Coolidge, claimed Republican credit for the prosperous times, lauded the protective tariff, and was hazy on labor, although admitting, out of deference to the labor vote, that the use of the injunction in labor disputes might have been abused. Unwilling in any way to offend the drys, it also favored the enforcement of the prohibition amendment, although Republican exertions to that end had been minimal. As for agriculture, it pledged the Republican party to create "a Federal farm board clothed with the necessary powers to promote the establishment of a farm-marketing system of farmer owned and controlled stabilization corporations or associations to prevent and control surpluses through orderly distribution." But it was adamant in its opposition to any program that would involve "putting the government into business," and the convention had specifically gone on record as opposed to the equalization fee. When Robert M. La Follette, Jr., submitted a substitute platform reflecting Progressive views, he was amiably, but overwhelmingly, voted down.[15]

Rebuffed at Kansas City, the McNary-Haugenites turned their eyes toward Houston, Texas, where the Democrats were to meet, June 26. But forces were at work within the Democratic party that in the end

[15] Walter Johnson, *William Allen White's America* (New York, 1947), pp. 401–405; *Official Report of the Proceedings of the Nineteenth Republican National Convention, 1928* (New York, 1928), pp. 113–131, 143; James E. Watson, *As I Knew Them; Memoirs of James E. Watson* (Indianapolis, 1936), pp. 254–259; R. V. Peel and Thomas C. Donnelly, *The 1928 Campaign; An Analysis* (New York, 1931), pp. 21–30.

were to make impossible any clear-cut referendum on relief for agriculture. It was almost as certain that the Democrats would nominate Alfred E. Smith as it had been that the Republicans would nominate Hoover, although the reasons were vastly different and went back at least as far as the storm-tossed Madison Square Garden convention of 1924. From that time forward the city democracies were obsessed by the determination to nominate their hero, Smith, not merely because they liked him, but principally as a means of demonstrating that the city voters must be recognized as a significant part of the Democratic party. They were tired of being passed over, and with McAdoo inactive and still smeared with oil they were presenting as their candidate the only outstanding Democratic national leader in sight. A belated effort by McAdoo to arouse interest in Senator Walsh of Montana won little support; Smith must have his chance if the city machines were to remain loyal to the party. That many Democrats would never vote for Smith was obvious, but the chance had to be taken; in the opinion of Franklin D. Roosevelt, Smith had "such a blind hero-worshipping personal following . . . that failure to nominate him would alienate from the party for a long time a tremendous vote in the eastern and middle western states." Among rural and southern Democrats there was even less enthusiasm for Smith at Houston than among Farmer-minded Republicans for Hoover at Kansas City. But in each case there was in reality no chance to restrain the majority.[16]

So the Democrats took Smith, a city-bred, Tammany Hall Roman Catholic and a thoroughgoing wet. To balance the ticket they nominated for Vice-President Senator Joseph T. Robinson of Arkansas, a Protestant from a state with no large cities and a thoroughgoing dry. In their platform they attempted to appeal to every element discontented with Republican rule. They denounced Republican corruption under Harding; they promised a tariff less tinctured with favoritism; they advocated collective bargaining for labor and greater restrictions on the use of the injunction in labor disputes; they favored retaining for the federal and state governments "absolute and exclusive sovereignty and control" over water-power resources; they demanded strict enforcement of the antitrust laws; they condemned the lack of a foreign

[16] E. A. Moore, *A Catholic Runs for President* (New York, 1956), pp. 103–105; Carroll Kilpatrick (ed.), *Roosevelt and Daniels, A Friendship in Politics* (Chapel Hill, N.C., 1952), pp. 86–90; Roosevelt to Daniels, June 23, 1927, Daniels Papers, Box 15, Library of Congress, Manuscripts Division.

policy on the part of the Republicans, urged noninterference in the internal affairs of other nations, including those of Latin America, and promised independence to the Philippines. On the subject of prohibition they pledged themselves to make an "honest effort" to enforce the Eighteenth Amendment, although Smith in his acceptance message to the convention demanded "fundamental changes in the present provisions for prohibition"—in other words, repeal. When it came to McNary-Haugenism, the Democrats adopted a plank prepared by Chester Davis, one of Peek's closest collaborators. If the Democratic stand on the subject was unsatisfactory, then, said Davis, "it is because we do not know how to use the English language." While the words "equalization fee" were studiously avoided, charges against "marketed units of the crop whose producers are benefited" were to pay for the disposal of farm surpluses.[17]

On the basis of the platforms, the way lay open for a battle of principle in the campaign, with the Democrats favoring McNary-Haugenism and the Republicans opposing it. But the obstacles that prevented the centering of attention on the farm issue were far greater than Peek, Davis, and their circle had anticipated. Smith himself proved to be difficult to nail down, probably because there was nothing in his experience to enable him to understand fully the farm problem. He told Peek flatly that he favored the principle of the equalization fee, but his later statements on the subject were vague and conflicting; while Peek never lost faith in Smith, many other McNary-Haugenites were filled with doubts. Moreover, in spite of the fact that both Hoover and Smith in their acceptance speeches devoted more attention to the farm issue than to any other, the debate on the farmer's ills ultimately became secondary to subjects that in the eyes of the public were far more important, principally (1) Smith's urban background, (2) his religion, and (3) his stand on prohibition. These, not the farm problem, proved to be the "paramount" issues of the campaign.[18]

It was little short of ironic that Smith should have been cast in the role of the farmer's champion, for in his life and person he reflected

[17] *Official Report of the Proceedings of the Democratic National Convention, 1928* (Indianapolis, 1928), pp. 186–200; Peel and Donnelly, *The 1928 Campaign,* pp. 9–15, 30–35; Fite, *Peek and the Fight for Farm Parity,* p. 207.

[18] *Ibid.,* pp. 208–211; *Republican Campaign Text-Book, 1928* (Chicago, 1928), pp. 22–26; *The Campaign Book of the Democratic Party, 1928* (New York, 1928), pp. 41–44; Peel and Donnelly, *The 1928 Campaign,* p. 66.

with complete accuracy the city, not the country. Born December 30, 1873, in the East Side tenement district of New York, of Irish-immigrant descent, he had worked his way up from the city sidewalks rather than from the country cornfields. He knew about poverty from experience as well as from observation, but it was the poverty of urban, industrial, sometimes hungry America that he had met at first hand, not the poverty of the economically distressed but usually well-fed countryside. He attended parochial school, but went to work at years earlier than college age because his family needed the money, and he never went to college. Blessed with a flair for public speaking and dramatics, he gravitated readily into politics by way of Tammany Hall, the only approach available to him if he wished that kind of career. For years a mere subpoena server, he eventually was rewarded by being nominated and elected to the state assembly. Bewildered at first by the complexities of law and government, he learned easily and acquitted himself well. Always loyal to the machine, he played the game squarely, according to the rules he knew, albeit with a jealous eye for the welfare of the working class from which he had sprung.

Smith's assembly service won him other rewards, for the machine was just to those who served it well. He became Sheriff of New York County for two years, a position made lucrative by fees, the only such political plum he ever held. Next he became president of the Board of Aldermen in New York City, where he served only one year of the four years' term to which he had been chosen; for in 1918 he was nominated and elected governor of the state, an office he retained during eight of the next ten years—his only defeat for re-election was in the Harding landslide of 1920. During these years he revealed a positive genius for political administration. He was liberal-minded, always the friend of the underprivileged, and he knew how to get things done even when he had to deal with a dominantly Republican legislature. Eminent Republicans spoke well of him. According to Charles Evans Hughes, Smith was "an expert in government" and "a master in the science of politics," who if he had lived in England would have been elevated to the peerage. "There is not in American life today," wrote William Allen White, the Republican sage of Emporia, Kansas, "a clearer, stronger, more accurately working brain in any man's head than Al Smith's brain." But, White might have added, it was a city man's brain and its judgments were conditioned by a city man's experience.

How could such a man represent the forever-embattled farmers of America?[19]

Could rural America, even if Smith's election meant better times for the farmers, vote for a man of his background for President? For one thing, there was a long-standing feud between city and country. City dwellers tended to look down on "country bumpkins" and to regard city achievements as in every way superior to anything the country had ever done, while for rural America the "agrarian myth" remained one of the strongest of realities. Americans who lived on the farms or in the country towns not only believed in their way of life as basic to the economic health of the country but they also had a deep suspicion that the city was fully as bad as the country was good. In the city vice was triumphant; it was here that farm boys and girls went wrong. City manipulators sucked the life blood out of the country; they bought at minimum prices what the farmer had to sell, and sold him in return at maximum prices what he had to buy. In the cities the law of the land was flouted, prohibition in particular; here gangsters and racketeers went unpunished, and even enjoyed the protection of the police. Immigrants from the Old World, including many criminals whose un-American names appeared every day in the press, had crowded into the cities, bringing with them foreign ways and subversive ideas—"50 per cent" Americans. One could even quote Scripture on the subject. Had not Jesus "beheld the city, and wept over it"?[20]

Then, too, there was the matter of Smith's religion. Stronger even than the agrarian myth in America was the Protestant myth. According to it the United States always had been and must forever remain a dominantly Protestant country. Never before Smith's time had a Roman Catholic seriously sought a presidential nomination. Anti-Catholic prejudice was an old American heritage that dated back to colonial times and had flared up strongly again with each major accretion of Catholic immigrants. To most Americans religious prejudice was principally a matter of feeling rather than of reason, but with

[19] Oscar Handlin, *Al Smith and his America* (New York, 1958), pp. 3–111; Norman Hapgood and Henry Moskowitz, *Up From the City Streets* (New York, 1927), pp. 27, 55–99, 165–217; *Campaign Book of the Democratic Party, 1928,* p. 28.

[20] Richard Hofstadter, "Myth of the Happy Yeoman," *American Heritage,* VII (Apr., 1956), 43–53; Dumas Malone, *Jefferson the Virginian* (Boston, 1948), p. 384; Paxton Hibben, *The Peerless Leader, William Jennings Bryan* (New York, 1929), pp. 311–318; Luke 19:41.

Smith's candidacy some intelligent questions began to be raised. Would a Catholic President of the United States owe a double allegiance, to a foreign potentate, the Pope of Rome, as well as to the American nation? Would he be free to support such fundamental American principles as the equality of all religions before the law, the separation of Church and State, and the American system of free public schools? Debate on these subjects reached a high plane in two *Atlantic Monthly* articles of 1927, one contributed by Smith himself, who asserted eloquently that his church loyalty left him free from any of the restraints alleged or implied and denounced with fervor the injection of the religious issue into politics. But only those were convinced who wished to be convinced, and Smith's nomination brought out anew every scurrilous anti-Catholic charge that had ever been made. Particularly in the South, where Protestantism was still militant, Smith's religion cost him many votes.[21]

Smith's uncompromising opposition to prohibition likewise evoked an intense emotional reaction. He was known to be a wet, but his virtual repudiation of the dry plank in his party's platform, made at the very close of the Democratic convention when perhaps a third of the delegates had gone home, elicited much angry reproach. The influential southern Methodist Bishop, James Cannon, Jr., of Virginia, one of Smith's most effective critics, claimed that if Smith's message had come earlier, the southern delegates would have bolted the convention and nominated a dry. Among the most convinced of the drys were many of the very farmers who, for economic reasons, might well have turned their votes to Smith, but much as they might covet government assistance to agriculture, if they could get help only by voting a wet into office, they would do without it. Furthermore, there was a plausible alternative. The Republican platform and the Republican candidate also made the farmers fine promises, while at the same time standing firm on prohibition. Had not Hoover defined prohibition as "a great social and economic experiment, noble in motive and far-reaching in purpose," whereas Smith had branded it as "entirely un-

[21] Moore, *A Catholic Runs for President*, pp. 15–19; Frank Graham, *Al Smith, American* (New York, 1945), pp. 195–201; Charles C. Marshall, "An Open Letter to the Honorable Alfred E. Smith," *Atlantic Monthly*, CXXXIV (Apr., 1927), 540–549; Alfred E. Smith, "Catholic and Patriot: Governor Smith Replies," *ibid.* (May, 1927), pp. 721–728; Michael Williams, *The Shadow of the Pope* (New York, 1932), pp. 183–205.

satisfactory to the great mass of our peoples" and had called outright for repeal?[22]

In striking contrast with Smith, Herbert Hoover possessed most of the qualifications for the Presidency that tradition-bound Americans had come to expect. He was born August 10, 1874, in West Branch, Iowa, a tiny midwestern country town. His parents and near relatives were devout Quakers, and he was reared in the ancestral faith. Left an orphan at an early age, he lived first with an uncle in Iowa, then with another uncle in Oregon. As a boy he conceived the idea of becoming a mining engineer, and with that aim in view enrolled at Stanford University in 1891, its first year, instead of at Earlham College, the Quaker institution his relatives had expected him to attend. Through an interested professor he obtained summer work with the United States Geological Survey that paid his way through college. Soon after graduation he got a start with a prominent San Francisco engineer, and his ability did the rest. All over the world—in Australia, China, Africa, Central and South America, Russia, and elsewhere—he demonstrated his talents, amassing in the process a considerable fortune. In London, when the First World War broke out, Wilson first made him chairman of the Committee for the Relief of Belgium, then later called him back to the United States to head the Food Administration. After the war, he served under Harding and Coolidge as Secretary of Commerce, and outshone them both. His life was the almost perfect embodiment of the American dream—the poor boy from the country who had made good in a big way. That he had acquired in the process the industrialists' point of view was obvious. But in 1928 the American businessman was at the peak of his eminence, and for a majority of Americans Hoover's economic principles were in no sense a disqualification. Even the farmers asked only to share the same prosperity that had come to business. Toward this goal Hoover promised to show them the way.[23]

The campaign of 1928 was therefore not to be the referendum on

[22] Virginius Dabney, *Dry Messiah; The Life of Bishop Cannon* (New York, 1949), pp. 173–189; Peel and Donnelly, *The 1928 Campaign,* p. 35; *Republican Campaign Text-Book, 1928,* p. 28.

[23] Richard Hofstadter, *The American Political Tradition* (New York, 1948), pp. 279–295; Robert S. Allen and Drew Pearson, *The Washington Merry-Go-Round* (New York, 1931), pp. 51–77; F. Wilson Smith, "Herbert Hoover's American Individualism in the History of American Thought," unpublished Master's Thesis, University of California, Berkeley, 1947.

McNary-Haugenism that Peek had envisaged. Most Republican politicians, even such an outspoken critic of Hoover as Senator Peter Norbeck of South Dakota, supported the Republican ticket. The only notable exception was Senator Norris of Nebraska, who found Smith's record on the power issue more to his liking than Hoover's. Nor, in spite of Norris's stand, were the issues weighted on the Republican side primarily in favor of industry and on the Democratic side primarily in favor of agriculture. Actually, Smith's economic views did not differ markedly from Hoover's. As time would soon demonstrate, he was not a serious critic of favoritism toward business, and during the campaign he did all he could to assure businessmen that neither he nor his party wished to offend them in any way.

He chose as his campaign manager John J. Raskob of General Motors, a businessman who had supported Coolidge in 1924 and favored Smith primarily because he, like Raskob, was a Roman Catholic and a wet. Smith hoped that his selection of Raskob would cut into the support business would naturally give Hoover, but it served mainly to offend the drys still further, and to raise doubts in the minds of liberals, a few of whom turned in despair to the Socialist candidate, Norman Thomas. Smith's stand on the tariff was also compromising. This was due partly to his friendliness to McNary-Haugenism, which was designed, as it was freely asserted, to get the farmer "up on stilts" alongside the manufacturer, but it was also due partly to the deference Smith had for big business as such. Actually a few prominent industrialists followed Raskob's example and lined up for Smith; they had every reason to believe that his election would not trouble them in the least. Also, Smith's pro-business attitude may have accounted for the virtual neutrality of the American Federation of Labor in the campaign.[24]

Smith ran for President, as he had run for governor, by taking his case directly to the people. At Omaha he endorsed the McNary-Haugen program of farm relief, including the equalization fee, if no better means of implementing it could be found. At Oklahoma City he defended the right of a Catholic to seek the Presidency, and denounced

[24] Gilbert C. Fite, *Peter Norbeck: Prairie Statesman* (Columbia, Mo., 1948), pp. 131–135; Karl Schriftgiesser, *This Was Normalcy* (Boston, 1948), pp. 250–262; Samuel G. Blythe, "The Fundamentals of the Campaign," *Saturday Evening Post*, CCI (Sept. 15, 1928), 6–7; Handlin, *Al Smith and His America*, pp. 116–129; Peel and Donnelly, *The 1928 Campaign*, pp. 78–79.

the spirit of intolerance that his candidacy had awakened. At Denver he discussed the water-power question, and held that the government, either national or state, must own both the principal power sites and the generating plants; his failure to insist on government distribution of power was a disappointment to many liberals. At Helena he attacked the Republican party's unconcern with the conservation of national resources, and its record on oil leases. At Louisville he set forth his views on the tariff, virtually abandoning the traditional Democratic attitude of a tariff for revenue only in favor of minimum protective duties. At Milwaukee and Philadelphia he denounced prohibition for its infringement of personal liberty and its promotion of lawlessness.[25]

Hoover's campaign was much less spectacular, with fewer speeches and more attention to the defense of American individualism in theory and practice. Hoover, as it turned out, had become the high priest and chief theologian of conservative Republicanism, a sort of St. Thomas Aquinas who reconciled the party's principles and stated them admirably. The prosperity of the time, he claimed, was due to the consistent way in which the Republican party had stood steadfastly by the ideal of free enterprise. "We in America today are nearer to the final triumph over poverty than ever before in the history of any land. The poorhouse is vanishing from among us. We have not reached the goal, but, given a chance to go forward with the policies of the last eight years, we shall soon with the help of God be in sight of the day when poverty will be banished from this nation."

Running through all of Hoover's addresses was a consistent defense of what he called "the American system." He probably did not invent the term "rugged individualism," but it came correctly to be closely associated with his name. Anything savoring of governmental participation in business he viewed with the gravest alarm, and he branded the somewhat less hard-boiled policies advocated by his Democratic opponent as sheer socialism. Throughout the campaign he avoided mentioning Smith's name, and assumed that there could be only one result, his own election.[26]

[25] Alfred E. Smith, *Campaign Addresses* (Washington, 1929); "Smith's Bid for the Farm Vote," *Literary Digest*, XCIX (Oct. 6, 1928), 5–7; "Smith's Conversion to Protectionism," *ibid.* (Oct. 27, 1928), pp. 7–9; James Murphy, "His Faith Is Slipping," *The Nation*, CXXVII (Sept. 24, 1928), 294–295.

[26] Herbert Hoover, *Memoirs* (New York, 1952), II, 197–209, and *The New Day; Campaign Speeches of Herbert Hoover, 1928* (Stanford, Calif., 1928), p. 16 and *passim*.

He was right, but the issues as stated and the issues in fact were by no means identical. Thanks in part to the radio, personalities came into the campaign to a remarkable degree. Smith in person was an eloquent public speaker who moved his audiences, but he could not stand still before a stationary microphone, the only kind then available, and for his radio listeners the effect was sometimes appalling. Moreover he talked with an exaggerated East Side New York accent that western and southern Americans could not always understand. Hoover, in contrast, was a stodgy public speaker who normally disappointed his immediate hearers. But he anchored himself to his lectern, poured what he had to say directly into the microphone, and it came out better than it went in; moreover, to most Americans there was nothing unfamiliar about his flat midwestern accent. On the stump, Smith's city mannerisms, his brown derby, and his half-chewed cigar aroused doubt and dismay; whereas Hoover's shyness, which the public mistook for modesty, and his generally dignified demeanor, inspired confidence and respect. With the radio available, the burden of the campaign fell more than ever before upon the two principals. The public wished to see and hear the candidates themselves rather than their defenders or detractors. In the end the issue was clear enough. Did the nation want a provincial New Yorker, the product of a city machine, a Roman Catholic, and a wet for President, or did it want a country boy who had made good, a great engineer rather than a politician, a Protestant, and dry? Had the times been out of joint, as in 1932, the results might have been different; but in 1928, with prosperity rampant except for agriculture, to ask the question was almost to answer it.[27]

On the surface at least, the election returns could hardly have been more convincing. Hoover carried forty states with 444 electoral votes, and Smith only eight states with 87 votes. The popular vote stood 21.4 million for Hoover to 15 million for Smith, 265,000 for Thomas, and insignificant numbers for the splinter-party candidates. Texas and every state of the upper South except Arkansas voted for Hoover, leaving only six southern states in the Democratic column. Smith also carried Massachusetts and Rhode Island, which the new immigration had

[27] Marjorie W. Lyman, "The Presidential Candidate and the Radio," unpublished Master's thesis, University of California, Berkeley, 1944, pp. 24–27; V. E. Simrell, "Oratory of the 1928 Presidential Campaign," *Quarterly Journal of Speech*, XV (Feb., 1929), 128–132; Handlin, *Al Smith and his America*, pp. 129–135.

made dominantly Catholic, urban, and wet. Both houses of Congress went to the Republicans, who in the first session of the Seventy-first Congress had 267 representatives to 163 for the Democrats and 56 senators to 39, with one Farmer-Laborite in each house. The governorships divided thirty for the Republicans to eighteen for the Democrats. Notably, while Smith failed to carry his own state, New York, the man he had hand-picked for governor, Franklin D. Roosevelt, won a slender victory. Also, except for the presidential candidates, the voting in the South was primarily Democratic. Southerners who deserted the white man's party were ordinarily better described as Hoover Democrats than as converts to Republicanism.[28]

Beneath the surface there was much more to the results than most contemporary observers were able to detect. The election of 1928 marked a significant change in the attitude of the urban masses. Both in 1920 and in 1924, the twelve largest cities in the United States had, taken together, given a decisive majority to the Republicans; now the tables were turned, and the Democrats came out ahead. This, as later elections were to prove, marked the beginning of a long-term urban trend. The "50 per cent" Americans of the great industrial cities were tired of being regarded as second-class citizens and were ready to pledge their allegiance to the Democratic party, which seemed more ready than the Republican to accord them equal status. It was their vote for Smith, the defeated candidate in 1928, rather than for Roosevelt, the victor in 1932, that first registered this change.

Hoover's triumph in carrying more than half the states of the old Confederacy won the headlines, but Smith's success in diverting 122 northern counties from the Republican to the Democratic column was the more important and the more permanent. A majority of these counties were predominantly Catholic, and in all of them recent immigrants and their descendants were numerous—in New England, for example, where the French Canadians and the Italian Americans almost unanimously became and were to remain Democrats. The proportion of such voters actually to cast their ballots was also higher than formerly; Catholic women, who had rarely voted before, turned out in impressive numbers to vote for Smith. In the heavy voting that characterized the election (67.5 per cent of the voters went to the polls)

[28] *Official Congressional Directory*, 71st Cong., 1st Sess., May 1, 1929 (Washington, 1929), pp. 135, 137, 246; Edgar E. Robinson, *The Presidential Vote, 1896–1932* (Stanford, Calif., 1934), pp. 24–27, 46.

Smith, despite his southern losses, received more ballots than had ever before been cast for a Democratic candidate, and approximately half of the new voters gave him their first votes. City voters of the older stock—the self-styled "100 per cent Americans"—remained dominantly loyal to the Republican party and voted for Hoover; it would take the depression to jar them loose. But the "50 per centers" were well on the way to becoming Democrats long before the New Deal.[29]

There was a similarly impressive minority shift in the eleven food-producing states that Peek had marked out for special attention. Thanks to Raskob and his rich friends, the Democrats had a campaign chest in 1928 that enabled them to keep within measurable distance of the heavy Republican expenditures. Peek planned and carried through an active campaign for Smith in Ohio, Indiana, Illinois, Wisconsin, Missouri, Iowa, Minnesota, the Dakotas, Nebraska, and Montana. Since all of these states voted for Hoover, Peek seemed to have little to show for his efforts—most midwestern farmers were unwilling to take a chance on Smith. But there were some striking changes in the pattern of voting. The Democrats, for one thing, gained almost two million votes over the totals their 1920 candidates had obtained in this area, and the Republicans gained only about a million and a half. In one state, North Dakota, the Democrats gained nearly 70,000 votes over the 1920 totals, while the Republicans actually lost nearly 30,000. Smith scored heavily in the Catholic counties, rural as well as city, although it is reasonable to assume that Hoover's anti-Catholic support at least compensated for all such Republican losses. Throughout the western farm belt, in the country as well as in the cities, the Democratic trend began with Smith rather than with Roosevelt. Careful analysis seems to indicate also that Smith got most of the midwestern support that had gone to La Follette four years before; in Wisconsin, to cite the most conspicuous case, the Democratic vote in 1924 was only about 68,000, whereas in 1928 it was over 450,000.[30]

Had the Republicans really been alert to the situation, they would have found little grounds for complacency in the 1928 results. Republican gains in the South meant next to nothing; they registered

[29] Samuel J. Eldersveld, "The Influence of Metropolitan Party Pluralities in Presidential Elections Since 1920," *American Political Science Review*, XLIII (Dec., 1949), 1193–1195; Samuel Lubell, *The Future of American Politics* (New York, 1952), pp. 34–41; Peel and Donnelly, *The 1928 Campaign*, p. 128.

[30] Fite, *Peek and the Fight for Farm Parity*, pp. 212–220.

merely the protest of the native-born Protestant drys against the nomination of Smith. In the overwhelmingly Negro counties, where the white voters still did practically all the voting, there was not even this protest. There, even in the presidential contest, the votes went to the white man's party, as usual. But in the North the situation was different. The recent immigrants and their children were no longer voting merely to support the local machine; they were now beginning to take an interest in national politics and to vote Democratic in larger numbers than ever before. And while most farmers in the breadbasket states clung to their Republican loyalties because they were predominantly native-born, Protestant, and dry, enough of them were drifting over to the Democrats to indicate a definite trend. As for the liberal intellectuals, they cast few votes, but the votes they cast were overwhelmingly for Smith. They liked his record as governor; they disliked the intolerance of his enemies—the Ku Klux Klan, the anti-Catholics, and the drys; and they continued to resent the way in which the Republican party accepted as gospel whatever principles of government the business world chose to maintain. Thus, while the election failed signally to dramatize the issue between agriculture and industry, it nevertheless revealed a degree of unrest among the underprivileged both in town and country that could not be suppressed for long.

CHAPTER 10

Hoover Takes Over

WHAT to do with a President-elect during the months immediately preceding his inauguration has always been a puzzle in American politics. Potentially such an individual is everything, but legally he is nothing. Hoover wisely turned this dilemma into an asset by scheduling a six weeks' "good will" tour of Latin America. The trip not only got the President-elect out of the country, where his presence would only have embarrassed the retiring administration, but it served also to promote better relations with the republics to the south. Everywhere he went he was received with the greatest courtesy. To emphasize the official nature of the trip, President Coolidge put the battleship *Maryland* at Hoover's disposal for the going journey and the *Utah* for the return.[1]

As an experienced business executive, Hoover gave much pre- and post-inauguration attention to the selection of his subordinates. He found to his great disappointment that few ambitious politicians were willing to accept the hazards of a Cabinet assignment, and the Cabinet he finally assembled was, with some exceptions, second-rate. For Secretary of State he turned to Henry L. Stimson of New York, an able and conscientious public servant, but despite his varied activities, including the Governor Generalship of the Philippines, not very well known to the public. For Secretary of the Treasury he continued Mellon until 1932, the longest term anyone had served in that office since Albert

[1] Alexander Moore, *Herbert Hoover's Latin American Policy* (Stanford, Calif., 1951), pp. 13–24.

Gallatin. Mellon's successor was another capitalist, Ogden Mills of New York, so that throughout Hoover's term business leadership held firmly to that strategic post. Hoover paid his respects to American history by making the current Charles Francis Adams his Secretary of the Navy, and he chose his friend, President Ray Lyman Wilbur of Stanford University, to be Secretary of the Interior. Outside the Cabinet he made some notable selections, as, for example, when he sent Charles Gates Dawes to Great Britain as ambassador, and made Charles Evans Hughes Chief Justice of the Supreme Court, and Benjamin N. Cardozo Associate Justice. But in general Hoover's high-ranking appointments were far less distinguished than he must have wished.[2]

Whatever the defects of his subordinates, Hoover was a skilled administrator, and soon showed it. The "transition from inertia to action in the directing head of the government" won much admiration, even in liberal circles. The new President substituted a secretariat for a secretary, with the duties of each administrative assistant assigned "with mathematical nicety." He instituted better relations with the press, and "ended the mask of anonymity" that attributed presidential statements to a White House spokesman. He cast mild aspersions on his two most recent predecessors by ordering the withdrawal of all oil lands within his legal reach from further leasing, and by ordering long overdue publicity for large-income tax refunds. He "does not run away from his troubles," commented the *New Republic;* "he feels competent to solve them, and acts in most cases with a promptness and decision which have not been seen in the White House since Mr. Wilson's early days." His "coordinating mind" and his ability "to consolidate, merge, standardize and drive" gave comfort to the business world, which expected no less from a great engineer and promoter. According to the *Magazine of Wall Street,* his accession to the Presidency marked "the end of political domination of the Federal government. Henceforth, economics, not politics, will be the chief concern of government." What early commentators failed to see was that Hoover's experience gave him far less understanding than he needed of the politicians with whom he would have to deal, particularly the senators and representatives in Congress, not one of whom could he fire for incompetence or disloyalty to his administration. His business habits had served him well in the

[2] Herbert Hoover, *The Memoirs of Herbert Hoover* (New York, 1952), II, 210–223, 268–269; Robert S. Allen and Drew Pearson, *Washington Merry-Go-Round* (New York, 1931), pp. 105–136, 163–183.

Commerce Department, where his subordinates had no choice but to obey him, but in the Presidency he had to deal with innumerable politicians for whom he could not lay down the law. Furthermore, he was the prisoner of his economic views; his strong convictions on the subject of what government had no right to do greatly narrowed the field of his possible activities.[3]

Whatever blurring of the issue had occurred during the campaign, there could be no question in any competent observer's mind that Hoover as President represented the triumph of industry over agriculture. But even conservative industrialists were concerned about the unhealthy status of agriculture, and were ready to give the farmer a helping hand if only in the process the sacred prerogatives of business could be fully conserved. There must be no equalization fees, price fixing, or any other such nonsense. Out of deference to the wishes of Senator Borah, who had supported him warmly during the campaign, Hoover had promised to call a special session of Congress early in his administration to raise the tariffs on agricultural products; in office he had no choice but to redeem his promise, and promptly did so. The President must have known that Congress, once assembled, could go as far as it chose with tariff revision, or any other subject, but he evidently hoped that it would confine its activities mainly to the relief of agriculture. His message of April 16 recommended, in addition to limited tariff revision, the creation of a "great instrumentality clothed with sufficient authority and resources" to aid the farmers in the effective marketing of their produce.[4]

But the Agricultural Marketing bill sponsored by the administration failed to satisfy the more militant advocates of farm relief, who wanted something more specific by way of aid to agriculture than Hoover had in mind. Their efforts centered mainly upon including in the proposed measure the "export debenture" plan, which Professor Charles L. Stewart of the University of Illinois had advocated as early as 1924, and which the National Grange had endorsed. This plan proposed a substantial bounty on agricultural exports; for each bushel of wheat sent abroad, for example, the exporter would receive from the govern-

[3] *New Republic,* LVIII (Mar. 20, 1929), 126, LIX (June 12, 1929), 88; (June 19, 1929), 124; *The Nation,* CXXVIII (Mar. 27, 1929), 359; (Apr. 3, 1929), 128; *Magazine of Wall Street,* XLIII (Mar. 9, 1929), 813.

[4] Hoover, *Memoirs,* II, 253–254, 292; *Congressional Record,* 71st Cong., 1st Sess., LXXI (April 16, 1929), 42.

ment approximately 20 cents, about half the existing duty on imported wheat. The payments were not to be made in cash, however, but in transferable treasury debentures that could be used by importers to balance off tariff charges. It was assumed that the debentures would sell at a discount and would therefore be readily marketable; by this clever device receipts from the protective tariff could be tapped directly to aid the farmer. Naturally Hoover threw the full weight of his administration against this plan, which he regarded as no less unsound than the McNary-Haugen proposals, and eventually it was defeated.[5]

By the Agricultural Marketing Act of June, 1929, Congress gave the President about what he wanted. It created a Federal Farm Board of nine members, eight of them to be appointed by the President and confirmed by the Senate, with the Secretary of Agriculture serving as an *ex officio* member. The Board was to have the assistance of a series of advisory committees, each to consist of seven members chosen by the co-operative associations handling any given agricultural commodity. It was provided with a revolving fund of $500 million, from which it might make loans to co-operative associations, and "upon application of the advisory committee for any commodity" to certain stabilization corporations that the law also authorized in case the need should arise. Each such stabilizing corporation was to deal only with the marketing of a single commodity, such as grain or cotton, and by a transparent device was not to be a federal agency. While any given stabilization corporation must adopt whatever rules the Federal Farm Board might require, it must be organized under the laws of some state or territory, with its voting stock and membership interests exclusively in the hands of the co-operative associations concerned. A stabilization corporation might buy, sell, store, and process "any quantity" of the commodity in which it dealt "for the purpose of controlling any surplus." It was not specifically authorized to fix prices, but the way was wide open toward that end since it was free to pay whatever prices it chose as long as the Federal Farm Board was willing to supply it with funds.[6]

The Federal Farm Board that Hoover appointed contained representative members of the various marketing associations, but was headed by Alexander Legge of Chicago, president of the International

[5] Theodore Saloutos and John D. Hicks, *Agricultural Discontent in the Middle West, 1900–1939* (Madison, Wis., 1951), pp. 406–407; Gilbert C. Fite, *George N. Peek and the Fight for Farm Parity* (Norman, Okla., 1952), pp. 160–161.

[6] *United States Statutes at Large* (Washington, 1931), XLVI, 11–19.

Harvester Company, an appointment that many farmers regarded with ill-concealed anxiety. In line with Hoover's views the Board undertook to co-ordinate, through over-all national agencies, the activities of the numerous co-operative associations, local, state, and regional. The grain trade, for example, was headed up by the Farmers' National Grain Corporation, which was incorporated on October 29, the worst day of the stock-market crash. The Farmers' National not only lent to the subordinate cooperatives but also attempted to support the price of wheat by purchases in the open market. But it was not long able to check the price decline, which by June, 1930, had brought wheat down to 90 cents a bushel. Other national marketing associations fostered by the Farm Board were similarly abortive.[7]

Reluctantly, the Board finally used its authority to bring about the creation of two stabilization corporations, one for grain and the other for cotton. But as a caustic critic observed, it had only found "a first-class way of throwing good money into a bottomless pit." These corporations, after speedily exhausting both their storage and financial resources, were obliged to confess defeat, and to allow prices to find their own levels. The average weighted farm price of wheat dropped from about $1.049 in 1929 to 68.1 cents in 1930, to 39.1 cents in 1931, and to 38.6 cents in 1932. For cotton the comparable figures were 16.8 cents per pound in 1929, 9.5 cents in 1930, 5.7 cents in 1931, and 6.5 cents in 1932. Other farm prices followed a similar pattern. After losing most of its capital in a vain effort to stabilize prices, the Federal Farm Board gave up that effort and began a campaign to cut down on production; but since it had no other inducements to offer than the common good, the results were notably insignificant.[8]

Hoover's proposal for a limited tariff revision, confined mainly to agricultural products, had a similarly unhappy ending. As originally presented by Representative Willis C. Hawley of Oregon, the House bill showed some tendency toward restraint, but individual congressmen

[7] Saloutos and Hicks, *Agricultural Discontent*, pp. 409–410, 414; Harris Gaylord Warren, *Herbert Hoover and the Great Depression* (New York, 1959), pp. 172–177.

[8] "Uncle Sam, Plunger," *The Nation*, CXXX (Mar. 26, 1930), 351; *Statistical Abstract of the United States, 1934* (Washington, 1934), p. 632; Chester C. Davis, "The Development of Agricultural Policy Since the End of the World War," Yearbook of Agriculture, 1940 (Washington, 1940), pp. 312–313; Ralph L. Dewey and James C. Nelson, "The Transportation Problem of Agriculture," *ibid.*, pp. 725–729.

were not long able to stand up against the demands for general revision that came from their constituents and from the innumerable lobbyists who descended on Washington. Increases in farm duties, however futile or insignificant, won general favor, but in a generous outburst of logrolling they were paralleled by higher duties on nearly everything else that might conceivably suffer from foreign competition. In the Senate there were some signs of revolt, and a Democratic-insurgent-Republican combination almost succeeded in passing a Borah-sponsored resolution to confine the revisions strictly to agricultural products. Senator Reed Smoot of Utah, who had charge of the tariff measure in the Senate, also had some initial trouble in lining up majorities for nonagricultural items. But in the end the opponents of general revision succumbed to the logrolling technique that had worked so successfully in the House. More powerful even than Smoot in obtaining the necessary votes was Joseph R. Grundy of Pennsylvania, president of the Pennsylvania Manufacturers' Association, who took office by appointment of the governor when the Senate refused to seat Senator-elect William S. Vare because of his excessive campaign expenditures. Grundy traded eastern support of agricultural duties for western support of industrial duties, and got a good deal better than he gave.[9]

Although the insurgent-Democratic bloc was unable to prevent final passage of the bill by the Senate, it did succeed, after a bitter struggle, in adding to the measure two amendments that were wholly unacceptable to the administration. One of these was the previously defeated export debenture plan; the other was a change in the flexible provision of the Fordney-McCumber Act that would have required Congress, rather than the President, to pass on each modification recommended by the Tariff Commission. Senator Borah led the fight for the latter amendment, raising doubts as to the constitutionality of Congress so delegating its legislative authority to the President, also pointing out the insignificance of the Presidential revisions downward in comparison with the far greater importance of the revisions upward. Since the House version of the bill excluded these two items, a long deadlock

[9] *Congressional Record*, 71st Cong., 1st Sess., LXXI (June 17, 1929), 2975; F. W. Taussig, *The Tariff History of the United States* (8th ed., New York, 1931), pp. 496–498. Senator Hiram Bingham of Connecticut, who had placed a manufacturer's lobbyist on the Senate payroll as an adviser, was, on motion of Senator Norris, officially censured for this impropriety. Alfred Lief, *Democracy's Norris* (New York, 1939), p. 330.

ensued in conference committee, with the President throwing the full weight of his office against the export debenture and the change in the flexible provision. Had Hoover shown equal stubbornness at the beginning of the session in resisting general revision, he might have prevented most of the excesses of the Hawley-Smoot Tariff, for by the threat of a veto he finally got rid of the two Senate amendments he disliked. As for the differences in schedules, the conferees had little difficulty in reaching agreements. In its final form the bill also included certain changes in the Tariff Commission. In order to give the President a chance to reconstitute its membership, the new commission was to consist of six, instead of seven, members; further, the commission might initiate investigations both upon its own authority and upon the request of the President or either house of Congress. Recommendations for increases and decreases, as formerly, might not exceed 50 per cent of the statute rates, and could be validated only by proclamation of the President, if in his judgment such changes seemed justifiable.[10]

At long last the conference bill passed the Senate, June 13, 1930, by a vote of 44 to 42, with fourteen Republican senators either voting or paired against it and five Democrats voting for it; the following day it passed the House, 222 to 153. In both Senate and House the majorities favoring the bill came principally from the industrial Northeast, where the most benefits were expected, and not from the agricultural South and West, for whom principally the revision was originally intended. On June 17, 1930, the President affixed his signature. By this time the stock-market panic was months in the past, and the depression was beginning to deepen. But it is worth noting that the Hawley-Smoot Tariff was essentially a pre-panic production, born of the boom days that preceded October, 1929.[11]

In its final form the new tariff act raised American import duties to an all-time high, with charges on raw materials from 50 to 100 per cent above those of the Fordney-McCumber tariffs, and with the average of ad valorem rates at 40.08 per cent as compared with the previous 33.22 per cent. The high rates on agricultural commodities, as usual, sounded better to the farmers than they were in fact. The two-cents-a-

[10] *Ibid.,* 328–329; *Congressional Record,* 71st Cong., 1st Sess., LXXI (Oct. 2, 1929), 4150; (Oct. 19, 1929), 4694; Claudius O. Johnson, *Borah of Idaho* (New York, 1936), pp. 436–443; Hoover, *Memoirs,* II, 292–297; *United States Statutes at Large* (Washington, 1931), XLVI, 696, 701.

[11] *Congressional Record,* 71st Cong., 2nd Sess., LXII (June 13, 1930), 10635; (June 14, 1930), p. 10789.

pound duty on raw sugar, for example, no doubt helped the mountain-state sugar-beet interests, which Reed Smoot so well represented, but for most American farmers the tariff on sugar meant, if anything, only a higher price for the sugar they had to buy. The tariff on hides, which were imported in considerable quantity and had previously been on the free list, was set at 10 per cent, but with compensating duties of 15 per cent on leather and 20 per cent on shoes; no doubt far more farmers wore shoes than sold hides. And so on down the list. Undoubtedly some of the duties served well certain local interests, California citrus fruits and long-staple cotton, for example, but for agriculture as a whole they provided little aid. As for the duties on manufactured products, some that were raised were already so high that the additional charges made little difference; others tended to stifle what minimum foreign competition still existed and to put new obstacles in the way of world trade. The principle of equalizing the cost of production at home and abroad, always so loudly proclaimed as the principal object of tariff protection, was almost completely ignored; pressures primarily, not principle or even reason, produced the new tariff rates.[12]

The Hawley-Smoot Tariff was so unsound economically that it drew the opposition of nearly every reputable economist in the United States; the month before its passage, 1,038 members of the American Economic Association, representing 46 states and 179 colleges and universities, presented a statement urging Congress not to pass the bill and the President to veto it if passed. The signers held that it would raise the cost of living and "injure the great majority of our citizens"; that it would encourage inefficient concerns to undertake production and thus subsidize waste; that it would hurt rather than help the vast majority of farmers, who had no competition in the home market, anyway, and as consumers stood only to lose; that it would hamper our export trade, including such items as copper, automobiles, agricultural machinery, and typewriters, since "countries cannot permanently buy from us unless they are permitted to sell to us"; that it would undoubtedly lead foreign nations to levy retaliatory tariffs against American goods; that it would handicap collections on the $12.5 to $14.5 billion that Americans had invested in foreign enterprises "entirely aside from the war debts"; that it would aggravate unemployment by restricting trade; and that it would inevitably inject a spirit of bitterness

[12] Taussig, *Tariff History,* pp. 500–521.

into international relations that the United States could ill afford to foster. But this lesson in elementary economics was totally lost upon both Congress and the President. In announcing his decision to sign the bill, Hoover admitted that it was not perfect, but pointed to the Tariff Commission as the means by which its injustices could be corrected and foreign reprisals prevented.[13]

Time was soon to prove the economists right in most of their predictions. Protests against the raising of the American tariff wall began to pour in from foreign nations while the bill was still in Congress; after its passage retaliatory tariffs became the order of the day. Americans who saw their foreign investments imperiled by the new rates cut down precipitately on their loans abroad, and dried up further the means of redressing a dangerously uneven balance of payments. If the members of Congress who were responsible for the Hawley-Smoot Tariff had taken careful thought on how they could hurt the United States most economically, they could hardly have done worse. Hoover's advance billing as an economist who would take politics out of government now had a strangely unconvincing sound; rather, the politicians seemed to have corrupted Hoover's economics. Nor were his promises to the farmers in any significant way fulfilled; despite Farm Board and tariffs, agricultural conditions grew steadily worse and worse. The ineptitude of business leadership, which had put a businessman in the White House and had called the signals for a majority of the politicians in Congress, was fully revealed. The business interest stood convicted of not even knowing what was good for business itself. Happily this was not true of all businessmen, especially those who understood the conditions of international trade and had products they wished to sell abroad. But theirs were minority voices. For the vast majority foreign competition was only an evil to be stamped out at whatever cost.[14]

The passage of the Hawley-Smoot Act was only an additional blow to an economy that had already suffered dire disaster. For in the fall of 1929 a stock-market panic had ended abruptly the overweening prosperity of the preceding years and had ushered in the "Great Depression." Appropriately, the signal that the boom was over came from the

[13] *The New York Times,* June 16, 1930, p. 1, col. 8; p. 2, col. 1; Warren, *Herbert Hoover,* pp. 92–94.

[14] *Ibid.,* pp. 94–97; Joseph M. Jones, Jr., *Tariff Retaliation; Repercussions of the Hawley-Smoot Bill* (Philadelphia, 1934), pp. 18–19; Broadus Mitchell, *Depression Decade; From New Era Through New Deal, 1929–1941* (New York, 1947), pp. 55, 61–62, 72–76.

nerve center of the American business world, the New York Stock Exchange, which handled the buying and selling of from three-fifths to three-fourths of the nation's corporate securities. By early September acute observers could see that the great bull market was at an end, and by mid-October the downward trend was frightening. But the worst period of panic was from October 24 through October 29. On the first of these days sales on the New York Exchange ran to nearly 13 million shares, and on the last to over 16 million. Efforts on the part of leading New York bankers to lend "organized support" to the market failed dismally. Stock prices fell catastrophically, and thousands of investors saw their fortunes vanish almost overnight. During the month of October listings on the New York Exchange declined in value by an average of 37.5 per cent, but this was not the end. Except for a period of three months during the spring of 1930, the trend of the market continued steadily downward until the summer of 1932. By that time few but the "blue chip" stocks survived, and what had happened to them strained credibility. American Telephone and Telegraph was down from a pre-panic high of 304 to 72, United States Steel from 262 to 22, General Motors from 73 to 8, and Montgomery Ward from 138 to 4. Meantime the total market value of all stocks listed on the New York Exchange had dropped from $89.6 billion on September 1, 1929, to $63.5 billion on December 1, 1929, and to $15.6 billion on July 1, 1932.[15]

In seeking to understand why all this had happened, one begins with the fact that to a remarkable extent American prosperity during the 1920's was corporate prosperity. The day of the great entrepreneur who owned and controlled his entire business was practically over; Henry Ford was almost the last of his kind. Now thousands, hundreds of thousands, or even millions of investors, large and small, supplied through the purchase of stocks and bonds the capital that the various enterprises required to carry on their activities. While Hoover denied the accuracy of the "oft-repeated statement that 200 corporations control 90 per cent of the nation's wealth," he admitted that the total holdings of American corporations, "outside of banking and insurance companies," constituted no less than 30 per cent of the national assets— a rather substantial fraction. To some observers, the fact that so many

[15] F. L. Allen, *Only Yesterday* (New York, 1931), pp. 320–338; *New York Stock Exchange Bulletin,* I (Apr. 1930), 6; III (July, 1932), 5; Mitchell, *Depression Decade,* pp. 28–30.

investors held a stake in American business was evidence that it had become more democratic. But as far as management was concerned, the exact reverse was true. In earlier days, with fewer investors, an individual who wished to control a given corporation must have in his grasp no less than 51 per cent of its voting stock; now, with ownership so widely diffused, 3 per cent, or even less, was ordinarily sufficient. The directors and a few insiders ran each corporation with little or no interference from the multitudes who owned the stock. And, as for these multitudes, they constituted all told only a few million persons. At most only about 7 or 8 per cent of the total American population owned stocks in 1929, and the amounts held by small investors were relatively insignificant.[16]

It is true, nevertheless, that during the flush years of the middle twenties prosperous Americans tended to invest an increasing portion of their savings in corporate stocks and bonds. Some of these issues were necessary to finance legitimate expansion, but others were far less defensible. The multiplication of holding companies, particularly in the public utility field, threw on the market many securities of dubious merit. Others resulted from the numerous mergers that characterized the times. Not since the early years of the century had so many corporations in so many different fields joined forces. This tendency was particularly marked among the new businesses, such as automobiles, radio, and chain stores; but it occurred all along the line, and extended even to banks, where chain banking brought many little firms into larger systems, and where consolidations were common, even among the titans. As a rule, whenever such a combination occurred, the new company issued securities that greatly exceeded in volume the sum total of all the issues of all the combining units, thus adding substantially to the supply of investments available to the public. Investment trusts provided still further new issues of securities. These organizations, which made their profits from investing in the stocks of other companies, were unimportant in the United States until the 1920's, but during that decade they grew mightily in number and in popularity. At best they served well the needs of uninformed purchasers who lacked the wisdom to select for themselves from among the innumerable offerings available.

[16] George Soule, *Prosperity Decade; From War to Depression: 1917–1929* (New York, 1947), pp. 293–298; Ray Lyman Wilbur and Arthur M. Hyde, *The Hoover Policies* (New York, 1937), p. 299; John Kenneth Galbraith, *The Great Crash, 1929* (Boston, 1955), pp. 71–72, 83.

But at worst they became gay deceivers who piled one investment trust upon another, after the holding company pattern, and produced fantastic profits for a favored few. As the speculative craze took hold of the country, there was much dividing and subdividing of high-priced stocks, or "stock splitting," while many "blue sky" concerns, with assets consisting mainly of hope or fraud, floated huge issues. Some of these offerings were too transparently worthless to be listed on the New York Exchange, but they all too frequently found their way to trusting purchasers through some outside market or the Curb.[17]

Brokerage firms in ordinary times sold their wares principally to two types of buyers. One type sought safe long-term investments that were expected to pay good dividends or interest. Such buyers usually advanced all the money needed to complete each transaction, put their securities in safe deposit, and left them there as long as the returns were good. The other type bought mainly with a view to speculation, finding their profits primarily in the shifting values of the securities they purchased. Such buyers cared little about the earnings of their holdings, and expected a rapid turnover; the game was principally to buy at a low price and sell at a higher price, the oftener the better. Not always, but usually, speculative purchasers bought on margin; that is, they put up only enough money to cover the probable range of fluctuation in the stocks they purchased and depended upon credit with their brokers to supply the rest. Margins varied in accordance with the caution exercised by the individual broker, and might run as high as 45 or 50 per cent, but were generally much less. The long period of rising stock values during the 1920's tended, however, to make speculators out of even the most conservative of investors. Solid businessmen and bankers who did not mean to take a chance, as well as many small purchasers, bought for the rise in values that they regarded as a certainty; about the only sure losers over a period of years were those who "sold short" in anticipation of a declining market that failed to appear.[18]

Since margin purchasers furnished most of the collateral upon which brokers obtained loans, the total volume of such borrowings at any given time provided a fair index of the existing speculation. Brokers' loans, or

[17] *Ibid.,* pp. 51–70; James C. Bonbright and Gardiner C. Means, *The Holding Company* (New York, 1932), pp. 109–110, 129, 261, 335; Soule, *Prosperity Decade,* 298–304.

[18] *Ibid.,* pp. 294, 304–306; Francis Wrigley Hirst, *Wall Street and Lombard Street* (New York, 1931), pp. 3–14; Irving Fisher, *The Stock Market Crash —and After* (New York, 1930), pp. 82–85; Galbraith, *The Great Crash,* p. 37.

call loans, as they were often termed because of their extreme liquidity, fluctuated during the early 1920's from $1 billion to $1.5 billion. By 1926 they had risen to about $3 billion, by 1927 to $4 billion, by 1928 to $6 billion, and before the crash to about $8.5 billion. The normal rate of interest on call money was about 5 per cent, but during the year 1928 the rate rose steadily until at the end of December it had reached 12 per cent. By March, 1929, when it had climbed to 20 per cent, the brokerage houses in some alarm lifted their margin requirements to 50 per cent, and so brought the interest rate down, but meantime money had flowed in from all over the world to support the wild American speculation. It seems incredible that so many supposedly competent observers failed to recognize the dangers inherent in the situation. Industrial stocks were selling at from sixteen to twenty times their earnings when eight or ten to one was the traditional margin of safety. Many stocks that had never paid a dividend brought fantastic figures, and soared ever upward. But Bernard Baruch claimed in June, 1929, that "the economic condition of the world seems on the verge of a great upward movement," Professor Irving Fisher of Yale University asserted a few weeks later that "Stock prices have reached what looks like a permanently high plateau," and Charles E. Mitchell of the National City Bank maintained even in early October that the "industrial condition of the United States is absolutely sound."[19]

A few prophets of gloom and doom raised their voices in warning. Alexander Dana Noyes, financial editor of *The New York Times,* saw the frenzy all along for what it was, and repeatedly told his readers what they might expect. Sir George Paish, an English economist, pointed out a year before the crash that the approaching end of "unlimited banking credit in America" presaged financial disaster for both Europe and America. Roger Babson, whose uninhibited hunches were often right, declared on September 5, 1929, that "Sooner or later a crash is coming, and it may be terrific." Some of the pessimists urged remedial action while there was yet time. Paul M. Warburg of the International Acceptance Bank earnestly besought the Federal Reserve Board to adopt restrictive policies that would call a halt to the "unrestrained speculation." Herbert Hoover, while still Secretary of Commerce, worked from the inside to reverse the "easy money policies" of

[19] *Ibid.,* pp. 26–27, 42, 75, 99; Soule, *Prosperity Decade,* p. 304; New York Stock Exchange, *Yearbook, 1929–30* (New York, 1930), pp. 95–107; Warren, *Herbert Hoover,* pp. 109–113.

the Coolidge administration, but was powerless to effect results. President Coolidge, as he left office, told the American people that their prosperity was "absolutely sound," and that stocks were "cheap at current prices."[20]

The "easy money policy" to which Hoover had objected was no mere accident. Both Coolidge and his far more perspicacious Secretary of the Treasury, Andrew W. Mellon, favored it. A decisive majority of the Federal Reserve Board were devoted adherents of the "let-business-have-its-head" school of thought, and business wanted easy money. The Board might at any time have diminished the amount of funds available for speculation by raising rediscount rates and by promoting the open-market sale of government and commercial securities, a course that would have sterilized in the Federal Reserve vaults much of the money the banks were lending. Eager to place the blame for the depression upon Europe rather than upon America, Hoover later made much of the fact that the premature restoration of the gold standard by England in 1925 and the general weakening of the European economy during the middle 1920's led to such insistent pressure from abroad for American credit inflation that the Federal Reserve Board yielded to it, first in 1925 and then again in 1927. Undoubtedly the Board yielded, but there were pressures from at home as well as from abroad; the American public liked the abundant prosperity that easy money seemed to promote, including the bull market, and wanted it to continue. And the men at the controls had neither the wit nor the will to resist the public demand.[21]

When Hoover became President, he tried, although somewhat feebly, to reverse the inflationary policies of his predecessor. First, he privately urged newspapers and magazines to warn their readers against speculation, then he persuaded Secretary Mellon to advocate that investors turn their stocks into bonds, and finally he asked Richard Whitney, president of the Stock Exchange, to "curb the manipulation of stocks." None of these efforts availed. Hoover believed that it would be futile for him to ask Congress to interfere in the stock market, and he told Whitney that he "had no desire to stretch the powers of the Federal

[20] Galbraith, *The Great Crash,* pp. 31, 78–79, 89; George Paish, "The United States and Europe," *Contemporary Review,* CXXXIV (Oct., 1928), 435–436; Hoover, *Memoirs,* II, 9–16.

[21] *Ibid.,* III, *The Great Depression, 1929–1941* (New York, 1952), pp. 2–14; Warren, *Herbert Hoover,* pp. 99–103.

Government" that far anyway. But he did back up the governor of the Federal Reserve Board in an effort "to refuse discounts to banks which were lending mainly on stocks," and in raising the rediscount rate to 5 per cent in June and to 6 per cent in August. The effect these measures had in producing the final denouement is difficult to estimate; probably the Bank of England's decision in late September to raise its rediscount rate to 6.5 per cent had more to do with the final collapse of the boom than any action taken by American officials. By this means the British authorities stopped the outward flow of gold from London to participate in the American speculation. Thereafter many large-scale speculators, both American and foreign, took the hint and sold out; a general collapse of confidence did the rest.[22]

Would the Panic of 1929 turn out to be merely a wholesome liquidation of stock-market gamblers? Or would it usher in a period of hard times, such as had followed the failure of Jay Cooke and Company in 1873 and the drop in the gold reserve below the $100-million mark in 1893? Business leaders talked optimistically to keep their courage up; American business, they recited almost in unison, was fundamentally sound and would carry on as usual. Political leaders, not to be outdone, chimed in with the same refrain. But they were all wrong. Prices dropped sharply, foreign trade fell off, factories closed, business failures multiplied, banks went under, unemployment began to mount—to five million in 1930, to nine million in 1931, to thirteen million in 1932. The horrors of these troubled times, unknown to later generations, were terribly real to those who lived through them. Savings disappeared; purchases made on installments had to be returned; substantial citizens lost their homes on mortgages; insurance companies had difficulty in meeting their obligations; stores closed for lack of customers; vandals or pranksters broke out the windows of vacant factory buildings; theaters went dark; university enrollments dropped abysmally, and faculty members lost their jobs or had their salaries cut; hospitals were short of patients; soup kitchens opened; bread lines began to form; local relief systems broke down; panhandlers roamed the streets; philanthropy dried up to a trickle; the jobless slept on park benches, in the doorways of public buildings, or on the ground; uncounted numbers knew the meaning of hunger and cold and fear. Furthermore, the contagion spread. With the collapse of American credit the nations

[22] *Ibid.*, pp. 17–19; Fisher, *The Stockmarket Crash*, pp. 1–2, 32; Soule, *Depression Decade*, pp. 306–311.

that had depended on it, particularly those of central and western Europe, soon suffered from the same ills that beset the United States, additional proof that isolation was only a myth.[23]

To explain this sudden descent from high prosperity to deep depression is not an easy task, for the factors that produced the cataclysm were many and complicated. Nor is it possible to assign percentage values to the various conditions that influenced the course of events. About all that a student of the period can do, even with the benefit of hindsight, is to list the weaknesses in the economy that combined in one fashion or another to bring it down, knowing full well that almost any other student of the period would for a certainty find fault with the list. Not many, however, would now dispute the assertion of John K. Galbraith, in *The Great Crash, 1929,* that American business, despite the contentions of its principal spokesmen, was "fundamentally unsound."[24]

1. One principal unsoundness, as Galbraith points out, was "the bad distribution of income" that resulted from the long profits business insisted on taking. During the prosperous years the poor may not have got poorer, but certainly the rich got richer with a vengeance—by the time the depression arrived, 5 per cent of the population contrived to absorb about "one-third of all the personal income." This was more than so few persons could spend, and the residue left over, plus the excessive surpluses that corporations regularly set aside for improvement and expanion, contributed to an immense overbuilding of industrial plants. The nation was set up to produce far more goods than it could absorb in ordinary times, or hope to market abroad. As Frank A. Vanderlip, a somewhat unorthodox banker, phrased it, "capital kept too much and labor did not have enough to buy its share of things." In fact, the shortage of customers was becoming apparent well before the panic broke. The boom in building construction, upon which so many other businesses depended, had reached its peak in 1925 and had been on the down grade ever since, while with 26.5 million cars of one kind or another in use the automobile market had begun to show unmistakable signs of being glutted. There was a limit to the number of

[23] *Ibid.,* pp. 311–314; W. S. Myers and W. H. Newton, *The Hoover Administration* (New York, 1936), pp. 21–22; Brookings Institution, *The Recovery Problem in the United States* (Washington, 1936), p. 135. Edward Angly (ed.), *Oh Yeah?* (New York, 1931), preserves many choice specimens of false optimism.

[24] Galbraith, *The Great Crash,* p. 182.

people who could afford to build houses and buy automobiles, a fact that the business world was unprepared to face. A willingness on the part of corporations to distribute their earnings more widely, particularly through the payment of higher wages, might have served to keep buying on an evener keel and to have prevented, or at least to have lessened, the final catastrophe.[25]

2. Technological unemployment due to the multiplication of labor-saving machines threw many workers out of jobs, at least temporarily. Since unemployment insurance was still virtually unknown in the United States, this meant a corresponding limitation on the buying power of the labor force. Nor did business often have the foresight to parallel the introduction of the new machines with higher wages, shorter hours, and added restrictions on the employment of women and children. In the end, the argument ran, the new machines would mean more jobs as well as more goods, but this was small comfort to those who found themselves out of work.[26]

3. Weaknesses in the corporate structure contributed materially to the fundamental unsoundness of American business. Holding companies, so rampant in the electric power field, were common enough elsewhere, particularly among light industries, banks, and railroads. They not only promoted monopoly, as intended, but they also made possible irresponsible minority control and the siphoning off of profits to a favored few. Together with investment trusts, they opened the way to a horde of conscienceless sharpsters bent on exploiting the gullibility of the public. When earnings fell off, something the creators of these enterprises had rarely foreseen, their jerry-built edifices came tumbling down.[27]

4. The American banking system suffered from certain elemental defects. Despite the services offered by the Federal Reserve System and the tendency in some sections toward chain banking, most American

[25] *The New York Times,* Jan. 13, 1931, p. 50, col. 1; Louis M. Hacker, *American Problems of Today* (New York, 1938), pp. 179–185; President's Research Committee, *Recent Social Trends in the United States* (2 vols., 1933), I, 173; Soule, *Depression Decade,* p. 164; Mitchell, *Prosperity Decade,* p. 447.

[26] President's Conference on Unemployment, *Recent Economic Changes in the United States* (2 vols., New York, 1929), I, 92–95; Stuart Chase, *Prosperity, Fact or Myth* (New York, 1930), pp. 152–161; *Congressional Record,* 71st Cong., 2nd Sess., LXII (June 13, 1930), p. 10686 (a report by William Green).

[27] Galbraith, *The Great Crash,* pp. 183–784; Hacker, *American Problems of Today,* pp. 97–98; Soule, *Depression Decade,* pp. 298–304.

banks were essentially independent units. Inadequate state regulation, bad management, overoptimism, and special local problems, such, for example, as crop failures in rural areas, could bring down a given bank and start a series of devastating runs on other banks nearby. Well before the Panic of 1929 this situation had become epidemic in the Middle West and the Southeast. During the years 1921–28, inclusive, no less than 5,000 banks closed their doors. Meantime, some of the great city banks, especially in New York, had fallen victims to the speculative fever. Their officers had indulged in such unseemly practices as dipping into depositors' money to play the market, speculating in their own bank stocks, covering their profits by fraudulent sales of securities to relatives at a loss in order to evade income taxes, and selling foreign bonds that they knew to be worthless in order to collect the commissions. Bank suspensions grew from 491 in 1928 to 642 in 1929 and to 1,345 in 1930, with a steadily increasing percentage of large city banks joining the procession. Small wonder that the very word "banker" became in popular parlance a term of opprobrium.[28]

5. Business control of government, so marked throughout the decade of the 1920's, made the regulation of business by government a farce. In particular, the Federal Reserve Board, which might have used its powers to restrain the boom, consistently promoted the inflation of credit that business demanded. This policy contributed not only to the wild speculation in stocks but also to industrial overexpansion, excessive installment buying, and ultimately, of course, to the stock-market collapse. Nor is it correct to assume that the Panic of 1929 was merely a surface phenomenon unrelated in any important way to the economic distress that followed it. Just as the existence of huge speculative profits had fed the boom, so their absence deepened the depression. A principal source of funds available for buying and investment had disappeared. Furthermore, the first violent contraction in the values of securities started a series of subsequent contractions that resulted in less business and greater unemployment year after year.[29]

6. The stubborn refusal of the business world to countenance any

[28] Hoover, *Memoirs*, III, 20–28; Galbraith, *The Great Crash*, pp. 152–159, 184–185; Ferdinand Pecora, *Wall Street under Oath* (New York, 1939), pp. 84–91; Mitchell, *Depression Decade*, pp. 155–156; Charles Michelson, *The Ghost Talks* (New York, 1944), p. 27.

[29] Hacker, *American Problems of Today*, p. 187; Hoover, *Memoirs*, III, pp. 6–11; William Allen White, *A Puritan in Babylon; The Story of Calvin Coolidge* (New York, 1938), pp. 289–294.

really effective measures for the relief of agriculture was likewise unfortunate. Agricultural overproduction had become chronic, and only the government had the power necessary to provide either for restrictions on production or the disposal of surpluses. But business leaders, backed by presidential vetoes, branded farmer proposals as economically unsound, and left the farmers to suffer from low prices, mortgage foreclosures, and, worst of all from the business point of view, inability to buy.[30]

7. The fact that international trade was out of balance put another strain on the American economy. With the First World War the United States had become a creditor nation, regularly selling to the outside world, especially to the war-ravaged nations of Europe, more than it bought in return. Had the debtor nations been able to market their wares freely in the United States, they might have cut down materially on their unfavorable balances, but the American tariff policy put an almost insuperable obstacle in the way of anything like an equal exchange of goods. Instead, American investors, aided by the easy-money policy of the Federal Reserve Board, lent generously to outside borrowers, mostly governments or governmental agencies, the funds needed to redress the balance of trade. This situation, grave enough in itself, was seriously worsened by the determination of the United States to collect back its war loans to the Allies, payments that the European nations could make only by borrowing. Thus, any letup in the steady flow of American money abroad was sure to spell disaster, both at home and overseas. After the stock-market crash the letup was not slow in coming.[31]

It seems strange that the darkening economic skies throughout the world should not have carried a message of warning to even the most isolationist of Americans. How long could the United States maintain its phenomenal prosperity when so many other nations were in chronic financial distress? How much further could the faith of American investors in the soundness of shaky foreign governments be stretched? How much gold could the United States safely acquire from abroad without undermining the very stability of the governments from which

[30] Mitchell, *Depression Decade*, pp. 183–185; Soule, *Prosperity Decade*, pp. 246–249.
[31] Brookings Institution, *Recovery Problem in the United States*, pp. 24–26; Galbraith, *The Great Crash*, pp. 185–187.

it expected payment in full of both their public and their private obligations? How certain could anyone be that the international tensions so apparent in Europe, Asia, and even the other Americas would not lead to war? But one of the most characteristic failures of the times was the inability of most Americans, either leaders or led, to think clearly about anything. For every voice raised in intelligent warning, there were hundreds ready to proclaim that all was well. Truly these were days in which the blind led the blind.[32]

Despite his strong convictions about the impropriety of governmental interference in business, Hoover made the nation's economic plight his concern to a degree that previous depression Presidents had never deemed necessary or feasible. Cleveland in the 1890's had acted to maintain the gold standard, and Theodore Roosevelt had taken a lively interest in arresting the Panic of 1907, but, in general, up to Hoover's time a President had thought of a depression as something with which business rather than government would have to deal. Hoover's first steps were far from drastic, for in common with most observers he failed to realize the gravity of the situation. But before his administration ended he was ready to throw the whole weight of the government into the balance to prevent the complete collapse of the capitalist system. In a sense the measures he ultimately felt obliged to support paved the way for the New Deal.[33]

Believing as he did in the fundamental soundness of the nation's business, Hoover's first instinct was to seek the co-operation of the business world itself in repairing the damage done by the stock-market crash. During the month of November, 1929, he held a series of White House conferences, with railroad presidents, with industrial leaders, with representatives of the building and construction interests, with prominent agriculturalists, and with public utility executives. "He calls here," Hiram Johnson complained, "those who have much and have lost little." The President urged strongly the maintenance of full employment at current wage levels, and no curtailment of construction programs. As for government, the Federal Reserve System promptly lowered its rediscount rate to 4.5 per cent, and promoted the expansion of credit by the purchase of government bonds and eligible commercial paper. The President also wired governors and mayors throughout the

[32] *Ibid.*, pp. 187–191.
[33] Hacker, *American Problems of Today*, pp. 192–193; Hoover, *Memoirs*, III, 41–60; Warren, *Herbert Hoover*, pp. 114–121.

country to do what they could to step up expenditures for public works, and promised to urge a similar policy upon Congress. When Congress met in December, the President was as good as his word, and in response Congress during the following year made substantial appropriations for river and harbor improvements, for new public buildings, for aid to the states in the construction of public roads, and for the building of Boulder Dam. All this, the President hoped, would serve to combat the growing trend toward unemployment.[34]

Hoover further recommended to Congress a tax cut, no doubt with the conviction that such a measure would increase buying power and so promote recovery. On this course Congress needed no urging. The first day of the session, December 2, 1929, saw the introduction of a tax-reduction measure, which within two weeks had passed both houses and received the President's signature. But taxes during the 1920's were too low to make the reductions voted of any great consequence. The normal rate on incomes under $4,000 was dropped from 1.5 to 0.5 per cent, on incomes from $4,000 to $8,000 from 3 to 2 per cent, and on those over $8,000 from 5 to 4 per cent. At the same time, the tax on corporate profits was lowered from 12 to 11 per cent. All this sounded good, but the amounts released from small incomes for buying purposes were insignificant. On a $4,000 income, for example, the reduction was from $5.63 to $1.88; on a $5,000 income, from $16.88 to $5.63; and for a $10,000 income, from $120 to $65. For the higher brackets the sums were correspondingly greater, but all the decreases taken together, although retroactive for the year 1929, were not drastic enough to prevent a slight increase in income-tax receipts for the fiscal year ending in June, 1930, and a balanced budget. Needless to say, this was the last balanced budget for many years to come.[35]

The Hoover administration accepted deficit financing, however, only as a temporary necessity and not as a policy; the President's aim remained at all times a balanced budget and a steady reduction in the national debt. Unfortunately the measures that he had hoped would effect a speedy upturn in business produced quite inadequate results. Industrial leaders who had promised him faithfully that they would not

[34] Myers and Newton, *The Hoover Policies,* pp. 23–31, 40; Hiram Johnson to sons, November 23, 1929, Johnson Papers, Bancroft Library, University of California.

[35] *United States Statutes at Large* (Washington, 1931), XLVI, 47; *Statistical Abstract of the United States, 1933* (Washington, 1933), pp. 159, 169; Galbraith, *The Great Crash,* pp. 142, 188.

cut down on planned expansion, curtail production, discharge employees, or lower wages soon found themselves obliged to forget their promises and do all these things. Credit inflation proved to be an equally disappointing remedy; who cared to borrow money in order to produce goods that he could not sell? Most local and state governments, short of revenue and engaged in a losing battle to provide relief for the unemployed, had no room in their budgets for expenditures on public works, while the starting of new federal projects was at best a slow-moving process. As incomes and profits fell off, government receipts declined correspondingly, the national budget automatically came unbalanced, and the national debt began to mount, from $16.2 billion in 1930, to $16.8 in 1931, to $19.5 billion in 1932, to $22.5 billion in 1933. Thus it was under Hoover, however much he may have deplored it, that the depression budget first got out of balance, and that deficit financing began.[36]

Whatever unusual expenditures the national government might have to make for other purposes, Hoover was adamant in his opposition to the direct use of federal funds for unemployment relief. The creation of a great national agency for handing out doles, he insisted, was not only unnecessary but it would serve also to "destroy local responsibility and introduce graft, politics, waste, and mismanagement." The task of relief, he maintained, must remain in the hands of state and local governments, with such supplemental aid as they might expect from private charity.

That state, local, and benevolent funds could turn out to be inadequate, however, became apparent during the summer and fall of 1930, when rainfall was below normal in forty of the forty-eight states and a great drought struck many farming areas, particularly in the lower Mississippi Valley, where ordinarily there was too much rather than too little water. The President took an immediate interest in the situation, obtained a 50 per cent reduction in railroad rates on foodstuffs hauled into the stricken areas, ordered an expansion of federal highway construction within their borders to provide supplementary employment, and supported the Red Cross in a drive for funds that added $10 million to the $5 million it had already allocated to meet

[36] Mitchell, *Depression Decade*, pp. 55–58, 82–84; David M. Schneider and Albert Deutsch, *The History of Public Welfare in New York State, 1867–1940* (Chicago, 1941), p. 298; *Statistical Abstract of the United States, 1935* (Washington, 1935), p. 199.

the emergency. In Congress there was a spirited attempt to appropriate $25 million in federal funds for use by the Red Cross, but this organization was unwilling on principle to accept contributions that might turn it from a private to a public agency, a stand that the President cordially approved. Nevertheless, the demands for relief compounded month by month, and the Red Cross was hard put to it to meet them. How much longer could the national government continue to dodge direct responsibility?[37]

From the Republican point of view the autumn of 1930 was a most inauspicious time to hold an election, but there was no way to escape the constitutional requirement. Democratic hopes were high. Between the normal mid-term trend against the party in power and the abnormal conditions resulting from the depression and the drought, a Democratic upsurge was almost inevitable. Furthermore, the Democratic organization was in better shape than it had been for many years. Thanks mainly to the generosity of John J. Raskob, who stayed on as National Chairman after Smith's defeat, the Democratic National Committee had a permanent paid director, Jouett Shouse, and a smart publicity agent, Charles Michelson. A stream of timely releases from Democratic headquarters blamed Hoover and the Republicans for the depression and for everything else that went wrong, and kept Democratic politicians well supplied with interesting ammunition.

Hoover, in a vigorous defense of his policies, October 2, 1930, before the American Bankers Association, did what he could to minimize the importance of the depression. Any recession in business that had occurred, he maintained, was only "a temporary halt in the prosperity of a great nation." The "cheerful courage and power of a confident people" would carry them through the crisis. The Washington *Post,* which supported Hoover warmly, went on to denounce the Democrats for trying to make prosperity a political issue. When "we give freedom to individuals and business," it argued, "we shouldn't blame the government if that freedom brings mistakes and depression and trouble." To this line of thought former Senator James A. Reed of Missouri replied bitingly that the Republican party had maintained for forty years that "it was the producer of prosperity, and now if it says it has no control over financial and economic conditions, it has perpetrated

[37] Hoover, *Memoirs,* III, 51–52, 55–56; F. R. Dulles, *The American Red Cross; A History* (New York, 1950), pp. 280–288; "Our Great Drought Still With Us," *Literary Digest,* CIII (Mar. 21, 1931), 23.

a 40 year fraud upon the American people and has gained and kept office by false pretenses." Or, more simply, as Chairman Shouse pointed out, the difference between what Hoover had promised in 1928 and what he had delivered was too great for the electorate to forgive.[38]

But the campaign was not waged entirely upon generalities. Republican responsibility for the Hawley-Smoot Tariff, commonly called by Democrats the "Grundy" tariff, was impossible to deny, so Republican orators undertook to defend it. Vice-President Curtis, for example, toured the country, recalling the great prosperity that had followed the passage of the Fordney-McCumber Act in 1922, and urging that the new tariff be given a fair chance to show what it could do. He denied that the American high rates had injured foreign trade, and pointed with pride to the flexible provision as a means of meeting new conditions. A Democratic victory, he said, would be sure to encourage tariff tinkering, and would serve further to unsettle business. The Democrats pointed out in return that foreign markets had declined, that American farmers were selling their produce at the lowest prices in decades, that business everywhere was on the downgrade, and that unemployment was rising.

Other specific issues also received attention. Hoover posed as the great friend of labor, but John J. Parker of North Carolina, whom Hoover had nominated for the Supreme Court in 1929, had failed of confirmation because of the support he had given as a circuit judge to the principle of the "yellow dog" contract. Not only did labor hold the nomination against the President but it also showed little friendship for Republican senators who had voted for Parker's confirmation. Nor was the Republican record on labor injunctions forgotten. The Democrats, on their part, were ready to strike out along new lines. Such leaders among them as Smith and Raskob called for a five-day week, a suggestion upon which Senator Fess of Ohio, speaking for the Republicans, heaped heavy ridicule. As for agriculture, the Hoover Farm Board program was already breaking down, and farmer disillusionment was growing. Both parties were split on the prohibition issue, but the Democrats were appreciably wetter than the Republicans. Not many of the latter had the courage to support the forthright stand in favor of re-

[38] Michelson, *The Ghost Talks,* pp. 14–35; A. M. Schlesinger, Jr., *The Age of Roosevelt; The Crisis of the Old Order* (New York, 1957), pp. 273–274; Myers and Newton, *The Hoover Administration,* p. 46; Washington *Post,* Oct. 3, 19, 26; Nov. 1, 1930.

peal taken by Dwight W. Morrow, Republican candidate for senator from New Jersey, but among the Democrats, especially in the city-filled industrial areas, opposition to prohibition was obviously on the march. Above all, the issue of federal participation in relief would not down. Was the Hoover administration doing enough to aid the jobless?[39]

Election results showed that the people had not as yet quite made up their minds; they were ready to administer a sharp rebuke to the Republicans, but they were still reluctant to give the Democrats complete control of Congress. Fear of a Democratic triumph, according to Hoover apologists, accounted for an additional stock-market decline of from 10 to 15 per cent during the month that preceded the voting. Without accepting this thesis, it is still possible to conclude that the electorate had its doubts about the Democrats. The outstanding certainty of the election was that the administration had lost control of both houses of Congress. In the new Senate, with forty-eight Republicans to forty-seven Democrats and one Farmer-Laborite, it was clear that the Republicans might have to use the casting vote of the Vice-President to retain even organizational control, while the balance of power would rest, as in the Seventy-first Congress, with the Republican insurgents. As for the House, the results immediately after the election indicated a majority of one for the Republicans, who had elected 218 representatives to 216 for the Democrats, and one for the Farmer-Laborites. But, as Speaker Longworth pointed out a little later, the division was so close that control of the chamber might rest eventually with whichever party suffered the fewer losses by death of its elected members during the months before the new Congress met. As it turned out, more Republicans (Longworth among them) died than Democrats, while in the resulting special elections more Democrats won than Republicans. With all vacancies filled, the House of Representatives in the Seventy-second Congress consisted of 214 Republicans, 220 Democrats, and one Farmer-Laborite. There were postelection changes in the Senate also, including one created by the death of Senator-elect Morrow, but in the new Senate the party lineup remained the same, and the right of the Republicans to choose committee majorities went unchallenged. The election showed that the wets were gaining, although

[39] *Ibid.*, Oct. 14–31, Nov. 1–4, 1930; Harold Nicholson, *Dwight Morrow* (New York, 1935), p. 379; Fite, *Peek and the Fight for Farm Parity*, p. 226; Myers and Newton, *The Hoover Administration*, p. 428.

they had less than a majority in either house. In three states, Rhode Island, Massachusetts, and Illinois, a popular referendum on repeal showed the opponents of prohibition far in the lead. Many factors, some of them purely personal, affected the results in the state elections, but when all the votes were counted the Republicans were left with only twenty-two governorships to twenty-five for the Democrats and one for the Farmer-Laborites. The re-election of Franklin D. Roosevelt in New York by a decisive majority put him in the best possible position to win his party's nomination for President in 1932.[40]

[40] *Ibid.*, pp. 54–55; Washington *Post*, Nov. 7–9, 1930; *The New York Times*, Apr. 10, 1931, p. 19, col. 2; *Congressional Directory*, 72nd Cong., 1st Sess., Jan., 1932, pp. iii, 145, 147, 249; Warren, *Herbert Hoover*, pp. 122–128. When the Seventy-second Congress met, the Democrats elected John N. Garner to the speakership by a vote of 218 to 207 for Bertrand N. Snell of New York, his Republican opponent. The lone Farmer-Laborite from Minnesota and four Wisconsin Republicans voted for George J. Schneider of Wisconsin. In the Senate, the Republican insurgents made a persistent, but futile, effort to replace the President pro tempore, George H. Moses of New Hampshire, with some other Republican more to their liking. *Congressional Record*, 72nd Cong., 1st Sess., LXXV (Dec. 7, 1931), 8; (Dec. 14, 1931), 439–440; (Jan. 4, 1932), 1198.

CHAPTER 11

Depression Diplomacy

HERBERT HOOVER by experience and disposition was incomparably better prepared than either Harding or Coolidge to deal with the foreign relations of the United States. No doubt he was more widely traveled than any of his predecessors in the Presidency, and his activities during the First World War had made him intimately aware of the problems from which European nations suffered. But he never forgot his Quaker principles when it came to war, or the threat of war. While he had supported with enthusiasm the Wilsonian program for world organization, he had accepted, almost without protest, the retreat of the United States to its traditional policy of isolation. To Hoover this did not mean a total unwillingness on the part of the American nation to participate in world affairs. He accepted the necessity of diplomatic negotiations, but American commitments must not go so far as to involve the United States in the risk of war. He favored adequate measures of national defense, but his definition of adequate seemed to be "a guaranty that no foreign soldier shall ever step upon the soil of our country."[1]

Hoover found himself in complete accord with the spirit of the Kellogg-Briand Peace Pact, but he was quite out of patience with the resumption of naval competition between the United States and Great Britain that had followed the failure of the Geneva Conference of 1927. Also, while the naval limitations agreed upon at Washington in

---

[1] Ray Lyman Wilbur and Arthur M. Hyde, *The Hoover Policies* (New York, 1957), pp. 570–583.

1922 were not due to expire until December 31, 1936, the replacement of overage capital ships was scheduled to begin on November 12, 1931. A Labour victory at the polls in Great Britain, May, 1929, brought into power a new government, headed by J. Ramsay MacDonald as Prime Minister, with which Hoover felt sure he could negotiate a new agreement. The President's experience in international affairs, however, had taught him the necessity of careful preliminary preparations in advance of any formal meeting, hence he initiated the discussions unobtrusively through his ambassador to Great Britain, Charles G. Dawes. When MacDonald proved to be extremely co-operative, Hoover invited him to visit the United States, in itself a gesture of good will much appreciated on both sides of the Atlantic. Working together admirably, the two men surmounted every important obstacle that stood in the way of a new program of limitation. Then and only then did an invitation to the proposed conference go forth. Furthermore, it came from the British government, and invited France, Italy, and Japan to join with the United States and Great Britain in the consultations. The opening date was finally set for January 17, 1930.[2]

The London Naval Conference accomplished about all that Hoover had expected of it. The American delegation, headed by Secretary of State Stimson, acquitted itself admirably. Besides Stimson it included three ambassadors—Dawes, Morrow, and Hugh Gibson (Belgium)— and two Senators, Reed of Pennsylvania and Robinson of Arkansas. It soon developed that whatever new agreements were reached would be primarily between the United States, Great Britain, and Japan. The French demanded naval superiority over Italy, and the Italians demanded complete parity with France. Since neither would yield on these points, the Conference largely passed them by. The difficulties between the United States and Great Britain over cruisers, which had seemed so impossible of settlement at Geneva, were resolved by a compromise arrangement. The British were given an advantage in light (six-inch-gun) cruisers, and the United States an equivalent advantage in heavy (eight-inch-gun) cruisers, with an approximately equal over-all tonnage limitation. To assuage Japanese pride, which had been deeply wounded by the 5:5:3 ration imposed at Washington, the ratio on cruisers was raised to about 10:10:6.5, and on destroyers to 10:10:7. Also, the United States agreed to delay the completion of its heavy-

[2] Henry L. Stimson and McGeorge Bundy, *On Active Service in Peace and War* (New York, 1958), pp. 163–167.

cruiser program until after 1936, and to reopen the whole question at that time. Both the United States and Great Britain were willing to eliminate submarines altogether, but since Japan and France insisted on retaining them, the United States, Great Britain, and Japan ultimately agreed to an identical tonnage limitation for each of the three. On capital-ship limitations, the 5:5:3 ratio of the Washington Conference was continued, but nine battleships—five British, three American, and one Japanese—that the earlier agreement had marked for eventual scrapping were to be scrapped immediately, while a building holiday on all such units was to extend to December 31, 1936. Provision was also made for a new conference in 1935, but any nation wishing to terminate the agreement at its concluding date, 1936, must give notice in 1934.[3]

LONDON CONFERENCE TONNAGE LIMITATIONS[4]

	United States	Great Britain	Japan
All categories	1,123,000	1,151,000	714,000
Heavy cruisers	180,000	146,800	108,400
Light cruisers	143,500	192,200	100,450
Destroyers	150,000	150,000	150,000
Submarines	52,700	52,700	52,700

The London decisions were fully ratified by the United States, Great Britain, and Japan, but they by no means satisfied the naval experts anywhere. Nor did all civilians regard them with favor. Winston Churchill argued that they relegated Great Britain to a position of inferiority as a sea power, and Hiram Johnson characterized them as "the wickedest thing that has been foisted on us since the effort to take us into the League of Nations." Events were soon to prove that again, as at Washington, the Japanese had done far better than appearances indicated. When war actually came, the Japanese were for years impregnable in the waters of eastern Asia, while the British and the Americans felt keenly the limitations that the conference had placed on them. It should be said in fairness, however, that neither the United

[3] *Ibid.*, pp. 167–174; Merze Tate, *The United States and Armaments* (Cambridge, Mass., 1948), pp. 175–181; Giovanni Engely, *The Politics of Naval Disarmament* (London, 1932), pp. 139–164. The treaty is printed in *United States Statutes at Large* (Washington, 1930), XLVI, 2858–2885.
[4] Tate, *United States and Armaments*, p. 179.

States nor Great Britain built up to its treaty rights, while Japan not only built to the limit but in 1934 denounced the treaty in order to build still more.[5]

The depression itself, like the problem of competition in armament, served as a heavy magnet to draw the United States ever more deeply into world affairs. In the buoyant days of inflation, American investors, with the tacit approval of their government, had lent recklessly to European and Latin-American borrowers, and then, without regard for the consequences, had suddenly ceased to lend and tried to collect. As American purchasing power declined, American importations from Europe likewise fell off, a situation which the unfortunate Hawley-Smoot Tariff, and the retaliatory measures it provoked, tended greatly to aggravate. This loss of American trade was a body blow to European economies that had begun confidently to depend on it. But Hoover chose to shut his eyes as much as possible to these facts, and as time went on to become more and more convinced that outside conditions over which the United States had little or no control were responsible for the American collapse. So believing, it was only natural for him to search out international remedies as the more important, and to regard as mere palliatives those aimed primarily at domestic reform.[6]

Designers of the Young Plan, which was projected before Hoover became President and put into effect shortly afterward, had expected it to make possible the continuation of reparations payments by Germany to the Allies, and of debt payments by the Allies to the United States. While the American government officially would never recognize that there was any relation between reparations and war debts, European governments owing money to the United States took a very different view of the matter; if they could not collect from Germany, the principal borrowers felt that they could not, or at least would not, pay the United States. Matters might have worked out as planned but for the growing unwillingness or inability of American investors to risk their money on European loans. As one means of facing up to this situation, the governments of Germany and Austria proposed in March, 1931, a customs union from which both countries hoped to reap important economic benefits. But this co-operative action the French gov-

[5] *Ibid.*, pp. 181–184; Johnson to sons, Johnson Papers, Bancroft Library of the University of California, Berkeley.

[6] Broadus Mitchell, *Depression Decade; From New Era Through New Deal, 1929–1941* (New York, 1947), pp. 58–61.

ernment refused to countenance, fearing that it might lead to an economic, or even political, union between its two former enemies. Partly as a result of this failure, but mainly because of the generally chaotic conditions that prevailed in Austria, that nation's largest bank, the Kreditanstalt, announced on May 11, 1931, that it would be unable to meet its obligations without immediate outside aid. Knowing that such a disaster would have far-reaching results, European nations hastily mobilized their financial resources to prevent the collapse, but psychologically the damage had been done. What the stock-market Panic of 1929 was to the United States, the Kreditanstalt insolvency of 1931 was to all central and western Europe. Distress in Germany became particularly acute, the Reichsbank took heavy losses in gold and foreign currency, and talk of a default on reparations payments began.[7]

President Hoover had kept in close touch with the situation all along, and would even have encouraged the Federal Reserve to participate in a loan to the Kreditanstalt had the opposition of France to the proposed customs union been less adamant. As the European depression deepened, he decided to intervene by asking for a general moratorium on all intergovernmental debts, both principal and interest, for a period of one year. Only Congress could grant this authority, but the President, after obtaining assurance from the leaders of both parties that they would back him up, decided to go ahead. On June 18 he received a moving communication from President Hindenburg, asking for help, and on June 20 he made his announcement. The joy with which it was received in most capitals was tempered by the fact that the French government chose to haggle over the terms, and to make embarrassing counterproposals. What worried the French most was their assumption, not without some basis in fact, that Hoover's primary purpose was to free Germany of her public debts in order to make her private debts, owing in large part to Americans, more collectable. Before the French finally gave in, there were further withdrawals of gold and foreign currency from Germany, and on July 13 the failure of the powerful Darmstädter and Nationalbank led to governmental restrictions on exchange and to bank holidays of the sort the United States would experience a little later on. A seven-power conference in London, to which the United States sent delegates, reached a "standstill agreement" not to withdraw existing foreign credits from Ger-

[7] *Ibid.*, pp. 10–13.

many, but this action was too little and too late. By this time not only Germany but all central Europe also was in the trough of depression.[8]

Could Great Britain, for so long the financial capital of the world, escape a similar catastrophe? Somewhat prematurely, and partly as a matter of pride, the British government in 1925, with Churchill as Chancellor of the Exchequer, had restored the gold standard with the pound at its prewar value. This action gave countries with depreciated currencies a decided advantage over Great Britain in international trade; moreover, the British government had taxed its resources to the limit in its frantic effort to keep central Europe afloat. Under the circumstances there was simply no chance of maintaining confidence in the British pound. By midsummer, withdrawals of gold from the Bank of England had reached £2.5 million daily, and it was obvious that British reserves could not much longer stand the strain. Finally, after the financial crisis proved too difficult for the Labour government to handle, a new national coalition was formed under MacDonald, which on September 21, 1931, surrendered to the inevitable and took Great Britain off the gold standard. The pound promptly dropped to about $3.49. The Scandinavian countries, Finland, all the nations of the British Commonwealth except South Africa, and many Latin-American countries followed the British in the abandonment of gold. Only the United States, France, Belgium, Italy, the Netherlands, and Switzerland among the western powers were still on the gold standard.[9]

For a brief period France, whose franc, although greatly devalued, was still pegged to gold, seemed to have escaped the calamities that had befallen so many of her neighbors. Indeed, after the fall of the pound a considerable quantity of American gold actually fled to France. But economic distress was too contagious and too near at hand for any European nation to escape for long. By late October, with signs of financial stress and strain in France steadily mounting, the French Premier, Pierre Laval, paid Hoover a visit, to obtain if possible a postmoratorium reduction in French war-debt payments. According to Hoover the only agreements of importance that the two men reached were with regard to the maintenance of the gold standard and the need

[8] William Starr Myers and Walter H. Newton, *The Hoover Administration; A Documented Narrative* (New York, 1936), pp. 88–95; Herbert Hoover, *The Memoirs of Herbert Hoover*, III, *The Great Depression, 1929–1941* (New York, 1952), 67–72; Stimson and Bundy, *On Active Service*, pp. 204–208.

[9] Mitchell, *Depression Decade*, pp. 13–14.

of stability in international exchange; but European nations chose to infer, quite inaccurately as it turned out, that Hoover was now ready to link war debts with reparations, and to consider plans for the permanent disposal of both.[10]

Pending the new settlement of "intergovernmental obligations," the various nations of Europe took whatever steps they could to restore their badly shattered economies. In international trade each made every effort to profit at the others' expense. "Tariffs, exchange restrictions, quotas, import prohibitions, barter trade agreements, central trade-clearing agreements" were multiplied furiously as every nation sought to expand its exports and contract its imports. Great Britain shattered long-established practice in early 1932 by abandoning free trade in favor of protection, and by signing a series of agreements at the Ottawa Imperial Conference of July-August, 1932, designed to pass around trade favors within the Empire and Commonwealth. Significantly, this conference was called by the Canadian government as a means of retaliating against the higher duties that the Hawley-Smoot Tariff had levied upon Canadian exports to the United States, and its decisions served materially to lessen the demand for American goods abroad. Among the weaker nations public debtors sought to ease their burden of private debt by substituting standstill agreements, interest revisions, and payments in scrip or blocked currency for the terms originally prescribed.[11]

Eventually the situation in Germany forced the calling of a new conference on reparations. The British and French governments would have preferred to settle for a one-year extension of the moratorium, but Chancellor Heinrich Bruening asserted flatly that, as far as Germany was concerned, reparations were over, and any further attempt "to uphold the political debt system would lead Germany and the world to disaster." Unfortunately political considerations delayed the opening of the conference until June, 1932, and by the time it met in Lausanne, Switzerland, Bruening the moderate was out as Chancellor, and Franz von Papen, soon to become a tool of Adolf Hitler, was in; thus it was to this charlatan that the Allies made the concessions that, if they had come earlier, might have prevented the German plunge into National

[10] William Starr Myers, *The Foreign Policies of Herbert Hoover, 1929–1933* (New York, 1940), pp. 180–187; Hoover, *Memoirs*, III, 96.

[11] Lionel Robbins, *The Great Depression* (London, 1934), pp. 100–124; Mitchell, *Depression Decade,* pp. 14–17.

Socialism. The Allies now agreed to scale down the total due from Germany to about $715 million, an insignificant fraction of the sum set by the Young Plan; furthermore, this obligation was to be met by depositing with the Bank for International Settlements bonds which were not to be negotiated for the next three years, and not even then if their sale would injure Germany's credit. Interestingly enough, the *quid pro quo* for this virtual cancellation of reparations was to come from the United States. By a "gentlemen's agreement" the Allied representatives promised not to ratify the new plan until they had reached a satisfactory settlement with their own creditors, that is, the United States.[12]

The Lausanne agreement was never ratified, for the United States remained unwilling to admit that the war debts had become uncollectable. On this matter President Hoover and Secretary of State Stimson disagreed. Hoover believed that the Allies, at least as soon as the depression was over, could pay their installments; while Stimson, impatient with the futile arguments over "these damn debts," became an outright cancellationist, a stand in which he was joined by most American bankers with international accounts, and by the unpredictable Borah. But the American people generally, and the overwhelming majority of both parties in Congress, regarded debt repayment by the Allies as a sacred obligation, and the "gentlemen's agreement" as little less than blackmail. Actually the Lausanne verdict on reparations, despite its failure to achieve ratification, marked the end of German payments. As for the war debts, Great Britain, Italy, Czechoslovakia, Lithuania, Latvia, and Finland paid the United States their installments in full on December 15, 1932, but France, Belgium, Hungary, Poland, and Yugoslavia defaulted. The next year Great Britain and some other nations made small token payments, but eventually all except Finland, whose debt was small and entirely of postwar origin, ceased to pay. Finland, by meeting its obligations in full, won great good will in the United States.[13]

The cancellation of war debts was not the only question upon which Hoover and Stimson disagreed; they were at odds also over what atti-

[12] Hoover, *Memoirs*, III, 172–173; *United States Statutes at Large* (Washington, 1933), XLVII, 3–4; Stimson and Bundy, *On Active Service*, pp. 211–212.

[13] *Ibid.*, pp. 213–215; Claudius O. Johnson, *Borah of Idaho* (New York, 1936), pp. 278–279; Myers and Newton, *The Hoover Administration*, pp. 229–230; *The New York Times*, Dec. 16, 1932, p. 17, col. 1.

tude the American government should take toward the Japanese attack on Manchuria in the fall of 1931, a challenge to the *status quo* in the Far East that deeply disturbed both the President and his Secretary of State. It was a matter of common knowledge that there existed in Japan an irresponsible military clique which, with some business backing, was bent on vigorous Japanese expansion regardless of world opinion. To American observers the failure of the current moderate government in Japan to hold this faction in leash was a great disappointment. What should the United States do, if anything, to maintain the sanctity of the treaties Japan had defied? Hoover soon made it clear that he was adamant in his opposition to any action that might point in the direction of war. Stimson, on the other hand, especially after the advent of a new and radical Japanese ministry in December, 1931, came to the conclusion that only force, or at least the threat of force, would ever induce the Japanese government to respect its treaty obligations.[14]

The Manchurian crisis was touched off by the so-called "Mukden incident" of September 18–19, 1931. Following "an alleged act of sabotage" by the Chinese on the Japanese-owned South Manchurian Railway, Japanese troops seized Mukden and began to expand against weak Chinese opposition throughout all South Manchuria. On the face of it this action was in complete defiance of the Nine Power Treaty, the Kellogg-Briand Peace Pact, and the Covenant of the League of Nations, to the first two of which the United States was a party. But the Japanese government took a very different view of the matter. Ever since the Russo-Japanese war Japan had held many special privileges in Manchuria, among them the right to keep troops as guards along Japanese-owned railroads; indeed, the exploitation of Manchurian natural resources and trade had become a settled aspect of Japanese policy. Meantime, however, the Chinese, who outnumbered the Japanese in Manchuria by about thirty million to one million, had come to resent more and more Japanese limitations on their national sovereignty and to resist Japanese authority all they dared. Chinese nationalism was on the rise; unless something drastic were done to arrest its progress in Manchuria, the Japanese feared they might even lose the foothold they

[14] Stimson and Bundy, *On Active Service,* pp. 226–239; R. N. Current, *Secretary Stimson; A Study in Statecraft* (New Brunswick, N.J., 1954), pp. 66–77; Wilbur and Hyde, *The Hoover Policies,* pp. 599–603.

had already achieved. The Mukden incident was Japan's answer to this threat.[15]

Had the League of Nations taken the lead in advocating the use of economic sanctions against Japan, it seems likely that Stimson would have favored giving it American support. But Hoover would not even consider such a move. The only weapon available to the United States, in the President's opinion, was moral condemnation. Since Hoover was President and Stimson was not, and since beyond a doubt the overwhelming majority of the American people agreed with Hoover and not with Stimson, the Secretary had no choice but to accept the decision of his chief. But the "Stimson doctrine" of nonrecognition that resulted was misnamed; it should have been called the "Hoover doctrine."[16]

The Japanese militarists had chosen an auspicious time for their great adventure. In the western world the depression was racing from bad to worse, with the nations of Europe now as deeply involved in the economic disaster as the United States. Political instability was the rule on both sides of the Atlantic, while international tensions over war debts, reparations, tariffs, and currencies could hardly have been worse. Naval strength in both Great Britain and the United States was at low ebb; if the test should come, Japan could probably hold her own against all adversaries in Far Eastern waters. The League of Nations, with no certainty of American support, would hardly dare take up the Japanese challenge, and the Kellogg-Briand Peace Pact was a mere scrap of paper. If Japan could get away with the control of Manchuria, the dreams of her imperialists for still further conquests might come true.[17]

The League of Nations proved to be about as ineffective as the makers of Japanese policy anticipated. China at once appealed to it under Article XI of the Covenant, which made "any war or threat of

---

[15] A. Whitney Griswold, *The Far Eastern Policy of the United States* (New York, 1938), pp. 410–415; Henry L. Stimson, *The Far Eastern Crisis; Recollections and Observations* (New York, 1936), pp. 31–37; Stimson and Bundy, *On Active Service*, pp. 220–226.

[16] Myers, *Foreign Policies of Herbert Hoover*, pp. 156–159; Stimson and Bundy, *On Active Service*, pp. 226–239; Griswold, *Far Eastern Policy*, pp. 415–426.

[17] "Hoover's Warning on Armament," *Literary Digest*, CXIV (Nov. 12, 1932), 5; Engely, *Politics of Naval Disarmament*, pp. 98–103; Walter Millis, *The Future of Sea Power in the Pacific* (New York, 1935), pp. 27–31.

war . . . a matter of concern to the whole League." Eventually the
League Council, after its resolutions urging the restoration of normal
relations failed to achieve results, voted on December 10 to send an
investigating committee to the Far East, a course to which the Japanese
had at first objected, but at length consented. The result was an able
commission of five, headed by an Englishman, Lord Lytton, and including one American, General Frank R. McCoy. The Lytton Commission
discharged its duties with diligence and deliberation, but in so doing it
gave the Japanese still further time to entrench themselves on the main-
land. The Lytton Report was not ready until September, 1932, and
was not made public until the month after that.[18]

From the very beginning Secretary Stimson had sought to collaborate
as closely as possible with the League, through which he hoped a way
might be found to curb Japan. When Aristide Briand, president of the
League Council, had sent identical telegrams on September 22, 1931,
to both China and Japan, urging them to refrain from further acts of
hostility and to find the means for withdrawing their troops, Stimson
had dispatched similar messages two days later. When the League
Council asked him, early in October, to send "a representative to sit at
the Council table" during discussions of the Sino-Japanese dispute, he
authorized Prentiss Gilbert, the American consul general at Geneva, to
undertake the task. Stimson's hope was that the moderates in the
Japanese Cabinet, including especially Baron Shidehira, the Foreign
Minister, would eventually "get control of the situation." But the
exact reverse happened; early in December a new Japanese Cabinet,
wholly friendly to what the army had done, took over with the clear
intent of holding fast to all territory taken. Indeed, on January 2, 1932,
Japanese forces occupied Chinchow, and by so doing "destroyed the
last remnant of Chinese authority in Manchuria."[19]

It was at this point that Stimson decided to act independently of the
League and turned to Hoover's suggestion of moral condemnation. On
January 7, 1932, he sent identical notes to both the Chinese and the
Japanese governments, informing them that the United States would

---

[18] Stimson, *Far Eastern Crisis,* pp. 38, 66–68; Stimson and Bundy, *On
Active Service,* p. 260; Current, Secretary Stimson, pp. 77–91; W. W.
Willoughby, *The Sino-Japanese Controversy and the League of Nations* (Balti-
more, 1935), pp. 172–200, 383.

[19] Stimson, *Far Eastern Crisis,* p. 46; Charles G. Dawes, *Journal as Ambassador to Great Britain* (New York, 1939), pp. 411–421; Stimson and Bundy,
On Active Service, pp. 227, 231.

neither admit the legality of any *de facto* situation, nor regard any treaty or agreement as binding that conflicted with the Open Door policy or had been brought about by means contrary to the Pact of Paris. This he meant to be a ringing denunciation of what the Japanese military had already done in Manchuria, and a deterrent against any further aggressions they might have in mind. If the other great powers would now join in similar statements, the Japanese government would at least know to what extent its actions ran counter to world opinion. But to Stimson's chagrin no other nation repaired to the standard that the United States had raised. Sir John Simon, the current British Foreign Minister, preferred to accept Japanese assurances, obviously contrary to fact, that Japan had no intention of violating the Open Door policy, and to forget about the Kellogg-Briand Pact. No doubt Sir John was influenced both by the eagerness of some British business-men to cultivate Japan in the interest of trade, and by his conviction that the United States would never use force to back up its words. At any rate, Stimson's reward for his efforts was a blunt rebuff, one which left the Japanese free to go as far as they chose. Naturally the attitude of Great Britain was echoed by other European powers. "What the British would not do the French would not do, nor the Dutch nor the Italians."[20]

That the Japanese expansionists had more in mind than Manchuria became evident when Japanese marines on January 28, 1932, advanced from the International Settlement of Shanghai into Chinese territory. The reason for this attack was in part the success of a Chinese boycott against Japanese trade, and in part the desire of the Japanese navy to emulate the exploits of the army in Manchuria. Chinese resistance proved to be much stronger than anticipated, and the Japanese admiral in charge of the operation ordered a bombing attack that cost the lives of many helpless civilians. It took heavy reinforcements from Japan and weeks of hard fighting before Chinese resistance was worn down. The vigor with which the Chinese troops fought back contrasted markedly with the weakness of their efforts in Manchuria, and aroused for China a degree of sympathy and admiration wholly lacking during the earlier incident. Moreover, the British were touched in a tender spot—they had important trade interests in Shanghai—and Simon now proved willing to co-operate far more cordially with Stimson than be-

[20] *Ibid.*, 237–238; Current, *Secretary Stimson*, pp. 92–113.

fore. The united Anglo-American stand, reinforced by League action, undoubtedly had much to do with the ultimate decision of the Japanese to draw their forces back within the International Settlement.[21]

Had Hoover been less determined in his opposition to sanctions, it is possible that Stimson might at least have tried to take advantage of the Shanghai attack to test out some kind of economic pressure as a means of checkmating Japan. But the President not only refused to consider such a course, he ultimately required also that Stimson announce publicly the decision of the United States not to use sanctions. Blocked at every other turn, Stimson finally, on February 23, 1932, embodied his views in a long letter to Senator Borah. If only the other nations of the world would take the position that the American government had taken, he argued, their action would "effectively bar the legality" of any title or right "obtained by pressure or treaty violation."[22]

Stimson's plea for international approval of his doctrine won a measure of support from the League of Nations, which called upon League members "not to recognize any situation, treaty or agreement which may be brought about by means contrary to the Covenant of the League of Nations or to the Pact of Paris." But the British Foreign Office showed no disposition to exert any pressure upon Japan beyond the minimum needed to end the Japanese trespass upon Chinese territory adjacent to Shanghai. As for Manchuria, Japan on February 18, 1932, recognized it as the "independent" state of Manchukuo, and shortly afterward made Henry Pu Yi, the deposed Chinese Emperor, its puppet ruler. All this happened before the appearance in October, 1932, of the Lytton Report, which found no adequate excuse either for the original Japanese attack or for the forcible seizure of "indisputably Chinese territory," and recommended the creation of an autonomous Manchuria under Chinese sovereignty but with full recognition of Japanese rights and interests. After a long debate, in which Simon took pains to emphasize the many provocations that Japan had suffered, the League Assembly voted on February 24, 1933, with only the Japanese dissenting, to adopt the report and to refuse recognition to Manchukuo. Japan, unimpressed and defiant, gave notice on March 27 of her intention to withdraw from the League of Nations.[23]

[21] Willoughby, *Sino-Japanese Controversy*, pp. 309–316, 323, 352, 357–360; Stimson and Bundy, *On Active Service*, pp. 239–242.

[22] *Ibid.*, pp. 243–256; Stimson, *Far Eastern Policy*, pp. 166–175.

[23] *Ibid.*, pp. 178, 230; Willoughby, *Sino-Japanese Controversy*, pp. 400, 404, 452, 595; Stimson and Bundy, *On Active Service*, pp. 248, 256–260.

Thus in the first real opportunity to exert its authority the League had demonstrated only that it could not discipline a nation bent on war. The results of this failure were soon apparent as one European power after another began to follow the example Japan had set. It is intersting to speculate on what might have happened (1) had the United States been an active member of the League, and (2) had Hoover been less unyielding in his determination not to use force or the threat of force against a nation guilty of treaty violations. As matters stood, British unwillingness to back up any punitive measures against Japan can be readily explained, if not condoned. It was perfectly clear that American co-operation with the League would extend only to condemning Japan; beyond that the American government would refuse to go. And Great Britain, to whom most of the fighting would fall if sanctions ended in war, had no interest in becoming so involved, with the United States sitting on the sidelines. The failure of the American President and the American people to see that they could not, without grave risk, take a high moral stand in international affairs, and at the same time refuse to back it up with appropriate action, was the root of the difficulty. Ten years later, at Pearl Harbor, the United States paid a high price for the nation's inadequate understanding of international realities.[24]

In Japan the conviction that the United States might talk against Japanese expansion, but would never act to prevent it, received added impetus from a vigorous American movement in the early 1930's in favor of granting independence to the Philippine Islands. Why should the United States plan a retreat from this outpost of empire if not primarily to escape from the risk of having to defend it against Japan? Possibly only a few of the many Americans who suddenly became interested in freedom for the Philippines had thought much about the danger to the islands from Japan. What these new crusaders for Philippine independence really had in mind was the exclusion of Philippine products from American markets. The same spirit of economic isolationism that had produced the Hawley-Smoot Tariff produced also a series of proposals, known as the Hawes-Cutting bills, for setting the Philippines free. Indeed, it was during the tariff debate that those who wished to discriminate against imports from the Philippines came to see in the independence movement the best possible

[24] *Ibid.,* pp. 261–264.

means of achieving the end they desired. Ultimate independence for the Philippines was generally taken for granted in the United States, and the Philippine leaders were deeply committed to the achievement of that goal. But somehow the time for action had never seemed quite ripe. Now, all of a sudden, considerations of internal American policy changed the situation completely, thus providing added evidence to the Japanese on how little Americans cared about their overseas interests, and why their foreign policy had gone soft.[25]

Politicians, at their wits' end for some kind of sop to throw the distressed American farmers, and urged along by the equally harassed leaders of farm organizations, were the most active proponents of Philippine independence. It was easy to pretend that the importation of Philippine coconut oil was a ghastly menace to American dairy, cottonseed oil, and fat-producing interests, all of which had certainly fallen on evil times. Actually, however, the domestic products competed more with each other than with the imports from the Philippines. Two-thirds of the imported coconut oil was turned into soap, for the manufacture of which the domestic oils and fats were not satisfactory substitutes. Oleomargarine could be made either from fats or from vegetable oils, and it would undersell butter whether the materials used were of domestic or of foreign origin. Probably coconut oil was preferable for this purpose to cottonseed oil, but so also were animal fats. If coconut oil could be kept out, more animal fats might be used in the manufacture of butter substitutes, and cottonseed oil might in turn gain on animal fats used for cooking purposes. It was that complicated, and in addition the quantities involved were not large enough to justify all the rhetoric expended on the subject.[26]

American sugar interests also professed to see a direct relation between the rising imports of Philippine sugar and the falling prices of sugar in the United States. As a matter of fact, American sugar prices were in line with world prices, plus the duty charged on Cuban sugar. The United States was unable to produce more than about one-fourth the sugar it consumed; another one-fourth came from Cuba; practically all the rest from the island possessions. Whatever additional imports came from the Philippines might diminish the amounts ob-

[25] Grayson Kirk, *Philippine Independence: Motives, Problems, and Prospects* (New York, 1936), pp. 102–105, 199–207; Ralston Hayden, "China, Japan and the Philippines," *Foreign Affairs*, XI (July, 1933), 711–715.

[26] Kirk, *Philippine Independence*, pp. 74–75, 78–81.

tained from Cuba, as indeed they had already done, but under existing laws that was about all that could be expected. There was in reality no important competition between Philippine and American sugar; such as existed was primarily between Philippine and Cuban sugar, a fact attested by the cheerful way in which the Cuban lobby made common cause with the American sugar interests.[27]

The other Philippine products that sold well in the United States included principally hemp and cordage. Naturally American manufactures of competitive items shared with the American farmers an interest in the equivalent of tariff protection, whether through independence or otherwise. That freedom of trade with the United States meant much to the Philippine economy was obvious, but that Philippine competition seriously injured either business or farming interests in the United States was more a myth than a reality.[28]

The original Hawes-Cutting program for severing ties with the Philippines would actually have granted tariff protectionists comparatively few immediate advantages. There was to be a long interim, or probationary, period in advance of independence, a gradual application of tariff duties, and a final plebiscite for or against independence. As finally passed, the measure made extensive modifications of all these stipulations. Congress gave the islands two years in which to draw up a constitution. The adoption of this document, provided it met the approval of the President of the United States, would then usher in a ten-year period of Commonwealth status. During this decade the United States would collect the regular American duties upon all except closely restricted quotas of Philippine products, while the Commonwealth, beginning with its sixth year, must impose a graduated duty on exports to the United States, with the export charges based upon American tariff rates and designed to pave the way for the ultimate application of full American duties. The Commonwealth, however, was given no similar right to limit or tax American imports into the Philippine Islands; moreover, instead of the final plebiscite on independence at the end of the ten-year trial period, the law asserted merely that, in case the Philippine voters accepted the constitution submitted to them, such action would be construed as an adequate expression of their desire for independence. Thus Philippine citizens who favored independence would have to vote for whatever constitution was

[27] *Ibid.*, pp. 89–93, 141–145.
[28] *Ibid.*, pp. 69–70, 75–76, 112–113, 148–150.

submitted, whether they liked it or not, or else have their votes counted against independence. There were still other clauses in the law that could hardly escape giving offense. One of them defined the Philippine people as aliens, and gave them an annual American immigration quota of fifty persons; another provided that the United States might retain such land or other property in the Philippines as the President might already have reserved for military or other purposes. Presumably, this provision would permit the construction of American naval bases on Philippine soil.[29]

The iniquities of this measure were so numerous that some who supported it must certainly have doubted if it ever could be put into effect. The intentions of its proponents were perfectly clear. "I believe it is time for the United States to stop acting as a good cousin or a good brother to the whole world, and . . . to stay at home and attend to its own business," said the President of the National Sugar-Beet Growers' Association, one of the insistent advocates of Philippine independence. Among the most earnest opponents of the bill was President Hoover, who promptly vetoed it in a stinging message that mercilessly revealed its many faults. But Congress, by a vote of 274 to 94 in the House and 66 to 26 in the Senate, unhesitatingly repassed the bill over his veto. The vote in favor of the measure was completely bipartisan, although the Republicans furnished whatever opposition to it there was. In the end it was the Philippine legislature, deeply as its members were committed to the idea of independence, which refused to go along, and thus nullified the action of Congress. No doubt the Philippine politicians hoped for better terms from the incoming Democratic administration, a hope in which they were for the most part doomed to disappointment. From almost any point of view, American withdrawal from the Philippines, as originally planned, was hardly less cynical than Japanese plans for the conquest of Manchuria. The chief difference lay in the fact that the Americans were determined to get out, and the Japanese were determined to stay in.[30]

Two other problems of international relations remained in the

---

[29] *Ibid.*, pp. 105–135; *United States Statutes at Large* (Washington, 1933), XLVII, 761–770; Wilbur and Hyde, *The Hoover Policies,* pp. 610–613.

[30] Kirk, *Philippine Independence,* p. 115; *Congressional Record,* 72nd Cong., 2nd Sess., LXXVI (Jan. 13, 1933), 1759–1761, 1768–1769; (Jan. 17, 1933), 1924–1925; Raymond Leslie Buell, "Hypocrisy and the Philippines," *The Nation,* CXXXV (Dec. 28, 1932), 639–640.

category of unfinished business at the close of the Hoover administration. One was a Conference on the Reduction and Limitation of Armaments, in session at Geneva. The other was a World Economic Conference, on which the President had set his heart, to be called sometime after the election, probably in early 1933.

The first of these conferences was the result of years of planning by a "Preparatory Commission" of the League of Nations. It opened in Geneva on February 2, 1932, with thirty-one nations in attendance, including the United States, the Soviet Union, and Germany. Since about all that could be expected by way of naval limitation had already been accomplished, the Geneva Conference concerned itself primarily with the reduction of land armaments. In this problem the United States, due to the insignificant size of its own army, was not primarily concerned, but after months of fruitless negotiations by the big-army nations, President Hoover instructed the American representative, Hugh Gibson, to present what Hoover believed to be some "practicable and far-reaching proposals." Hoover's plan called for (1) the reduction of all armies to one-third more strength than would be required to maintain internal order, and (2) the abolition of weapons designed essentially for offensive operations. The Hoover proposals got exactly nowhere, and the conference adjourned on July 23 to meet again on January 19, 1933. Its second session was marked by the same exercises in futility as the first; in the end German truculence was to destroy all hope of agreement.[31]

The main purpose of the World Economic Conference, which Prime Minister MacDonald agreed to invite to London, and to which the League of Nations had also given its blessing, was to take steps toward world stabilization of currencies and international exchange. Proper action by the conference, Hoover believed, would do much toward the restoration of prosperity everywhere. Before the election of 1932 he had already decided on the personnel of the American delegation, but his defeat in November made further action, without the co-operation of the incoming administration, seem inexpedient. Hoover made an earnest effort to induce Roosevelt to join him in selecting an American delegation, but the President-elect refused to make any commitments in advance of taking office. The conference was postponed until the

[31] Herbert Hoover and Hugh Gibson, *The Problems of Lasting Peace* (New York, 1942), pp. 160–164; Wilbur and Hyde, *Hoover Policies*, pp. 605–610.

summer of 1933, and when it met its accomplishments were negligible.[32]

On the whole, the record of the Hoover administration on international relations was as good as could be expected in view of the intense isolationism of the American people, and the aversion of the President to using the threat of force as a diplomatic weapon. On naval limitations and Far Eastern affairs the President's attitude, despite the importance of American overseas commitments, undoubtedly represented accurately the will of the American people. On war debts, reparations, and independence for the Philippines, his views were far more enlightened than those of most Americans; but, especially during the last half of his administration, he found it very difficult to mold public opinion his way. His insistence that the United States had had little to do with bringing on the depression was unfortunate only in so far as it made him less concerned with domestic remedies than he might otherwise have been; what he did toward the restoration of Europe was all to the good. It was a pity that both Hoover and the American people failed to realize that the United States, and the United States alone, was in a position to assert world leadership, but the decision to reject the League and the outside world antedated Hoover's administration, and he should not be blamed for the mistaken policies he inherited. Once Theodore Roosevelt had said: "The United States has not the option as to whether it will or will not play a great part in the world. It *must* play a great part. All that it can decide is whether it will play that part well or badly." In effect the United States, instead of playing a minor role well during these years, played a major role badly. Perhaps Stimson had this thought in mind on one occasion when he denounced "the timidity of governments" and "said that the time had come when somebody has got to show some guts."[33]

[32] *Ibid.*, pp. 494–506.

[33] A. B. Hart and H. R. Ferleger (eds.), *Theodore Roosevelt Cyclopedia* (New York, 1914), p. 184; Stimson and Bundy, *On Active Service*, p. 281.

CHAPTER 12

The Years of the Locust

BAFFLING as were the problems of foreign affairs that harassed the Hoover administration, conditions on the home front were even worse. With the coming of the depression the problem of prohibition came to a head, and a decision on that touchy subject had to be reached. Agricultural distress, despite the best efforts of the Federal Farm Board, refused stubbornly to yield to the remedies prescribed for it. Industrial enterprise dropped steadily to new lows, and unemployment rose correspondingly to new highs. The President could not have taken his responsibilities more seriously, but somehow each new crisis seemed only to lead to another. By the end of his term the very bottom had dropped out of the depression. Elected as the business world's answer to what the country needed by way of a President, Hoover failed dismally, perhaps because he represented business so well, to come up with a successful formula for business recovery.

Before the crash in 1929 the *status quo* on prohibition seemed to satisfy an overwhelming majority of Americans; the drys had their law and the wets had their liquor. Most of the state codes on prohibition were fully as drastic as the Volstead Act, some of them even more so. Indeed, new and stiffer penalties for those who broke prohibition laws were rarely difficult to obtain. But when it came to actual enforcement, neither the states nor the nation made anything like adequate efforts. The total expenditures for this purpose in all the states, taken together, came to less than $700,000 in 1927, while in some states the amounts expended were next to nothing, less than $1,000 in each of three states, and between $1,000 and $25,000 in each of seven others. The national government, proportionately, did little better; that same year, 1927, the total appropriated for national enforcement was under $12 million, about ten cents per capita. Efforts to spend substantially more money on making the law effective won little support in Congress. When in early 1929 Senator Bruce of Maryland, a wet, slipped an amendment into an appropriation bill adding $256 million to the budget of the Prohibition Bureau—enough to make a real try at enforcement—both drys and wets were thoroughly upset, and united in restoring the item to its normal insignificance.[1]

The election of 1928 seemed to demonstrate that most Americans had no very great objection to prohibition as long as it failed to prohibit. But Smith's candidacy also brought out the fact that an increasingly vocal minority had begun to think in terms of repeal. Should a free people be required to accept laws that trespassed so glaringly on their personal liberties? Was it decent and proper to leave on the statute books laws that were not seriously intended to be enforced? What could the national Prohibition Bureau, with only a few thousand employees and a strictly limited budget, ever hope to do against the widespread tendency in most cities and some whole states to ignore the law? Or what would happen to state and local authority if the nation should build up a bureaucracy strong enough to make prohibition really effective? Was prohibition responsible for the growth of racketeering, and for the frightening disrespect for law in general that seemed to have engulfed the land? For a long time these questions could hardly be heard above the din raised in favor of prohibition by the Anti-Saloon League and other dry organizations. But by the late 1920's the Association Against the Prohibition Amendment (backed by du Pont funds), the Moderation League, and other antiprohibition societies were also raising a din. Furthermore, state referendums and *Literary Digest* polls revealed that the opposition organizations were at least reflecting, if not actually creating, a steadily growing sentiment for repeal.[2]

[1] Charles Merz, *The Dry Decade* (New York, 1931), pp. 206, 231–236, 329; *Congressional Record*, 70th Cong., 2nd Sess., LXX (Feb. 19, 1929), 3742; (Feb. 28, 1929), 4796; (Mar. 2, 1929), 4968; Harris Gaylord Warren, *Herbert Hoover and the Great Depression* (New York, 1959), pp. 210–212.

[2] Fabian Franklin, *What Prohibition Has Done to America* (New York, 1922), pp. 121–129; Gilman M. Ostrander, *The Prohibition Movement in California, 1848–1933* (Berkeley, Calif., 1957), pp. 169–181; John C. Gebhart, "Move-

As President, Hoover had to face up to the pledges he had made during the 1928 campaign. One of them, stated in his acceptance speech, had called for a "searching investigation" of the prohibition situation, both as to "fact and cause." Possibly his ultimate decision to extend the investigation to "the whole of the law enforcement machinery" indicated a desire to relegate prohibition to a place of lesser importance, and to shift the emphasis from whether it was enforceable or not to how it could best be enforced. But the eleven-member Commission on Law Enforcement and Observance, which he appointed late in May, 1929, left few aspects of the subject unstudied. Headed by former Attorney General George W. Wickersham, it took its duties seriously, and in its final report, January 20, 1931, branded prohibition enforcement as a failure, noted the increase in corruption that had accompanied it, deplored its undermining of law enforcement generally, and regarded with alarm its demoralizing effect on the federal judicial system and on the nation's prison problem. Superficially, at least, the report seemed to favor the retention of prohibition, possibly with a revision of the Eighteenth Amendment which would merely grant Congress authority "to regulate or to prohibit the manufacture, traffic in or transportation of intoxicating liquors." But the individual opinions of the eleven members were so at variance that even this deduction seems open to question. Two commissioners favored the retention of the Eighteenth Amendment, two favored its immediate repeal, seven favored revision with the ultimate goal of national and state monopoly. The report, whatever its authors meant to recommend, revealed fully the existing discontent with prohibition and the need for decisive action.[3]

Just as the Eighteenth Amendment was the child of the First World War, so its repeal was the child of the Great Depression. Wet propagandists, adapting to their ends the techniques of the Anti-Saloon League, which in its day had attributed practically all evil to the liquor traffic, now pinned the same accusation on prohibition: "Every time

---

ment Against Prohibition," *Annals of the American Academy of Political and Social Science,* CLXIII (Sept., 1932), 176–178.

[3] *Ibid.*, 174–175; Merz, *Dry Decade,* p. 237; Ray Lyman Wilbur and Arthur M. Hyde, *The Hoover Policies* (New York, 1937), p. 551. The Report of the Wickersham Commission is printed in House Document No. 722, 71st Cong., 3rd Sess. (Washington, 1931), ser. 9361. See also Fletcher Dobyns, *The Amazing Story of Repeal; An Exposé of the Power of Propaganda* (Chicago, 1940), pp. 88–89; Warren, *Herbert Hoover,* pp. 212–218.

a crime is committed, they cry prohibition. Every time a girl or boy goes wrong, they shout prohibition. Every time a policeman or politician is accused of corruption, they scream prohibition. As a result, they are gradually building up in the public mind the impression that prohibition is a major cause of the sins of society."[4]

There was much argument, too, as to the cost of prohibition in taxes lost, jobs destroyed, farm produce unsold, buildings untenanted, and the like; no doubt some citizens were influenced by the economic motive, and hoped that repeal might pave the way toward lowered taxes, balanced budgets, and greater prosperity. But in the main it was the psychology of depression that made people change their minds. In prosperous times the voters could tolerate the inefficiency of prohibition, make jokes about it, let it ride. But with the advent of depression its every fault was magnified, and the best jokes turned stale. The people were in a mood for change. Zealots who had promised the millennium as a result of prohibition, and had delivered bootleggers and racketeers instead, were in a class with politicians who had promised prosperity and delivered adversity. It was about time to wipe the slate clean and start over.[5]

Hoover did what he could to enforce prohibition. He reorganized and enlarged the Prohibition Bureau, transferred it to the Department of Justice, and placed its personnel under civil service. But federal enforcement without state and local support was still a failure. In those localities, mostly rural, where public sentiment favored the law and supported enforcement, it was enforced; elsewhere it was the same old false pretense as under Harding and Coolidge. Eventually Hoover, who hated the saloon and deplored intemperance as much as anyone, made up his mind that the Eighteenth Amendment would have to go, and on August 11, 1932, almost three months before the election, announced his decision to the nation. Since the Democratic platform of 1932 also favored repeal, there could be but one end in sight. After the election, in February, 1933, the last lame-duck Congress submitted the repeal amendment, and before the end of the year it became a part of the Constitution. The repeal of racketeering was not so simple, but one device of great effectiveness in dealing with leading criminals, prosecution for income-tax evasion, had already netted an important victory

4 Peter H. Odegard, *The American Public Mind* (New York, 1930), p. 180.
5 Dobyns, *Amazing Story*, pp. 375–381; Warren, *Herbert Hoover*, pp. 218–223.

as early as 1931 with the arrest and conviction of Al Capone, king of
the Chicago underworld. The crime-control acts that led to the later
effectiveness of the Federal Bureau of Investigation were not passed
until the spring of 1934.[6]

If the farmers were satisfied with prohibition, they were not very
happy about anything else. The failure of the Federal Farm Board to
live up to expectations had left rural America in a cruel predicament.
Farm production continued at high levels, but farm prices dropped
catastrophically; gross farm income in 1932 was less than half as much
as in 1929. The decline in farm prices was at its worst in the great
basic crops that affected the greatest numbers: wheat, cotton, and tobacco—all export crops which suffered disastrously from the collapse of
foreign markets. According to Department of Agriculture estimates, the
average farmer's net annual income after cost of production, rent,
interest, and taxes was not more than $230. The value of capital em-
ployed in agriculture declined from $79 billion in 1919 to $58 billion in
1929, and to only $38 billion in 1932. Efforts of the Federal Farm
Board to promote acreage reductions brought mainly jeers and ridicule.
What else was the farmer to do if not to farm? According to Senator
Brookhart the F.F.B., in order to achieve the results it sought, would
"pretty near have to kill off 20 per cent of the farmers." But as a matter
of fact, for the first time since 1922, farm population in 1931 was up,
with an increase of 206,000 over the preceding year; unemployment in
the cities kept the farmers on the land, while some city job seekers
drifted to the country in their frantic search for work.[7]

The Hoover administration did much to alleviate the distress in agriculture, but little to cure it. After the drought of 1930 Congress appropriated $45 million for the Department of Agriculture to use in
making advances to farmers for the purchase of seed, stock feed, fuel
for farm tractors, and the like. Such grants were intended as loans,
however, not gifts, and the Secretary of Agriculture was authorized to

[6] Merz, *Dry Decade,* p. 243; William Starr Myers and Walter H. Newton,
The Hoover Administration; A Documented Narrative (New York, 1936), pp.
535–536, 552–556; Don Whitehead, *The FBI Story* (New York, 1956), pp.
15, 102, 104.

[7] Chester C. Davis, "The Development of Agricultural Policy Since the End
of the World War," Yearbook of Agriculture, 1940 (Washington, 1940), pp.
313–314; Theodore Saloutos and John D. Hicks, *Agricultural Discontent in
the Middle West, 1900–1939* (Madison, Wis., 1951), p. 419; Broadus Mitchell,
Depression Decade; From New Era Through New Deal, 1929–1940 (New
York, 1947), p. 67.

obtain first liens on crops by way of security. That this appropriation served a useful purpose is indicated by the fact that during the winter and spring of 1931–32 over 385,000 borrowers obtained loans under its terms. In answer to the tightening of credit in rural districts, the President recommended to Congress an appropriation of $125 million to strengthen the Federal Land Banks. The added capital, he hoped, would enable the Banks to "grant extensions to worthy borrowers," and to make new loans where needed. Congress voted the whole sum requested. As a means of reducing rural unemployment Congress also voted extra funds for building forest roads and trails, for highway construction, and for the control of "animals injurious to agriculture and forestry."[8]

The nearest approach to direct relief that Hoover was willing to accept was also closely related to the farm problem. The Federal Farm Board, thanks to its efforts at price control, had at its disposal huge quantities of wheat and cotton, the very existence of which tended to depress prices. With starvation in the face of plenty, the President somewhat reluctantly affixed his signature to a series of measures that turned over to the Red Cross 85 million bushels of wheat held by the Grain Stabilization Corporation and 844,000 bales of cotton held by the Cotton Stabilization Corporation. To the Red Cross organization fell the somewhat unwelcome, but well-discharged, task of arranging for the milling of the wheat, the processing of the cotton, and the distribution to the needy of flour, foodstuffs, cloth, and clothing. According to the official historian:

The statistics of this vast operation are overwhelming. Over 27,000 carloads of wheat, 30,000 of flour and 7,800 of stock feed were shipped the length and breadth of the land. These supplies ultimately reached all but 17 of the 3,098 counties in the United States, and the result was the distribution of over 10,000,000 barrels of flour to 5,000,000 families. In cotton distribution, 540,000 bales of finished garments, 211,000 of yard goods, and 92,000 blankets and comforters were handled. Approximately the same number of families as were given flour were the recipients of over 66,000,000 ready-made garments, 38,000,000 chapter-made garments, and 3,000,000 blankets.[9]

[8] *Ibid.*, pp. 67–68; Myers and Newton, *The Hoover Administration*, pp. 59, 129; *United States Statutes at Large* (Washington, 1931), XLVI, 1032; (Washington, 1933), XLVII, 36.
[9] Foster Rhea Dulles, *The American Red Cross; A History* (New York, 1950), pp. 290–293.

Handouts were not what the American farmers wanted. They raised enough, except during such emergencies as the drought of 1930. What they wanted was a chance to sell their produce at decent prices. By the end of 1931 they had lost confidence in the Federal Farm Board; indeed, during the final year of the Hoover administration, this organization, having used up its capital, became virtually moribund. What was to replace it? A few agricultural economists, notably Professor John D. Black of Harvard University, were ready to turn to a "domestic allotment" plan for limiting the sales permitted to individual producers, but this idea had not yet percolated down to the grass roots. At a Washington meeting of farm leaders, held in January, 1932, representatives of the Farm Bureau, the Grange, and the Farmers' Union attempted to agree on a new program for agriculture, but the recommendations they adopted failed to reconcile the differences that divided them. The Farm Bureau still hankered after the McNary-Haugen program, equalization fee and all; the Grange continued to prefer its export debenture plan; and the Farmers' Union embraced a newer formula, "cost of production plus a reasonable profit." As everyone knew, there was practically no chance of implementing any of these programs as long as Hoover was President. Further, there was something to the Farm Board's argument that low farm incomes only reflected low consumer incomes, both at home and abroad, and that farm recovery, all by itself, could never be accomplished.[10]

It is not surprising that some farmers, in the depths of their desperation, were tempted to violence and embraced the "farm strike" as a means of forcing action favorable to their demands. The strike idea was by no means new; indeed, Iowa farmers had resorted to it only recently in a vain effort to halt the state program of testing dairy herds for tuberculosis. As early as 1930 one Farmers' Union leader suggested that "if the farmers of the nation would band together and for sixty days neither sell nor buy from industry, the farm problem would be solved any way farmers wanted it solved." There were two fundamental troubles with this suggestion: (1) getting the farmers to band together, and (2) finding out what the farmers really wanted. Nevertheless, under the noisy leadership of an ex-McNary-Haugenite, Milo Reno, a

[10] Murray Benedict, *Farm Policies of the United States, 1750–1950* (New York, 1953), p. 264; John D. Black, *Agricultural Reform in the United States* (New York, 1929), pp. 271–301; Warren, *Herbert Hoover*, pp. 172–177; Saloutos and Hicks, *Agricultural Discontent*, pp. 433–434.

"farm holiday" program was launched in Iowa during the spring and summer of 1932. Its slogan was "Stay at Home—Buy Nothing—Sell Nothing." Mass meetings in various Iowa counties built up sentiment for the strike, and the movement spread into several neighboring states. With eggs selling at 22 cents, oats at 11 cents, butter at 18 cents, and other items correspondingly low, there might be little incentive to sell, but everyone realized that it would take more than talk to keep some of the farmers from hauling their produce to market. At various points angry mobs blocked roads, dumped milk, paraded streets with placards such as "In Hoover we trusted, now we are busted," and halted foreclosure proceedings.[11]

After the election there was a general slackening up, perhaps to allow the incoming administration time to show what it could do, but a farm-holiday convention held in Bismarck, North Dakota, just before Roosevelt took office urged the farmers to organize county defense councils ". . . to prevent foreclosures, and any attempt to dispossess those against whom foreclosures are pending if started; and to retire to our farms, and there barricade ourselves to see the battle through until we either receive cost of production or relief from the unfair and unjust conditions existing at present; and we hereby state our intention to pay no existing debts, except for taxes and the necessities of life, unless satisfactory reductions in accordance with prevailing farm prices are made on such debts." Obviously such groups meant to serve notice on the new Democratic regime that it must do something for agriculture, and do it in a hurry.[12]

Hard times were nothing new to the farmers of the United States; they had known little else since 1920. But the industrial areas were attuned to prosperity and poorly prepared for the steady deepening of the depression. They had at first accepted at face value the optimistic predictions that emanated from Washington. But times refused stubbornly to follow the official predictions. Senator Simeon D. Fess of Ohio, chairman of the Republican National Committee, complained bitterly that there must be "some concerted effort on foot to utilize the stock market as a method of discrediting the administration. Every time an Administration official gives out an optimistic statement about business conditions, the market immediately drops." When sixty-six banks went down in Arkansas on a single day, November 17, 1930, it

[11] *Ibid.*, pp. 441–446.
[12] *Ibid.*, p. 447, quoting *Farm Holiday News,* Feb. 20, 1933.

was possible to blame local drought conditions for the calamity; but when the Bank of United States in New York City, with 400,000 depositors and $180 million in deposits, closed its doors, December 12, 1930, even Hoover's most ardent supporters had to admit that the failure "had an alarming effect upon the public mind."[13]

Times got steadily worse, not better. Some employers staggered their work loads so as to spread the work. The *Wall Street Journal* reported on April 28, 1931, that 32 per cent of the Ford employees were working five days a week, 18 per cent four days, and 50 per cent three days. But less than four months later Ford shut down his Detroit factories almost completely, throwing 75,000 men out of work. On September 23, 1931, newspapers announced that United States Steel and Bethlehem Steel had decided to cut the wages of the men they still employed by 10 per cent. "During 1931," Roger Babson recited, "we had bank-closings, dividend slashings, collapsing stock-markets, slipping commodity prices, bond-defaultings, breadlines, foreclosures, failures, unemployment and world-chaos." But Babson's attempt to cheer the public up with the thought that all this had happened in earlier business cycles, and that eventually business had always revived, elicited little enthusiasm; past triumphs were small consolation in the face of present woes. In point of fact, business steadfastly refused to revive, unemployment grew, the bread lines lengthened.[14]

Hoover's insistence that the problem of relief was not a proper charge on the federal government found an echo during the early part of the depression in the readiness of states and municipalities to turn the whole burden over to private charity. At first private welfare agencies and emergency relief committees raised money in surprisingly large amounts and expended it with considerable wisdom; in New York City, for example, they even set up a creditable program of work relief. As private benevolence dried up (former contributors themselves often became candidates for relief), municipal authorities fought desperately to avoid taking responsibility for the administration of relief. They preferred, when they could, to sponsor work projects that would help make jobs for the needy, or to contribute public funds for the use of

[13] Edward Angly (ed.), *Oh Yeah?* (New York, 1931), pp. 17, 25, 27; C. W. Wilson, "Famine in Arkansas," *Outlook*, CLVII (Apr. 29, 1931), 596; Myers and Newton, *Hoover Administration*, p. 59.

[14] Angly, *Oh Yeah?*, pp. 29, 33; Roger W. Babson, *Cheer Up! Better Times Ahead!* (New York, 1932), p. 23.

private relief agencies. Only when there was no other available alternative were they willing to appropriate funds for direct relief and to turn the task over to public welfare departments or other public bodies, many of which had to be created for the purpose. Sometimes there was excellent co-operation between public and private agencies; sometimes there was friction. Sometimes local relief was well administered; sometimes it was badly managed. But one development seemed to be inevitable everywhere. Eventually, when the proportion of those unemployed in any given area reached a high enough level, local resources, whether public or private or both, became inadequate, and state aid a necessity.[15]

Urged on by Governor Roosevelt, New York took the lead among the states in accepting state responsibility for the relief program. A joint investigation of unemployment and relief, conducted during the winter of 1930–31 by the State Department of Social Welfare and the State Charities Aid Association, reported (1) that the major cost of relief for the future would have to be paid for out of public funds, and (2) that the municipalities could not much longer raise by taxation or borrowing all the money they would need for relief purposes. Called into special session by the governor, the state legislature took the next logical step in September, 1931, when it set up a Temporary Emergency Relief Administration (TERA) to aid city and county governments in their problems of relief. New York was the first state to take such action, and not many other states went as far toward the centralization of administration, but in one fashion or another, despite great initial reluctance, nearly every state became deeply involved in the business of relief. Appropriations varied in accordance with the degree of the emergency and the condition of the state's finances.[16]

It took little perspicacity to foresee that when state resources gave out the nation would have to step in. After all, was not the problem of unemployment national in scope rather than merely state or local, and therefore a national responsibility? But to postpone, and if possible head off, any such development became almost an obsession with the

[15] Mitchell, *Depression Decade,* p. 102; David M. Schneider and Albert Deutsch, *The History of Public Welfare in New York State, 1867–1940* (Chicago, 1941), p. 299; J. J. Hanna, "Urban Reaction to the Great Depression in the United States, 1929–1933," unpublished doctoral dissertation, University of California, Berkeley, 1956, p. 103.

[16] *Ibid.,* pp. 101–102, 118–119; Schneider and Deutsch, *Public Welfare in New York,* pp. 307–310.

President. Three weeks before the elections of 1930 he had established a President's Committee for Unemployment Relief under the chairmanship of Colonel Arthur Woods, former police commissioner of New York City. The Woods committee, with only limited funds available (its total expenditures amounted to about $157,000), could do little more than stress the virtues of re-employment and offer encouragement to local authorities in charge of relief. In August, 1931, it was succeeded by a somewhat larger President's Unemployment Relief Organization, which conducted "a nation-wide drive to aid the private relief agencies," and did whatever else it could to forestall the need of federal intervention. But by 1932, as the American Association of Social Workers pointed out, the situation had passed "beyond local control and local experience," and "needed the utmost which the whole Nation could give from its material resources and from its great capacity for guidance and leadership." In New York City families receiving aid were by this time getting an average of $2.39 per week; in Toledo, Ohio, the allowance per relief meal was 2.14 cents; in Pennsylvania, with three million people—one third of the state's population—on relief, a $10-million appropriation by the legislature, available in April, would be used up in July. In Chicago, by May, 1932, the unemployed numbered 700,000, or 40 per cent of the normal working population. In Houston, Texas, applications for relief from unemployed Mexican or colored families were no longer being taken. "They are being asked to shift for themselves."[17]

The President, in his frantic struggle to keep the federal government pure from relief contamination, had his troubles with Congress. Immediately after the election of 1930, seven leading Democrats—James M. Cox, John W. Davis, Alfred E. Smith, Joe T. Robinson, John N. Garner, John J. Raskob, and Jouett Shouse—issued a statement promising that the Democratic party would not seek to embarrass the President, and would co-operate with him to the full in his efforts to stimulate business and restore prosperity. But as *The Nation* pointed out, there might not have been any pro-Democratic upheaval on November 4 had the people known this attitude in advance. Whatever the signers of this extraordinary document may have meant, the Democrats in Congress lost no time in aligning themselves against the Presi-

[17] *Ibid.*, p. 318; Herbert Hoover, *The Memoirs of Herbert Hoover,* III, *The Great Depression, 1929–1941* (New York, 1952), 53, 150; Mitchell, *Depression Decade,* pp. 103–105; Warren, *Herbert Hoover,* pp. 188–208.

dent's attitude on relief. During the lame-duck session of the Seventy-first Congress, which followed immediately after the election, they bombarded the Republican majority with proposals for the direct organization of relief by the federal government, and for federal relief appropriations. All this, the President insisted, was merely "playing politics at the expense of human misery." When it came to the use of federal funds for public works, the President's conscience troubled him far less, although appropriations for such purposes tended greatly to exceed actual expenditures. In the interest of efficiency, however, Hoover recommended to Congress in December, 1931, the creation of a single Public Works Administration to take over all governmental construction, except for naval and military purposes. But Congress did not respond, and the establishment of such an agency awaited the coming of the New Deal.[18]

Hoover's willingness to aid distressed corporations, particularly banks, contrasted markedly with his policy of no federal doles to individuals. By the autumn of 1931, thanks in part to the European financial crisis, there was grave danger that many of the larger as well as smaller banks might go down. The President countered first by asking the stronger banks to provide a credit pool of $500 million for use in shoring up the weaker banks. But when the resulting National Credit Association proved inadequate for the task, Hoover yielded to pressure for the establishment of a new Reconstruction Finance Corporation comparable to the old War Finance Corporation of 1918. On the President's recommendation Congress, by an act of January 22, 1932, authorized the creation of such an organization, with a capital stock of $500 million to be subscribed by the Treasury, and with the right to borrow three times that amount in tax-exempt, government-guaranteed obligations. The agency might lend on appropriate security to banks and other financial corporations, to insurance companies, to agricultural credit associations, and, with the approval of the Interstate Commerce Commission, to railroads. The President wished to include also loans to industry for the improvement of plants, and to public bodies for reproductive public works, but Congress at the time refused this additional authority. An Emergency Relief and Construction Act,

---

[18] *The New York Times,* Nov. 8, 1930, p. 1, col. 8; *The Nation,* CXXXI (Nov. 19, 1930), p. 539; Myers and Newton, *Hoover Administration,* p. 59; Schneider and Deutsch, *Public Welfare in New York,* p. 318; Wilbur and Hyde, *Hoover Policies,* pp. 569–570.

passed six months later, still denied loans to industry, but went along with the President's idea on public works, more than doubled the amount of private funds the R.F.C. could raise, appropriated $322 million for specified "non-productive" federal projects, and authorized the use of $300 million in 3 per cent loans to the states for relief purposes, the first recognition that the federal government could not refuse help when the states had exhausted their resources.[19]

The R.F.C. operated with smooth efficiency. Under the direction of former Vice-President Dawes, now a Chicago banker, it made loans, before the Hoover administration ended, of well over $1.5 billion, most of which went to banks and trust companies, mortgage loan companies, and the like. Next highest on the list of private borrowers came the railroads, then insurance companies, then the various agricultural credit corporations, which received only minor amounts. Relief payments to the states did not quite reach the $300 million earmarked for the purpose, and loans for self-liquidating public works came to less than $19 million, although contracts for numerous large expenditures of this type were authorized.[20]

One provision of the Emergency Relief and Construction Act Hoover regarded as "terribly dangerous." It required the R.F.C. to report regularly to the President and Congress on the identity of all borrowers and the amounts borrowed. Hoover feared that if such information should reach the public, it might destroy confidence in borrowing banks and lead to disastrous runs. Out of deference to the President's wishes, congressional leaders agreed that all such information should be regarded as confidential. But such self-imposed restrictions were hard to maintain, and later on an R.F.C. loan of $92 million to the Dawes bank in Chicago received much adverse publicity. Actually, Dawes at the time was no longer associated with the R.F.C., and the loan was perfectly legitimate. The real trouble with the Hoover policies was not favoritism toward any particular bank or bankers, but favoritism toward the great business corporations in general. For them he was ready enough to dole out federal loans of gigantic proportions, but when it came to

[19] Hoover, *Memoirs*, III, 85, 107–111, 153–154; *United States Statutes at Large* (Washington, 1933), XLVII, 5–14, 710–714; Myers and Newton, *Hoover Administration*, pp. 161, 163, 165, 232.

[20] Bascom N. Timmons, *Portrait of an American; Charles G. Dawes* (New York, 1953), pp. 314–315; Hoover, *Memoirs*, III, 168–169; Mitchell, *Depression Decade*, pp. 76–78.

the relief of distressed individuals he regarded the use of federal funds as well-nigh calamitous. As later events seemed to prove, money poured in at the top of the economic system tended to stay there, whereas money poured in at the bottom tended to rise through all levels of business and to strengthen the economy as a whole.[21]

During the fall and winter of 1931–32, Hoover and the Treasury Department became concerned not only with the condition of the nation's banks but also with the condition of the nation's Treasury. Between the declining economy and the unwillingness or inability of Congress to vote adequate new taxes, receipts were on the downgrade, $2.1 billion in 1932 as compared to over $4 billion in 1929. On the ordinary expenditures of government the Hoover administration made a good record for economy; but with emergency expenditures on the increase, borrowing to balance the budget became a chronic necessity. While the Treasury had no difficulty in raising money by loans, insiders were soon aware of an alarming situation with reference to gold. The withdrawal of gold from the United States by foreigners, and the hoarding of gold and currency by Americans, reached such proportions by early 1932 that Secretary Ogden Mills actually feared that the nation might be forced off the gold standard, something that both he and the President regarded as close to the ultimate calamity. As the law stood, Federal Reserve currency issues must be covered by at least 40 per cent in gold and the rest in securities eligible for discount by the Federal Reserve Banks. But with business at such low ebb, the restrictions on "eligible" securities turned out to be too severe. The result was that the gold coverage of currency issues had risen to about 70 per cent, and the Treasury's supply of gold for other needs was steadily drying up. Urged on by the President and Secretary Mills, who took congressional leaders into their confidence, Congress on February 17, 1932, passed the Glass-Steagall Act, which broadened the eligibility of securities available for Federal Reserve discount and so took much of the pressure off the gold in the Treasury. The new law, according to the President, would enable the Federal Reserve Banks "to meet any conceivable demands that might be made on them at home or from

[21] *Ibid.,* pp. 78–81; Warren, *Herbert Hoover,* pp. 145–147; Hoover, *Memoirs,* III, 169–171; Timmons, *Portrait of an American,* pp. 316–324. Charles A. Miller of Utica, New York, succeeded Dawes. Myers and Newton, *Hoover Administration,* p. 239.

abroad," and would serve also to arrest the "gradual credit contraction" that had characterized the preceding months.[22]

Another measure designed to ease the credit stringency was the Federal Home Loan Bank Act, passed by Congress in July, 1932. The President had long stressed the inadequacy of the nation's mortgage machinery, and had advocated the creation of "a national system of mortgage discount institutions," which would parallel the Federal Reserve System. The measure that Congress finally passed did not go as far as Hoover wished, but it did create a series of Federal Home Loan Banks for the discount of home mortgages that at least greatly diminished the problems of the building and loan associations, the savings banks, and the insurance companies dealing in loans of this type. The measure also no doubt cut down materially on foreclosures, and it may have promoted some new construction, but unfortunately many home owners had already lost their property. As Hoover himself pointed out, "The literally thousands of heart-breaking instances of inability of working people to attain renewal of expiring mortgages on favorable terms, and the consequent loss of their homes, have been one of the tragedies of this depression."[23]

Eager as he was to help the working people by helping the private-enterprise system to provide them with work, Hoover's opposition to whatever he regarded as illegitimate raids on the Treasury continued firm to the end. He vetoed, in July, 1932, a bill sponsored by Representative Garner and Senator Wagner on the ground that it oversupplied the R.F.C. with funds for expenditure on nonproductive public works, and overextended the list of eligible borrowers to which the agency could make loans. The measure, if passed, he declared, "would place the government in private business in such fashion as to violate the very principle of public relations upon which we have builded our nation, and would render insecure its very foundations." And he headed off by veto, or otherwise, a variety of other measures that he regarded as extravagant, or inflationary, or both.[24]

The President's hostility to unorthodox expenditures brought him into constant conflict with the veterans, who early in the depression

[22] *Ibid.*, pp. 179, 182, 185–188, 532; Wilbur and Hyde, *Hoover Policies,* pp. 446–448; Hoover, *Memoirs,* III, 115–119.

[23] *Ibid.,* 111–115; Wilbur and Hyde, *Hoover Policies,* pp. 332, 422, 436–441.

[24] Hoover, *Memoirs,* III, 162–163; Myers and Newton, *Hoover Administration,* pp. 226–229.

began an insistent demand for additional relief. The strength of the veterans' vote, not to mention the persuasiveness of their lobbyists, made it difficult for congressmen to resist their pressure, and early in 1931, with the Republicans still in control of both houses, Congress over the President's veto authorized loans up to 50 per cent on the adjusted compensation certificates of 1924. This measure, to the President's great distress, imposed a cash obligation on the Treasury of about $1.7 billion, but even so the unemployed veterans were soon out of funds, a condition that led their spokesmen to advocate immediate payment in full of the remaining 50 per cent. Hoover made a special trip to the American Legion Convention at Detroit in September, 1931, to speak against this proposal, and the Legion refused to endorse it. When the Seventy-second Congress convened, Congressman Wright Patman of Texas promptly presented a bill for the issuance of $2.4 billion in fiat money to be used in payment of the additional claims. In the spring of 1932 thousands of ex-servicemen—the "Bonus Expeditionary Force"—began to converge on Washington with the express purpose of remaining there until their demands were met.[25]

By summer the "Bonus Army" numbered perhaps 11,000 persons, including wives and children. Some of the invaders took over unoccupied buildings near the Capitol; others built shacks on Anacostia Flats, the kind of "Hooverville" that had appeared during the hard times on the outskirts of every sizable American city. Finally the House of Representatives, on June 15, passed the Patman bill, but two days later the Senate turned it down. At Hoover's urging Congress provided funds for the members of the B.E.F. to return home, but about 2,000 of them stayed on defiantly, a course that both frightened and irritated the President. Eventually he ordered the Washington superintendent of police, General Pelham D. Glassford, to clear out the veterans from the buildings they occupied on Pennsylvania Avenue. This was done on July 28 with a minimum of resistance, although the police, in the process, shot and killed two veterans. Thereupon the President called in an impressive array of troops from Fort Myer—four troops of cavalry, four infantry companies, and tanks—who cleared all the members of the Bonus Army from the District of Columbia, burning the Anacostia

[25] *Ibid.*, pp. 68–69; Wilbur and Hyde, *Hoover Policies*, pp. 199–200; Mitchell, *Depression Decade*, pp. 108–110; W. W. Waters and William C. White, *B.E.F.; The Whole Story of the Bonus Army* (New York, 1933), pp. 103–114.

shacks to the ground. Politically speaking, the President could hardly have made a more disastrous blunder. His contention that the bonus seekers were infiltrated by "Communists and persons with criminal records" carried little weight with the voters, too many of whom understood by that time all too well the motives of the unemployed veterans who had marched on Washington.[26]

Hoover believed that the United States reached the "bottom of the depression pit" in midsummer, 1932. After that time, as he saw it, an upward turn began which, in his judgment, would have continued through to full recovery, except for the sudden realization of the business world early in the fall that the Democrats were going to win the election of 1932. The returns from the voting in Maine on September 14 were what awakened the nation to the impending calamity; thereafter, the "prices of commodities and securities began to decline, and unemployment increased." The Hoover thesis seems somehow a little too pat to be given much credence, especially since most political observers for the preceding two years had foreseen a Democratic victory in 1932. Why the sudden fright? Moreover, Hoover had a long record of pointing confidently to upward turns that for unanticipated reasons suddenly turned downward again.[27]

It seems improbable that the November defeat of Hoover and the Republicans by Roosevelt and the Democrats was the sole reason for the business decline of late 1932. More to the point was the deepening disillusionment of the American people with business leadership. According to Joseph P. Kennedy, "The belief that those in control of the corporate life of America were motivated by honesty and ideals of honorable conduct was completely shattered." Andrew Mellon was no longer the greatest Secretary of the Treasury since Alexander Hamilton, but only since Carter Glass. American businessmen who had peddled the wares of Ivar Krueger, the Swedish "Match King," could not have been very smart; not until his suicide in March, 1932, did they discover that he was only a daring international swindler. The crash of the Insull empire at about the same time was another blow; Insull, charged with embezzlement, fled the country, while many of the stocks

---

[26] Myers and Newton, *Hoover Administration*, pp. 498–502; Hoover, *Memoirs*, III, 225–230; Arthur M. Schlesinger, Jr., *The Age of Roosevelt; The Crisis of the Old Order, 1919–1933* (Boston, 1957), 256–265; Warren, *Herbert Hoover*, pp. 224–236.

[27] Hoover, *Memoirs*, III, 38–40, 80, 155, 176. The election of 1932 will be covered in a later volume of this series.

he had created and sold became virtually valueless. A Senate investigating committee certified as true the stories of how supposedly reputable business leaders connived at income-tax evasion, gave special favors to insiders, and sold to the public securities that they knew to be worthless. With the chief exponents of economic orthodoxy in ill repute, a few still-credulous citizens listened with perhaps more hope than belief to a group of economic freethinkers, led by Howard Scott, who proposed to junk the whole price system and substitute for it something they called "Technocracy." But even the Technocrats seemed not to know exactly what they were talking about, and the craze they started in 1932 subsided in 1933.[28]

Lack of confidence in bankers and their methods certainly had as much to do with setting the scene for the Bank Panic of February, 1933, as the impending inauguration of Franklin D. Roosevelt. The "singular weakness" of the nation's banking structure, as Hoover himself pointed out, had helped to bring on the depression and had stood in the way of recovery all along. Bank failures had become chronic well before the fear of Roosevelt could have gripped the land. There were 1,345 of them in 1930, 2,298 in 1931, and 1,456 in 1932; as time went on larger and larger banks joined the dismal procession into oblivion. Generous loans from the R.F.C. temporarily averted disaster for many banks, although the fact that they had to borrow so heavily understandably worried their depositors. But according to the Hoover version, although the banks had begun to show signs of strain during "the first seventy days after the election," there was "no panic in the public mind" until mid-January, 1933. Then the shadow of coming events really began to work its mischief. Following earlier precedents in Nevada and Louisiana, the governor of Michigan closed the banks of his state on February 14 for an eight-day period, after which extended banking holidays became epidemic. Before inauguration day, March 4, the banks were closed in twenty-two states, and an agreement between

[28] Schlesinger, Age of Roosevelt, pp. 254–255, 458–459, 461–463, 478; William E. Leuchtenburg, The Perils of Prosperity, 1914–32 (Chicago, 1958), pp. 258–259; Mitchell, Depression Decade, pp. 154–157; Wayne Andrews, Battle for Chicago (New York, 1946), pp. 277–282; Ferdinand Pecora, Wall Street Under Oath; The Story of our Modern Money Changers (New York, 1939), pp. 28–29; Myers and Newton, Hoover Administration, pp. 184, 245; "Technocracy, Good Medicine or a Bedtime Story," New Republic, LXXIII (Dec. 28, 1932), 178–180. See ante, p. 123 n.

the outgoing and the incoming administrations on that day resulted in their closing in practically all the rest.[29]

Hoover could have been saved most of his postelection dilemmas, and undoubtedly the country would have been better off, had the Twentieth Amendment to the Constitution achieved early enough ratification. The man who had sponsored this reform, Senator George W. Norris of Nebraska, finally saw his patient efforts rewarded when Congress, on March 3, 1932, submitted the amendment to the states for ratification. Its purpose was to eliminate the "lame duck" session of the old Congress after election by requiring each new Congress to meet for its first session early in January, and by advancing the date of inauguration to a little later in the same month. But ratification was not fully accomplished until February, 1933, so Hoover and the old Congress had no choice but to retain office until March 4. Seemingly it never occurred to the outgoing President that lack of confidence in the banks and in his administration could have had any responsibility for the financial disintegration that characterized his closing months in office. The sole trouble, as he saw it, was fear that the incoming administration might depart from the sound policies he had advocated. His only recourse, therefore, seemed to him to be an appeal to Roosevelt for help in dispelling the fears that the Democratic victory had inspired.[30]

The full story of these negotiations, like the story of the election itself, will be left to a later book in this series. Shortly after the election, Roosevelt, at Hoover's invitation, came to the White House for a fruitless discussion of Hoover's plans for a renewal of the war-debts negotiations. Twice later the President also sought in vain to obtain the co-operation of the President-elect, once with reference to the proposed World Economic Conference, then high on the Hoover agenda, and once about the bank panic. But Roosevelt was wary, and consistently refused to commit his administration to anything in advance. Hoover was not a very subtle person, but in his proposals regarding foreign affairs he may have had in mind obtaining from Roosevelt some kind of endorsement of his theory that the causes and

[29] Hoover, *Memoirs* III, 21–23, 160–161; Mitchell, *Depression Decade,* pp. 78, 127–131; Myers and Newton, *Hoover Administration,* pp. 347–360; Keith Sward, *The Legend of Henry Ford* (New York, 1948), pp. 249–254; Henry Barnard, *Independent Man; The Life of Senator James Couzens* (New York, 1958), p. 226.

[30] Alfred Lief, *Democracy's Norris; The Biography of a Lonely Crusade* (New York, 1939), pp. 408–409; Hoover, *Memoirs,* III, 196–198.

cure of the depression were primarily external, not internal, in character. As for his banking proposals, he admitted that the statements he
had hoped to obtain from Roosevelt would have involved "the aban-
donment of 90% of the so-called new deal."[31]

The note of unrelieved tragedy that marked the closing weeks of the
Hoover administration served only to emphasize the deep disillusionment the American people had begun to feel about their whole way of
life. For a dozen years they had seen their highest hopes dashed, time
after time; theirs had become indeed an age of disillusionment. The
first blow fell when they realized that the great crusade they had fought
in Europe "to make the world safe for democracy," and to end all war,
had fallen far short of those goals. Oversold on idealism, they did not
bother to reflect that temporarily, at least, they had made the world
safe for the United States; all they could think of was that almost
everywhere democracy was declining, not advancing, and that the seeds
of future wars were starting to grow. To save America from another
false step they put their faith in disarmament, in meaningless peace
pacts, and in isolation, only to find that each new effort to withdraw
from the world seemed only to draw the nation farther in. They tried
out prohibition and woman suffrage, but neither did much toward the
cleansing of society; evil seemed as rampant as ever, and evildoers even
less repentant. In government and politics they turned their backs on
reforms and reformers, and handed the country over to the hard-boiled
conservatives who controlled the Republican party after Theodore
Roosevelt led the progressives into the wilderness and left them there.
But the Harding scandals and the general inferiority of the politicians
out in front offended and disgruntled the people. They might have
swung back to the reformers again, but the progressives of the 1920's
had not progressed very far. Such ideas as they propounded seemed
better suited to the nineteenth century than to the twentieth, and to
rural rather than urban America. Only the business world seemed
sound, so the people shunned the professional politicians all they could,
conservatives and progressives alike, and with great confidence handed
over the nation to business leadership, the Presidency along with the
rest. But business leadership led straight to the Panic of 1929, then on
deeper and deeper into the worst depression the western world had

[31] *Ibid.*, 178–191; *The New York Times,* Dec. 16, 1932, p. 17, col. 1; Myers
and Newton, *Hoover Administration,* pp. 295, 338–341, 351.

ever known in modern times. "Stay yourselves, and wonder; cry ye out, and cry; they are drunken, but not with wine; they stagger, but not with strong drink. . . . And the vision of all is become unto you as the words of a book that is sealed."[32]

It was not so much with great expectations that the country turned in the election of 1932 to Roosevelt and the Democrats; by this time disillusionment had become too deeply ingrained in the people, and faith too dim. There was simply nowhere else to go.

[32] Isaiah 29:9, 11.

Bibliographical Essay

Personal Papers, Documents, Newspapers, Periodicals

Manuscript collections that throw light on the period covered by this volume are numerous, but scattered. The most valuable concentration is in the Library of Congress, which houses among others the papers of Charles Evans Hughes, William E. Borah, George W. Norris, Thomas J. Walsh, William Gibbs McAdoo, Josephus Daniels, Bronson Cutting, Ogden Mills, Gifford Pinchot, Albert J. Beveridge, Warren G. Harding, Calvin Coolidge, William Mitchell, Frederick Lewis Allen, and (of considerable consequence) the League of Women Voters. The papers of Frank P. Walsh are in the possession of the New York Public Library; those of Hiram Johnson, Chester Rowell, and Thomas J. Mooney in the Bancroft Library of the University of California; those of Father John A. Ryan at the Catholic University of America, Washington, D.C. The New York Public Library check list on collections of personal papers locates the Hans Kaltenborn papers in the State Historical Society of Wisconsin; the William Lemke papers in the Libby Collection, Library of Congress; the Sinclair Lewis papers, bequeathed to Yale University; the Charles A. Lindbergh, Sr., papers in the Minnesota Historical Society; the Charles A. Lindbergh, Jr., papers in the Missouri Historical Society; and the Ida M. Tarbell papers in Allegheny College, Meadville, Pa. The papers of Franklin D. Roosevelt are easily accessible at Hyde Park, N.Y.; those of Herbert Hoover are completely inaccessible in the Hoover Library, Stanford University. George E. Mowry, *The Era of Theodore Roosevelt* (New York, 1958), pp. 297–301, provides an excellent guide to manuscript collections of use for the early twentieth century, many of which have a bearing on the 1920's.

The difficulties in making use of personal papers are not confined merely to the overcoming of the large distances that separate the various depositories. Despite the best efforts of dedicated librarians, most of the larger collections are almost impenetrable jungles. If one knows the right questions he can sometimes, without too great an investment of time, find the right answers, but in general it takes the work of many patient monographers to extract the secrets that the manuscript collections make it their business to conceal. The same is true of the immense stores of documents in the National Archives and its subsidiaries, in the various state archives and their local counterparts, and in the growing collections of accessible corporate records. Historical research has become of necessity a collective enterprise; no one person can expect to accomplish very much without thousands of assists from others working in the same field. The author of this volume certainly makes no pretense of having seen all of the manuscript and archival collections here mentioned, or of having worked adequately any single item on the list.

Some types of sources may almost be taken for granted. It is hardly necessary to mention the various congressional documents, such as the *Congressional Record,* the Census reports, the *Statistical Abstracts,* the *United States Statutes at Large, Foreign Relations,* and the *United States Reports.* Newspapers, too, are a part of the general stock in trade for all writers of recent American history, *The New York Times,* because of its index, being a universal favorite. In general the newspapers of the 1920's all carried much the same national news, although the Hearst journals, the Chicago *Tribune,* and a few others suffered in varying degrees from personality problems. The periodicals of the period include several that have vanished, such as the *Outlook,* the *Literary Digest,* the *World's Work,* and the *American Review of Reviews,* but others that are still with us, such as *The Nation,* the *New Republic, Time, Current History,* and *Foreign Affairs.* Of enduring value, also, are the various yearly compilations, such as the *New International Yearbook,* the *Americana Annual,* the *World Almanac,* and the like.

General Accounts

Several excellent books by Frederick Lewis Allen, *Only Yesterday* (New York, 1931), *Since Yesterday* (New York, 1939), and *The Big Change* (New York, 1952), have done much to set the pattern of thought on the period. William E. Leuchtenburg, *The Perils of Prosperity, 1914–1932* (Chicago, 1958), is a delightful reinterpretation, somewhat selective in coverage. Arthur M. Schlesinger, Jr., *The Age of Roosevelt,* I, *The Crisis of the Old Order* (Boston, 1957), although mainly concerned with setting the stage for the New Deal, is brilliantly conceived and executed. Karl Schriftgiesser, *This Was Normalcy* (Boston, 1948), covers the period of the Republican ascendancy, with little quarter for the party in power, while Malcolm Moos, *The Republicans* (New York, 1956), falls somewhat short of redressing the balance. Harold U. Faulkner, *From Versailles to the New Deal* (New Haven, 1951), is brief and uncontroversial. James C. Malin, *The United States after the World War* (Boston, 1930), is tightly organized and mainly factual. Louis M. Hacker, *American Problems of Today* (New York, 1938), covers both the Old Deal and the New Deal, with the emphasis mainly on economic developments. Bruce Minton and John Stuart, *The Fat Years and the Lean* (New York, 1940), deals with practically the same period, but from a strictly Marxist point of view.

Books of a general nature that center on economic, social, or cultural history are likewise numerous. This list begins properly with two formidable co-operative undertakings, one sponsored by the President's Conference on Unemployment, *Recent Economic Changes in the United States* (2 vols., New York, 1929), and another by the President's Research Committee on Social Trends, *Recent Social Trends in the United States* (2 vols., New York, 1933). The best of the economic histories are George Soule, *Prosperity Decade* (New York, 1947), and Broadus Mitchell, *Depression Decade* (New York, 1947). On social history Preston Slosson, *The Great Crusade and After, 1914–1928* (New York, 1930), and Dixon Wecter, *The Age of the Great Depression, 1929–1941* (New York, 1948), are still the best general accounts, but other books of this type worth mentioning include Lloyd Morris, *Postscript to Yesterday* (New York, 1947); Lawrence Greene, *The Era of Wonderful Nonsense* (Indianapolis, 1939); and Isabel Leighton (ed.), *The Aspirin Age* (New York, 1949). Thomas C. Cochran and William Miller, *The Age of Enterprise* (New York, 1942), reaches far back into the nineteenth century for a start, while Thomas Cochran, *The American Business System* (Cambridge, 1957), covers only the twentieth century. James Prothro, *Dollar Decade; Business Ideas in the 1920's* (Baton Rouge, 1954), draws its conclusions mainly from the records of the National Association of Manufacturers and the United States Chamber of Commerce. On cultural history there are two valuable general treatments, Ralph Henry Gabriel, *The Course of American Democratic Thought* (New York, 1940), and Henry Steele Commager, *The American Mind* (New Haven, 1950). Merle Curti, *The Growth of American Thought* (New York, 1943), has two excellent chapters on the post-World War I period.

On foreign affairs the best one-volume texts are S. F. Bemis, *A Diplomatic History of the United States* (4th ed., New York, 1955); Thomas A. Bailey, *A Diplomatic History of the American People* (5th ed., New York, 1955); Robert H. Ferrell, *American Diplomacy, A History* (New York, 1959); and Julius W. Pratt, *A History of United States Foreign Policy* (Englewood Cliffs, N.J., 1955). Excellent for the European situation between the wars is a co-operative undertaking, Floyd A. Cave and associates, *The Origins and Consequences of World War II* (New York, 1948). Other books on the European background include Raymond Leslie Buell, *Europe; A History of Ten Years* (New York, 1928); George Seldes, *You Can't Print That; The Truth Behind the News, 1918–1928* (Garden City, 1929); and Leopold Schwarzchild, *World in Trance; From Versailles to Pearl Harbor* (New York, 1942). Accounts dealing with the general aspects of American diplomacy during these troubled years include Allan Nevins, *The United States in a Chaotic World* (New Haven, 1951); James T. Shotwell, *On the Rim of the Abyss* (New York, 1937); William E. Rappard, *The Quest for Peace Since the World War* (Cambridge, Mass., 1940); Frank H. Simonds, *Can America Stay at Home?* (New York, 1932); Eugene J. Young, *Powerful America; Our Place in a Rearming World* (New York, 1936); and R. Palme Dutt, *World Politics, 1918–1936* (New York, 1936), a pro-Soviet view. Ruhl J. Bartlett (ed.), *The Record of American Diplomacy* (New York, 1947), is a useful collection of documents.

Memoirs and Autobiographies

The recollections of participants are bafflingly numerous. Most useful of these writings, despite the unwillingness of the author to concede that he could ever have been wrong on anything, are *The Memoirs of Herbert Hoover* (3 vols., New York, 1951–52). By way of contrast, *The Autobiography of Calvin Coolidge* (New York, 1929), is of negligible importance. Bernard M. Baruch, *Baruch: My Own Story* (New York, 1957), is valuable both for political and economic observations. Henry L. Stimson and McGeorge Bundy, *On Active Service in Peace and War* (New York, 1947), records Stimson's extensive activities under Coolidge and Hoover. Raymond B. Fosdick, *Chronicle of a Generation* (New York, 1958), has several chapters of general interest on the period. Henry Ford and Samuel Crowther, *My Life and Work* (Garden City, 1923), and *Today and Tomorrow* (Garden City, 1926), present cogently the business ideas of the great automobile manufacturer. The persistent reader can also pick up gleanings from such varied recollections as Walter E. Edge, *A Jerseyman's Journal* (Princeton, 1948); James M. Cox, *Journey through My Years* (New York, 1946); James E. Watson, *As I Knew Them* (Indianapolis, 1936); George W. Norris, *Fighting Liberal* (New York, 1945); Alice Roosevelt Longworth, *Crowded Hours* (New York, 1933); Alfred E. Smith, *Up to Now* (New York, 1929), and *The Citizen and His Government* (New York, 1935); Edmund W. Starling and Thomas Sugrue, *Starling of the White House* (New York, 1946); Clarence Darrow, *The Story of My Life* (New York, 1932); Morris Hillquit, *Loose Leaves from a Busy Life* (New York, 1934); and *The Autobiography of William Allen White* (New York, 1946). O. G. Villard, *Fighting Years* (New York, 1939), and Samuel Gompers, *Seventy Years of Life and Labor* (New York, 1957), are both more useful for earlier periods than for the 1920's. Louis B. Wehle, *Hidden Threads of History; Wilson through Roosevelt* (New York, 1953), is an interesting outgrowth of Columbia University's oral-history project.

Biographies

Among the best of the biographies that involve all or a considerable part of the period under review are Merlo J. Pusey, *Charles Evans Hughes* (2 vols., New York, 1951); William Allen White, *A Puritan in Babylon; The Story of Calvin Coolidge* (New York, 1938); C. M. Fuess, *Calvin Coolidge; The Man from Vermont* (Boston, 1940); Walter Johnson, *William Allen White's America* (New York, 1947); Margaret L. Coit, *Mr. Baruch* (Boston, 1957); William T. Hutchinson, *Lowden of Illinois; The Life of Frank O. Lowden* (2 vols., Chicago, 1957); Catherine D. Bowen, *Yankee from Olympus; Justice Holmes and His Family* (Boston, 1944); Alfred Lief, *Democracy's Norris* (New York, 1939); Richard L. Neuberger and Stephen B. Kahn, *Integrity; The Life of George W. Norris* (New York, 1937); Claudius O. Johnson, *Borah of Idaho* (New York, 1936); Josephine O'Keane, *Thomas J. Walsh* (Francestown, N.H., 1955); Rixey Smith and Norman Beasley, *Carter Glass* (New York, 1939); Harold Nicolson, *Dwight Morrow* (New York, 1935); Harry Barnard, *Independent Man: The Life of Senator James Couzens* (New York, 1958); Keith Sward, *The Legend of Henry Ford* (New York, 1948); Frank Freidel, *Franklin D. Roosevelt*, II, *The Ordeal* (Boston, 1954), and III, *The Triumph* (Boston, 1956); Gilbert C. Fite, *Peter Norbeck: Prairie Statesman* (Columbia, Mo., 1948); Raymond B. Fosdick, *John D. Rockefeller, Jr., A Portrait* (New York, 1956); John Tebbel, *The Life and Good Times of William Randolph Hearst* (New York, 1952); Ray Ginger, *The Bending Cross; A Biography of Eugene Victor Debs* (New Brunswick, N.J., 1949).

Biographers are seldom impartial. Harvey O'Connor, *Mellon's Millions; The Life and Times of Andrew W. Mellon* (New York, 1933), suffers from an acute anti-Mellon bias, while Philip H. Love, *Andrew W. Mellon; The Man and His Work* (Baltimore, 1929), is overadulatory. Saul Alinsky, *John L. Lewis; An Unauthorized Biography* (New York, 1949), and Cecil Carnes, *John L. Lewis; Leader of Labor* (New York, 1936), are both decidedly friendly to Lewis. Matthew Josephson, *Sidney Hillman, Statesman of American Labor* (Garden City, 1952), and Rowland H. Harvey, *Samuel Gompers, Champion of the Toiling Masses* (Stanford, Calif., 1935), are similarly laudatory. Belle C. La Follette and Fola La Follette, *Robert M. La Follette* (New York, 1953), is a faithful family chronicle based on La Follette's private papers. Oswald G. Villard, *Prophets True and False* (New York, 1928), records Villard's opinion of several Americans prominent during the 1920's. Walter Lippmann, *Men of Destiny* (New York, 1927), consists of similarly colored biographic studies. Henry F. Pringle, *Big Frogs* (New York, 1928), is also a series of pen portraits, usually somewhat exaggerated, beginning with Herbert Hoover; Eugene Lyons, *The Herbert Hoover Story* (Washington, 1959), vindicates Hoover and victimizes Roosevelt with equal vehemence.

Party Politics

Every period in American history pays a heavy tribute to politics. Two excellent introductions to this subject are Wilfred E. Binkley, *American*

Political Parties (3d ed., New York, 1958), and V. O. Key, Jr., *Politics, Parties, and Pressure Groups* (4th ed., New York, 1958). An older study, reflecting the attitudes of the 1920's, is Charles E. Merriam and Harold F. Gosnell, *The American Party System* (4th ed., New York, 1949). Samuel Lubell, *The Future of American Politics* (New York, 1952), also deals cogently with the past. For each presidential election each party publishes the *Proceedings* of its national nominating convention, and a campaign *Textbook* for the guidance of the faithful. Kirk H. Porter and Donald Bruce Johnson (eds.), *National Party Platforms* (Urbana, Ill., 1956), includes all platforms through 1956. Louise Overacker, *The Presidential Primary* (New York, 1926), and Louise Overacker and Victor J. West, *Money in Elections* (New York, 1932), deal with problems of continuing importance. Eugene H. Roseboom, *A History of Presidential Elections* (New York, 1957), extends beyond elections to the intervening political history.

Edgar E. Robinson, *The Presidential Vote, 1896–1932* (Stanford, Calif., 1934), is a convenient statistical compilation. Frank R. Kent, *The Great Game of Politics* (Garden City, 1935), is full of behind-the-scenes political lore. Nathan J. Fine, *Labor and Farmer Parties in the United States, 1828–1928* (New York, 1928), is better on the labor than on the farmer side. Richard Hofstadter, *The Age of Reform* (New York, 1955), touches only lightly on the 1920's. Russel B. Nye, *Midwestern Progressive Politics* (East Lansing, Mich., 1951), is excellent on recent third-party movements. David A. Shannon, *The Socialist Party of America* (New York, 1955), is a model study of its kind. Most of the writing on communism is highly controversial, but the principal facts come out in Theodore Draper, *The Roots of American Communism* (New York, 1957); James Oneal and G. A. Werner, *American Communism* (New York, 1947); Benjamin Gitlow, *The Whole of Their Lives* (New York, 1948); Irving Howe and Lewis Coser, *The American Communist Party: A Critical History* (Boston, 1957).

Presidential elections offer tempting subjects for monographic study. Those that deal with the campaign of 1924 center primarily on the La Follette candidacy. Kenneth C. MacKay, *The Progressive Movement of 1924* (New York, 1947), is the most comprehensive printed account, but is less satisfactory in some respects than James H. Shideler, "The Neo-Progressives; Reform Politics in the United States, 1920–1925," unpublished Ph. D. dissertation, University of California, Berkeley, 1945. See also, by the same author, "The Disintegration of the Progressive Movement of 1924," in the *Historian*, XIV (Spring, 1951), 189–201, and Vincent P. Carosso, "The Conference for Progressive Political Action, 1922–1925," unpublished M.A. thesis, University of California, Berkeley, 1944. Good background material on progressivism is available in F. E. Haynes, *Social Politics in the United States* (Boston, 1924). Robert A. Woods, *The Preparation of Calvin Coolidge*

(Boston, 1924), and Theodore A. Huntley, *The Life of John W. Davis* (New York, 1924), are the customary not-very-good campaign biographies. J. Leonard Bates, "The Teapot Dome Scandal and the Election of 1924," *American Historical Review,* LX (Jan., 1955), 303–322, points out the bipartisan effects of the oil scandal. Mary Synon, *McAdoo, The Man and His Times* (Indianapolis, 1924), records the life history of the principal Democratic also-ran.

For the election of 1928, Roy V. Peel and Thomas C. Donnelly, *The 1928 Campaign* (New York, 1931), provides little more than the bare essentials. Much more satisfactory is E. A. Moore, *A Catholic Runs for President* (New York, 1956). Oscar Handlin, *Al Smith and His America* (New York, 1958), overemphasizes the importance of the Catholic issue in the final decision. The questions raised by Smith's religion are discussed on a high plane in two articles, Charles C. Marshall, "An Open Letter to the Honorable Alfred E. Smith," *Atlantic Monthly,* CXXXIV (Apr., 1927), 540–549, and Alfred E. Smith, "Catholic and Patriot; Governor Smith Replies," *ibid.* (May, 1927), 721–728. Alfred E. Smith, *Campaign Addresses* (Washington, 1929), and Herbert Hoover, *The New Day; Campaign Speeches of Herbert Hoover, 1928* (Stanford, Calif., 1929), reveal the high level on which the two principals conducted their campaign. Marjorie W. Lyman, "The Presidential Candidate and the Radio," unpublished University of California M.A. thesis, Berkeley, 1944, demonstrates the importance of the radio in the campaign. Roy V. Peel and Thomas C. Donnelly, *The 1932 Campaign* (New York, 1935), is somewhat reminiscent of the 1928 campaign. There are many biographies of Smith and Hoover. For the former, the principal items are Henry Moskowitz, *Up From the City Streets* (New York, 1927); Henry F. Pringle, *Alfred E. Smith* (New York, 1927); and Frank Graham, *Al Smith, American* (New York, 1945). For Hoover, roughly comparable studies are Will Irwin, *Herbert Hoover* (New York, 1928); Edwin Emerson, *Hoover and His Times* (Garden City, 1932); and Samuel Crowther, *The Presidency vs. Hoover* (Garden City, 1928). On the inconspicuous part played by the Communists in 1928, see Vaugn Davis Bornet, "The Communist Party in the Presidential Election of 1928," *Western Political Quarterly,* VI (Sept., 1958), 514–538.

The Harding Administration

Harding's short presidential term has received more attention, perhaps, than it deserves. Frederic L. Paxson, *American Democracy and the World War,* III, *Postwar Years, Normalcy, 1918–1923* (Berkeley, Calif., 1948), achieves an unusual degree of detachment. Mark Sullivan, *Our Times, The United States, 1900–1925,* VI, *The Twenties* (New York, 1935), is the conscientious work of a keen newspaper reporter. Samuel Hopkins Adams,

Incredible Era: The Life and Times of Warren Gamaliel Harding (Boston, 1939), is unrestrainedly sensational. Harry M. Daugherty and Thomas Dixon, *The Inside Story of the Harding Tragedy* (New York, 1932), is a sustained but unconvincing apology for Harding. Joe Mitchell Chapple, *Life and Times of Warren G. Harding* (Boston, 1924), wins even less respect; while Gaston B. Means and May Dixon Thacker, *The Strange Death of President Harding* (New York, 1930), is obviously the product of overactive imagination. William Allen White, *Masks in a Pageant* (New York, 1928), has a concluding section on the 1920's. Stewart H. Holbrook, *Lost Men of American History* (New York, 1946), contains a chapter "In Praise of the Harding Era." Nan Britton, *The President's Daughter* (New York, 1927), charges Harding with the paternity of an illegitimate child. M. E. Ravage, *The Story of Teapot Dome* (New York, 1924), deals effectively with one of the worst of the Harding scandals, but see also Burl Noggle, "The Origins of the Teapot Dome Investigation," *Mississippi Valley Historical Review*, XLIV (Sept., 1957), 237–266. Charles Gates Dawes, *The First Year of the Budget of the United States* (New York, 1923), is an illuminating account. F. W. Taussig, *The Tariff History of the United States* (8th ed., New York, 1931), has an excellent chapter on tariff legislation during Harding's administration, but see also Abraham Berglund, "The Tariff Act of 1922," *American Economic Review*, XIII (Mar. 1923), 14–33.

Any study of Harding's foreign policy may well begin with the excellent book by Selig Adler, *The Isolationist Impulse; Its Twentieth Century Reaction* (New York, 1957). Illuminating, also, is Dexter Perkins, *Charles Evans Hughes and American Democratic Statesmanship* (Boston, 1956). The settlement with Columbia is reviewed in E. Taylor Parks, *Columbia and the United States, 1765–1934* (Durham, N.C., 1935); J. Fred Rippy, *The Capitalists and Colombia* (New York, 1931); and Watt Stewart, "The Ratification of the Thompson-Urrutia Treaty," *Southwestern Political and Social Science Quarterly*, X (Mar., 1930), 416–428. Anglo-American oil rivalry is treated in J. A. Spender, *Weetman Pearson, First Viscount Cowdray* (London, 1930); Ludwell Denny, *We Fight for Oil* (New York, 1928); and E. H. Davenport and S. R. Cooke, *The Oil Trusts and Anglo-American Relations* (New York, 1924); J. Saxon Mills, *The Genoa Conference* (London, 1922); and Sister Gertrude Mary (Gray), "Oil in Anglo-American Diplomatic Relations, 1920–28," unpublished Ph. D. dissertation, University of California, Berkeley, 1950.

For the Washington Conference, the official record is in *Conference on the Limitation of Armament*, Senate Document 126, 67th Cong., 2nd Sess. (Washington, 1922). An excellent account is presented in Henry C. Beerits, "The Washington Conference," unpublished manuscript in the Charles Evans Hughes Papers, Library of Congress, Manuscript Division. Harold and

Margaret Sprout, *Toward a New Order of Sea Power* (Princeton, 1946), is probably the most scholarly study of the conference, although the atmosphere in which it was staged is best captured by Mark Sullivan, *The Great Adventure at Washington* (Garden City, 1922). Merze Tate, *The United States and Armaments* (Cambridge, Mass., 1948), deals with all the major efforts at disarmament in which the United States participated. Other useful books are R. L. Buell, *The Washington Conference* (New York, 1922); C. L. Hoag, *Preface to Preparedness; The Washington Conference and Public Opinion* (Washington, 1941); Tatsuji Takeuchi, *War and Diplomacy in the Japanese Empire* (Garden City, 1935); Rolland A. Chaput, *Disarmament in British Foreign Policy* (London, 1935); H. G. Wells, *Washington and the Riddle of Peace* (New York, 1922); Yamato Ichihashi, *The Washington Conference and After* (Stanford, Calif., 1928); S. F. Bemis (ed.), *The American Secretaries of State and Their Diplomacy* (New York, 1929), X. Rear Admiral Harry S. Knapp, U.S.N., Ret., "The Limitation of Armament at the Conference of Washington," *Proceedings of the American Society of International Law, 1922* (Washington, 1922), voices the American Navy's objections to the Washington limitations. See also J. Bartlet Brebner, "Canada, the Anglo-Japanese Alliance and the Washington Conference," *Political Science Quarterly*, L (Mar., 1935). Herbert O. Yardley, *The American Black Chamber* (Indianapolis, 1931), maintains that the United States had broken the Japanese code and made good use of this advantage.

The Coolidge Administration

In addition to items already mentioned there are several Coolidge biographies, none of which rises above the mediocrity of its subject: R. M. Washburn, *Calvin Coolidge; His First Biography* (Boston, 1924); William Allen White, *Calvin Coolidge; The Man Who Is President* (New York, 1925); Edward E. Whiting, *President Coolidge; A Contemporary Estimate* (Boston, 1923); and Cameron Rogers, *The Legend of Calvin Coolidge* (Garden City, 1928). Alfred P. Dennis, *Gods and Little Fishes* (Indianapolis, 1931), contains an interesting study of Coolidge. So also does Peter R. Levin, *Seven by Chance; The Accidental Presidents* (New York, 1948). Some of the independents who sought to disturb Coolidge's calm are sketched in Ray Tucker and Frederick R. Barkley, *Sons of the Wild Jackass* (Boston, 1932). Interesting comments from the sidelines appear in Carroll Kilpatrick (ed.), *Roosevelt and Daniels; A Friendship in Politics* (Chapel Hill, N.C., 1952); Horace Wilson Stokes (ed.), *Mirrors of the Year* (New York, 1928); and Will Rogers, *Letters of a Self-Made Diplomat to His President* (New York, 1926). Carroll W. Wooddy, *The Case of Frank L. Smith* (Chicago, 1931), throws light on the political standards of the middle 1920's. Coolidge's speeches say much and tell little. Some of them are published under the titles *The Price of*

Freedom (New York, 1925), and *Foundations of the Republic* (New York, 1926). Eric F. Goldman, *Rendezvous with Destiny* (New York, 1952), has an interesting chapter on "The Shame of the Babbitts" that stresses the eclipse of reform during the 1920's. But see also Arthur S. Link, "What Happened to the Progressive Movement in the 1920's?" *American Historical Review,* LXIV (July, 1959), 833–851.

On immigration restriction, the *Annual Report of the Commissioner General of Immigration, 1924* (Washington, 1924), is useful. So also is the thoughtful study by John Higham, *Strangers in the Land* (New Brunswick, N.J., 1955). Robert DeC. Ward, "Our New Immigration Policy," *Foreign Affairs,* III (Sept. 15, 1924), 99–111, defends the principle of exclusion. Pertinent information is also available in R. L. Garis, *Immigration Restriction* (New York, 1927); Edward Corsi, *In the Shadow of Liberty; The Chronicle of Ellis Island* (New York, 1935); Antonio Stella, *Some Aspects of Italian Immigration to the United States* (New York, 1924); Robert E. Park, *The Immigrant Press and Its Control* (New York, 1922); Theodore Saloutos, *They Remember America; The Story of the Repatriated Greek-Americans* (Berkeley, Calif., 1956); O. Fritiof Ander, "The Effects of the Immigration Law of 1924 upon a Minority Immigrant Group," *Annual Report of the American Historical Association,* 1942, III (Washington, 1944), 343–352; Charles P. Howland, *Survey of American Foreign Relations, 1929* (New Haven, 1929), Sec. III. On the problem of Japanese exclusion the best study is R. W. Paul, *The Abrogation of the Gentlemen's Agreement* (Cambridge, Mass., 1936).

On the war debts problem, Harold G. Moulton and Leo Pasvolsky, *War Debts and World Prosperity* (Washington, 1932), is the standard citation, but this may be supplemented by Wildon Lloyd, *The European War Debts and their Settlement* (New York, 1934); H. E. Fisk, *The Inter-Ally Debts* (New York, 1924); John F. Bass and Harold G. Moulton, *America and the Balance Sheet of Europe* (New York, 1922); George P. Auld, *The Dawes Plan and the New Economics* (Garden City, 1928); Charles P. Howland, *Survey of American Foreign Relations, 1928* (New Haven, 1928), Sec. IV; James T. Gerould and Laura Shearer Turnbull (eds.), *Selected Articles on Interallied Debts and Revision of the Debt Settlements* (New York, 1928); Albert J. Nock, *The Myth of a Guilty Nation* (New York) 1922; Paul R. Leach, *That Man Dawes* (Chicago, 1930); and Bascom N. Timmons, *Portrait of an American, Charles G. Dawes* (New York, 1953).

On the various movements for world peace, see Merle Curti, *Peace or War, The American Struggle, 1636–1936* (New York, 1936); John H. Clarke, *America and World Peace* (New York, 1925); Irving Fisher, *League or War?* (New York, 1923); and Henry Cabot Lodge, Jr., *The Cult of Weakness* (Boston, 1932). The League of Nations, *Ten Years of World Co-Operation*

(London, 1930), is a comprehensive study of League activities. William E. Rappard, *Uniting Europe* (New Haven, 1930), deals with efforts at unity both within and without the League. Denna F. Fleming, *The United States and the World Court* (Garden City, 1945), follows through painstakingly the various efforts to induce the United States to support the Court. John Bassett Moore, *International Law and Some Current Illusions, and Other Essays* (New York, 1924), has an excellent section on the nature of the Court. On the abortive Geneva Conference of 1927, the official account is printed in *Records of the Conference for the Limitation of Naval Armament*, Senate Document 55, 70th Cong., 1st Sess. (Washington, 1928). H. C. Englebrecht and F. C. Hanighen, *Merchants of Death* (New York, 1934), is much over-drawn. Richard Hooker, "The Geneva Naval Conference," *Yale Review*, new series, XVII (Jan., 1928), 263–280, is more dependable. Robert H. Ferrell, *Peace in Their Time; The Origins of the Kellogg-Briand Pact* (New Haven, 1952), is a meticulous study of the negotiations that led to the Paris Pact. James T. Shotwell, *War as an Instrument of National Policy and its Renunciation in the Pact of Paris* (New York, 1929), is written by one who played a principal role in the formulation of the pact. John E. Stoner, *S. O. Levinson and the Pact of Paris* (Chicago, 1943), is the biography of another prime mover.

On hemispheric relations, a useful commentary is Arthur P. Whitaker, *The Western Hemisphere Idea; Its Rise and Decline* (Ithaca, N.Y.. 1954). Among the best of the general treatises on the relations between the United States and its southern neighbors are S. F. Bemis, *The Latin American Policy of the United States* (New York, 1943); Graham H. Stuart, *Latin America and the United States* (New York, 1955); Alexander DeConde, *Herbert Hoover's Latin-American Policy* (Stanford, Calif., 1951); Arthur P. Whitaker, *The United States and South America* (Cambridge, Mass., 1948); Clarence H. Haring, *South America Looks at the United States* (New York, 1929); Charles E. Hughes, *Our Relations to the Nations of the Western Hemisphere* (Princeton, 1928); Luis Quintanilla, *A Latin American Speaks* (New York, 1943); Max Winkler, *Investments of United States Capital in Latin America* (Boston, 1929). On relations with Mexico, the best general study is Charles W. Hackett, *The Mexican Revolution and the United States, 1910–1926*, World Peace Foundation, Pamphlets, IX (Boston, 1926). Harold Nicolson, *Dwight Morrow* (New York, 1935), is excellent on the Morrow mission. Other studies worth noting are Henry L. Stimson, *American Policy in Nicaragua* (New York, 1927); I. J. Cox, *Nicaragua and the United States, 1909–1927* (Boston, 1927); Sumner Welles, *Naboth's Vineyard; The Dominican Republic, 1844–1924* (2 vols., New York, 1928); Melvin M. Knight, *The Americans in Santo Domingo* (New York, 1928); Carleton Beale, *The Crime of Cuba* (Philadelphia, 1933); Margaret A. Marsh, *The Bankers in Bolivia*

(New York, 1928); Gaston Nerval, *An Autopsy on the Monroe Doctrine* (Washington, 1930). The shift in American foreign policy away from the Roosevelt Corollary is stated in J. Reuben Clark, *Memorandum on the Monroe Doctrine* (Washington, 1930).

On Canadian-American relations, see Hugh L. Keenlyside and Gerald S. Brown, *Canada and the United States* (New York, 1952); Carl Wittke, *A History of Canada* (New York, 1941); C. P. Wright, *The St. Lawrence Deep Waterway; A Canadian Appraisal* (Toronto, 1935); H. G. Moulton and others, *The St. Lawrence Navigation and Power Project* (Washington, 1929).

The Business Boom

The literature of American business activities during the 1920's is bafflingly plentiful, and only a few of the many relevant titles may be mentioned. An official defense of American business concepts is provided by the Economic Principles Commission of the National Association of Manufacturers, *The American Individual Enterprise System* (2 vols., New York, 1946). Henry Ford's own views are presented in Henry Ford and Samuel Crowther, *Moving Forward* (Garden City, 1930). Contemporary studies by economists include William Z. Ripley, *Main Street and Wall Street* (Boston, 1927); Paul M. Mazur, *American Prosperity; Its Causes and Consequences* (New York, 1928); Rexford G. Tugwell, *Industry's Coming of Age* (New York, 1927), and Tugwell (ed.), *The Trend of Economics* (New York, 1924), a symposium. The rapid drift toward consolidation is the principal theme of Harry W. Laidler, *Concentration of Control in American Industry* (New York, 1931); Adolph A. Berle and Gardiner C. Means, *The Modern Corporation and Private Property* (New York, 1933); and Henry R. Seager and Charles A. Gulick, Jr., *Trust and Corporation Problems* (New York, 1929). James C. Bonbright and Gardiner C. Means, *The Holding Company* (New York, 1932), studies one of the principal devices used to promote business concentration. Several books by Simon Smith Kuznets, *National Income and Its Composition, 1919–1938* (New York, 1941), *National Product Since 1869* (New York, 1946), and *Economic Change* (New York, 1953), center attention on the total output of the American economic plant, a subject studied also in Robert F. Martin, *National Income in the United States* (New York, 1939). Thomas C. Blaisdell, Jr., *The Federal Trade Commission* (New York, 1932), reveals the facts about federal regulation. W. J. A. Donald, *Trade Associations* (New York, 1933); J. H. Foth, *Trade Associations, Their Services to Industry* (New York, 1930); and H. L. Childs, *Labor and Capital in National Politics* (Columbus, 1930), explain the growing part played by trade associations in American business. Sharply critical of prevailing behavior are such books as Thurman W. Arnold, *The Folklore of Capitalism* (New Haven, 1937); Ferdinand Lundberg, *America's 60 Families* (New York, 1937);

Stuart Chase, *Prosperity: Fact or Myth?* (New York, 1929); Louis Brandeis, *Other People's Money* (new ed., New York, 1932); Stuart Chase and F. J. Schlink, *Your Money's Worth* (New York, 1927); John T. Flynn, *Investment Trusts Gone Wrong!* (New York, 1930), and, by the same author, *Graft in Business* (New York, 1931).

Various types of American industry come in for special treatment. The expansion of public utilities, particularly power, claimed much attention, most of it unfavorable, for example, Gifford Pinchot, *The Power Monopoly* (Milford, Pa., 1928); Ernest Gruening, *The Public Pays* (New York, 1931); Jack Levin, *Power Ethics* (New York, 1931); H. S. Raushenbush and Harry W. Laidler, *Power Control* (New York, 1928); and Carl D. Thompson, *Confessions of the Power Trust* (New York, 1932). There is an interesting chapter on Insull in Wayne Andrews, *Battle for Chicago* (New York, 1946). Forrest McDonald, *Let There Be Light; The Electric Utility Industry in Wisconsin, 1881–1955* (Madison, Wis., 1957), is, by way of contrast, friendly to the industry it studies. The automobile industry has also attracted much attention. In addition to the books about himself that Ford sponsored, one should consult Ralph C. Epstein, *The Automobile Industry* (Chicago, 1928); E. D. Kennedy, *The Automobile Industry* (New York, 1941); C. B. Glasscock, *The Gasoline Age* (Indianapolis, 1937); and Allan Nevins and Frank Hill, *Ford: Expansion and Challenge: 1915–1932* (New York, 1957). The importance of highway construction is featured in C. L. Dearing, *American Highway Policy* (Washington, 1941), and F. L. Paxson, "The Highway Movement, 1916–1935," *American Historical Review*, LI (Jan., 1946). On the railroads, see D. Philip Lochlin, *Railroad Regulation since 1920* (Chicago, 1928); and W. N. Leonard, *Railroad Consolidation under the Transportation Act of 1920* (New York, 1946). On the real estate boom, see Homer Vanderblue, "The Florida Land Boom," *Journal of Land and Public Utility Economics,* III (May, 1927), 113–131; and Homer Hoyt, *One Hundred Years of Land Values in Chicago* (Chicago, 1933).

Overseas business expansion and its results have inspired many excellent studies, among them Herbert Feis, *The Diplomacy of the Dollar, First Era, 1919–1932* (Baltimore, 1950), and, the same author, *The Changing Pattern of International Economic Affairs* (New York, 1940); Cleona Lewis, *America's Stake in International Investments* (Washington, 1938); Muriel F. Jolliffe, *The United States as a Financial Center, 1919–1933* (Cardiff, Wales, 1935); J. T. Madden and others, *America's Experience as a Creditor Nation* (New York, 1937); Julius Klein, *Frontiers of Trade* (New York, 1929). The efforts of the United States to maintain an effective merchant fleet are reviewed in Paul M. Zeis, *American Shipping Policy* (Princeton, 1938); National Industrial Conference Board, *The American Merchant Marine Problem* (New York, 1929); and John B. Hutchins, "The American Shipping Industry Since 1914," *Business History Review,* XXVIII (June, 1954), 105–127.

On the problems of labor in boom and depression the excellent compilation by Maurice F. Neufeld, *A Bibliography of Labor Union History* (Ithaca, N.Y., 1958), provides ample references. The most comprehensive history of labor is John R. Commons (ed.), *History of Labor in the United States, 1896–1932* (New York, 1935), III, IV. Other standard works are Leo Wolman, *The Growth of American Trade Unions, 1880–1923* (New York, 1924); Lewis Lorwin, *The American Federation of Labor* (Washington, 1933); and C. R. Daugherty, *Labor Problems in American Industry* (Boston, 1933). Still others, with varying emotional overtones, are H. M. Kallen, *Education, the Machine, and the Worker* (New York, 1925); David J. and Bertha T. Saposs, *Readings in Trade Unionism* (New York, 1927); John A. Fitch, *The Causes of Industrial Unrest* (New York, 1924); and Thomas Nixon Carver, *The Present Economic Revolution in the United States* (Boston, 1925). The Socialist point of view is well set forth in two books by Norman Thomas, *What Is Industrial Democracy?* (New York, 1925), and *Human Exploitation in the United States* (New York, 1934). The plight of the southern textile-mills worker is described in Tom Tippett, *When Southern Labor Stirs* (New York, 1931). On the Negro in industry, see Sterling D. Spero and Abram L. Harris, *The Black Worker* (New York, 1931); on the Herrin massacre of 1922, Paul M. Angle, *Bloody Williamson* (New York, 1952); on the silk workers and the Paterson strike, Grace Hutchins, *Labor and Silk* (New York, 1929); on coal miners, Isador Lubin, *Miner's Wages and the Cost of Coal* (New York, 1924); on real wages, Paul H. Douglas, *Real Wages in the United States, 1890–1926* (Boston, 1930); on the I.W.W., J. S. Gambs, *The Decline of the I.W.W.* (New York, 1932); on labor espionage, Leo Huberman, *The Labor Spy Racket* (New York, 1937). Coburn Allen, *The Law of the Jungle* (New York, 1926), is a frankly anticapitalist tract. Philip Taft, *The AF of L from the Death of Gompers to the Merger* (New York, 1959), is a valuable new synthesis.

American Society

Writings on American society during the 1920's are superabundant, but generally lacking in perspective. Henry F. May, "Shifting Perspectives on the 1920's," *Mississippi Valley Historical Review,* XLIII (Dec., 1956), 405–427, attempts with some success to set the record straight, and provides also many useful citations. Clarke A. Chambers, "The Belief in Progress in Twentieth-Century America," *Journal of the History of Ideas,* XIX (Apr., 1958), 198–224, is similarly useful. D. D. Egbert and Stow Persons (eds.), *Socialism and American Life* (2 vols., Princeton, 1952), is encyclopedic in scope and contains much more than merely Socialist propaganda. Warren S. Thompson, *Population Problems* (New York, 1953), is an excellent demographic study. See also, by the same author, *Population, The Growth of Metropolitan*

Districts in the United States: 1900–1940 (Washington, 1947). Robert S. and Helen Merrell Lynd, *Middletown* (New York, 1929), reveals the everyday life and thought of a typical small American city. James T. Adams, *Our Business Civilization* (New York, 1929), is the conscientious work of a self-appointed critic. André Siegfried, *America Comes of Age* (New York, 1927), is a keenly penetrative French analysis. Joe Alex Morris, *What a Year!* (New York, 1956), surveys the American social scene during the last year of the boom. Other useful accounts of American life during the 1920's are Lloyd Morris, *Not So Long Ago* (New York, 1949); Charles Merz, *The Great American Band Wagon* (New York, 1928); E. Haldeman-Julius, *The Big American Parade* (Boston, 1929); Wm. H. Wise & Co. (pubs.), *The American Scrapbook: The Year's Golden Harvest of Thought and Achievement* (New York, 1928); Shaw Desmond, *Stars and Stripes* (London, 1932), a caustic Irish view; and George H. Knoles, *The Jazz Age Revisited; British Criticism of American Civilization during the 1920's* (Stanford, Calif., 1955).

Attempts by contemporaries to deal philosophically with the basic problems of an industrial society are plentiful. Among those worth noting are Floyd Dell, *Looking at Life* (New York, 1924); Walter B. Pitkin, *The Twilight of the American Mind* (New York, 1928); Charles W. Wood, *The Passing of Normalcy* (New York, 1929); Waldo Frank, *The Rediscovery of America* (New York, 1929); Hoffman Nickerson, *The American Rich* (Garden City, 1930); Glenn Frank, *Thunder and Dawn* (New York, 1932); Burton Rascoe, *We Were Interrupted* (Garden City, N.Y., 1947). There was a rash, too, of iconoclastic symposia. Most famous of these was a compilation by America's original beatnik, Harold E. Stearns (ed.), *Civilization in the United States; An Inquiry by Thirty Americans* (New York, 1922). Others in somewhat similar vein are Fred J. Ringel (ed.), *America as Americans See It* (New York, 1932); Samuel D. Schmalhausen (ed.), *Behold America!* (New York, 1931); and Oliver M. Sayler (ed.), *Revolt in the Arts* (New York, 1930). Somewhat more optimistic are William A. Neilson (ed.), *Roads to Knowledge* (New York, 1932), and Paul D. Schilpp (ed.), *Higher Education Faces the Future* (New York, 1930). Broader in scope is Charles A. Beard (ed.), *A Century of Progress* (New York, 1933).

On the subject of religion and morality, probably the most notable publication of the period was Walter Lippmann, *A Preface to Morals* (New York, 1929), a book which recommended humanism as a substitute for atheism to those who rejected supernatural faith. Relevant also at this point is David E. Weingast, *Walter Lippmann; A Study in Personal Journalism* (New Brunswick, N.J., 1949). Norman Furniss, *The Fundamentalist Controversy, 1918–1931* (New Haven, 1954), deals with the problems of those who still believed. H. Paul Douglass, *Protestant Cooperation in American Cities* (New York, 1930), and Paul A. Carter, *The Decline and Revival of the Social*

Gospel, 1920–40 (Ithaca, N.Y., 1956), are based upon painstaking research. Ben B. Lindsey and Wainwright Evans, *The Revolt of Modern Youth* (New York, 1925), draws upon Judge Lindsey's extensive experience in juvenile court. W. G. McLoughlin, *Billy Sunday Was His Real Name* (Chicago, 1955); Nancy Barr Mavity, *Sister Aimee* (Garden City, 1931); and Lately Thomas, *The Vanishing Evangelist* (New York, 1959), tell the life stories of Billy Sunday and Aimee McPherson. Stanley Walker, *City Editor* (New York, 1934), examines the American behavior pattern from a particularly revealing angle. Polly Adler, *A House Is Not a Home* (New York, 1954), gets even further down to fundamentals.

Literary history and criticism are outside the scope of this volume, but a few titles may not be amiss. Frederick J. Hoffman, *The Twenties* (New York, 1949), is not only the best such book on the period but it also contains an excellent bibliography, pp. 431–434. One of the most prolific writers of the time, H. L. Mencken, was also much written about, for example, Edgar Kemler, *The Irreverent Mr. Mencken* (Boston, 1950); William Manchester, *Disturber of the Peace; The Life of H. L. Mencken* (New York, 1950); Charles Angoff, *H. L. Mencken; A Portrait from Memory* (New York, 1956); Alistair Cooke (ed.), *The Vintage Mencken* (New York, 1955); Alfred A. Knopf (pub.), *Menckeniana, A Schimpflexikon* (New York, 1928). Arthur Mizener, *The Far Side of Paradise; A Biography of F. Scott Fitzgerald* (Boston, 1951), is sympathetic and understanding. See also Robert H. Elias (ed.), *Letters of Theodore Dreiser* (3 vols., Philadelphia, 1959); Harrison Smith (ed.), *From Main Street to Stockholm; Letters of Sinclair Lewis* (New York, 1952); Ben Hecht, *A Child of the Century* (New York, 1954); Howard Mumford Jones and Walter Rideout (eds.), *The Letters of Sherwood Anderson* (Boston, 1953).

Many of the books already mentioned devote space to the effects on American society of the movies, the radio, the airplane, the automobile, and other mechanical devices, but some special studies should be noted. The *Annals of the American Academy of Political and Social Science,* CCLIV (Nov., 1947), is an indispensable symposium on motion pictures, which may be supplemented by Lewis Jacobs, *The Rise of the American Film* (New York, 1939), and Arthur Mayer, *Merely Colossal* (New York, 1953). Paul Schubert, *The Electric Word; The Rise of the Radio* (New York, 1928), does a similar service for the radio. Henry Ladd Smith, *Airways; The History of Commercial Aviation in the United States* (New York, 1942), points out the parallels between the growth of the aviation industry and that of other American big businesses. For colorful details, see R. S. Holland, *Historic Airships* (Philadelphia, 1928), and Charles A. Lindbergh, *The Spirit of St. Louis* (New York, 1953). An interesting result of the automobile is exploited by Earl Pomeroy, *In Search of the Golden West; The Tourist in Western*

America (New York, 1957). On recreational activities in general, the best accounts are F. R. Dulles, *America Learns to Play* (New York, 1940), and J. A. Krout, *Annals of American Sport* (New Haven, 1929).

Prohibition, Racketeering, the Ku Klux Klan

The experiment with prohibition, whether success or failure, certainly produced a formidable body of literature. Charles Merz, *The Dry Decade* (New York, 1931), is still the best book on the subject, but the *Annals of the American Academy of Political and Social Science,* CLXIII (Sept., 1932), presents in addition a valuable symposium. Peter Odegard, *Pressure Politics; The Story of the Anti-Saloon League* (New York, 1928), shows how the sentiment for prohibition was created. Herbert Asbury, *The Great Illusion: An Informal History of Prohibition* (Garden City, 1950), is comprehensive and perspicacious. Irving Fisher and H. Bruce Brougham, *The "Noble Experiment"* (New York, 1930), attempts to analyze the social effects of prohibition. Gilbert M. Ostrander, *The Prohibition Movement in California, 1848–1933* (Berkeley, Calif., 1957), studies one of the states in which prohibition was most highly experimental. Mabel Walker Willebrandt, *The Inside of Prohibition* (Indianapolis, 1929), features the difficulties of enforcement. Justin Steuart, *Wayne Wheeler, Dry Boss* (New York, 1928), and Virginia Dabney, *Dry Messiah; The Life of Bishop Cannon* (New York, 1949), are excellent biographies of leading prohibitionists. Fabian Franklin, *What Prohibition Has Done to America* (New York, 1922), was an early effort to arouse repeal sentiment. Fletcher Dobyns, *The Amazing Story of Repeal* (New York, 1940), is an exposé of antiprohibition propaganda. William G. McAdoo, *The Challenge; Liquor and Lawlessness versus Constitutional Government* (New York, 1928), is a series of addresses on prohibition and its consequences. John Erskine, *Prohibition and Christianity and Other Paradoxes of the American Spirit* (Indianapolis, 1927), is a series of interpretative essays.

On lawlessness and racketeering, the results of the most pretentious study appear in *Report of the National Commission on Law Enforcement,* House Document 722, 71st Cong., 3rd Sess. Edward D. Sullivan, *Rattling the Cup on Chicago Crime* (New York, 1929); Walter N. Burns, *The One-Way Ride; The Red Trail of Chicago Gangland from Prohibition to Jake Lingle* (Garden City, 1931); Fred D. Pasley, *Al Capone: The Biography of a Self-Made Man* (Garden City, 1930); and Lloyd Wendt and Herman Kogen, *Big Bill of Chicago* (Indianapolis, 1953), all ring the changes on Chicago's misconduct. Books that undertake a similar mission for New York include Norman Thomas and Paul Blanshard, *What's the Matter with New York* (New York, 1932); Gene Fowler, *Beau James; The Life and Times of Jimmy Walker* (New York, 1949); Walter Chambers, *Samuel Seabury, A Challenge*

(New York, 1932); Milton Mackaye, *The Tin Box Parade: A Handbook for Larceny* (New York, 1934); William B. and John B. Northrop, *The Insolence of Office* (New York, 1932). Courtenay Terrett, *Only Saps Work: A Ballyhoo for Racketeering* (New York, 1930), traces the taint of dishonesty into many aspects of American life. The somewhat halting efforts of the law to keep apace with crime are revealed in Max Lowenthal, *The Federal Bureau of Investigation* (New York, 1950), and Don Whitehead, *The FBI Story* (New York, 1956). The unsavory history of the Ku Klux Klan has not yet been adequately told, but the best book available is still J. M. Mecklin, *The Ku Klux Klan; A Study of the American Mind* (New York, 1924). Emerson H. Loucks, *The Ku Klux Klan in Pennsylvania* (New York, 1936), is good on the state studied. Stanley Frost, *The Challenge of the Klan* (Indianapolis, 1924), is a contemporary reaction. Horace M. Kallen, *Culture and Democracy in the United States* (New York, 1924), has a chapter on the Klan. Oscar Ameringer, *If You Don't Weaken* (New York, 1940), contains some useful material on the Klan in Oklahoma. Michael Williams, *The Shadow of the Pope* (New York, 1932), examines anti-Catholic propaganda in the United States, of which Paul M. Winter, *What Price Tolerance* (Hewlett, N.Y., 1928), provides a good example.

The Hoover Administration

The best single volume on the Hoover regime, although restricted mainly to domestic affairs, is Harris Gaylord Warren, *Herbert Hoover and the Great Depression* (New York, 1959). A short pro-Hoover brochure, William Starr Myers, *The True Republican Record* (New York, 1939), is an earlier, but less successful, effort to set the record straight. Thorough documentation was a specialty of the Hoover administration. Two difficult volumes, William Starr Myers and Walter H. Newton, *The Hoover Administration; A Documented Narrative* (New York, 1936), and Ray Lyman Wilbur and Arthur M. Hyde, *The Hoover Policies* (New York, 1937), undertake to tell the whole story, although strictly from the President's point of view. Hoover's official pronouncements are available in William Starr Myers (ed.), *The State Papers and Other Public Writings of Herbert Hoover* (2 vols., Garden City, 1934). His political and economic views are recorded in Herbert Hoover, *American Individualism* (Garden City, 1922), *The Challenge to Liberty* (New York, 1934), and *Addresses upon the American Road, 1933–1938* (New York, 1938). Biographical material on Hoover is also abundant, but mostly of indifferent value because of its extreme bias, either pro or con. Among the books of this type not previously mentioned are John Hamill, *The Strange Career of Herbert Hoover under Two Flags* (New York, 1931); John Knox, *The Great Mistake; Can Herbert Hoover Explain His Past?* (Baltimore, 1930); Walter W. Liggett, *The Rise of Herbert Hoover* (New

York, 1932); and Eugene Lyons, *Our Unknown Ex-President; A Portrait of Herbert Hoover* (Garden City, 1950). Richard Hofstadter, *The American Political Tradition and the Men Who Made It* (New York, 1948), contains an admirable interpretative essay on Hoover. Carroll H. Wooddy, *The Growth of the Federal Government, 1915–1932* (New York, 1934), contains much valuable data on administrative history. William P. Helm, *Washington Swindle Sheet* (New York, 1932), reveals the generosity of some public servants with public money. Robert S. Allen and Drew Pearson, *The Washington Merry-Go-Round* (New York, 1931), is bitingly sarcastic of Washington officialdom in general. Ray Thomas Tucker, *The Mirrors of 1932* (New York, 1931), concentrates its attack on potential presidential nominees for 1932. Edwin C. Hill, *The American Scene* (New York, 1933), attempts to describe and evaluate the leading events of the year 1932. Charles Michelson, *The Ghost Talks* (New York, 1944), tells the inside story of the post-1928 Democratic revival. Joseph M. Jones, *Tariff Retaliation* (Philadelphia, 1934), assesses the reactions of foreign nations to the Hawley-Smoot Tariff.

The diplomatic history of the Hoover administration is summarized officially in William Starr Myers, *The Foreign Policies of Herbert Hoover, 1929–1933* (New York, 1940). The growth of fascism and communism in Europe is the principal subject of two books by Gilbert Seldes, *You Can't Print That; The Truth Behind the News, 1918–1928* (Garden City, 1929), and *Can These Things Be!* (Garden City, 1931). Ludwell Denny, *America Conquers Britain; A Record of Economic War* (New York, 1930), sketches grimly the background of the London Conference. Worth consulting on the problem of disarmament are Drew Pearson and Constantine Brown, *The American Diplomatic Game* (Garden City, 1935); Jonathan Mitchell, *Goose Steps to Peace* (Boston, 1931); Frank H. Simonds, *Can Europe Keep the Peace?* (New York, 1931); and Gerald W. Wheeler, "Japan's Influence on American Naval Policies, 1922–1931," unpublished Ph. D. dissertation, University of California, Berkeley, 1954. On the London Conference proper, see Department of State, *Proceedings of the London Naval Conference of 1930* (Washington, 1931); also Giovanni Engely, *The Politics of Naval Disarmament* (London, 1932). On the Far East, Henry L. Stimson, *The Far Eastern Crisis* (New York, 1936); Charles E. Martin and K. C. Leebrick (eds.), *The Pacific Area* (Seattle, 1929); W. W. Willoughby, *The Sino-Japanese Controversy and the League of Nations* (Baltimore, 1935). On the abortive Geneva Conference of 1932, Herbert Hoover and Hugh Gibson, *The Problems of Lasting Peace* (New York, 1942). On the Philippines, Grayson Kirk, *Philippine Independence* (New York, 1936); Harriet Moore, "The American Stake in the Philippines," *Foreign Affairs,* XI (Apr., 1933), 517–520; and Ralston Hayden, "China, Japan and the Philippines," *ibid.* (July, 1933), 711–715.

Agriculture

The decade of the twenties witnessed a steady build-up of agricultural discontent, culminating during the Hoover administration. Various aspects of this movement are treated in the Yearbook of Agriculture, 1940, *Farmers in a Changing World* (Washington, 1940), an admirable symposium on the agricultural history of the two preceding decades. Two other volumes, Murray R. Benedict, *Farm Policies of the United States, 1790–1950* (New York, 1953), and Theodore Saloutos and John D. Hicks, *Agricultural Discontent in the Middle West, 1900–1939* (Madison, Wis., 1951), also touch on nearly every phase of the subject. James H. Shideler, *Farm Crisis, 1919–1923* (Berkeley, Calif., 1957), is an excellent study of the first few postwar years. Robert L. Morlan, *Political Prairie Fire; The Non-Partisan League, 1915–1922* (Minneapolis, 1955), centers on a leading feature of the farmers' revolt. Gilbert C. Fite, *George N. Peek and the Fight for Farm Parity* (Norman, Okla., 1952), is an admirably effective account of McNary-Haugenism in its various manifestations. W. R. Sutherland, *A Debate Handbook on the McNary-Haugen Agricultural Surplus Control Act* (Lexington, Ky., 1927), presents practically all the arguments on the subject, both pro and con. Orville M. Kile, *The Farm Bureau Movement* (New York, 1921), shows how one important agricultural organization came into being. Lewis F. Carr, *America Challenged* (New York, 1929), emphasizes the danger to the United States in the decline of agriculture. Alonzo E. Taylor, *Corn and Hog Surplus of the Corn Belt* (Stanford, Calif., 1932), centers on a single critical problem. Henry A. Wallace, *New Frontiers* (New York, 1934), reviews the history of the farm problem during the years of Republican supremacy. John D. Black, *Agricultural Reform in the United States* (New York, 1929), is scholarly and objective. Edwin G. Nourse, *Government in Relation to Agriculture* (Washington, 1940), is a convenient summary of the subject. Foster F. Elliott, *Types of Farming in the United States* (Washington, 1933), is an indispensable guide to the geographic distribution of farm activities. Of great biographic interest is Russell Lord, *The Wallaces of Iowa* (Boston, 1947).

Panic and Depression

Such earlier efforts to explain the Panic of 1929 as Irving Fisher, *Stock Market Crash—and After* (New York, 1930), and Brookings Institution, *The Recovery Problem in the United States* (Washington, 1936), have been largely superseded by John Kenneth Galbraith, *The Great Crash, 1929* (Boston, 1955), a brilliant analysis. Lionel Robbins, *The Great Depression* (London, 1934), provides a British; M. J. Bonn, *The Crisis of Capitalism in America* (New York, 1932), a German; and Richard T. Ely, *Hard Times: The Way In and the Way Out* (New York, 1932), an American view of the business boom and its collapse. Stock-market activities and their consequences come to light in Francis W. Hirst, *Wall Street and Lombard Street* (New York, 1931); E. H. H. Simmons, *Cooperation against Security Frauds and Other Addresses* (New York, 1924); Lawrence H. Sloan, *Security Speculation; The Dazzling Adventure* (New York, 1926); Ferdinand Pecora, *Wall Street under Oath* (New York, 1939); and Bernard J. Reis, *False Security; The Betrayal of the American Investor* (New York, 1937).

Contemporary efforts to explain the lengthening period of depression were occasionally on the optimistic side, as Roger W. Babson, *Cheer Up! Better Times Ahead!* (New York, 1932), but more often dubious and cynical, as Edward Angly (ed.), *O Yeah?* (New York, 1931). See, for example, Gilbert Seldes, *The Years of the Locust, America, 1929–1932* (Boston, 1933); Edmund Wilson, *The American Jitters; A Year of the Slump* (New York, 1932); Walter Lippmann, *Interpretations, 1931–1932* (New York, 1932); Lawrence Dennes, *Is Capitalism Doomed?* (New York, 1932); Max Lowenthal, *The Investor Pays* (New York, 1933); Stuart Chase, *The Nemesis of American Business and Other Essays* (New York, 1931). Contemporary symposia sought earnestly to provide guidance: Felix Morley (ed.), *Aspects of the Depression* (Chicago, 1932); Samuel Crowther and others, *A Basis of Stability* (Boston, 1932); J. G. Smith (ed.), *Facing the Facts; An Economic Diagnosis* (New York, 1932). Daniel Aaron (ed.), *America in Crisis* (New York, 1952), has an interesting chapter by Walter Hamilton, "When the Banks Closed." The problems of unemployment and relief led to a continuing procession of books, among them James D. Mooney, *Wages and the Road Ahead* (London, 1931); Mary S. Callcott, *Principles of Social Legislation* (New York, 1932); David M. Schneider and Albert Deutsch, *The History of Public Welfare in New York State* (Chicago, 1941); James M. Williams, *Human Aspects of Unemployment and Relief* (Chapel Hill, N.C., 1933); Clinch Calkins, *Some Folks Won't Work* (New York, 1930). Premonitory of the New Deal are Jay Franklin, *What This Country Needs* (New York, 1931) and *What We Are About to Receive* (New York, 1932); Stuart Chase, *A New Deal* (New York, 1932); Mauritz A. Hallgren, *Seeds of Revolt* (New York, 1933); George Soule, *The Coming American Revolution* (New York, 1934); James P. Warburg, *The Money Muddle* (New York, 1934); Walter Lippmann, *The Method of Freedom* (New York, 1934). The overseas economic crisis receives attention in Paul M. Mazur, *America Looks Abroad* (New York, 1930); Paul Einzig, *Behind the Scenes of International Finance* (London, 1931); and Lothrop Stoddard, *Europe and Our Money* (New York, 1932). Two useful books published as this study went to press are Arthur Mann, *LaGuardia* (Philadelphia, 1959), and Howard Zinn, *LaGuardia in Congress* (Ithaca, 1959). See also John D. Hicks, "Two Postwar Decades," *Nebraska History*, XL (Dec., 1959), 243–264.

Index

Adams, Charles Francis, Navy Secretary, 216
Adjusted Compensation Act, 52
Advertising techniques, 119
Agriculture, postwar status, 17; tenancy, 18; price decline, 19; Farm Bloc, 54; in politics, 92; limited prosperity, 127; Agricultural Credits Act, 193; co-operatives, 194; tariffs, 196, 202; exportable surplus, 197; McNary-Haugenism, 198; Republican pledges (1928), 202; Democratic pledges (1928), 204; "agrarian myth," 206; export debenture plan, 217; Agricultural Marketing Act, 218; overproduction, 233; hit by drought, 236; in 1930 campaign, 238; Philippine competition, 255; farm incomes, 264; farm holiday program, 266
Agriculture Department, inspection powers, 55; Division of Co-operative Marketing, 195; on farm incomes, 264
Airplanes, military effectiveness, 44; manufacture of, 111; discounted by Army and Navy, 174; Air Commerce Act, 176
Alabama Power Company, 64
Aleutian Islands, 40
Aluminum Company of America, 108
American Bankers Association, 237
American Farm Bureau Federation, origins, 20; growth, 21; *Weekly News Letter*, 85; McNary-Haugen plan, 266
American Federation of Labor, strength, 13; *American Federation-ist*, 85; third party faction, 86; endorses La Follette, 99; in 1928 campaign, 209
American Legion, veterans' lobby, 52; on history teaching, 183; addressed by Hoover, 275
American literature, 185, 186
American Mercury, 185
American plan (open shop), 68
American Society of Equity, 19
American Telephone and Telegraph Company, 11, 224
American valuation (tariff), 57
Amos 'n' Andy, radio team, 173
Anderson, Sherwood, 186
Anglo-Japanese Alliance, objections to, 34; end of, 40
Anti-Saloon League, activities of, 177; methods imitated, 261
Argentine, trade with United States, 163
Arizona, copper production, 7; Boulder Dam agreement, 125
Arkansas, agriculture, 17; bank failures in, 267
Army, United States, discounts airplane, 174; insignificant size of, 258
Atlantic Monthly, on Smith's religion, 207
Australia, opposes Japanese immigration, 36
Austria, separate peace with United States, 31; Kreditanstalt failure, 245
Automobiles, postwar output, 5; competition with railroads, 60; manu-

facture of, 111; numbers of, 114; influence of, 115, 169

Aviation. See Airplanes

Babson, Roger, predicts panic, 227; predicts prosperity, 268

Baker, Newton D., favors League, 96

Balfour, Arthur, at Washington Conference, 37

Bank for International Settlements, 248

Banking in United States, weaknesses of, 231; bank failures, 232, 267, 268, 277; Glass-Steagall Act, 273. *See also* Federal Reserve Board

Bara, Theda, screen star, 171

Beard, C. A., on United States and the League, 145

Belgium, invited to Washington Conference, 34; debt to United States funded, 138

Bennett, Floyd G., explorer, 176

"Best Minds," under Harding, 27

Black, John D., economist, 266

Blaine, John J., Senator, 129; votes against Paris Peace Pact, 151

Bolton, Herbert E., on hemispheric solidarity, 163; Latin-Americanist, 190

Bonus Army (B.E.F.), in Washington, 275

Bonus bills, in Congress, 52; Patman bill (1932), 275

Boone, Joel T., medical officer, 79

Borah, William E., on treaty with Colombia, 30; on disarmament conference, 32; opposes Fordney-McCumber Act, 56; Republican insurgent, 86; meets with Progressive block, 89; refuses vice-presidential nomination, 91; favors Russian recognition, 134; on war guilt, 139; on Geneva Conference, 149; favors outlawry of war, 150; on Paris Peace Pact, 152; on Mexican intervention, 156; obtains special session, 217; on Tariff Commission, 220; Stimson's letter to, 253

Boston, police strike broken, 81; Watch and Ward Society, 183

Boulder Dam, projected, 125; authorized, 126; appropriations for, 235

Bow, Clara, screen star, 171

Brazil, boundary dispute, 159

Briand, Aristide, at Washington Conference, 37; proposes Peace Pact, 150; on Manchurian crisis, 251

British Commonwealth of Nations, 164, 247

Brookhart, Smith W., Senator, 86; views on Federal Farm Board, 264

Brown, W. F., Postmaster General, 177

Bruce, W. C., Senator, 261

Bryan, C. W., candidate for Vice-President, 97; defeated, 102

Bryan, W. J., at Scopes trial, 182

Bryan-Chamorro Treaty, with Nicaragua, 157

Budget and Accounting Act, 51

Bureau of Foreign and Domestic Commerce, 67

Bureau of Standards, 67

Burke, John J., mission to Mexico, 156

Business, postwar boom, 6; varieties of, 10; 1920 decline, 22; political power of, 50, 73; views on taxation, 53; aided by Department of Commerce, 67; recovery from depression, 83; favors from Republicans, 91; boom under Coolidge, 109; public utilities, 121; Mexican interests, 155; Latin-American interests, 162; promotes philanthropy, 191; dominates Republican party, 202; wooed by Democrats, 209; Panic of 1929, 224; fundamentally unsound, 230; refuses aid to agriculture, 233; alliance with Republicans, 237; depression aids from government, 276; failure of business leadership, 279

Butler, Nicholas Murray, 144

Butler, Smedley D., heads Philadelphia police, 179

Butler, William B., Senator, 129

Byrd, Richard E., explorer, 176

California, Oriental residents, 3; oil output, 7; agriculture, 17, 118; Boulder Dam agreement, 125; Fruit Growers Association, 194

Calles, Plutarco Elías, Mexican President, 155; sends arms to Nicaragua, 158

Canada, on Anglo-Japanese Alliance, 34; emigration to United States, 132; relations with United States, 163; member British Commonwealth, 164; St. Lawrence Seaway, 165

Cannon, James, Jr., Methodist bishop, 207

Capone, Al, racketeer, 178; conviction of, 264

Capper-Volstead Act (1922), 194

Cardozo, Benjamin N., Associate Justice, 216

Carnegie Endowment for International Peace, 144

Carranza, Venustiana, Mexican President, 154

Catholics, numbers of, 3; strength among immigrants, 93; opposed by Ku Klux Klan, 94; problems in Mexico, 156; parochial schools, 183; in 1928 campaign, 206, 212

Chamber of Commerce of the United States, 13

Chamberlin, C. D., flies Atlantic, 176

Chaplin, Charlie, screen actor, 170

Chase, Stuart, on prosperity, 127

Chicago bootlegging, 178; racketeering, 179; relief problem, 270

Child labor laws, opposed, 72

China, invited to Washington Conference, 35; Nine Power Treaty, 46; Shantung agreement, 47; attacked in Manchuria, 249; in Shanghai, 252

Chinese, number in United States, 3

Christensen, Parley P., presidential candidate (1920), 87

Churchill, Winston, on London Naval Conference, 243

Cities, growth in 1920's, 4; radicalism in, 168; political machines, 93; prohibition in, 178; racketeering, 179; rural fear of, 206; vote for Smith (1928), 212

Clark, J. Reuben, Memorandum, 162

Clarke, Edward Y., Klan leader, 94

Clarke, John H., League advocate, 144

Clayton Act, Supreme Court on, 72

Coal, production in United States, 7; declining importance of, 69; strike of 1922, 70; Coal Commission report, 71; use to create power, 124

Colombia, treaty with United States, 28; trade with United States, 30; boundary dispute, 159

Colorado, Boulder Dam agreement, 125

Columbia Broadcasting Company, 172

Columbia River, power potential, 125

Colver, W. B., on Progressive defeat, 103

Commerce Department, under Hoover, 67; promotes aviation, 176

Commerce of United States, postwar, 9; Merchant Marine Act, 61; aided by Hoover, 67; with Latin America, 162; affected by tariff, 222; out of balance, 233; continued decline, 244; with Philippines, 255

Commercial and Financial Chronicle, 13

Commission on Law Enforcement and Obedience, 262

Committee for Progressive Political Action (C.P.P.A.), in 1922 election, 87; in 1924 election, 89, 97

Committee of Forty-eight, urges third party, 87; in 1924 election, 97

Commons, John R., economist, 86

Communists, postwar status, 15; in 1924 election, 97; critics of America, 168

Compton, Arthur H., scientist, 189

Congress of United States, bonus legislation, 52; reduces taxes, 53; Farm Bloc measures, 55; supports War Finance Corporation, 55; passes Muscle Shoals bills, 64; creates Coal Commission, 71; after 1922 election, 88; after 1924 election, 102; after 1926 election, 129; restricts immigration, 132; creates War Debt Commission, 137; adopts naval building program, 149; Air Commerce Act, 176; on agricultural credits, 193; passes McNary-Haugen bill, 198; after election of 1928, 212; Agricultural Marketing Act, 218; Hawley-Smoot Act, 221; after election of 1930, 239; speakership contest, 240n.; drought appropriations, 264; creates R.F.C., 271

Constitution of 1917 (Mexico), 154

Constitution of United States, adaptability, 167; Eighteenth Amendment, 177; Nineteenth Amendment, 181; Twentieth Amendment, 278

Construction industry, in 1920's, 115

Continental Trading Company, Ltd., Canadian corporation, 76; activities, 77

Coolidge, Calvin, policy on shipping, 61; nominated for Vice-President, 80; career of 81; liquidates Harding scandals, 82; appointees, 83; nomination (1924), 84; election, 102; second term, 106; lauds tax reduction, 107; opposes Tennessee Valley development, 125; on Boulder Dam, 126; accepts Japanese exclusion, 132; on war debts, 136; on World Court, 146; calls Geneva Conference, 147; favors naval construction, 149; sends Morrow to Mexico, 157; Nicaraguan policy, 158; Mitchell inquiry, 175; endorses co-operative marketing, 195; vetoes McNary-Haugen bill, 199; does not choose to run, 201

Coolidge, Mrs. Calvin, renovates White House, 83

Coontz, Robert E., at Washington Conference, 38

Co-operative Marketing, legalized, 194; limitations of, 195

Corporations, taxation of, 54, 106; net incomes of, 110; new industries, 111; holding companies, 121; public utilities, 123, 127; methods of finance, 224; overexpansion, 230; structural weaknesses, 231; government relief for, 271

Correll, C. J., radio star, 173

Cotton, production of, 17; in McNary-Haugen bills, 198; depression prices, 219; tariff on, 222; stabilization corporation, 265

Cox, James M., Democratic leader, 270

Crime, facilitated by automobile, 169; bootlegging, 178; racketeering, 179;

Lindbergh case, 180; investigated, 262

Crissinger, D. R., governor of Federal Reserve Board, 65

Cristeros, Mexican faction, 156

Chrysler, Walter, manufacturer, 112

Croly, Herbert, editor of *New Republic*, 85; *Promise of American Life*, 184

Cuba, Platt Amendment, 161; interest in Philippine independence, 256

Culbertson, W. S., Tariff Commissioner, 66

Cunningham, E. H., member Federal Reserve Board, 65

Curtis, Charles, nominated for Vice-President, 201; elected, 211

Darrow, Clarence, at Scopes trial, 182

Daugherty, Harry M., opposes League, 25; obtains labor injunction, 72; relations with "Jess" Smith, 74; involved in Harding scandals, 75; removed from office, 83; third-party target, 88

Daugherty, Mal S., in Harding scandals, 75

Davis, Chester, on Democratic pledges (1928), 204

Davis, J. J., Labor Secretary, 26

Davis, John W., Democratic nominee (1924), 97; defeated, 102; promises Hoover co-operation, 270

Dawes, Charles G., Director of the Budget, 51; nominated for Vice-President, 91; attacks La Follette, 100; on Warren's confirmation, 107; "Dawes Plan," 141, 143; Ambassador to Great Britain, 216; at London Naval Conference, 242; heads Reconstruction Finance Corporation, 272

Dearborn Independent, 183

Debt of United States, postwar increases, 5, 6; payments on, 107; during depression, 235, 236

de Mille, Cecil, movie producer, 170

Democrats, oppose Four Power Pact, 48; tariff views, 57; divisions among, 92; Madison Square Convention, 95; Klan issue, 96; campaign of 1924, 100; on Coolidge

administration, 128; platform
(1928), 203; election results, 211;
win new voters, 213; depression upsurge, 237; in 1930 campaign, 238;
promises to Hoover, 270; depression
victory, 278, 280

Denby, Edwin, Navy Secretary, 26;
oil scandal, 75

Depressions, postwar, 22; Panic of
1929, 223; causes of, 230; politics
of, 237; Hoover's views on, 276

Dewey, John, 187

Díaz, Adolfo, President of Nicaragua,
158

Díaz, Porfirio, President of Mexico,
154

Disarmament, Borah's resolution on
(1921), 33; Washington Conference, 37; naval limitations, 44;
Geneva Conference, 147; London
Naval Conference, 242; Preparatory Commission, 258

Doheny, Edward L., relations with
Secretary Fall, 75; retains McAdoo,
94; Mexican oil interests, 155

Dominican Republic, marines with-
.drawn, 160

Donovan, W. J., in Justice Department, 108

Dos Passos, John, 186

du Pont, Pierre, backs General Motors,
112; backs Prohibition repeal, 261

Durant, William C., manufacturer,
112

Education, pattern in United States, 3;
American belief in, 167; changes in,
169; use of radio, 172; Dewey's
influence, 187; professional schools,
188; scientific research, 189; the
social studies, 190

Eighteenth Amendment, 177. See also
Prohibition

Einstein, Albert, 189

Elections, (1922), 88; (1924), 94,
102; (1926), 128; (1928), 201,
212; (1930), 237, 239; (1932),
276, 278, 280

Eliot, T. S., 186

Elk Hills, oil scandal, 75; Supreme
Court opinion, 77

Emergency Quota Act, 131

Emergency Relief and Construction
Act, 272

Empire State Building, 115

Esch, J. J., Interstate Commerce Commissioner, 65

Europe, borrowings from United
States, 6; exchange problems, 21;
reaction to Washington Conference,
47; American investments in, 59;
private loans to, 109; United States
immigrant quotas, 131; war debt
problem, 136; Locarno Pact, 147;
relations with Latin America, 163;
depression in, 230; financial relations with United States, 233; trade
problems, 244

Experimental College, Wisconsin, 189

Export Debenture Plan, 217

Fairbanks, Douglas, screen actor, 170

Fall, A. B., Secretary of Interior, 26;
on treaty with Colombia, 28; involved in Harding scandals, 75;
conviction, 76

Farm Bloc, formed, 54; obtains legislation, 55; favors high tariffs, 56;
disappointing results, 193; promotes co-operative marketing, 194

Farm Bureau. See American Farm
Bureau Federation

Farm Holiday movement, 267

Farmer-Laborites, in 1920 campaign,
87; in Congress, 129, 212, 239

Farmers' National Grain Corporation,
219

Farmers' Union, founded, 20; favors
cost-plus prices, 266

Faulkner, William, 186

Federal Bureau of Investigation, under
J. Edgar Hoover, 180; effectiveness,
264

Federal Farm Board, created, 218;
failures, 219, 239; efforts, 260, 264

Federal Highways Act, 8

Federal Home Loan Bank Act, 274

Federal Land Banks, 193, 265

Federal Power Commission, regulatory
authority, 63; ineffectiveness, 66,
124

Federal Radio Commission, 173

Federal Reserve Board, war record,
11; rediscount policy (1919–20),

21; appointments to, 65; low rediscount rates, 109; agricultural credit, 193; easy money policy, 228, 232, 233; raises rediscount rates, 229, 234

Federal Trade Commission, powers of, 64; on aluminum trust, 108

Fess, Simeon D., on labor reforms, 23; on business and politics, 267

Finland, debt to United States, 138; continues payments, 246

Fisher, Irving, economist, 227

Fitzgerald, F. Scott, 186

Florida, agriculture, 17; real estate boom, 117

Forbes, Charles R., in Harding scandals, 74

Ford, Henry, methods of production, 5; bid for Muscle Shoals, 62; candidate for Senate, 88n.; Model T, 111; Model A, 113; anti-Semitism, 183

Fordney-McCumber Act, passed, 57; high rates, 58; unpopularity of, 88; effect on Canada, 164; flexible provision, 220

Fosdick, Raymond B., 144

Four Power Pact, on Pacific affairs, 41; ratified, 49

France, invited to Washington Conference, 35; discontented with results, 42, 48; funds debt to United States, 138; invades Ruhr, 140; Briand's peace proposals, 150; accepts Paris Peace Pact, 151; at London Naval Conference, 242; financial distress, 246

France, Joseph I., Senator, 134; favors loan to Russia, 135

Frankfurter, Felix, 86

Frazier, Lynn J., Senator, 86

Freeman, The, liberal journal, 185

Freud, Sigmund, influence of, 168, 181

Fundamentalism, in religion, 168, 182

Galbraith, John K., The Great Crash, 230

Garner, John N., promises Hoover co-operation, 270; favors increased R.F.C. appropriations, 274

General Motors Company, 112

Geneva Conference (1927), called, 147; failure of, 148, 241, 242

Geneva Conference (1932), 258

Genoa Conference, 135

Gentlemen's Agreement, abrogated, 132

Germany, peace treaty with United States, 31; not invited to Washington Conference, 34; feared by France, 42; reparations problem, 139; Dawes Plan, 141; Young Plan, 142; borrowings, 143; admitted to League, 147; accepts Paris Peace Pact, 151; economic distress in, 245

Gibson, Hugh, at Geneva Conference (1927), 148; at London Naval Conference, 242; at Geneva Conference (1932), 258

Gilbert, Prentiss, American observer, 251

Gilbert, S. Parker, Dawes Plan adviser, 142

Gilfillan, S. C., sociologist, 174

Ginn, Edwin, League supporter, 144

Glass, Carter, on Paris Peace Pact, 151; sponsors Glass-Steagall Act, 273

Glassford, Pelham D., superintendent of police, 275

Gold, flows to United States, 136; British efforts to hold, 229; abandoned as British standard, 246; withdrawals from American Treasury, 273

Gompers, Samuel, heads American Federation of Labor, 13; voluntarism, 15; death, 16; co-operation with Progressives, 89; on Boston Police Strike, 82; political neutrality, 93

Gosden, Freeman F., radio star, 173

Grange, farm order, 19; supports Export Debenture Plan, 217, 266

Great Britain, oil rivalry with United States, 28; naval rivalry, 33; invited to Washington Conference, 35; naval limitations, 42; Far Eastern concessions, 47; war debts, 138; opposes Ruhr invasion, 140; Geneva Conference (1927), 148; Commonwealth of Nations, 164;

London Naval Conference, 242; abandons gold standard, 246

Great Lakes-St. Lawrence Seaway, 165

Great Plains, agriculture, 17; Boulder Dam agreements, 125

Green, William, heads American Federation of Labor, 16

Griffiths, D. W., movie producer, 170

Grundy, Joseph R., Senator, 220

Guam, proposed naval base, 39

Guatemala, boundary dispute, 159

Haiti, marines in, 160

Hammond, John Hays, heads Coal Commission, 71

Harding, Warren G., addresses Congress, 8; on merchant marine, 10; sketch of, 24; cabinet, 26; policies, 27; signs separate peace with Germany, 31; calls Washington Conference, 35; deference to business interests, 50; budget estimates, 51; opposes Bonus, 52; appointments criticized, 65; opens coal mines, 71; scandals under, 73; trip to Alaska, 79; death of, 80; appointments to Debt Commission, 137; favors St. Lawrence Seaway, 165

Harding, Mrs. Warren G., favors isolation, 25; with Harding at death, 80

Harvey, George, Ambassador to Great Britain, 26; supports Coolidge (1924), 101; in war debts negotiations, 138

Haugen, Gilbert N., Representative from Iowa, 197

Hawaii, naval importance, 39

Hawes-Cutting Act, for Philippines, 256

Hawley-Smoot Act, effect on Canada, 165; high tariffs, 221; criticisms of, 222; retaliatory measures, 223, 244, 247

Hays, Will H., Postmaster General, 26; motion picture "czar," 171

Hemingway, Ernest, 185, 186

Herrin Massacre, 70

Highways, postwar expansion, 9; competition with railroads, 60; expenditures for, 115; accidents on, 169

Holding companies, in public utilities, 121; multiplication of, 225; weaknesses of, 231

Hollywood, California, 111, 170

Holt, Hamilton, League advocate, 144

Honduras, boundary dispute, 159; United States intervention, 160

Hoover, Herbert, favors trade associations, 12; Cabinet, 26; on League of Nations, 32; on Ford's Muscle Shoals offer, 62; as Secretary of Commerce, 67; on tour with Harding, 84; on credit to Europe, 109; opposes Tennessee Valley development, 125; on Boulder Dam, 126; on War Debt Commission, 137; interest in aviation, 176; wins Republican nomination (1928), 201; business-mindedness, 202; sketch of, 208; elected President, 211; Latin-American tour, 215; as administrator, 216; represents industry, 217; appoints Federal Farm Board, 219; signs Hawley-Smoot Act, 221; opposes easy money, 228; fights depression, 234; advocates lower taxes, 235; Quaker ideas, 241; favors naval limitation, 242; agreement with Laval, 246; differences with Stimson, 248; on Manchurian crisis, 250; opposed to sanctions, 253; proposals to Geneva Conference (1932), 258; unwillingness to use force, 259; on Prohibition, 263; agricultural policy, 264; favors public works, 271; relief principles, 272; on Bonus Army, 275; seeks Roosevelt's co-operation, 278

Hoover, J. Edgar, heads F.B.I., 180

Hopkins, J. A. H., heads Committee of 48, 87

House of Representatives, initiates tariff bill, 55; after 1922 election, 88; after 1924 election, 102; after 1926 election, 129; after 1928 election, 212; after 1930 election, 239

Hudson, Manley O., peace advocate, 144

Hughes, Charles Evans, Secretary of State, 26; separate peace with Germany, 31; at Washington Conference, 36; dealings with League, 130; criticizes Japanese exclusion,

133; opposes Russian recognition, 134; on War Debt Commission, 137; on reparations, 141; favors World Court, 145; negotiates with Mexico, 154; Latin-American policy, 159; at Havana Conference, 161; promotes St. Lawrence Seaway, 165; on Alfred E. Smith, 205; becomes Chief Justice, 216

Humphrey, William E., Federal Trade Commissioner, 65

Hungary, treaty with United States, 31

Hunt, C. W., Federal Trade Commissioner, 65

Hylan, John F., New York mayor, 183

Idaho, lead and zinc production, 7

Illinois, coal and oil production, 7

Immigrants, in American cities, 2; political allegiance, 93; restrictions on immigration, 131; quotas allowed, 132; Asiatic and Latin-American, 133; voting in 1928, 212, 214

Indians, number in United States, 3

Industrial Workers of the World, 16

Insull, Samuel, interests of, 121; sketch of, 123; campaign contributions, 129; failure of, 276

Interior Department, acquires naval oil reserves, 75

International Joint Commission, on Canadian-American relations, 165

Interstate Commerce Commission, sets railroad rates, 7, 60; powers of, 64; appointments to, 65

Investment trusts, multiply securities, 225; weaknesses of, 231

Iowa, farm holiday program, 267

Isolationism, retreat to, 25; Hughes's views on, 31, 130; leads to naval reductions, 49; in 1924 election, 94, 96; difficulties of, 144; generally accepted, 167; results of, 259

Italy, invited to Washington Conference, 35; wins equality with France, 42; immigration discriminations against, 133; funds debt to United States, 138; accepts Paris Peace Pact, 151; at London Naval Conference, 242

James, G. R., member of Federal Reserve Board, 65

Japan, nationals in United States, 3; naval rivalry with, 33; invited to Washington Conference, 35; bargaining efforts, 39; successes, 41; Shantung treaty, 47; reaction to Conference, 47; resents exclusion policy, 132; at Geneva Conference (1927), 148; accepts Paris Peace Pact, 151; at London Naval Conference, 242; attacks Manchuria, 249; attacks Shanghai, 252

Jews, minority status, 3; among city voters, 93; and Ku Klux Klan, 94; attacks on, 183

Johnson, Hiram, opposes League, 25; votes for Fordney-McCumber Act, 56; Republican insurgent, 86; seeks Republican nomination (1924), 90; on Boulder Dam, 126; critic of Hughes, 131; correspondence on war debts, 136; on Paris Peace Pact, 152; on Hoover, 234; on London Naval Conference, 243

Johnson, Hugh S., promotes two-price system, 197; shapes McNary-Haugen bill, 199

Johnson, Magnus, Senator, 86

Jung, Carl, influence of, 168, 181

Justice Department, involved in scandal, 74; cleaned up by Stone, 83; drops Aluminum Trust charges, 108; prohibition enforcement, 179, 263

Kellogg, Frank P., on treaty with Colombia, 30; becomes Secretary of State, 150; signs Paris Peace Pact, 151; Mexican negotiations, 156

Kendrick, J. B., on oil scandals, 75

Kennedy, Joseph P., on American business, 276

Kentucky, agriculture, 17; Co-operative Act of 1922, 195

King, John T., in Harding scandals, 75

Knapp, Harry S., on Washington Conference, 41

Knox, D. W., on Washington Conference, 42

Knox, Philander C., negotiates with Colombia, 29

Krueger, Ivar, failure of, 276

Ku Klux Klan, origins of, 94; divides Democratic party, 96; decline of, 128; joiners of, 168; discredited, 182; opposed by intellectuals, 214

Labor, postwar status, 13; unemployment in 1920, 22; textile strike, 68; coal strike, 69; Railroad Shopmen's strike, 72; "yellow-dog" contracts, 73; unrest, 84; journals of, 85; political loyalties, 92; Gompers' policy, 93; new needs of, 127; Democratic policy on, 238

Ladd, Edwin F., Senator, 86

La Follette, Robert M., friend of labor, 16; opposes Mellon's tax program, 54; opposes Fordney-McCumber Act, 56; opposes Harding appointees, 65; helps uncover oil scandals, 76; in 1920 election, 87; heads Progressive bloc, 89; supported for Republican nomination, 90; denounces Communists, 97; in 1924 campaign, 98; defeat of, 101; death of, 103

La Follette, Robert M., Jr., elected to Senate, 103; at Republican Convention (1928), 202

La Guardia, Fiorello, friend of labor, 16; member, Progressive bloc, 86, 89

Lardner, Ring, 186

Lasker, Albert D., heads Shipping Board, 61

Latin America, United States oil interests in, 28; emigration from, to United States, 133; objectors to Paris Peace Pact, 152; Monroe Doctrine, 153; United States policy toward, 159; trade with United States, 162; relations with Europe, 163; historians of, 190; Democratic stand on (1928), 204; trade during depression, 244

Lausanne Agreement, negotiated, 247; unratified, 248

Laval, Pierre, visits United States, 246

League of Nations, opposed by Harding, 25; Hughes's plans for, 31; opposed by Republicans (1924), 90; divides Democrats, 95; Hughes's relations with, 130; American support for, 144; disarmament activities of, 147; ignored by Japan, 249; on Manchurian attack, 251; Japan withdraws from, 253

League of Women Voters, 181

Legge, Alexander, heads Federal Farm Board, 218

Levine, C. A., flies Atlantic, 176

Levinson, Salmon O., advocates outlawry of war, 149; Paris Peace Pact, 151

Lewis, John L., heads United Mine Workers, 69; coal settlement, 71

Lewis, Sinclair, 186

Lindbergh, Charles A., flies Atlantic, 150; flies to Mexico, 157; ovations for, 176; son's death, 180

Lippmann, Walter, favors League, 144

Locarno, treaties of, 147

Lodge, Henry Cabot, on treaty with Colombia, 29; at Washington Conference, 36; by-passed by Coolidge, 90

London Imperial Conference (1926), 164

London Naval Conference, called, 242; sets tonnage limitations, 243

Long, Huey P., Louisiana politician, 92

Longworth, Alice Roosevelt, 74

Longworth, Nicholas, Speaker, 239

Los Angeles, business boom, 118; motion picture center, 170

Louisiana, agriculture, 17; bank holiday, 277

Lowden, Frank O., refuses vice-presidential nomination (1924), 91; seeks presidential nomination (1928), 201; business-mindedness, 202

Lutherans, parochial schools, 3

Lynd, Robert S. and Helen M., Middletown, 190

Lytton Report, on Manchuria, 251, 253

McAdoo, William G., on Harding, 24; seeks Democratic nomination

(1924), 94; defeated, 97; on Ford in politics, 112; promotes Walsh (1928), 203

McCarl, John R., Comptroller General, 51

McCoy, Frank R., member Lytton Commission, 251

McCumber, Porter J., Senator, 56

MacDonald, J. Ramsay, calls London Naval Conference, 242; forms national government, 246; agrees to World Economic Conference, 258

McDowell, C. K., mining superintendent, 70

McNary-Haugen bills, details of, 198; vetoed by Coolidge, 199; in campaign of 1928, 201; Democratic stand on, 204; favored by Farm Bureau, 266

McPherson, Aimee Semple, evangelist, 182

Magazine of Wall Street, 216

Maine, agriculture, 17

Manchuria, Japanese attack on, 249; condemned by United States, 250; Lytton Report on, 251; becomes Manchukuo, 253

Manufacturing, new methods in, 5; tariff protection for, 57, 222; new products, 111; automobiles, 112; mass production, 119; radio, 172; aircraft, 174

Marvin, T. O., tariff commissioner, 66

Marxists, critics of America, 168, 184

Massey, Vincent, Canadian minister, 164

Meiklejohn, Alexander, educator, 189

Mellon, Andrew W., Secretary of the Treasury, 26; financial program, 53; member Federal Reserve Board, 65; principal victories, 106; debt policy, 107; on war debts, 137; endorses Hoover, 201; retained by Hoover, 215; favors easy money, 228; declining popularity, 276

Mencken, Henry L., journalist, 185

Merchant Marine Act (1920), purpose, 10; operations, 61; revised (1928), 62

Merton, Richard, in Harding scandals, 75

Methodists, denounced by Mencken, 185; Bishop Cannon, 207

Mexico, immigration from, 133; relations with United States, 153; Constitution of 1917, 154; discriminations against foreigners, 155; anti-Catholic legislation, 156; Morrow's mission to, 157

Miami, real estate boom, 117

Michelson, Charles, Democratic publicity agent, 237

Michigan, iron and copper production, 7; bank holiday, 277

Middle Atlantic States, prosperity of, 128

Middle West, food production in, 17; prosperity of, 128; criticized by Mencken, 185; Democratic gains in, 213; bank failures in, 232

Miller, Thomas W., in Harding scandals, 74

Millikan, Robert A., scientist, 189

Mills, Ogden, Treasury Secretary, 216; gold policy, 273

Minnesota, iron ore, 7; Non-Partisan League, 20

Mississippi, population, 2

Missouri, lead and zinc production, 7; Kansas City Convention (1928), 202

Mitchell, Charles E., banker, 227

Mitchell, William, sinks *Ostfriesland*, 43; court-martialed, 175

Moncada, José María, Nicaraguan President, 158

Monroe Doctrine, and United States oil interests, 27; and Paris Peace Pact, 151; Roosevelt's Corollary, 153; resented by Latin America, 159; Clark Memorandum, 161

Moody, Dwight L., evangelist, 182

Moratorium, proposed by Hoover, 245; extension sought by Laval, 246

Morrow, Dwight W., mission to Mexico, 157; heads Mitchell inquiry, 175; opposes Prohibition, 238; at London Naval Conference, 242

Moses, George H., characterizes insurgents, 86n.; favors Coolidge for

President, 90; President pro tem of Senate, 240n.
Motion pictures, growth of, 111; effect of, 170; foreign influence of, 172
Mukden incident, 249
Muscle Shoals, United States policy toward, 62; Ford's bid for, 63; saved by Norris, 64
Mussolini, Benito, colonial policy, 133

Nathan, George Jean, journalist, 189
Nation, The, Norris article in, 66; represents liberals, 85, 185; on 1930 statement by Democratic leaders, 270
National Broadcasting Company, 172
National Credit Association, 271
National Non-Partisan League, 20
Nation's Business, 13
Navy, United States, building program, 33; Washington limitations on, 40, 43; decline during 1920's, 49; plans for rebuilding, 149; discounts air power, 175; tonnage limitations (1930), 243
Negroes, number in United States, 2; Republican partisans, 92; Ku Klux Klan persecutions, 94; political discriminations against, 214
Netherlands, The, invited to Washington Conference, 34
Nevada, Boulder Dam agreement, 125; bank holiday, 277
Newberry, Truman H., Senator, 88n.
New England, agriculture, 17; declining prosperity, 128; Democratic gains (1928), 212
New Masses, leftist journal, 185
New Mexico, Boulder Dam agreement, 125
New Republic, liberal journal, 85, 185; views on Hoover, 216
Newspapers, favor business, 13; on sex and crime, 180
New York (state), agriculture, 17; elects Smith governor, 88; opposes St. Lawrence Seaway, 165; elects Roosevelt governor, 212; relief program, 269
New York (city), growth of, 4; Tammany Hall, 92; Madison Square Convention, 95; skyline, 113, 115; textbook restrictions, 183; Greenwich Village, 184; Smith's career in, 205; stock-market panic, 224; bank failures in, 232; relief program, 268, 270
Nicaragua, relations with United States, 157; Stimson's mission to, 158
Nine Power Treaty, on Far East, 46; ratified, 49; violated by Japan, 249
Nineteenth Amendment, 181
Nobel prizes, 189
Norbeck, Peter, supports Hoover, 209
Norris, George W., friend of labor, 16; saves Muscle Shoals, 63; criticizes Presidential appointments, 66; influence of, 86; joins Progressive bloc, 89; on aluminum trust, 108; on power trust, 126; on Mexico, 156; favors price fixing, 195; mentioned for President (1928), 201; supports Smith (1928), 209; promotes Lame Duck Amendment (20th), 278
North Central States, prosperity in, 128
North Dakota, Non-Partisan League in, 20; Republicans for La Follette, 90; Coolidge vacation in, 201; farm-holiday convention, 267
Noyes, Alexander Dana, business warnings, 229
Nye, Gerald P., Senator, 129

Obregón, Alvaro, Mexican President, 154
O'Fallon Case, on railroad regulation, 60
Ogburn, W. F., sociologist, 174
Ohio Gang, Harding's cronies, 27
Oil, production in United States, 7; in diplomacy, 27, 30; naval reserve scandals, 75; use to create power, 124; American interests in Mexico, 155; in Latin America, 163; oil land withdrawals, 216
Oklahoma, oil output, 7
O'Neill, Eugene, 186
Open Door policy, supported in Nine Power Pact, 46; violated by Japan, 252
Open shop, favored by business, 68

Oregon, textbook restrictions, 183
Ostfriesland, sunk by bombers, 41, 44
Ottawa Conference (1932), 165, 247
Ozawa v. *United States,* naturalization case, 133

Pacific Coast, Oriental residents, 3; agriculture, 17; prosperity of, 128
Packers and Stockyards Act, 55
Paish, Sir George, economist, 227
Panama, boundary dispute, 159
Panama Canal, competition with railroads, 60; diplomatic protection of, 160
Pan-American Conferences, 161
Panic of 1929, effect on Latin America, 163; drop in stock prices, 224; causes of, 225; relation to depression, 232
Paris Peace Pact, signed, 151; ratifications, 152; applied to Latin America, 161; violated by Japan, 252
Parker, John J., Federal judge, 238
Patman bonus bill, 275
Patrons of Husbandry. *See* Grange
Peace Movement, organizations, 144; outlawry of war, 150; Paris Peace Pact, 151; in Central America, 160; in Latin America, 161
Peek, George N., promotes two-price system, 197; shapes McNary-Haugen bill, 199; supports Smith (1928), 204; in 1928 campaign, 213
Pennsylvania, coal output, 7; agriculture, 17; elects Pinchot governor, 88
Peru, boundary dispute, 159
Peters, Andrew, mayor of Boston, 82
Philanthropy, 191
Philippine Islands, proposed naval base, 39; Democratic pledges on, 204; movement for independence, 254; Hawes-Cutting program, 256; Congress on, 257
Phillips, Wendell, minister to Canada, 164
Pickford, Mary, screen actress, 170
Pinchot, Gifford, governor of Pennsylvania, 88; on public power, 124
Platt Amendment, 161

Plumb Plan, for railroads, 15, 87
Pomerene, Atlee, oil prosecutor, 83
Population, 14th Census, 1; homogeneity, 3; mobility, 169
Portugal, invited to Washington Conference, 34
Post Office Department, 176
Pound, Ezra, 186
Power industry, expansion of, 111, 120; activities of, 126
Pratt, William V., naval expert, 38
Preparatory Commission, on disarmament, 258
Progress, idea of, 167
Progressives, in 1922 elections, 89; in 1924, 97; La Follette platform, 99; decline of, 103; oppose Mellon, 106; defeat Warren, 107; support Smith in 1928, 213; favor Schneider for Speaker, 240n.
Prohibition, ignored in White House, 74; divides Democrats (1924), 96; as war measure, 177; enforcement problems, 178; in 1928 campaign, 204, 207; opposed by liberals, 214; repeal sentiment, 240; expenditures for, 260; anti-Prohibitionists, 261; Wickersham Report, 262; repeal, 263
Prosperity, postwar, 6; under Coolidge, 108; analyzed, 128; associated with isolationism, 130; Hoover on, 210; Panic of 1929, 224; claimed by Republicans, 237
Public utilities, expansion of, 121; profits of, 122; Insull interests, 123; regulation of, 124
Public works, favored by Hoover, 235; recommends P.W.A., 271
Puerto Rico, immigration from, 133
Puritanism, criticisms of, 168

Racketeering, operators, 178; profits from, 179; gang warfare, 180
Radio, creates new industry, 111; broadcasting networks, 172; advertising, 173
Railroad Brotherhoods, affiliated with A.F. of L., 15; in shopmen's strike, 71
Railroads, returned to owners, 7;

Plumb Plan, 15; O'Fallon case, 60; shopmen's strike, 72

Railway Labor Board, 71

Raskob, John J., Democratic campaign manager (1928), 209; aids Democratic finances, 213, 237; calls for five-day week, 238

Real estate, boom in, 18, 116

Reconstruction Finance Corporation, created, 271; Hoover's views on, 274

Red Cross, drought relief, 236; work of, 265

"Red hysteria," abatement of, 16; Coolidge on "reds," 82; participants in, 168; Mencken on, 185

Reed, David A., Senator, 242

Reed, James A., on Republican record, 237

Reform, before World War I, 23; journals of, 85; leaders, 86; railroad workers' demands, 87; in 1922 election, 88; in 1924 election, 98; F. D. Roosevelt on, 104; in 1926 election, 129; agricultural, 197; in 1928 election, 213; in 1930 election, 239

Religion, varieties in United States, 3; Mexican laws on, 154, 156; Church and State, 167; moral standards, 181; evangelism, 182; Mencken on, 185; in 1928 election, 206

Reno, Milo, farm leader, 266

Reparations problem, and war debts, 137; agreements on, 140

Republicans, pledges on League, 32; favor Washington treaties, 49; favor high tariffs, 57; on business recovery, 84; party composition, 91; on Coolidge prosperity, 128; losses in 1926, 129; nominate Hoover, 201; agricultural pledges, 202; gains in South, 211; 1930 losses, 239

Roberts, Owen J., oil prosecutor, 83

Robins, Raymond, influence on Borah, 134

Robinson, Joseph T., nominated for Vice-President, 203; at London Naval Conference, 242; promises Hoover co-operation, 270

Rockefeller, John D., Jr., ousts

Colonel Stewart, 77; philanthropies, 191

Rocky Mountains, agriculture, 17

Roosevelt, Franklin D., appeals to Democrats, 104; prophesies 1932 victory, 105; favors Smith's nomination (1928), 203; elected governor, 212; re-elected, 240; on World Economic Conference, 238; relief program, 269; President-elect, 277

Roosevelt, Theodore, as reform leader, 23; offends Colombia, 29; Corollary to Monroe Doctrine, 153, 159; on United States in world affairs, 259

Roosevelt, Theodore, Jr., in Washington Conference, 38

Root, Elihu, at Washington Conference, 36; favors League of Nations, 144; helps create World Court, 145

Rowell, Chester H., reform leader, 86

Ruhr Valley, occupied, 140; troops withdrawn, 142

Russia. See Soviet Russia

Sacasa, Juan B., Nicaraguan rebel, 158

St. Lawrence Seaway, power possibilities, 125; efforts to obtain, 165

Salesmanship, techniques of, 120

Sandino, Augusto, Nicaraguan rebel, 158

Sapiro, Aaron, co-operative organizer, 195

Sargent, John G., Attorney General, 108

Sawyer, Charles E., Harding's physician, 79

Schlesinger, Arthur M., historian, 190

Schools. See Education

Scopes trial, 182

Scott, Howard, Technocrat, 277

Scott, James Brown, World Court advocate, 145

Senate, United States, ratifies treaty with Colombia, 30; separate peace with Germany, 31; Washington treaties, 49; on bonus bill, 52; tariff deliberations, 56; after 1922 election, 88; after 1924 election, 102;

refuses to confirm Warren, 108; after 1926 election, 129; rejects World Court, 145, 146; ratifies Paris Peace Pact, 151; defeats St. Lawrence Seaway, 165; rejects Patman bill, 275

Shanghai, Japanese attack on, 252

Shearer, William Baldwin, lobbyist, 148

Sheffield, James R., Ambassador to Mexico, 156

Shenandoah, destroyed, 175

Shipping. *See* United States Shipping Board

Shipstead, Henrik, Senator, 129

Shotwell, James T., historian, 149

Shouse, Jouett, Democratic chairman, 237; promises Hoover co-operation, 270

Silver, Gray, Farm Bureau lobbyist, 21

Simmons, William J., Klan leader, 94

Simon, Sir John, British foreign minister, 252

Sinclair, Harry F., relations with Fall, 76

Skyscrapers, multiplied, 113, 115

Slemp, C. Bascom, Coolidge's private secretary, 83; influences southern delegates, 90

Smith, Alfred E., governor of New York, 88; seeks Democratic nomination (1924), 97; nominated by Roosevelt, 105; wins nomination (1928), 203; sketch of, 204; religion, 206; on prohibition, 207; campaign, 209; defeat, 211; wins new voters, 212; favors five-day week, 238; promises Hoover co-operation, 270

Smith, Frank L., elected senator, 129

Smith, "Jess," involved in Harding scandals, 74

Smith-Hughes Act, 187

Smith-Lever Act, 187

Smoot, Reed, Senator, 222

Smoot-Hawley Act. *See* Hawley-Smoot Act

Social conditions, housing needs, 115; general, 167; changed by automobile, 168; motion picture influence, 170; radio influence, 172; airplanes, 174; prohibition, 177;

racketeering, 180; new standards, 181; religion, 182; anti-Semitism, 183; critics of, 184; Mencken on, 185; literature and art, 186; education, 187; science, 189

Socialists, postwar status, 15; in 1924 election, 97; ideas of, 184; in 1928 election, 209, 211

Social security, opposition to, 73; under city machines, 93

South, the, Negroes in, 3; agriculture, 17; spotty prosperity, 128; criticized by Mencken, 185; Republican gains in, 211; bank failures in, 232

South Carolina, population, 2

Soviet Russia, excluded from Washington Conference, 34; problem of recognition, 134; problem of trade, 135; war debts, 139; signs Paris Peace Pact, 150; attends Preparatory Commission, 258

Speculation, in land, 18, 117; Florida boom, 118; on New York Stock Exchange, 225; warnings against, 227; money for, 228

State Department, arranges for Washington Conference, 34; advises on foreign investments, 66; considers Briand peace proposals, 150; issues Clark Memorandum, 162; under Stimson, 215; Manchurian crisis, 248

Stearns, Harold, literary rebel, 184

Stewart, Charles L., proposes export debenture plan, 217

Stewart, Robert W., Standard Oil executive, 77

Stimson, Henry L., mission to Nicaragua, 158; Secretary of State, 215; at London Naval Conference, 242; on war debts, 248; Stimson doctrine, 250; letter to Borah, 253; on timidity of governments, 259

Stock Exchange, New York, panic on, 224; margin purchases, 226; call loans, 227

Stone, Harlan Fiske, Attorney General, 83; Associate Justice, 107

Straight, Willard and Dorothy, back *New Republic,* 85

Strikes, textiles (1922), 68; coal miners (1922), 69; railroad shopmen (1922), 71; Boston police (1919), 81

Submarine, no limitations on (1922), 44; equal quotas (1930), 243

Sunday, "Billy," evangelist, 182

Supreme Court, upholds trade associations, 12; Harding's appointments to, 26; O'Fallon case, 60; on labor injunctions, 72; on labor contracts, 73; on oil scandals, 77; campaign issue (1924), 100; *Ozawa* v. *United States*, 133; Hoover's appointments to, 216

Tacna-Arica dispute, 159

Taft, William Howard, Chief Justice, 26

Tammany Hall, Democratic machine, 92; anti-Klan, 95; rewards Smith, 205

Tariff Commission, activities of, 57, 58; packed with protectionists, 66; revised (1930), 220, 221

Tariffs, Emergency (1921), 54; Fordney-McCumber (1922), 56, 59; Hawley-Smoot (1930), 221; effects on Europe, 233; proposed extension to Philippines, 256

Taxation, Mellon's views on, 53; reductions voted, 54, 106; Coolidge on, 107; lowered in 1929, 235

Taylor, Frederick W., efficiency expert, 5

Teapot Dome, oil scandals, 76; Supreme Court on, 77

Technocracy, rise and fall, 277

Television, unused in 1920's, 174

Temporary Emergency Relief Administration (New York), 269

Tennessee Valley, power development, 62, 125

Texas, oil output, 7; agriculture, 17; Houston Convention (1928), 202; votes for Hoover, 211; relief policies, 270

Thomas, Norman, Socialist nominee (1928), 109; votes for, 211

Thompson, "Big Bill," Chicago mayor, 179

Thompson-Urrutia treaty, proposed, 28; ratified, 30

Townley, Arthur C., Non-Partisan leader, 20

Trade associations, 12

Transportation Act of 1920, terms of, 7; effects of, 59; Esch's part in, 65

Treasury Department, postwar borrowing, 5; tax refunds, 53; repayments on national debt, 84; surplus, 107; on war debt agreements, 139; collections on war debts, 143; Prohibition enforcement, 179; under Mellon and Mills, 216; gold withdrawals, 273

Treaties, United States, with Colombia, 30; Versailles, 31; with Germany, 31; Paris Peace Pact, 151; Bryan-Chamorro, 157

Tugwell, Rexford G., economist, 200

Twentieth Amendment ("lame duck"), 278

Underwood, Oscar, Senator, 36

Unemployment, in 1920, 22; during prosperity, 127; during depression, 229; relief measures, 236; in 1931, 268; New York relief program, 269; President's committee on, 270

United Artists Corporation, 170

United Mine Workers, strike of 1922, 69; decline of, 71

United States Shipping Board, 10, 61

Utah, Boulder Dam agreement, 125

Valentino, Rudolph, screen star, 171

Vanderlip, Frank A., banker, 230

Van Fleet, V. W., Federal Trade Commissioner, 65

Vare, Wm. S., elected Senator, 129; endorses Hoover, 201; denied Senate seat, 220

Versailles, Treaty of, defeated, 31; war guilt clause, 139; affects Canadian-American relations, 164

Veterans' Bureau, scandals in, 74

Victory Loan (1919), 6

Villard, O. G., edits *The Nation*, 85; co-operates with Progressives, 89; demands "a new deal," 105

Viviani, René, French premier, 37

Volstead Act, 178, 260

Wadsworth, James W., Senator, 129

Wagner, Robert F., Senator, 129; favors R.F.C. appropriations, 274

Wallace, Henry C., Secretary of Agriculture, 26; edits *Wallace's Farmer*, 85; favors McNary-Haugenism, 198

Wall Street Journal, financial organ, 13; on employment, 268

Walsh, David I., Senator, 129

Walsh, Thomas J., investigates oil scandals, 76; on party issues, 94; on aluminum trust, 108; on Ford in politics, 112; in 1928 election, 203

Warburg, Paul M., banker, 227

War Debts, contracted by European nations, 6; problem of repayment, 136; funded, 138; payments on, 143; Hoover's Moratorium, 245; cancellation proposals, 248

War Finance Corporation, 55

War Guilt clause, 139

Warren, Charles B., fails of confirmation, 107

Washington Conference, plans for, 34; invitations to, 35; opened, 37; naval ratio, 39; Pacific agreement, 40; Four Power Pact, 41; limitations, 43; Nine Power Pact, 46; ratification, 48; ratios revised, 242

Waterpower, Muscle Shoals, 63; government interest in, 124; projects for development, 125; Boulder Dam, 126

Watson, John B., *Behaviorism*, 191

Weeks, John W., Secretary of War, 26; asks bids for Muscle Shoals, 62

Weimar Republic, 140

Welfare capitalism, advocated, 15; in practice, 191

West Virginia, coal and oil, 7

Wheat, price supports, 18; surplus production, 195; marketing problems, 196; export debenture plan, 217; depression prices, 219; Grain Stabilization Corporation, 265

Wheeler, Burton K., Senator, 86; joins Progressive bloc, 90; nominated for Vice-President, 98

White, William Allen, Progressive Republican, 86; favors League, 144; on Alfred E. Smith, 205

White Sox scandal (1919), 181

Whitney, Richard, President of New York Stock Exchange, 228

Wickersham, George W., heads Law Enforcement Commission, 262

Wilbur, Ray Lyman, diagnoses Harding's illness, 80; Secretary of Interior, 216

Wilkerson, James, Federal judge, 72

Williamson County, Ill., labor troubles, 70

Wilson, Woodrow, as reform leader, 23; vetoes separate peace with Germany, 31; telegram to Coolidge, 82

Wilson Dam, on Tennessee River, 62; completed, 64

Wisconsin, supports La Follette, 90; enacts textbook restrictions, 183; Democratic gains in, 213

Women's rights, labor laws, 73; Nineteenth Amendment, 181

Wood, Leonard, Philippine governor, 26

Woodlock, Thomas F., Interstate Commerce Commissioner, 65

Woodrow Wilson Foundation, 144

Woods, Arthur, heads relief committee, 270

Wooley, Robert W., Interstate Commerce Commissioner, 65

World Court, American rejection of, 145; Coolidge's attitude on, 146

World Economic Conference (1933), proposed, 258; Hoover consults Roosevelt on, 278

World Peace Foundation, 144

Wyoming, Boulder Dam agreement, 125

Yap, United States-Japanese agreement, 47

"Yellow-dog" contracts, favored by employers, 14; sustained by Supreme Court, 73; defeat Parker, 238

Young, Owen D., on German reparations, 142; Young Plan, 143, 244, 248

Yugoslavia, debt to United States, 138

hARpER ✦ ꭲoRChbooks

American Studies: General

HENRY ADAMS Degradation of the Democratic Dogma. ‡ *Introduction by Charles Hirschfeld.* TB/1450

LOUIS D. BRANDEIS: Other People's Money, *and How the Bankers Use It. Ed. with Intro, by Richard M. Abrams* TB/3081

HENRY STEELE COMMAGER, Ed.: The Struggle for Racial Equality TB/1300

CARL N. DEGLER: Out of Our Past: *The Forces that Shaped Modern America* CN/2

CARL N. DEGLER, Ed.: Pivotal Interpretations of American History
Vol. I TB/1240; Vol. II TB/1241

LAWRENCE H. FUCHS, Ed.: American Ethnic Politics TB/1368

ROBERT L. HEILBRONER: The Limits of American Capitalism TB/1305

JOHN HIGHAM, Ed.: The Reconstruction of American History TB/1068

ROBERT H. JACKSON: The Supreme Court in the American System of Government TB/1106

JOHN F. KENNEDY: A Nation of Immigrants. *Illus. Revised and Enlarged. Introduction by Robert F. Kennedy* TB/1118

RICHARD B. MORRIS: Fair Trial: *Fourteen Who Stood Accused, from Anne Hutchinson to Alger Hiss* TB/1335

GUNNAR MYRDAL: An American Dilemma: *The Negro Problem and Modern Democracy. Introduction by the Author.*
Vol. I TB/1443; Vol. II TB/1444

GILBERT OSOFSKY, Ed.: The Burden of Race: *A Documentary History of Negro-White Relations in America* TB/1405

ARNOLD ROSE: The Negro in America: *The Condensed Version of Gunnar Myrdal's* An American Dilemma. *Second Edition* TB/3048

JOHN E. SMITH: Themes in American Philosophy: *Purpose, Experience and Community* TB/1466

WILLIAM R. TAYLOR: Cavalier and Yankee: *The Old South and American National Character* TB/1474

American Studies: Colonial

BERNARD BAILYN: The New England Merchants in the Seventeenth Century TB/1149

ROBERT E. BROWN: Middle-Class Democracy and Revolution in Massachusetts, 1691–1780. *New Introduction by Author* TB/1413

JOSEPH CHARLES: The Origins of the American Party System TB/1049

WESLEY FRANK CRAVEN: The Colonies in Transition: 1660-1712† TB/3084

CHARLES GIBSON: Spain in America † TB/3077

CHARLES GIBSON, Ed.: The Spanish Tradition in America + HR/1351

LAWRENCE HENRY GIPSON: The Coming of the Revolution: 1763-1775. † *Illus.* TB/3007

JACK P. GREENE, Ed.: Great Britain and the American Colonies: 1606-1763. + *Introduction by the Author* HR/1477

AUBREY C. LAND, Ed.: Bases of the Plantation Society + HR/1429

PERRY MILLER: Errand Into the Wilderness TB/1139

PERRY MILLER & T. H. JOHNSON, Ed.: The Puritans: *A Sourcebook of Their Writings*
Vol. I TB/1093; Vol. II TB/1094

EDMUND S. MORGAN: The Puritan Family: *Religion and Domestic Relations in Seventeenth Century New England* TB/1227

WALLACE NOTESTEIN: The English People on the Eve of Colonization: 1603-1630. † *Illus.* TB/3006

LOUIS B. WRIGHT: The Cultural Life of the American Colonies: 1607-1763. † *Illus.* TB/3005

YVES F. ZOLTVANY, Ed.: The French Tradition in America + HR/1425

American Studies: The Revolution to 1860

JOHN R. ALDEN: The American Revolution: 1775-1783. † *Illus.* TB/3011

RAY A. BILLINGTON: The Far Western Frontier: 1830-1860. † *Illus.* TB/3012

STUART BRUCHEY: The Roots of American Economic Growth, 1607-1861: *An Essay in Social Causation. New Introduction by the Author.* TB/1350

NOBLE E. CUNNINGHAM, JR., Ed.: The Early Republic, 1789-1828 + HR/1394

GEORGE DANGERFIELD: The Awakening of American Nationalism, 1815-1828. † *Illus.* TB/3061

† The New American Nation Series, edited by Henry Steele Commager and Richard B. Morris.
‡ American Perspectives series, edited by Bernard Wishy and William E. Leuchtenburg.
a History of Europe series, edited by J. H. Plumb.
§ The Library of Religion and Culture, edited by Benjamin Nelson.
‖ Researches in the Social, Cultural, and Behavioral Sciences, edited by Benjamin Nelson.
Σ Harper Modern Science Series, edited by James A. Newman.
° Not for sale in Canada.
+ Documentary History of the United States series, edited by Richard B. Morris.
# Documentary History of Western Civilization series, edited by Eugene C. Black and Leonard W. Levy.
∧ The Economic History of the United States series, edited by Henry David et al.
¶ European Perspectives series, edited by Eugene C. Black.
** Contemporary Essays series, edited by Leonard W. Levy.
* The Stratum Series, edited by John Hale.

CLEMENT EATON: The Freedom-of-Thought Struggle in the Old South. *Revised and Enlarged. Illus.*   TB/1150

CLEMENT EATON: The Growth of Southern Civilization, 1790-1860. † *Illus.*   TB/3040

ROBERT H. FERRELL, Ed.: Foundations of American Diplomacy, 1775-1872 +   HR/1393

LOUIS FILLER: The Crusade against Slavery: 1830-1860. † *Illus.*   TB/3029

WILLIM W. FREEHLING: Prelude to Civil War: *The Nullification Controversy in South Carolina, 1816-1836*   TB/1359

PAUL W. GATES: The Farmer's Age: *Agriculture, 1815-1860* △   TB/1398

THOMAS JEFFERSON: Notes on the State of Virginia. ‡ *Edited by Thomas P. Abernethy*   TB/3052

FORREST MCDONALD, Ed.: Confederation and Constitution, 1781-1789 +   HR/1396

JOHN C. MILLER: The Federalist Era: 1789-1801. † *Illus.*   TB/3027

RICHARD B. MORRIS; The American Revolution Reconsidered   TB/1363

CURTIS P. NETTELS: The Emergence of a National Economy, 1775-1815 △   TB/1438

DOUGLASS C. NORTH & ROBERT PAUL THOMAS, Eds.: *The Growth of the American Economy ot 1860* +   HR/1352

R. B. NYE: The Cultural Life of the New Nation: 1776-1830. † *Illus.*   TB/3026

GILBERT OSOFSKY, Ed.: Puttin' On Ole Massa: *The Slave Narratives of Henry Bibb, William Wells Brown, and Solomon Northup* ‡   TB/1432

JAMES PARTON: The Presidency of Andrew Jackson. *From Volume III of the* Life of Andrew Jackson. *Ed. with Intro. by Robert V. Remini*   TB/3080

FRANCIS S. PHILBRICK: The Rise of the West, 1754-1830. † *Illus.*   TB/3067

MARSHALL SMELSER: The Democratic Republic, 1801-1815 †   TB/1406

JACK M. SOSIN, Ed.: The Opening of the West +   HR/1424

GEORGE ROGERS TAYLOR: The Transportation Revolution, 1815-1860 △   TB/1347

A. F. TYLER: Freedom's Ferment: *Phases of American Social History from the Revolution to the Outbreak of the Civil War. Illus.*   TB/1074

GLYNDON G. VAN DEUSEN: The Jacksonian Era: 1828-1848. † *Illus.*   TB/3028

LOUIS B. WRIGHT: Culture on the Moving Frontier   TB/1053

American Studies: The Civil War to 1900

W. R. BROCK: An American Crisis: *Congress and Reconstruction, 1865-67* °   TB/1283

T. C. COCHRAN & WILLIAM MILLER: The Age of Enterprise: *A Social History of Industrial America*   TB/1054

W. A. DUNNING: Reconstruction, Political and Economic: 1865-1877   TB/1073

HAROLD U. FAULKNER: Politics, Reform and Expansion: 1890-1900. † *Illus.*   TB/3020

GEORGE M. FREDRICKSON: The Inner Civil War: *Northern Intellectuals and the Crisis of the Union*   TB/1358

JOHN A. GARRATY: The New Commonwealth, 1877-1890 †   TB/1410

JOHN A. GARRATY, Ed.: The Transformation of American Society, 1870-1890 +   HR/1395

HELEN HUNT JACKSON: A Century of Dishonor: *The Early Crusade for Indian Reform.* † *Edited by Andrew F. Rolle*   TB/3063

WILLIAM G. MCLOUGHLIN, Ed.: The American Evangelicals, 1800-1900: An Anthology ‡   TB/1382

JAMES S. PIKE: The Prostrate State: *South Carolina under Negro Government.* ‡ *Intro. by Robert F. Durden*   TB/3085

FRED A. SHANNON: The Farmer's Last Frontier: *Agriculture, 1860-1897*   TB/1348

VERNON LANE WHARTON: The Negro in Mississippi, 1865-1890   TB/1178

American Studies: The Twentieth Century

RICHARD M. ABRAMS, Ed.: The Issues of the Populist and Progressive Eras, 1892-1912 +   HR/1428

RAY STANNARD BAKER: Following the Color Line: *American Negro Citizenship in Progressive Era.* ‡ *Edited by Dewey W. Grantham, Jr. Illus.*   TB/3053

RANDOLPH S. BOURNE: War and the Intellectuals: *Collected Essays, 1915-1919.* ‡ *Edited by Carl · Resek*   TB/3043

A. RUSSELL BUCHANAN: The United States and World War II. † *Illus.*
Vol. I TB/3044; Vol. II TB/3045

THOMAS C. COCHRAN: The American Business System: *A Historical Perspective, 1900-1955*   TB/1080

FOSTER RHEA DULLES: America's Rise to World Power: 1898-1954. † *Illus.*   TB/3021

HAROLD U. FAULKNER: The Decline of Laissez Faire, 1897-1917   TB/1397

JOHN D. HICKS: Republican Ascendancy: 1921-1933. † *Illus.*   TB/3041

WILLIAM E. LEUCHTENBURG: Franklin D. Roosevelt and the New Deal: 1932-1940. † *Illus.*   TB/3025

WILLIAM E. LEUCHTENBURG, Ed.: The New Deal: *A Documentary History* +   HR/1354

ARTHUR S. LINK: Woodrow Wilson and the Progressive Era: 1910-1917. † *Illus.* TB/3023

BROADUS MITCHELL: Depression Decade: *From New Era through New Deal, 1929-1941* △   TB/1439

GEORGE E. MOWRY: The Era of Theodore Roosevelt and the Birth of Modern America: 1900-1912. † *Illus.*   TB/3022

GEORGE SOULE: Prosperity Decade: *From War to Depression, 1917-1929* △   TB/1349

TWELVE SOUTHERNERS: I'll Take My Stand: *The South and the Agrarian Tradition. Intro. by Louis D. Rubin, Jr.; Biographical Essays by Virginia Rock*   TB/1072

Art, Art History, Aesthetics

ERWIN PANOFSKY: Renaissance and Renascences in Western Art. *Illus.*   TB/1447

ERWIN PANOFSKY: Studies in Iconology: *Humanistic Themes in the Art of the Renaissance. 180 illus.*   TB/1077

OTTO VON SIMSON: The Gothic Cathedral: *Origins of Gothic Architecture and the Medieval Concept of Order. 58 illus.*   TB/2018

HEINRICH ZIMMER: Myths and Symbols in Indian Art and Civilization. *70 illus.*   TB/2005

Asian Studies

WOLFGANG FRANKE: China and the West: *The Cultural Encounter. 13th to 20th Centuries. Trans. by R. A. Wilson*   TB/1326

L. CARRINGTON GOODRICH: A Short History of the Chinese People. *Illus.*   TB/3015

Economics & Economic History

C. E. BLACK: The Dynamics of Modernization: *A Study in Comparative History* TB/1321

GILBERT BURCK & EDITOR OF *Fortune:* The Computer Age: *And its Potential for Management* TB/1179

SHEPARD B. CLOUGH, THOMAS MOODIE & CAROL MOODIE, Eds.: Economic History of Europe: *Twentieth Century #* HR/1388

THOMAS C. COCHRAN: The American Business System: *A Historical Perspective, 1900-1955* TB/1180

HAROLD U. FAULKNER: The Decline of Laissez Faire, 1897-1917 △ TB/1397

PAUL W. GATES: The Farmer's Age: *Agriculture, 1815-1860* △ TB/1398

WILLIAM GREENLEAF, Ed.: American Economic Development Since 1860 + HR/1353

ROBERT L. HEILBRONER: The Future as History: *The Historic Currents of Our Time and the Direction in Which They Are Taking America* TB/1386

ROBERT L. HEILBRONER: The Great Ascent: *The Struggle for Economic Development in Our Time* TB/3030

DAVID S. LANDES: Bankers and Pashas: *International Finance and Economic Imperialism in Egypt. New Preface by the Author* TB/1412

ROBERT LATOUCHE: The Birth of Western Economy: *Economic Aspects of the Dark Ages* TB/1290

W. ARTHUR LEWIS: The Principles of Economic Planning. *New Introduction by the Author°* TB/1436

ROBERT GREEN MC CLOSKEY: American Conservatism in the Age of Enterprise TB/1137

WILLIAM MILLER, Ed.: Men in Business: *Essays on the Historical Role of the Entrepreneur* TB/1081

HERBERT A. SIMON: The Shape of Automation: *For Men and Management* TB/1245

Historiography and History of Ideas

J. BRONOWSKI & BRUCE MAZLISH: The Western Intellectual Tradition: *From Leonardo to Hegel* TB/3001

WILHELM DILTHEY: Pattern and Meaning in History: *Thoughts on History and Society.° Edited with an Intro. by H. P. Rickman* TB/1075

J. H. HEXTER: More's Utopia: *The Biography of an Idea. Epilogue by the Author* TB/1195

H. STUART HUGHES: History as Art and as Science: *Twin Vistas on the Past* TB/1207

ARTHUR O. LOVEJOY: The Great Chain of Being: *A Study of the History of an Idea* TB/1009

RICHARD H. POPKIN: The History of Scenticism from Erasmus to Descartes. *Revised Edition* TB/1391

MASSIMO SALVADORI, Ed.: Modern Socialism # HR/1374

BRUNO SNELL: The Discovery of the Mind: *The Greek Origins of European Thought* TB/1018

History: General

HANS KOHN: The Age of Nationalism: *The First Era of Global History* TB/1380

BERNARD LEWIS: The Arabs in History TB/1029

BERNARD LEWIS: The Middle East and the West ° TB/1274

History: Ancient

A. ANDREWS: The Greek Tyrants TB/1103

THEODOR H. GASTER: Thespis: *Ritual Myth and Drama in the Ancient Near East* TB/1281

MICHAEL GRANT: Ancient History ° TB/1190

History: Medieval

NORMAN COHN: The Pursuit of the Millennium: *Revolutionary Messianism in Medieval and Reformation Europe* TB/1037

F. L. GANSHOF: Feudalism TB/1058

F. L. GANSHOF: The Middle Ages: *A History of International Relations. Translated by Rémy Hall* TB/1411

ROBERT LATOUCHE: The Birth of Western Economy: *Economic Aspects of the Dark Ages* ° TB/1290

HENRY CHARLES LEA: The Inquisition of the Middle Ages. || *Introduction by Walter Ullmann* TB/1456

History: Renaissance & Reformation

JACOB BURCKHARDT: The Civilization of the Renaissance in Italy. *Introduction by Benjamin Nelson and Charles Trinkaus. Illus.* Vol. I TB/40; Vol. II TB/41

JOHN CALVIN & JACOPO SADOLETO: A Reformation Debate. *Edited by John C. Olin* TB/1239

FEDERICO CHABOD: Machiavelli and the Renaissance TB/1193

THOMAS CROMWELL: Thomas Cromwell: *Selected Letters on Church and Commonwealth, 1523-1540.* ¶ *Ed. with an Intro. by Arthur J. Slavin* TB/1462

FRANCESCO GUICCIARDINI: History of Florence. *Translated with an Introduction and Notes by Mario Domandi* TB/1470

WERNER L. GUNDERSHEIMER, Ed.: French Humanism, 1470-1600. * *Illus.* TB/1473

HANS J. HILLERBRAND, Ed., The Protestant Reformation # HR/1342

JOHAN HUIZINGA: Erasmus and the Age of Reformation. *Illus.* TB/19

JOEL HURSTFIELD: The Elizabethan Nation TB/1312

JOEL HURSTFIELD, Ed.: The Reformation Crisis TB/1267

PAUL OSKAR KRISTELLER: Renaissance Thought: *The Classic, Scholastic, and Humanist Strains* TB/1048

PAUL OSKAR KRISTELLER: Renaissance Thought II: *Papers on Humanism and the Arts* TB/1163

PAUL O. KRISTELLER & PHILIP P. WIENER, Eds.: Renaissance Essays TB/1392

DAVID LITTLE: Religion, Order, and Law: *A Study in Pre-Revolutionary England. § Preface by R. Bellah* TB/1418

NICCOLO MACHIAVELLI: History of Florence and of the Affairs of Italy: *From the Earliest Times to the Death of Lorenzo the Magnificent. Introduction by Felix Gilbert* TB/1027

ALFRED VON MARTIN: Sociology of the Renaissance. ° *Introduction by W. K. Ferguson* TB/1099

GARRETT MATTINGLY et al.: Renaissance Profiles. *Edited by J. H. Plumb* TB/1162

J. H. PARRY: The Establishment of the European Hegemony: 1415-1715: *Trade and Exploration in the Age of the Renaissance* TB/1045

PAOLO ROSSI: Philosophy, Technology, and the Arts, in the Early Modern Era 1400-1700. || *Edited by Benjamin Nelson. Translated by Salvator Attanasio* TB/1458

R. H. TAWNEY: The Agrarian Problem in the Sixteenth Century. *Intro. by Lawrence Stone* TB/1315

H. R. TREVOR-ROPER: The European Witch-craze of the Sixteenth and Seventeenth Centuries and Other Essays ° TB/1416

VESPASIANO: Rennaissance Princes, Popes, and XVth Century: The Vespasiano Memoirs. Introduction by Myron P. Gilmore. Illus. TB/1111

History: Modern European

MAX BELOFF: The Age of Absolutism, 1660-1815 TB/1062

D. W. BROGAN: The Development of Modern France ° Vol. I: From the Fall of the Empire to the Dreyfus Affair TB/1184 Vol. II: The Shadow of War, World War I, Between the Two Wars TB/1185

ALAN BULLOCK: Hitler, A Study in Tyranny. ° Revised Edition. Illus. TB/1123

JOHANN GOTTLIEB FICHTE: Addresses to the German Nation. Ed. with Intro. by George A. Kelly ¶ TB/1366

ALBERT GOODWIN: The French Revolution TB/1064

H. STUART HUGHES: The Obstructed Path: French Social Thought in the Years of Desperation TB/1451

JOHAN HUIZINGA: Dutch Civilization in the 17th Century and Other Essays TB/1453

JOHN MCMANNERS: European History, 1789-1914: Men, Machines and Freedom TB/1419

FRANZ NEUMANN: Behemoth: The Structure and Practice of National Socialism, 1933-1944 TB/1289

DAVID OGG: Europe of the Ancien Régime, 1715-1783 ° α TB/1271

ALBERT SOREL: Europe Under the Old Regime. Translated by Francis H. Herrick TB/1121

A. J. P. TAYLOR: From Napoleon to Lenin: Historical Essays ° TB/1268

A. J. P. TAYLOR: The Habsburg Monarchy, 1809-1918: A History of the Austrian Empire and Austria-Hungary ° TB/1187

J. M. THOMPSON: European History, 1494-1789 TB/1431

H. R. TREVOR-ROPER: Historical Essays TB/1269

Literature & Literary Criticism

JACQUES BARZUN: The House of Intellect TB/1051

W. J. BATE: From Classic to Romantic: Premises of Taste in Eighteenth Century England TB/1036

VAN WYCK BROOKS: Van Wyck Brooks: The Early Years: A Selection from his Works, 1908-1921 Ed. with Intro. by Claire Sprague TB/3082

RICHMOND LATTIMORE, Translator: The Odyssey of Homer TB/1389

Philosophy

HENRI BERGSON: Time and Free Will: An Essay on the Immediate Data of Consciousness ° TB/1021

H. J. BLACKHAM: Six Existentialist Thinkers: Kierkegaard, Nietzsche, Jaspers, Marcel, Heidegger, Sartre ° TB/1002

J. M. BOCHENSKI: The Methods of Contemporary Thought. Trans by Peter Caws TB/1377

CRANE BRINTON: Nietzsche. Preface, Bibliography, and Epilogue by the Author TB/1197

ERNST CASSIRER: Rousseau, Kant and Goethe. Intro by Peter Gay TB/1092

WILFRID DESAN: The Tragic Finale: An Essay on the Philosophy of Jean-Paul Sartre TB/1030

MARVIN FARBER: The Aims of Phenomenology: The Motives, Methods, and Impact of Husserl's Thought TB/1291

PAUL FRIEDLANDER: Plato: An Introduction TB/2017

MICHAEL GELVEN: A Commentary on Heidegger's "Being and Time" TB/1464

G. W. F. HEGEL: On Art, Religion Philosophy: Introductory Lectures to the Realm of Absolute Spirit. || Edited with an Introduction by J. Glenn Gray TB/1463

G. W. F. HEGEL: Phenomenology of Mind. ° || Introduction by eGorge Lichtheim TB/1303

MARTIN HEIDEGGER: Discourse on Thinking. Translated with a Preface by John M. Anderson and E. Hans Freund. Introduction by John M. Anderson TB/1459

F. H. HEINEMANN: Existentialism and the Modern Predicament TB/28

WERER HEISENBERG: Physics and Philosophy: The Revolution in Modern Science. Intro. by F. S. C. Northrop TB/549

EDMUND HUSSERL: Phenomenology and the Crisis of Philosophy. § Translated with an Introduction by Quentin Lauer TB/1170

IMMANUEL KANT: Groundwork of the Metaphysic of Morals. Translated and Analyzed by H. J. Paton TB/1159

IMMANUEL KANT: Lectures on Ethics. § Introduction by Lewis White Beck TB/105

QUENTIN LAUER: Phenomenology: Its Genesis and Prospect. Preface by Aron Gurwitsch TB/1169

GEORGE A. MORGAN: What Nietzsche Means TB/1198

H. J. PATON: The Categorical Imperative: A Study in Kant's Moral Philosophy TB/1325

MICHAEL POLANYI: Personal Knowledge: Towards a Post-Critical Philosophy TB/1158

WILLARD VAN ORMAN QUINE: Elementary Logic Revised Edition TB/577

JOHN E. SMITH: Themes in American Philosophy: Purpose, Experience and Community TB/1466

MORTON WHITE: Foundations of Historical Knowledge TB/1440

WILHELM WINDELBAND: A History of Philosophy Vol. I: Greek, Roman, Medieval TB/38 Vol. II: Renaissance, Enlightenment, Modern TB/39

LUDWIG WITTGENSTEIN: The Blue and Brown Books ° TB/1211

LUDWIG WITTGENSTEIN: Notebooks, 1914-1916 TB/1441

Political Science & Government

C. E. BLACK: The Dynamics of Modernization: A Study in Comparative History TB/1321

KENNETH E. BOULDING: Conflict and Defense: A General Theory of Action TB/3024

DENIS W. BROGAN: Politics in America. New Introduction by the Author TB/1469

LEWIS COSER, Ed.: Political Sociology TB/1293

ROBERT A. DAHL & CHARLES E. LINDBLOM: Politics, Economics, and Welfare: Planning and Politico-Economic Systems Resolved into Basic Social Processes TB/3037

ROY C. MACRIDIS, Ed.: Political Parties: Contemporary Trends and Ideas ** TB/1322

ROBERT GREEN MC CLOSKEY: American Conservatism in the Age of Enterprise, 1865-1910 TB/1137

JOHN B. MORRALL: Political Thought in Medieval Times TB/1076

KARL R. POPPER: The Open Society and Its
Enemies *Vol. I: The Spell of Plato* TB/1101
*Vol. II: The High Tide of Prophecy: Hegel,
Marx, and the Aftermath* TB/1102
HENRI DE SAINT-SIMON: Social Organization, The
Science of Man, and Other Writings. ||
*Edited and Translated with an Introduction
by Felix Markham* TB/1152
JOSEPH A. SCHUMPETER: Capitalism, Socialism
and Democracy TB/3008

Psychology

LUDWIG BINSWANGER: Being-in-the-World: *Se-
lected Papers.* || *Trans. with Intro. by Jacob
Needleman* TB/1365
HADLEY CANTRIL: The Invasion from Mars: *A
Study in the Psychology of Panic* || TB/1282
MIRCEA ELIADE: Cosmos and History: *The Myth
of the Eternal Return* § TB/2050
MIRCEA ELIADE: Myth and Reality TB/1369
MIRCEA ELIADE: Myths, Dreams and Mysteries:
*The Encounter Between Contemporary Faiths
and Archaic Realities* § TB/1320
MIRCEA ELIADE: Rites and Symbols of Initiation:
The Mysteries of Birth and Rebirth §
TB/1236
SIGMUND FREUD: On Creativity and the Uncon-
scious: *Papers on the Psychology of Art,
Literature, Love, Religion.* § *Intro. by Ben-
jamin Nelson* TB/45
J. GLENN GRAY: The Warriors: *Reflections on
Men in Battle. Introduction by Hannah
Arendt* TB/1294
WILLIAM JAMES: Psychology: *The Briefer
Course. Edited with an Intro. by Gordon
Allport* TB/1034
KARL MENNINGER, M.D.: Theory of Psychoan-
alytic Technique TB/1144

Religion: Ancient and Classical, Biblical and
Judaic Traditions

MARTIN BUBER: Eclipse of God: *Studies in the
Relation Between Religion and Philosophy*
TB/12
MARTIN BUBER: Hasidism and Modern Man.
Edited and Translated by Maurice Friedman
TB/839
MARTIN BUBER: The Knowledge of Man. *Edited
with an Introduction by Maurice Friedman.
Translated by Maurice Friedman and Ronald
Gregor Smith* TB/135
MARTIN BUBER: Moses. *The Revelation and the
Covenant* TB/837
MARTIN BUBER: The Origin and Meaning of
Hasidism. *Edited and Translated by Maurice
Friedman* TB/835
MARTIN BUBER: The Prophetic Faith TB/73
MARTIN BUBER: Two Types of Faith: *Interpene-
tration of Judaism and Christianity* ° TB/75
MALCOLM L. DIAMOND: Martin Buber: *Jewish
Existentialist* TB/840
M. S. ENSLIN: Christian Beginnings TB/5
M. S. ENSLIN: The Literature of the Christian
Movement TB/6
HENRI FRANKFORT: Ancient Egyptian Religion:
An Interpretation TB/77
ABRAHAM HESCHEL: God in Search of Man: *A
Philosophy of Judaism* TB/807
ABRAHAM HESCHEL: Man Is not Alone: *A Phil-
osophy of Religion* TB/838
T. J. MEEK: Hebrew Origins TB/69
H. J. ROSE: Religion in Greece and Rome
TB/55

*Religion: Early Christianity Through
Reformation*

ANSELM OF CANTERBURY: Truth, Freedom, and
Evil: *Three Philosophical Dialogues. Edited
and Translated by Jasper Hopkins and Her-
bert Richardson* TB/317
JOHANNES ECKHART: Meister Eckhart: *A Mod-
ern Translation by R. Blakney* TB/8
EDGAR J. GOODSPEED: A Life of Jesus TB/1
ROBERT M. GRANT: Gnosticism and Early Christi-
anity TB/136
ARTHUR DARBY NOCK: St. Paul ° TR/104
GORDON RUPP: Luther's Progress to the Diet of
Worms ° TB/120

Religion: The Protestant Tradition

KARL BARTH: Church Dogmatics: *A Selection.
Intro. by H. Gollwitzer. Ed. by G. W. Bro-
miley* TB/95
KARL BARTH: Dogmatics in Outline TB/56
KARL BARTH: The Word of God and the Word
of Man TB/13
WILLIAM R. HUTCHISON, Ed.: American Prot-
estant Thought: *The Liberal Era* ‡ TB/1385
SOREN KIERKEGAARD: Edifying Discourses. *Edited
with an Intro. by Paul Holmer* TB/32
SOREN KIERKEGAARD: The Journals of Kierke-
gaard. ° *Edited with an Intro. by Alexander
Dru* TB/52
SOREN KIERKEGAARD: The Point of View for My
Work as an Author: *A Report to History.* §
Preface by Benjamin Nelson TB/88
SOREN KIERKEGAARD: The Present Age. § *Trans-
lated and edited by Alexander Dru. Intro-
duction by Walter Kaufmann* TB/94
SOREN KIERKEGAARD: Purity of Heart. *Trans. by
Douglas Steere* TB/4
SOREN KIERKEGAARD: Repetition: *An Essay in
Experimental Psychology* § TB/117
WOLFHART PANNENBERG, et al.: History and Her-
meneutic. *Volume 4 of* Journal for Theol-
ogy and the Church, *edited by Robert W.
Funk and Gerhard Ebeling* TB/254
F. SCHLEIERMACHER: The Christian Faith. *Intro-
duction by Richard R. Niebuhr.*
Vol. I TB/108; Vol. II TB/109
F. SCHLEIERMACHER: On Religion: *Speeches to
Its Cultured Despisers. Intro. by Rudolf
Otto* TB/36
PAUL TILLICH: Dynamics of Faith TB/42
PAUL TILLICH: Morality and Beyond TB/142

*Religion: The Roman & Eastern Christian
Traditions*

A. ROBERT CAPONIGRI, Ed.: Modern Catholic
Thinkers II: *The Church and the Political
Order* TB/307
G. P. FEDOTOV: The Russian Religious Mind:
*Kievan Christianity, the tenth to the thir-
teenth Centuries* TB/370
GABRIEL MARCEL: Being and Having: *An Ex-
istential Diary. Introduction by James Col-
lins* TB/310
GABRIEL MARCEL: Homo Viator: *Introduction to
a Metaphysic of Hope* TB/397

Religion: Oriental Religions

TOR ANDRAE: Mohammed: *The Man and His
Faith* § TB/62
EDWARD CONZE: Buddhism: *Its Essence and De-
velopment.* ° *Foreword by Arthur Waley*
TB/58

EDWARD CONZE et al, Editors: Buddhist Texts through the Ages TB/113
H. G. CREEL: Confucius and the Chinese Way TB/63
FRANKLIN EDGERTON, Trans. & Ed.: The Bhagavad Gita TB/115
SWAMI NIKHILANANDA, Trans. & Ed.: The Upanishads TB/114

Religion: Philosophy, Culture, and Society

NICOLAS BERDYAEV: The Destiny of Man TB/61
RUDOLF BULTMANN: History and Eschatology: The Presence of Eternity ° TB/91
LUDWIG FEUERBACH: The Essence of Christianity. § Introduction by Karl Barth. Foreword by H. Richard Niebuhr TB/11
ADOLF HARNACK: What Is Christianity? § Introduction by Rudolf Bultmann TB/17
KYLE HASELDEN: The Racial Problem in Christian Perspective TB/116
IMMANUEL KANT: Religion Within the Limits of Reason Alone. § Introduction by Theodore M. Greene and John Silber TB/67
H. RICHARD NIEBUHR: Christ and Culture TB/3
H. RICHARD NIEBUHR: The Kingdom of God in America TB/49

Science and Mathematics

W. E. LE GROS CLARK: The Antecedents of Man: An Introduction to the Evolution of the Primates. ° Illus. TB/559
ROBERT E. COKER: Streams, Lakes, Ponds. Illus. TB/586
ROBERT E. COKER: This Great and Wide Sea: An Introduction to Oceanography and Marine Biology. Illus. TB/551
F. K. HARE: The Restless Atmosphere TB/560
WILLARD VAN ORMAN QUINE: Mathematical Logic TB/558

Science: Philosophy

J. M. BOCHENSKI: The Methods of Contemporary Thought. Tr. by Peter Caws TB/1377
J. BRONOWSKI: Science and Human Values. Revised and Enlarged. Illus. TB/505
WERNER HEISENBERG: Physics and Philosophy: The Revolution in Modern Science. Introduction by F. S. C. Northrop TB/549
KARL R. POPPER: Conjectures and Refutations: The Growth of Scientific Knowledge TB/1376
KARL R. POPPER: The Logic of Scientific Discovery TB/576

Sociology and Anthropology

REINHARD BENDIX: Work and Authority in Industry: Ideologies of Management in the Course of Industrialization TB/3035
BERNARD BERELSON, Ed., The Behavioral Sciences Today TB/1127
KENNETH B. CLARK: Dark Ghetto: Dilemmas of Social Power. Foreword by Gunnar Myrdal TB/1317

KENNETH CLARK & JEANNETTE HOPKINS: A Relevant War Against Poverty: A Study of Community Action Programs and Observable Social Change TB/1480
LEWIS COSER, Ed.: Political Sociology TB/1293
ALLISON DAVIS & JOHN DOLLARD: Children of Bondage: The Personality Development of Negro Youth in the Urban South || TB/3049
ST. CLAIR DRAKE & HORACE R. CAYTON: Black Metropolis: A Study of Negro Life in a Northern City. Introduction by Everett C. Hughes. Tables, maps, charts, and graphs Vol. I TB/1086; Vol. II TB/1087
PETER F. DRUCKER: The New Society: The Anatomy of Industrial Order TB/1082
CHARLES Y. GLOCK & RODNEY STARK: Christian Beliefs and Anti-Semitism. Introduction by the Authors TB/1454
ALVIN W. GOULDNER: The Hellenic World TB/1479
R. M. MACIVER: Social Causation TB/1153
GARY T. MARX: Protest and Prejudice: A Study of Belief in the Black Community TB/1435
ROBERT K. MERTON, LEONARD BROOM, LEONARD S. COTTRELL, JR., Editors: Sociology Today: Problems and Prospects || Vol. I TB/1173; Vol. II TB/1174
GILBERT OSOFSKY, Ed.: The Burden of Race: A Documentary History of Negro-White Relations in America TB/1405
GILBERT OSOFSKY: Harlem: The Making of a Ghetto: Negro New York 1890-1930 TB/1381
TALCOTT PARSONS & EDWARD A. SHILS, Editors: Toward a General Theory of Action: Theoretical Foundations for the Social Sciences TB/1083
PHILIP RIEFF: The Triumph of the Therapeutic: Uses of Faith After Freud TB/1360
JOHN H. ROHRER & MUNRO S. EDMONSON, Eds.: The Eighth Generation Grows Up: Cultures and Personalities of New Orleans Negroes || TB/3050
ARNOLD ROSE: The Negro in America: The Condensed Version of Gunnar Myrdal's An American Dilemma. Second Edition TB/3048
GEORGE ROSEN: Madness in Society: Chapters in the Historical Sociology of Mental Illness. || Preface by Benjamin Nelson TB/1337
PHILIP SELZNICK: TVA and the Grass Roots: A Study in the Sociology of Formal Organization TB/1230
PITIRIM A. SOROKIN: Contemporary Sociological Theories: Through the First Quarter of the Twentieth Century TB/3046
MAURICE R. STEIN: The Eclipse of Community: An Interpretation of American Studies TB/1128
FERDINAND TONNIES: Community and Society: Gemeinschaft und Gesellschaft. Translated and Edited by Charles P. Loomis TB/1116
W. LLOYD WARNER and Associates: Democracy in Jonesville: A Study in Quality and Inequality || TB/1129
W. LLOYD WARNER: Social Class in America: The Evaluation of Status TB/1013
FLORIAN ZNANIECKI: The Social Role of the Man of Knowledge. Introduction by Lewis A. Coser TB/1372